ARCHITECTURE
FOR CULTURE

ARCHITECTURE FOR CULTURE

Rethinking Museums

Béatrice Grenier

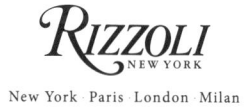

New York · Paris · London · Milan

Table of Contents

Foreword by	**Chris Dercon**	7
Introduction	**Rethinking Museums**	9
The museum is	**SCROLL PAINTING**	13
	CITY	45
	DRIVE-THROUGH	69
	MACHINE	85
	LANDSCAPE	107
	THE IN-BETWEEN	129
	FICTION	155
	SPROUT	173
	PLANET	195
Afterword by	**Shohei Shigematsu**	219

Foreword by Chris Dercon
Director of the Fondation Cartier pour l'art contemporain

In 1974, William Rubin, the fabled curator of the Museum of Modern Art in New York, admitted during an interview that "The museum concept is not infinitely expandable." At the time, he ascribed this notion to the emerging rupture between the traditional aesthetic categories of painting and sculpture and the land art and conceptual art that were all the rage in those days. According to Rubin, this latter category called for an entirely different museum environment. Three years later, when the Centre Pompidou opened its doors in Paris, the sociologist Pierre Bourdieu, prophesized that the desacralization of cultural objects in such a desacralized environment—as he described this newly built museum—would change the concept of a museum forever.

Forty years later, Rubin and Bourdieu could not have imagined that so many novel plans to build, expand, or renovate museums would, and still are, transforming the very concept of the museum!

Indeed, as museums began examining their future needs, they realized that they required not only more space but also fundamentally different spaces from the existing ones. Spaces that would allow museums to realize their intellectual and programmatic goals in line with the evolving needs of their time. For instance, one might even go so far as to say that today the architecture of museums are, and partly serve as, representation models in and of themselves.

The contemporary museums that Béatrice Grenier presents and lucidly comments on are illustrations of these developments, whereby architecture plays a role in "formulating the museum's new selves." Indeed, we are presently witnessing a shift in the historical relationship between architecture and collecting practices, which inherited conceptions of the museum can no longer describe. New cultural practices and the presence of all possible disciplines in museums require totally new kinds of spaces and spatial relationships.

Moreover, a significant amount of social space is required in today's museums for many different activities, diverse and younger audiences, and a rapidly growing number of visitors in general. We live in a curatorial age, there are so many things to select and choose from, to comment on or to understand. What boundaries still exist? Architects, therefore, play a role in rethinking museums. In this context, design is a form of anticipation with which museums can help us to think about our future collectively.

So, is museum architecture as we know it, losing part of its mandate? Or can it be recaptured by becoming part of the extensions, those very different museum buildings, so excitingly explored by Grenier? The architectural historian Mark Wigley was right when he stated, "Architects are always talking about things that don't change, but their idea of what is not changing keeps changing, and that is great by the way."

It is the architects and commissioning bodies of museums that embrace changing things—those supposedly unchanging—who will build tomorrow's museums. You'll find a great selection of these in this book, perfectly titled *Architecture for Culture*.

Introduction Rethinking Museums

New museums are being built and emerging all over the world, despite all odds, given the advent of the digital revolution. Indeed, there is a paradox whereby knowledge today is more accessible through the digital realm, where we live in a landscape of archives, and the latter outnumber the world of experience in terms of size and density. Every day, through the immense accumulation of images, words, sounds, and forms stored on tiny silicon surfaces, our archives are growing faster than Le Corbusier's wildest dreams, which he sketched out in the *Musée à croissance illimitée* or "Museum of Unlimited Growth," whose walls were meant to be infinitely extended to accommodate ever-expanding collections.

We no longer need to go to the museum or the library, as knowledge has become ubiquitous and accessible to all at all times. Our contemporary condition, whereby we can hold the museum in the palm of our hands, was foreseen by André Malraux in his concept of *Le Musée imaginaire* or "Museum Without Walls" (1947), for whom photography permitted the joining of artifacts belonging to any civilization into a kind of supramuseum that would flatten—or put on the same level of importance—any artwork from any culture. But of course, this would only be possible in the form of a book, or today, in the form of a digital museum. And so it would seem that this concentrated physical space of knowledge is no longer necessary in the city.

Yet the museum, its architectural self, persists, and too little critical attention has been given to the role and agency of architecture in defining its new forms. This book aims to address this gap by rethinking and reinterpreting what stands today as one of the most important and innovative architectural typologies of recent decades. The architectural challenge of the museum designer is no longer a question of creating a virtually unlimited archive in one place, nor of proposing itineraries within a space that defines it and ensures its chronological narration, or even a question of being a space that is opposed to the city as an environment of display, as the white cube proposed.

The radical redefinition of the role of the museum as an incubator and laboratory of urban culture is studied in nine chapters, inviting the reader to reconsider architecture's agency in formulating the museum's new selves. The first chapter, "Scroll Painting" (page 13), addresses one of the most inventive architectural iterations for a novel type of museum in China. Amateur Architecture's project for the National Archives of Publications and Culture in Hangzhou departs from a masterpiece of Chinese painting as the blueprint for the architecture of a new type of institution, which is at once a library and a center for exhibiting state-owned collections. By equating artwork to architecture, the museum is the place where culture becomes the concrete form of this world.

While not aiming to be comprehensive, this text cites examples from around the globe selected for their paradigmatic nature. In Paris, the city itself is an encyclopedic museum, with collections spread across different museum buildings in Abu

Dhabi, the Louvre, designed by Jean Nouvel (examined in the chapter "City," page 45), is a universal city in itself: a shallow cupola of superimposed metal mesh serves as the dome under which a classic representation of the heavens and a metaphor for universality is articulated. Built on a non-place, a tabula rasa of sand, the Gulf iteration of these universalizing ambitions reimagines the spatial idea of the Louvre and its Paris satellites, bringing times, places, and ideas together with far greater efficiency than in France's capital.

Both historical and contemporary examples are considered. The architecture of the Pompidou (examined in the chapter "Drive-Through," page 69), remains vibrant and critical today, as it was instrumental in crystallizing a new idea for a museum at the time of its conception in the early 1970s—a flagship of symbolic commitment to futurist technology amid an iconic nineteenth-century material heritage. The Centre Pompidou was not the first material manifestation of an architecture that seeks to respond to the advent of technology in the urban context, in this case, the car, a phenomenon that can be traced back to the first architecture of the World Expositions in London and Paris. The architectural impetus of the museum accelerated thanks to these urban-scale exhibitions, which created a direct relationship with the city and its technology, and in turn pushed the museum to depart from the refuge of urban life that its historical forms, such as the Kunstkammer and university collections, had heretofore maintained. In the chapter "Machines" (page 85), the museum is postulated as a "machine," which surveys different types of dynamic architectures that suggest cultural institutions should be the site of the invention of culture by provoking different typologies of programming where hybridity of expression is encouraged, and events in which the exhibition, theater performance, concert, and immersive experience all merge into one. Architecture has the potential to foster both a new kind of art and a new kind of institution.

Today, a veritable collection of museum architecture exists on a planetary scale, in forms we do not fully suspect or recognize as such. Art and architecture have left the exhibition space of the traditional museum, revealing a museological reality that is elsewhere—from architectural gestures such as the disappearance into a landscape—the Zaishui Museum by Junya Ishigami, which questions the divide between nature and culture (chapter "Landscape," page 107), to the preserved socialist modern architectural heritage of Zanzibar City (chapter "The In-Between," page 129). Architectural preservation can be understood as a global geopolitical curatorial project, with entire urban fragments being preserved while others are demolished, critically defining the memory of our past human culture. Further, the museum is considered a representation of the gesture through which architecture affirms the canon and its presence in the urban environment, which is evident in the global ambition and planetary relevance of an institution like M+ in Hong Kong, where both architecture and the museum's collection work together to affirm a new cosmological order (chapter "Fiction," page 155).

The twenty-first-century museum is redefining the spaces and roles of the museum, which is no longer to be infinitely extensible, either at a local or planetary scale, nor to provide a mere container for ephemeral exhibitions—rather, this new museum becomes the place where life happens, a meeting ground where knowledge circulates through social means, exemplified by the renovated Grand Palais in Paris or the Arkansas Museum of Fine Arts in Little Rock (chapter "Sprout," page 173). Finally, the museum represents the topology through which the very soil of our planet emerges as an archive of human culture. This is the point made by the museum-city of Michael Heizer's latest and most ambitious work in the Nevada desert (chapter "Planet," page 195).

At the heart of the investigation into architecture's role in articulating the forms of new museums lies a profound optimism and belief in the museum's ability to play a defining role in the formulation of our future societies. Contemporary architecture transforms the museum's definition itself as the enabler of a different kind of space for the encyclopedia to come, as the instigator for questioning the dichotomy between the urban and the wild, or the natural and the built as false absolutes; as exacerbating its democratization potential by including new forms of technology as forms of knowledge and culture. As a cognitive space that serves as a privileged gateway to contemporary art, museum architecture today has the potential to define the space for the enactment of contemporary culture and be the site for the incubation of our future cities.

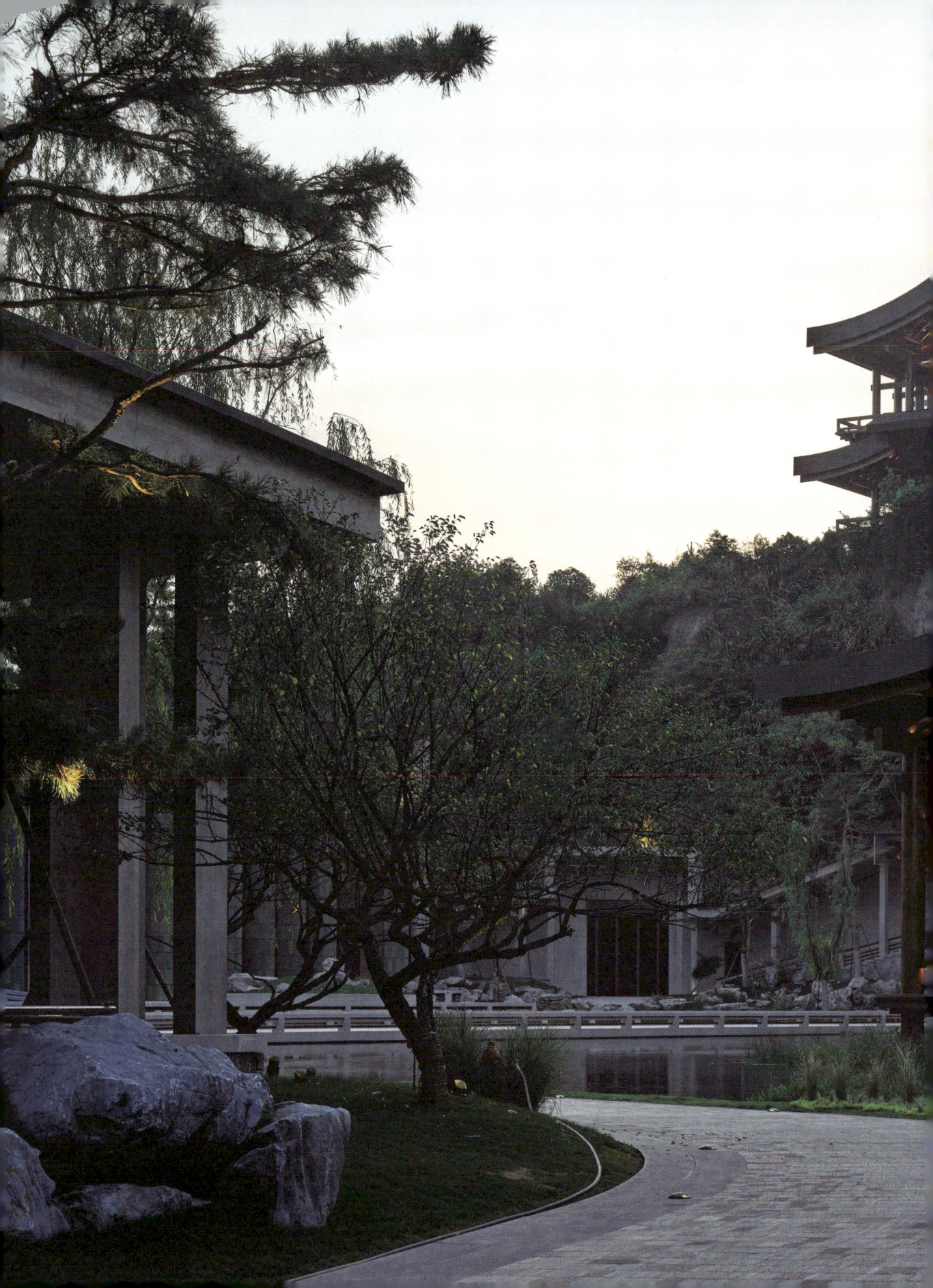

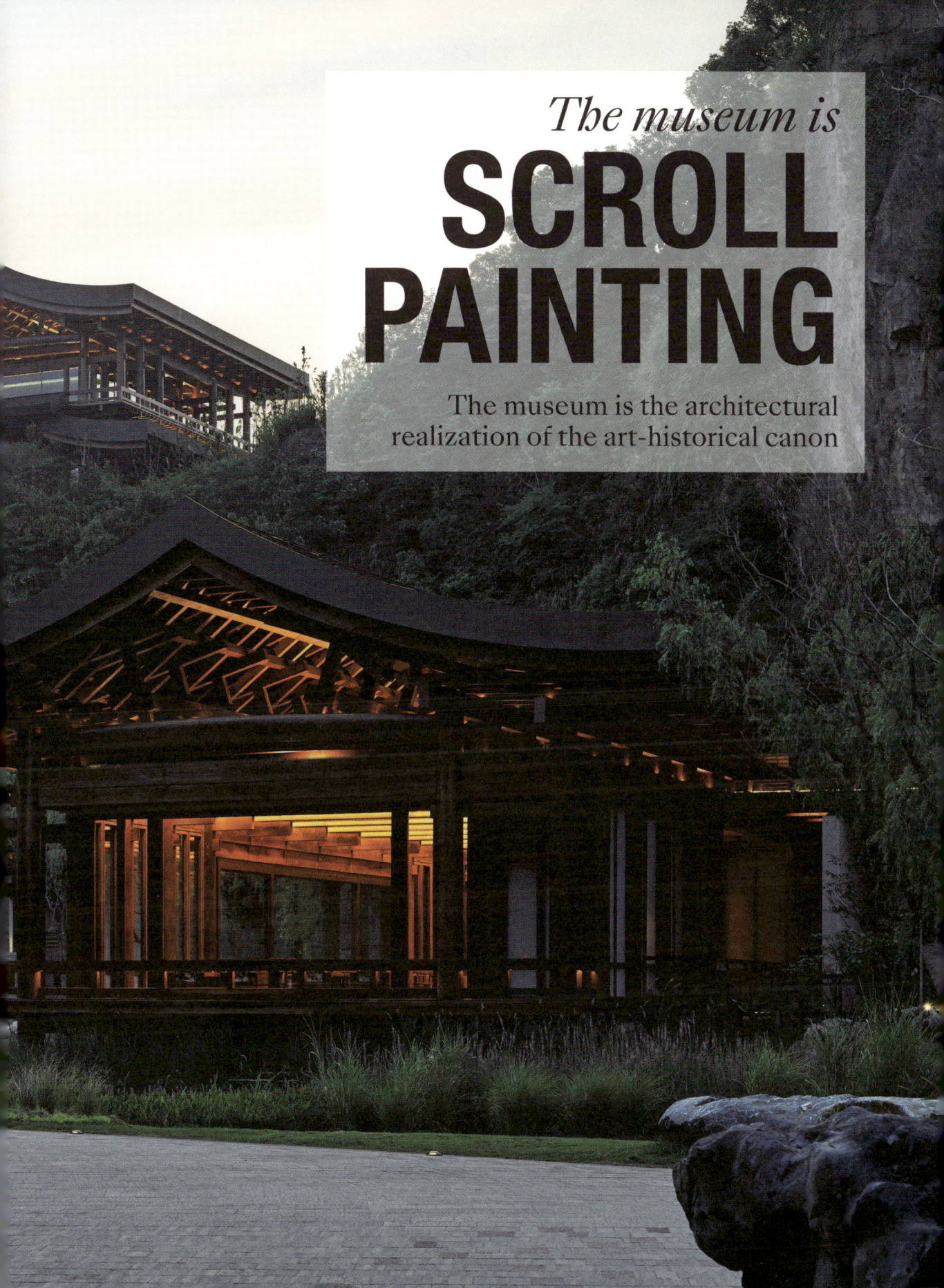

The museum is SCROLL PAINTING

The museum is the architectural realization of the art-historical canon

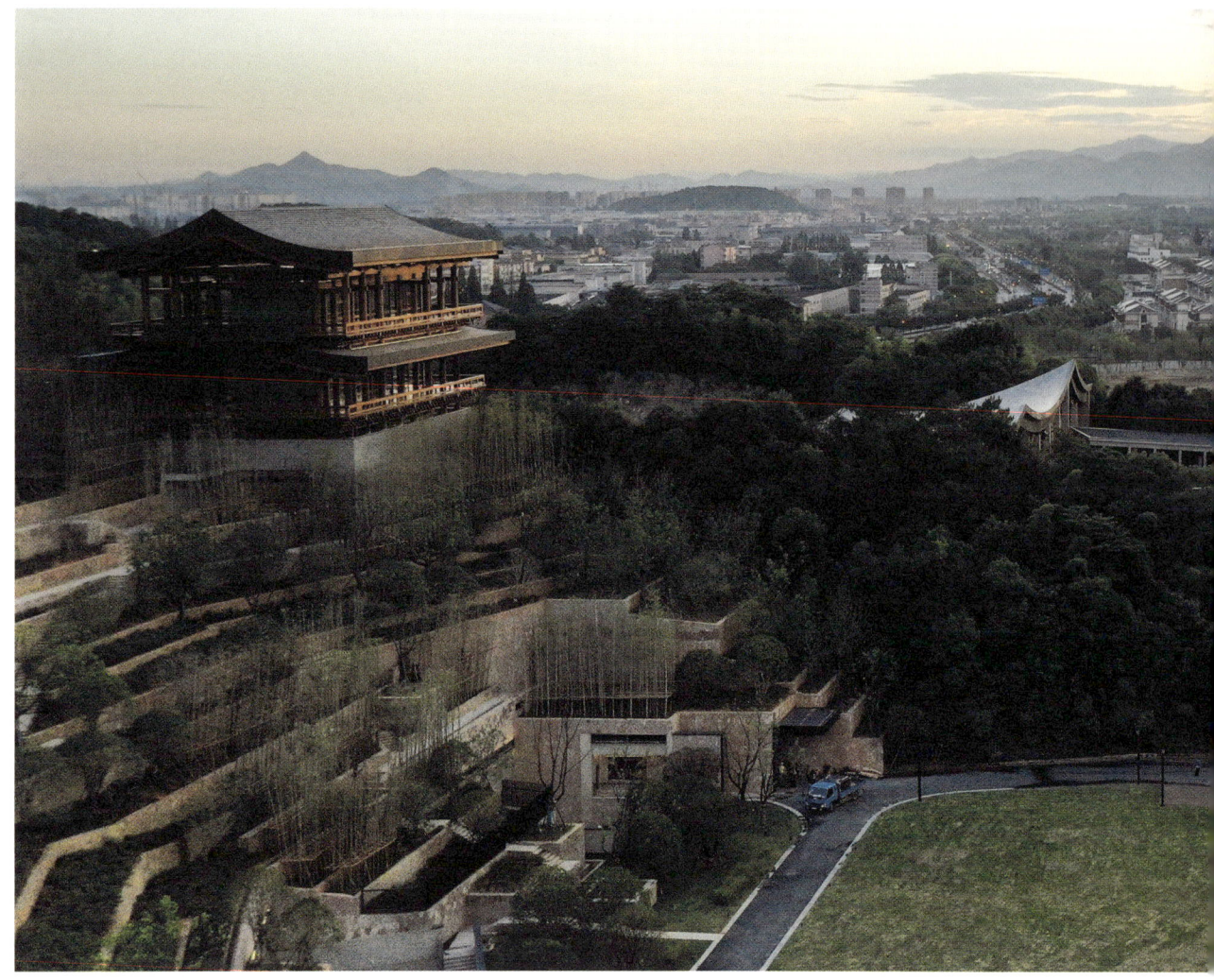

"If you would like to go to the library, you may come here; if you would like to go to the museum, you could also come here; if you would like to see an exhibition or consult an archive, you can also come here!"[1] boasts a promotional video introducing the National Archives of Publication and Culture, a new typology for a cultural institution created by the Chinese government in 2022. The National Archives are the home of an atypical amalgam of collections that span the entire history of China. To date, it has no European or American equivalent—at once a library, museum, and archive, it holds ancient texts, imperial records, books, paintings, calligraphy, and woodblock prints of all dates, with a common foundation in the written word. In terms of the timespan they cover, the collections can be compared to those of an institution like the British Museum; in terms of variety, they represent the equivalent of those of the Bibliothèque Nationale de France and

---

1. The promotional video features a young man giving a tour of the new spaces to advertise the multimedia dimension of the collections, which treat both artifacts and books as having equal status, a concept that does not exist in Western culture and contemporary forms of the museum. "如果你想去图书馆你可以来这儿，你如果想去博物馆你也可以来这儿，如果你想去美术馆，展览馆，档案馆你都可以来这儿 […] 这是国家版本馆"

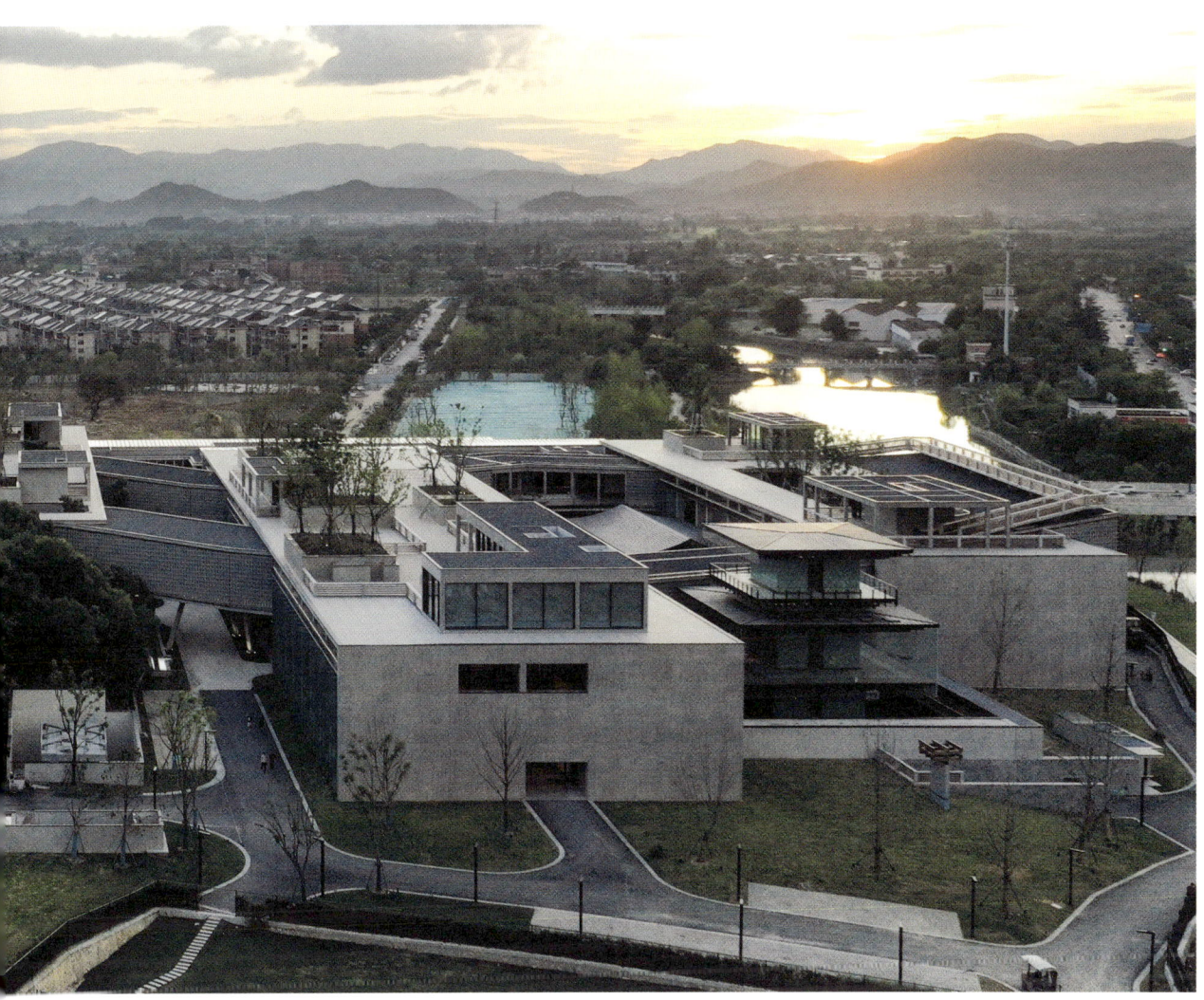

the Louvre gathered in a single place. Visitors can try to decipher the earliest form of writing found on bamboo slips from the third century BCE, admire some of China's most revered scroll paintings, or read sections of the Yongle Dadian, until recently the world's largest encyclopedia, commissioned in the early fifteenth century by the Ming dynasty Yongle Emperor. In terms of visitor experience, the National Archives are like a cross between the New York Public Library and the Metropolitan Museum of Art: spanning the cultural spectrum from high to low, ancient to contemporary, elitist to popular, they elevate the status of the book and the written word to the same level as the museum.

Previous pages: The pavilions of the National Archives of Publications and Culture are multifunctional and can adapt to various forms of programming.

Above: The campus of the National Archives is perched on a hill overlooking the countryside of Hangzhou and comprises different galleries for exhibitions as well as archival storage for consultation.

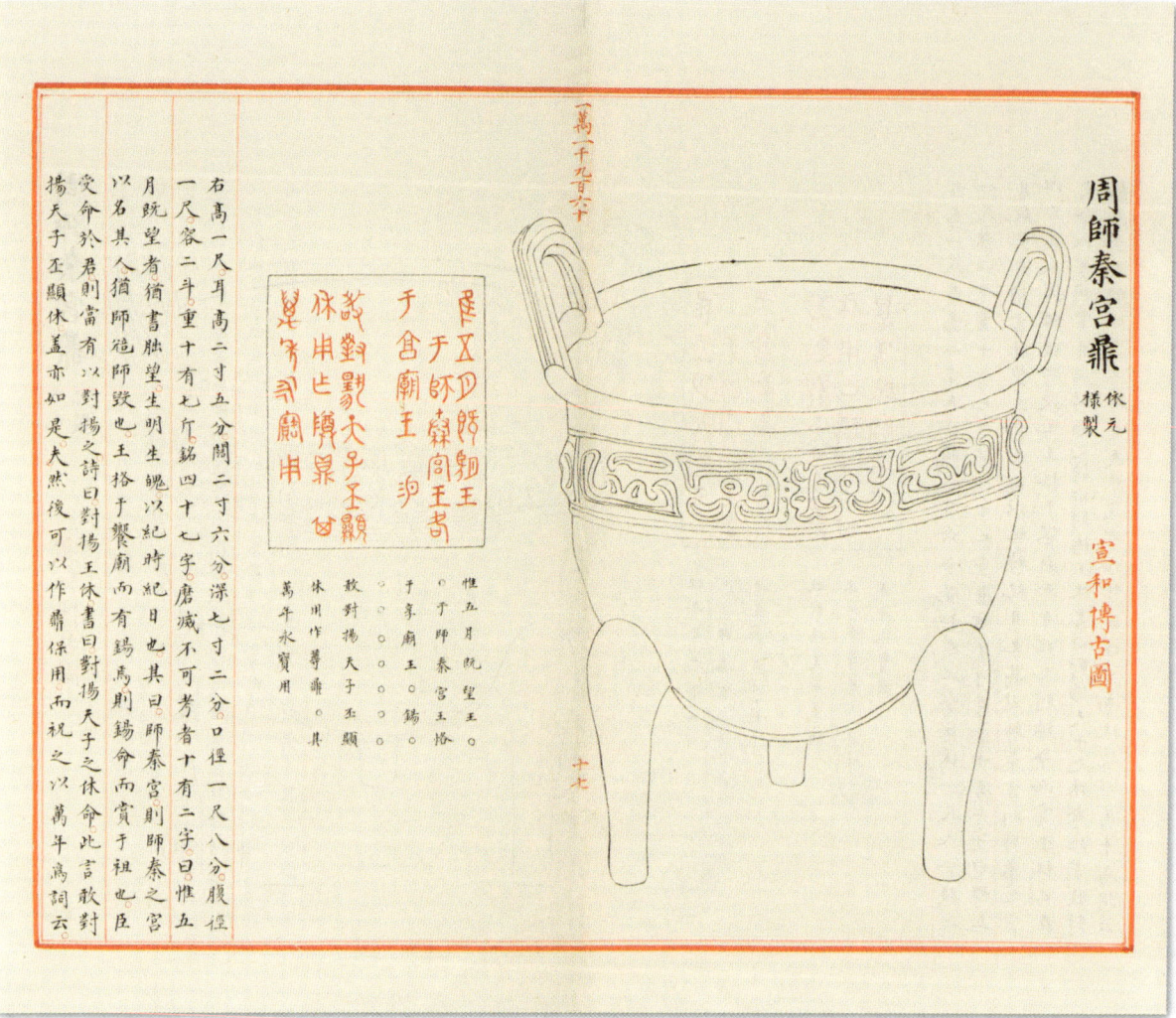

In China, the written word holds a special status that differs from that in Western cultures.² While language and visual images are indeed two distinct forms of expression in Chinese, the imposition of one on the other can either enhance or detract from their individual impact. Throughout Chinese history, the relationship between words and images has constantly alternated between complementary illustration and integration.³ By brushing a poem onto a painting so that word and image combine, the artist creates a verbal discourse and a broader context that co-exist as a system of shared visual thinking. Yet, in some art forms where no visual representation is apparent, such as poetry or calligraphy, language bears the responsibility of creating scenes of concentrated images.⁴ Furthermore, the dynamism of the scroll format, where texts are read in the same movement as a painting,

---

2. For more on the status of writing see research of sinologis Thomas S. Mullaney, *The Chinese Typewriter* (Cambridge, MA: MIT Press, 2018).
3. Scholar Wen C Fong has done tremendously important work on this topic, see "Why Chinese Painting is History," *The Art Bulletin*, vol. 85, no. 2 (June 2003), 258–80.
4. See Shuai Yuan, "Comparative Study on 'Images' in Chinese and Western Culture and Art," paper presented at the International Conference on Arts, Design and Contemporary Education, 2015.

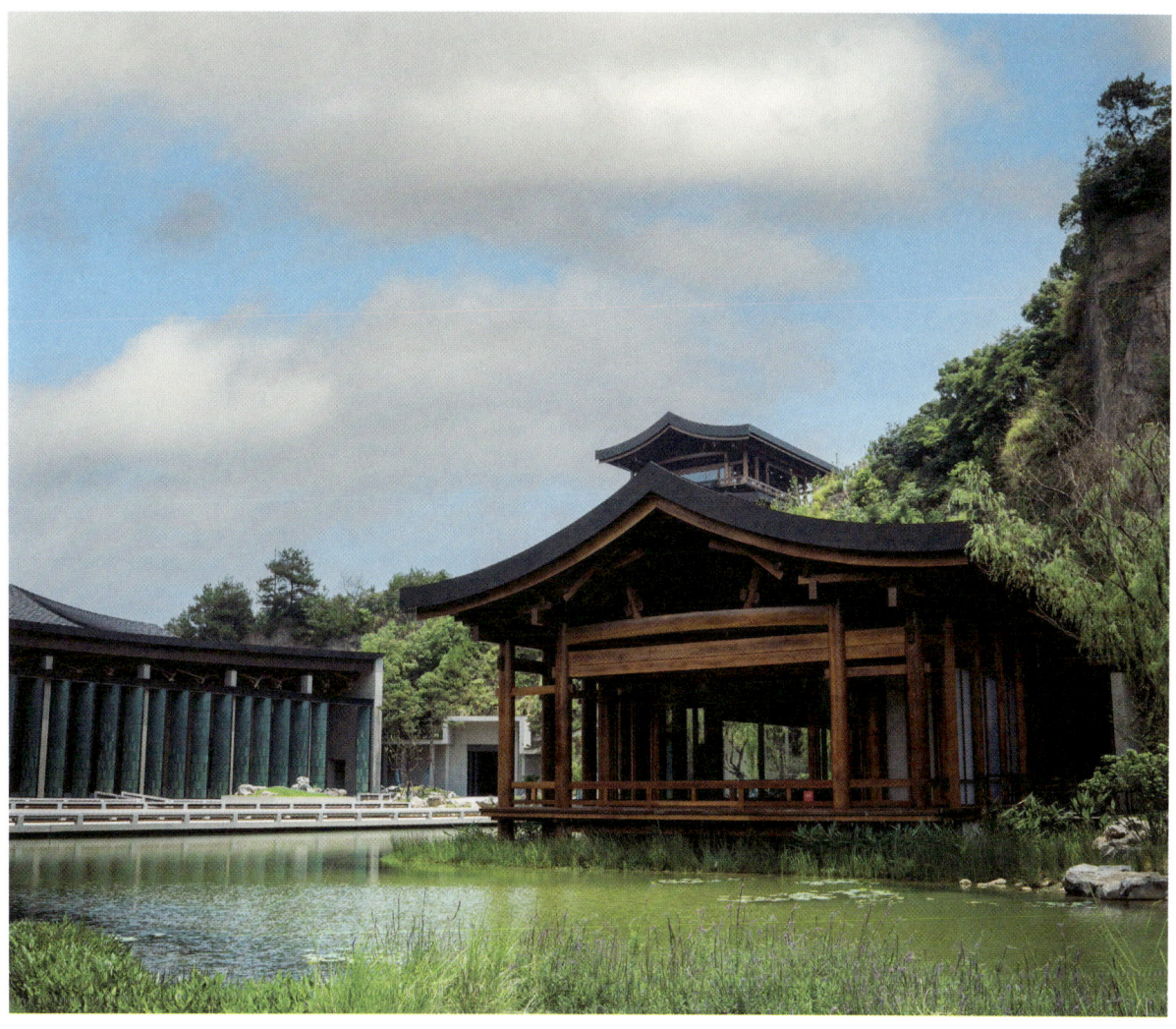

renders the relationship between word and image even more ambiguous.

This fluidity between the written word and the image—which is also embedded in Chinese characters—is what enables the vast conceptual expanse of the National Archives. In the Chinese media, the new institution has been described as a "repository of the genes of Chinese culture" (中华文化种子基因库 *zhonghua wenhua zhongzi jiyinku*), a place that seeks to collect all forms of cultural artifacts that record Chinese civilization. In English, "the National Archives of Publications and Culture" is a rather awkward rendering, as an exact translation is impossible given the all-encompassing meaning of *ban ben* (版本)—a loose term that is

Opposite: A spread of the Yongle Dadian, a canonical encyclopedia, commissioned in the early fifteenth century by the Ming dynasty Yongle Emperor.

Above: A pavilion on the campus echoes traditional architecture of the Song with modern features of stacked open plans and a glass facade.

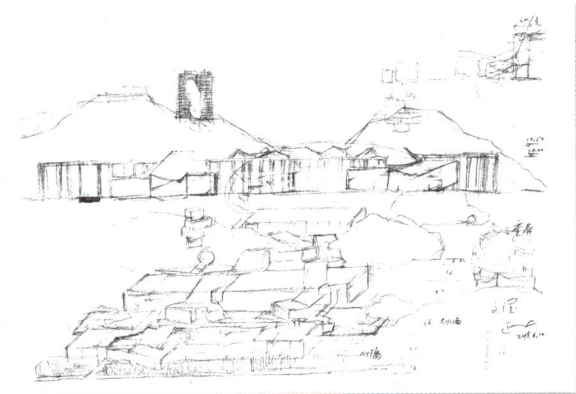
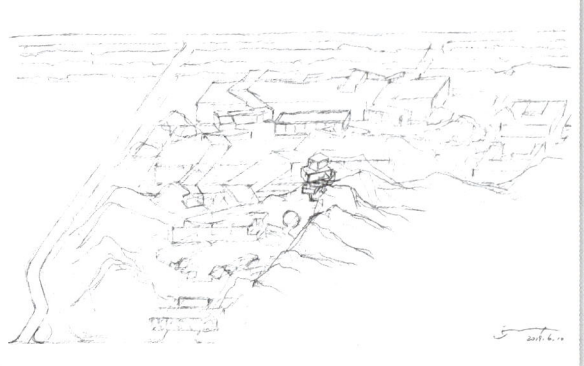
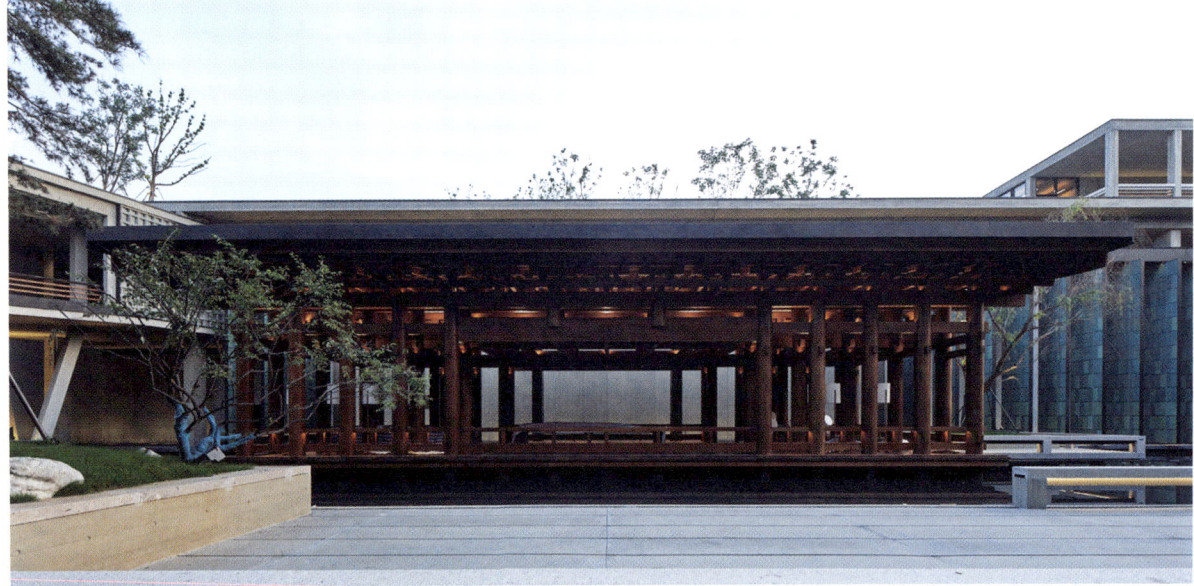

principally related to the notion of "publication," but which could also mean edition, version, or proof. The institution could simply have been called "National Archives" (*guojia wenxian guan* 国家文献馆), with the word *wenxian* (文献) referring specifically to documents of historical or literary value. However, both the nature of the collections and the choice of *ban ben* 版本 as a concept to anchor the institution's mandate broaden its scope, enabling an understanding of its holdings as encompassing "anything that is liable to record Chinese culture."

What kind of architecture could manifest the meeting point of the written word and the image, the book and the artifact, as the National Archives attempts to do, across all temporalities of what is considered Chinese civilization? This was the task of architects Wang Shu and Lu Wenyu, who were commissioned to conceive the Hangzhou branch in their home base, where the duo has also built the campus of the China Academy of Fine Arts, southern China's largest humanities and arts school.[5] The architectural response to the program of this institution crystallizes its philosophy in architectural form. They achieve this by using a historical canonical

---

5. For more on the duo's practice, see Wang Shu, *The Beginning of Design* (Beijing: China Building Press, 2022); and Wang Shu, 造房子 *To Make a Home* (Changsha: Hunan Fine Art Publishers, 2012).

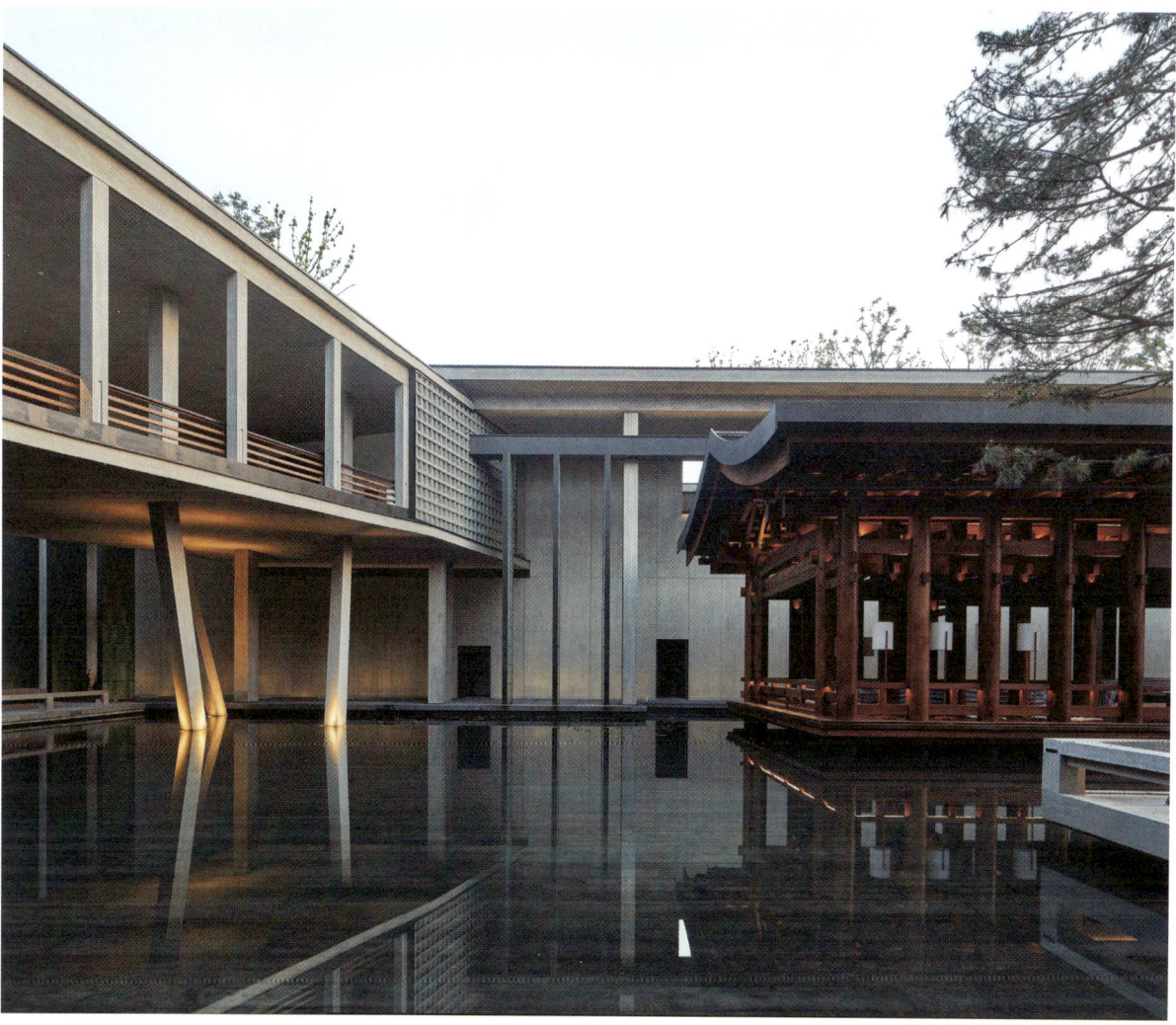

painting as the blueprint for the design of the site and building, turning a two-dimensional scroll into an architectural experience. Much like the institution treats the written record of history and art as a testament to culture, the architects treat an artifact as a historical truth, carrying in its essence a symbol of Chinese culture, which they express in three-dimensional form.

As visitors climb the front steps of the Hangzhou branch of China's National Archives of Publications and Culture, they have little idea of what awaits them behind the first gate. "When you step into the building," says Lu Wenyu, cofounder with her husband Wang Shu of the Hangzhou-based office Amateur

Opposite, top: Sketches of the National Archives by one of the architects of Amateur Architecture Studio, Wang Shu. **Bottom:** Overall, the design of the campus provides visitors with the emotions and vistas traditionally incorporated in the architecture of Song dynasty landscape painting, which was an important inspiration for the architects.

Above: The winding paths under the covered visitor pathways lead through a series of pavilions of different scales.

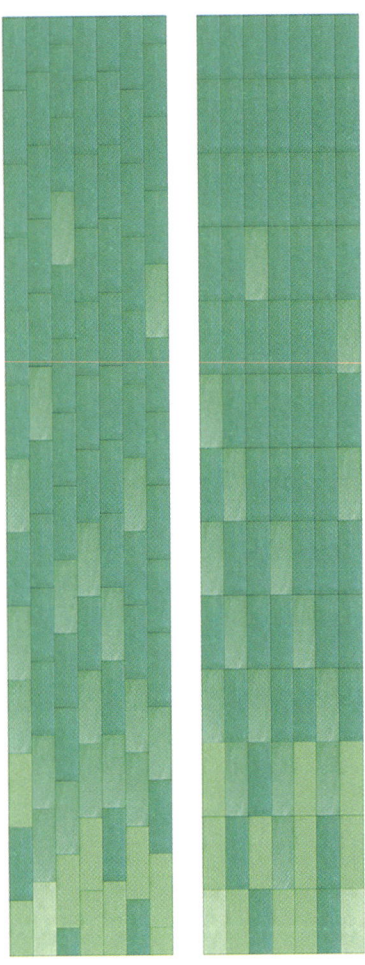  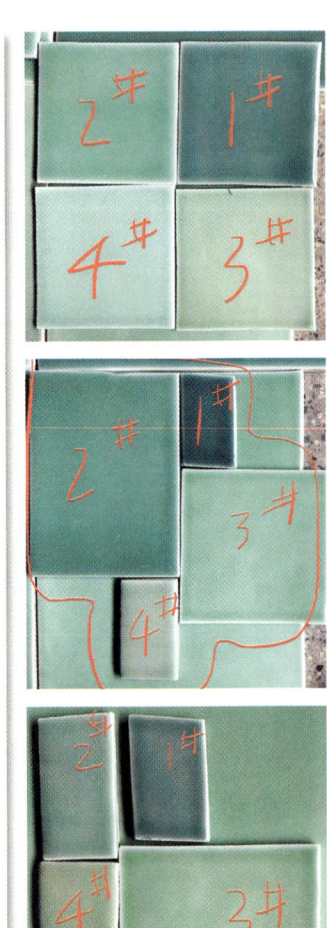

Architecture Studio, which completed the project in 2022, "you feel as if you've walked into a landscape painting."[6] Just as traditional Chinese scroll paintings give the sense of wandering through a scene rather than viewing it from a fixed perspective, the Hangzhou National Archives take visitors on a journey. Articulated as a series of pavilions that wrap around courtyards and are connected by zigzagging pathways, the complex offers a seemingly unlimited number of outdoor and indoor rooms that ceaselessly respond to one another and to the entire work. A sum of parts you can never fully grasp, the building reveals itself from within as you experience its different depths, heights, and angles.

Both inside and out, the architecture presents visitors with an impression of abundance and variety, its many different materials chosen for both their intrinsic properties and their historical symbolism. Ascending the site in concert with pools, terraces, pavilions, and stairs, poured-concrete buildings bear the imprint of bamboo stems and are punctuated with bands of packed dirt and stone. Giant greenware tile screens in four different shades

---

6. Lu Wenyu and Wang Shu interview with the author, July 24, 2024. For an overview of the Amateur Architure Studio see Michael Juul Holm, Kjeld Kjeldsen and Mette Kallehauge, eds., *Wang Shu Amateur Architecture Studio* (Louisiana Museum of Modern Art and Baden: Lars Muller, 2017).

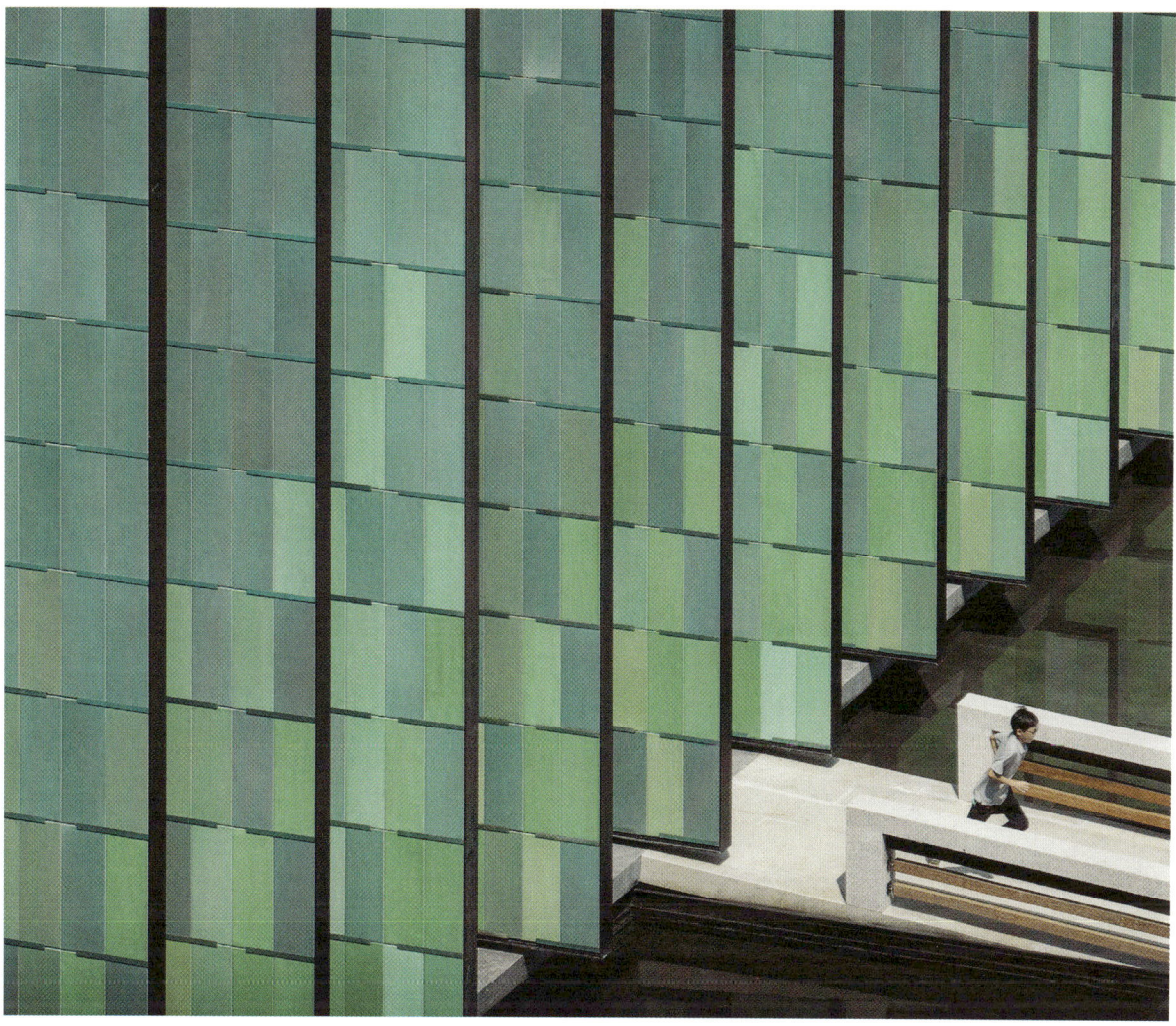

pay monumental homage to the ancient craft techniques of the local Longquan kilns, which have been operating in the region since the tenth century. Hand-assembled according to traditional construction principles, the timber pavilions at the complex's center use no metal or decorative elements in their connective joints, which are an integral part of the structures' vocabulary. These innovative uses of historical architectural principles and traditional techniques engage in an interdependent dialogue with one another.

Gentle sloping walkways throughout the campus allow visitors to reach various levels, offering changing perspectives on the site's topography. The surrounding greenery

Opposite and above: Giant greenware tile screens, in four different shades, pay monumental homage to the ancient craft techniques of the local Longquan kilns, which have been operating in the region since the tenth century.

Following pages : Innovative uses of historical architectural principles and traditional techniques dialogue in interdependent relation to one another.

Pages 24–25, left: Timber pavilions at the complex's center are hand-assembled according to traditional construction principles, using no metal or decorative elements in their connective joints. **Right:** *A Solitary Temple Amid Clearing Peaks*, a masterpiece attributed to the literati painter Li Cheng (919–967), inspired the blueprints of the National Archives.

THE MUSEUM IS SCROLL PAINTING

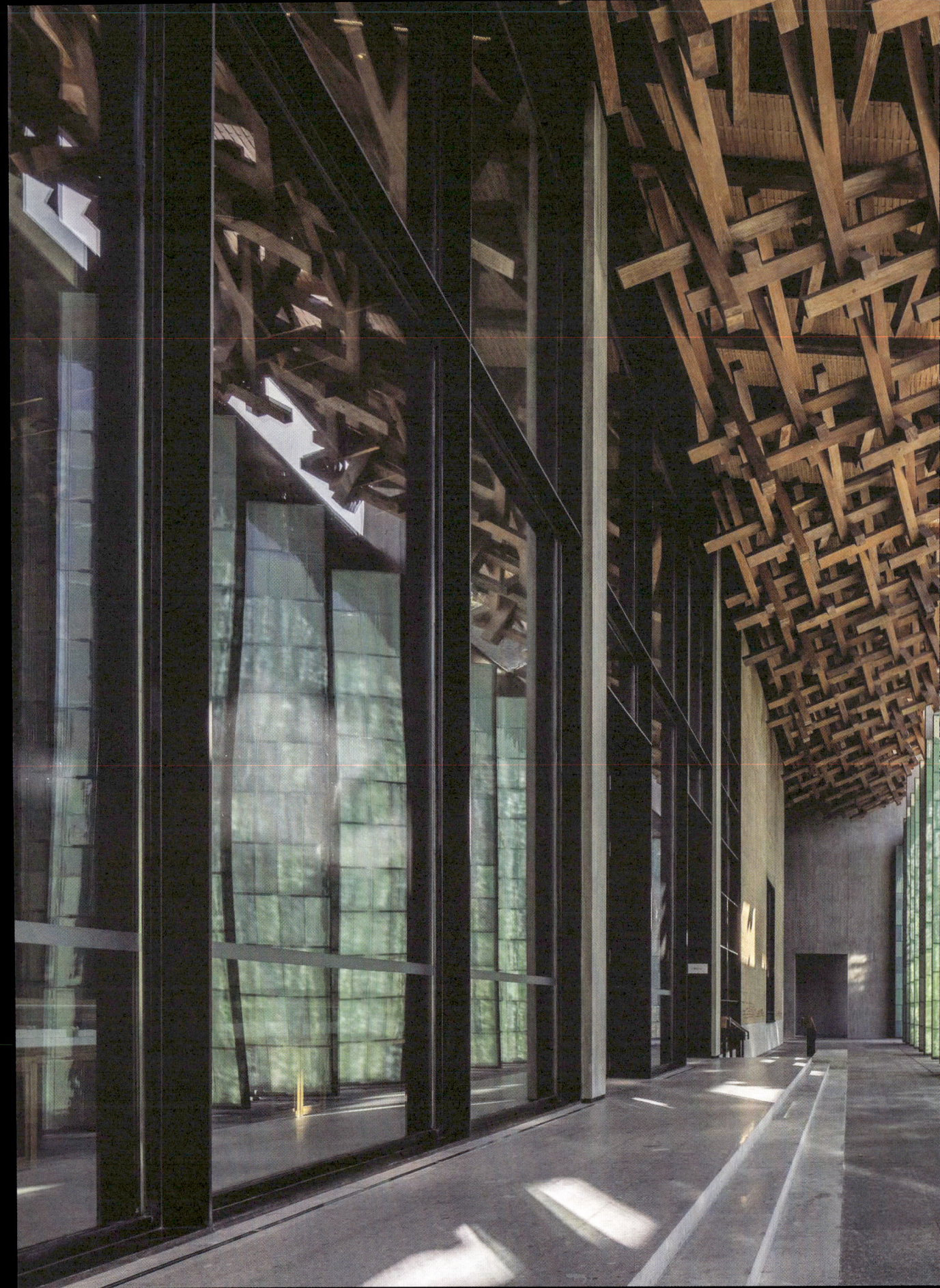

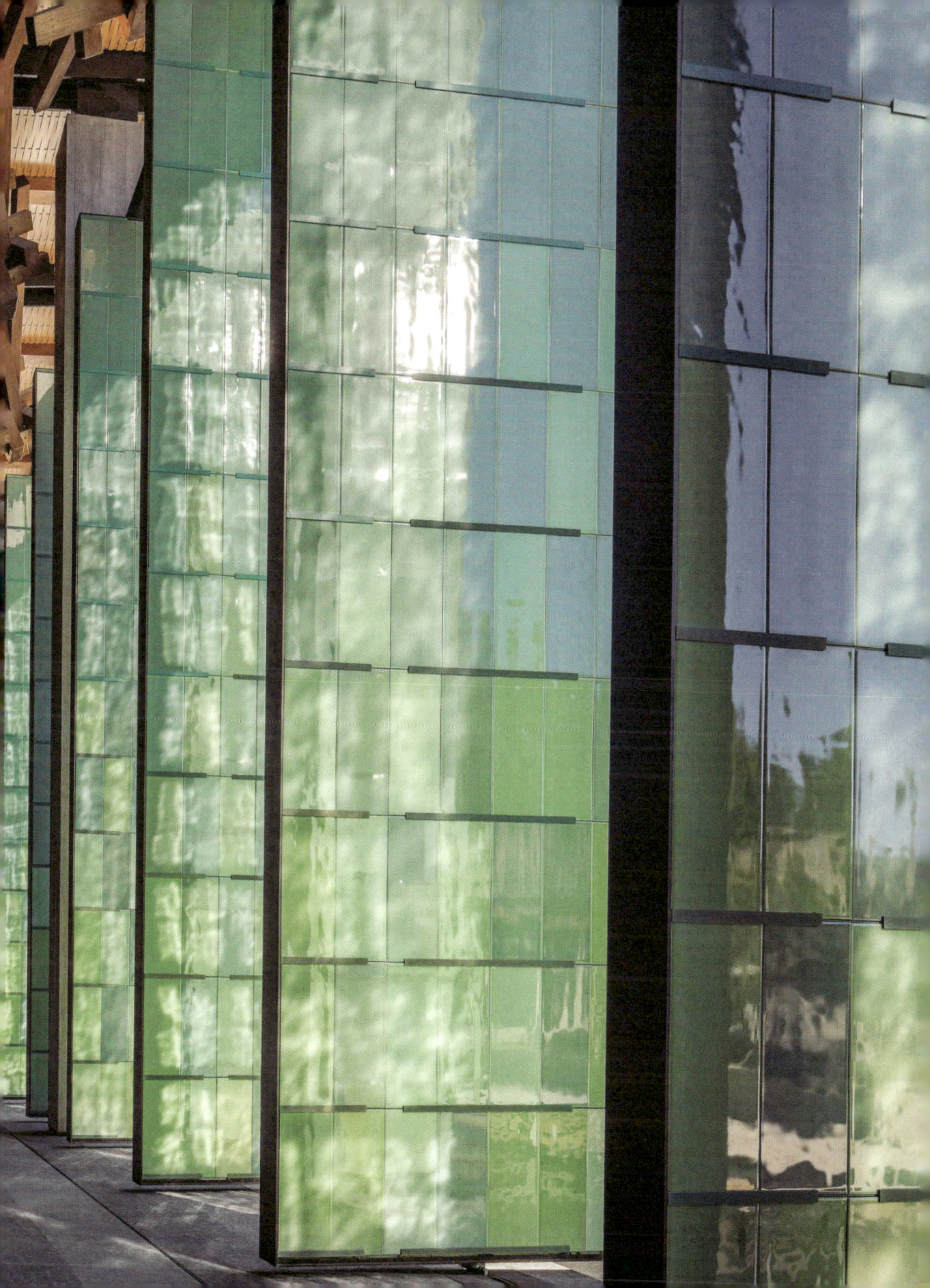

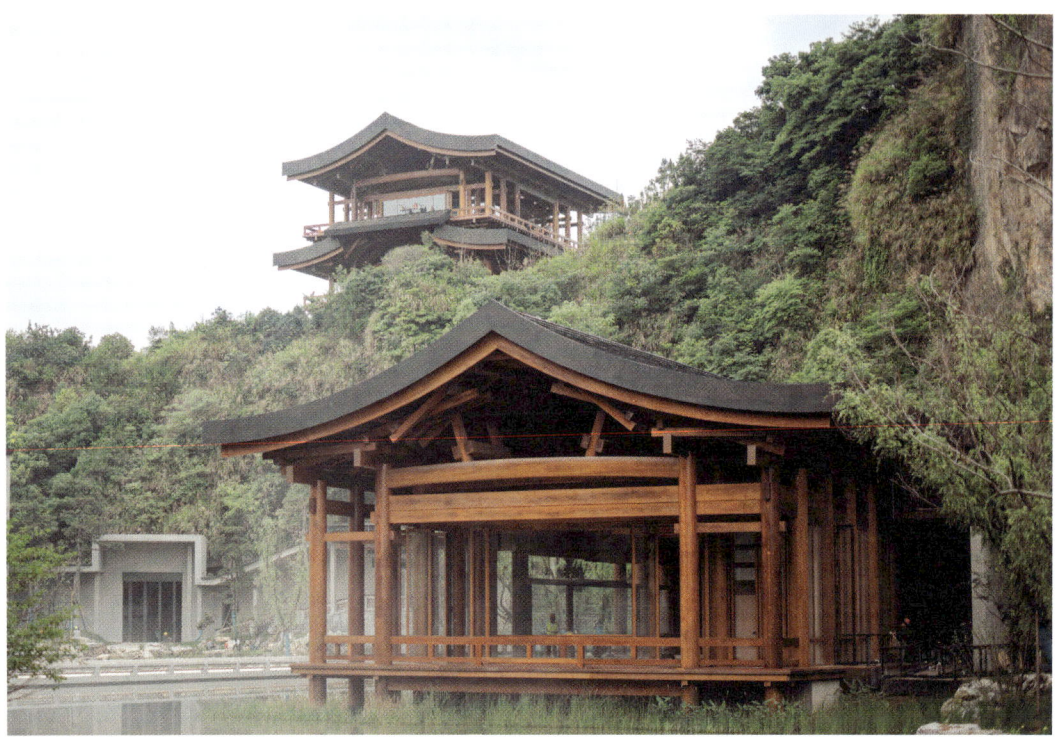

is framed by apertures in the successive passageways, which, akin to the literati gardens that flourished in the Hangzhou-Suzhou region during the Song dynasty (960–1279), invite contemplation.[7] In line with the fundamental principles of literati-garden design, which acknowledge the impossibility of complete representation—similar to those of landscape painting—the visitor's gaze, aided by the low height of the frames, is encouraged to ponder the various metaphors of nature in its different scales and depths of field. Available via a series of staircases set among a Longjing tea field, the topmost pavilion offers views over the complex's undulating roofs, constructed using a technique derived from a traditional tile-roofing system.

At the Hangzhou National Archives, Wang Shu and Lu Wenyu aimed to recreate the experience of a specific, canonical painting, not just any Song dynasty landscape representation. They drew inspiration from the hanging scroll *A Solitary Temple Amid Clearing Peaks*, a masterpiece attributed to the literati painter Li Cheng (919–967).[8] Born into an aristocratic family, Li gained recognition as one of the creators of the northern landscape style. His elegant and peaceful vistas, which also incorporated elements of the southern style, were seen as symbols of China's unification under the Song dynasty. *A Solitary Temple Amid Clearing Peaks* features many architectural details, including a fragment of a Song village with a temple, bridges, pagodas, pavilions, and pathways, creating a dream world that reflects the cosmological order of the new empire. The Son of Heaven, as the emperor was styled, is represented by the dominant mountain in the background, while his ministers and associates are depicted by the subordinate ranges and foothills. The entire vast structure appears as ordered, clear, and infinite as the great empire of China itself. There is no dust or dirt, no violence or disorder; nature is placid and benevolent, governed by the power and wisdom of the enlightened ruler who

---

7. For more on the Chinese garden, see Maggie Keswick, *The Chinese Garden: History, Art Architecture*. (Cambridge, MA: Harvard University Press, 2003); Ron Henderson, *The Gardens of Suzhou* (University Park: Pennsylvania University Press, 2012).
8. Now in the collections of the Nelson Atkins Museum of Art, Kansas City. For a complete testimony of the research and material insvestigation of the National Archives by the architects, see 杭州版本馆：创新设计与理念 [The National Archives, Creating and Designing Theory] (Hangzhou: Zhejiang University Press, 2022).

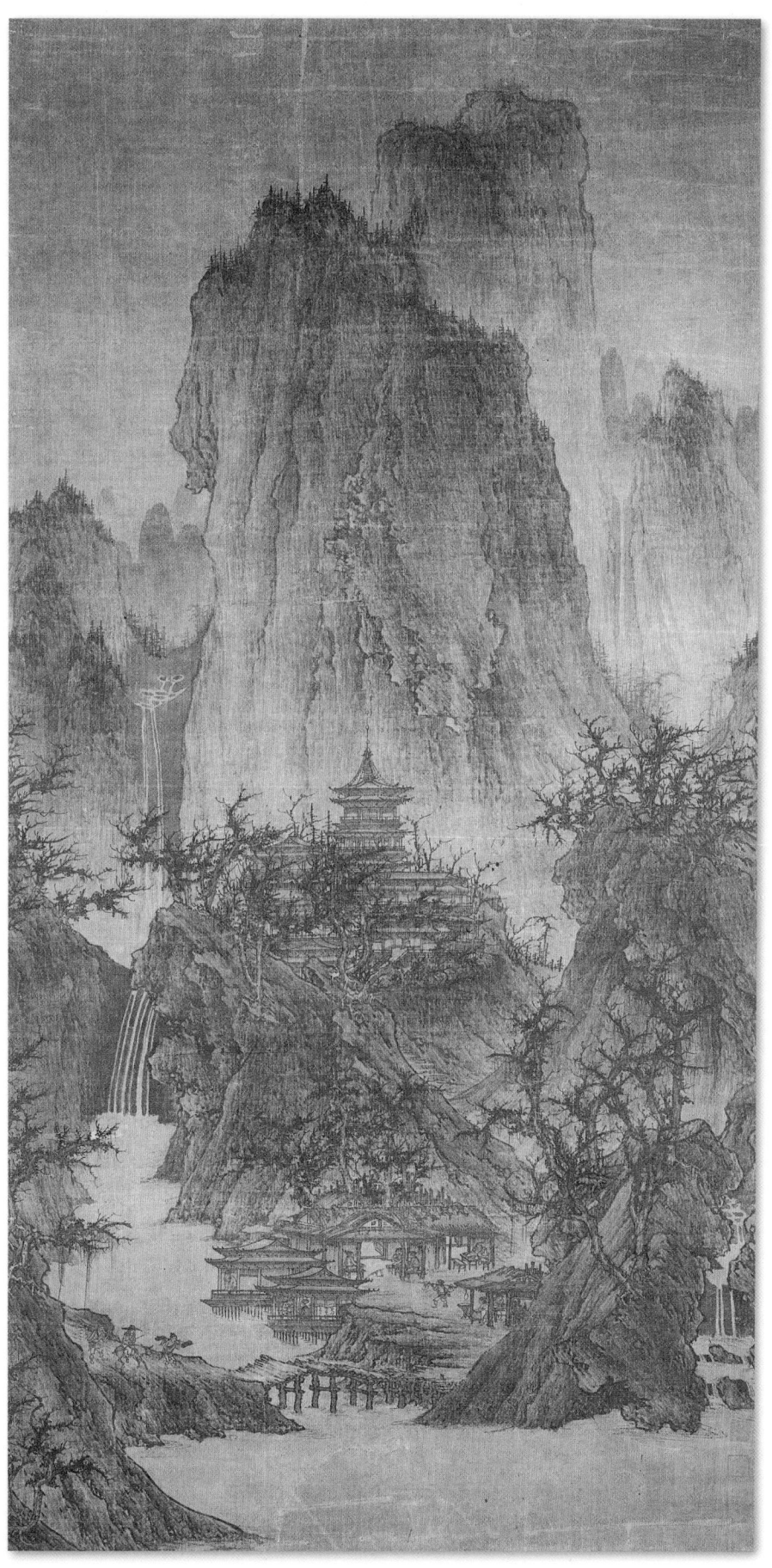

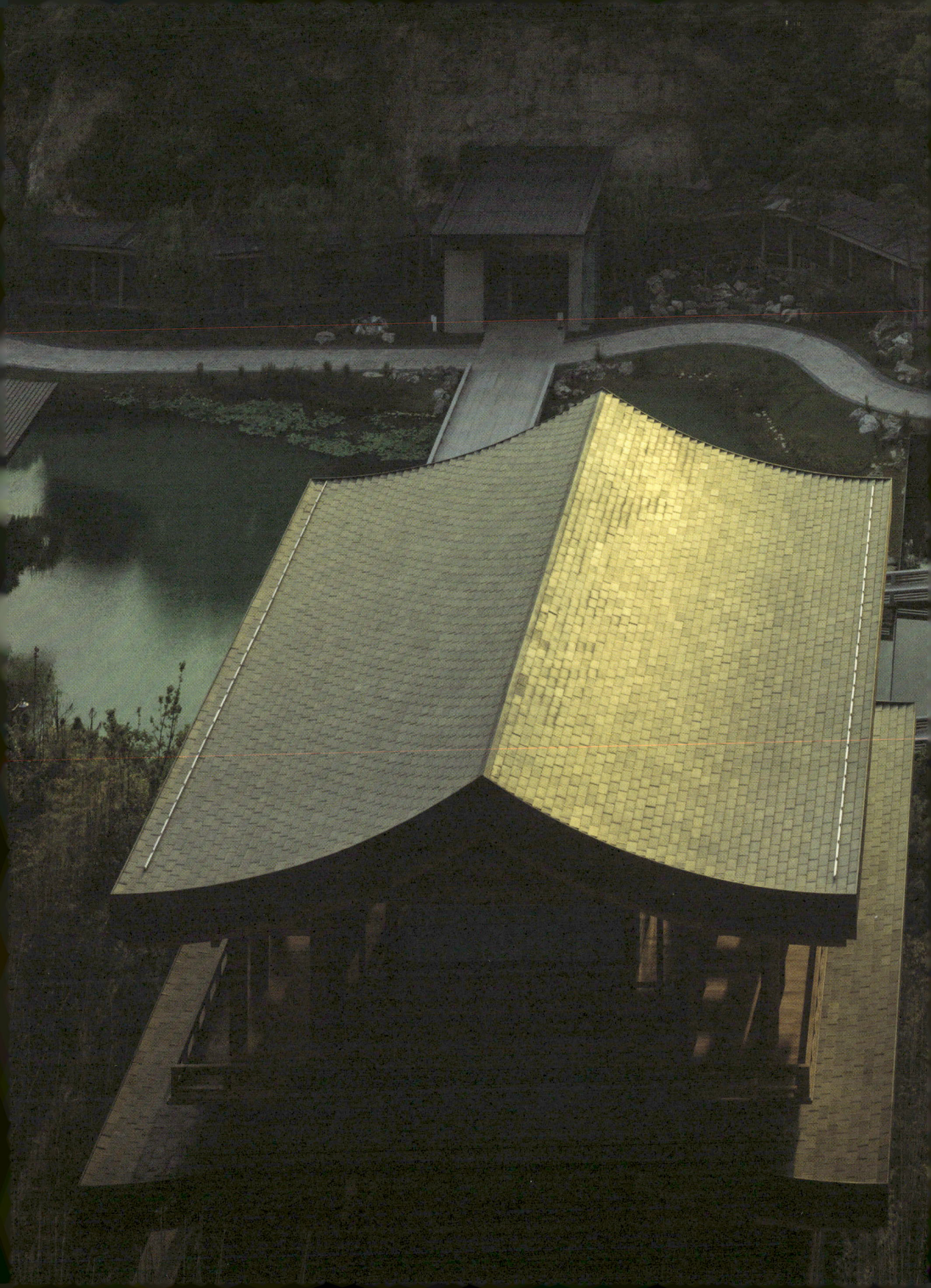

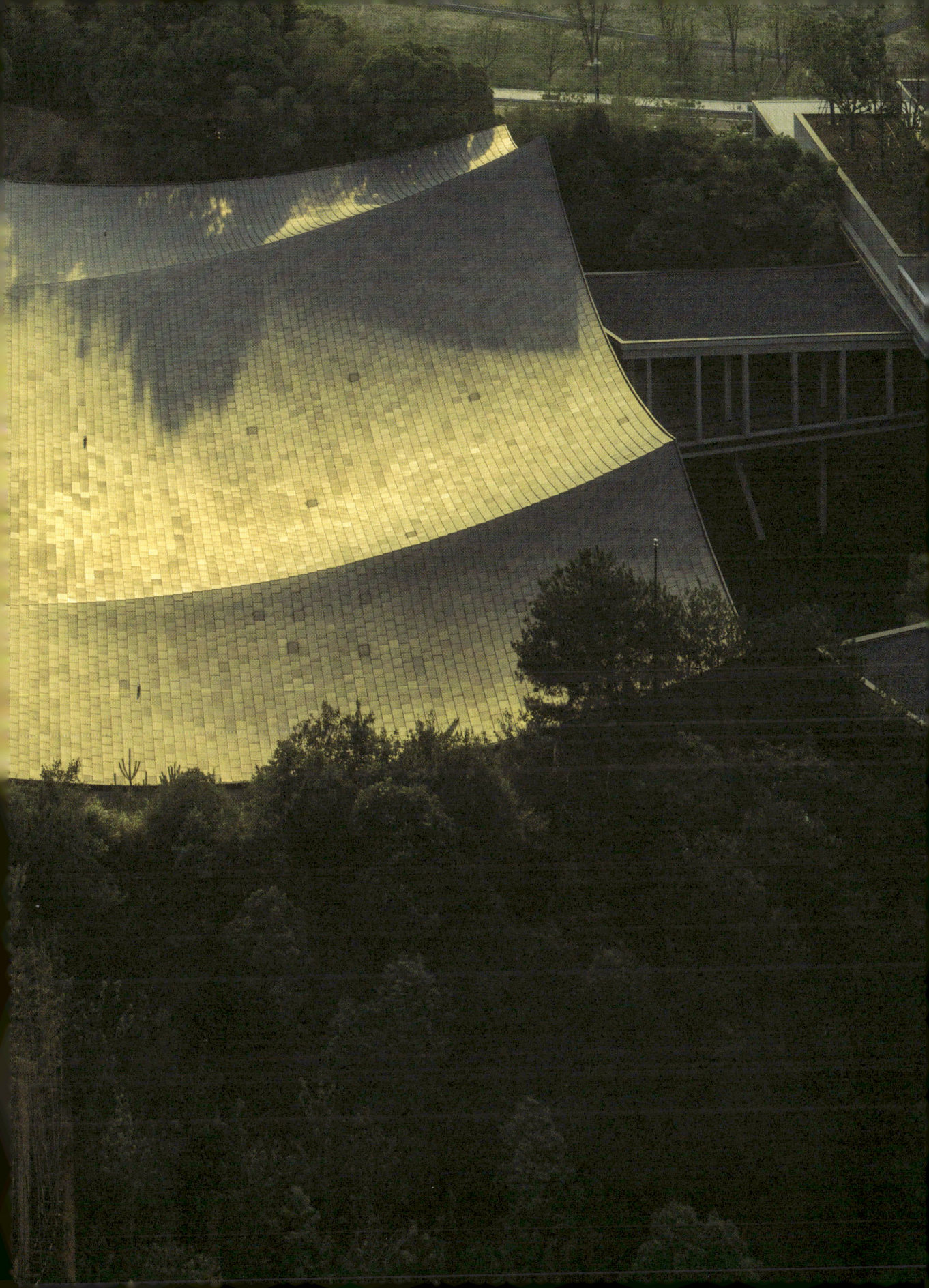

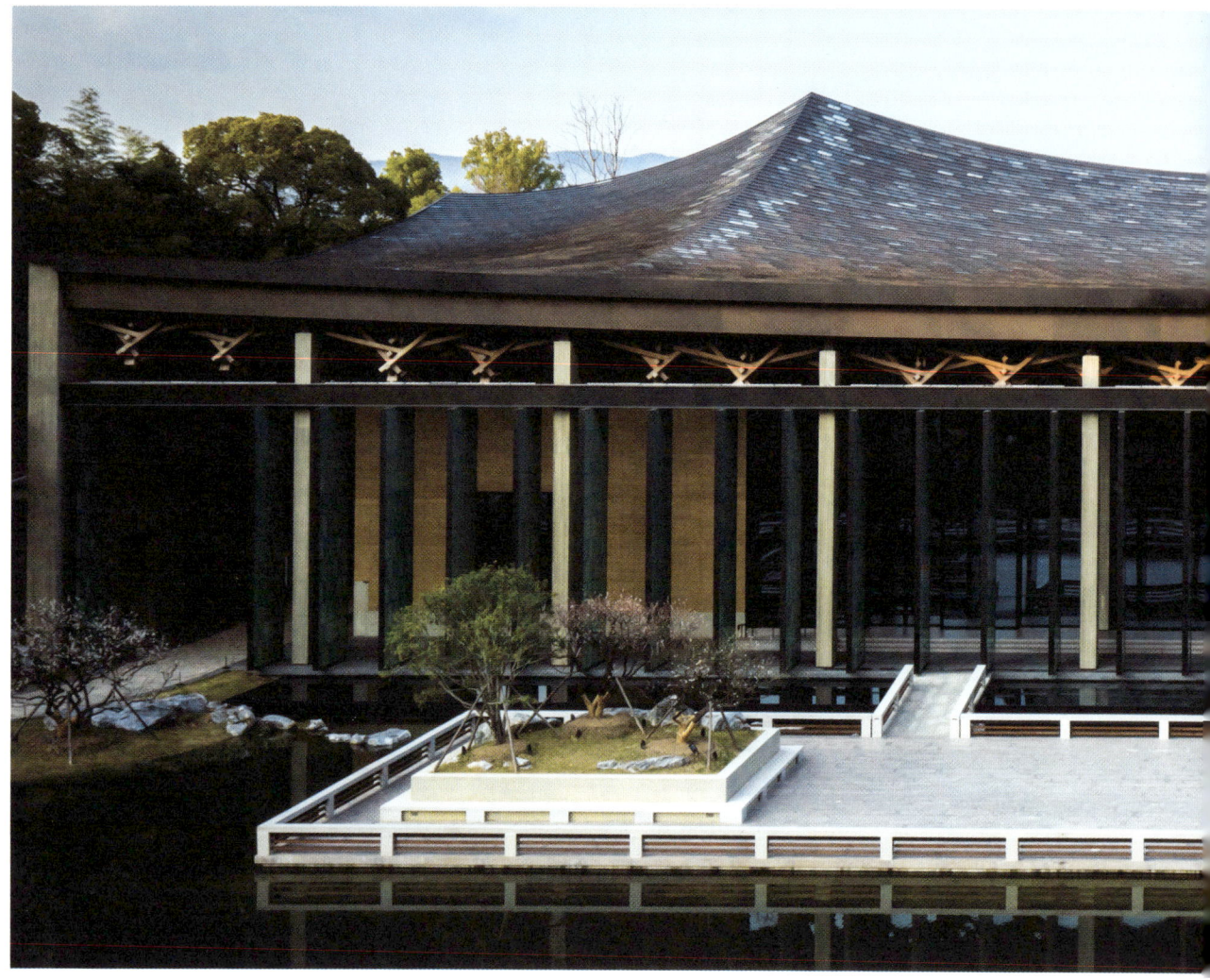

has brought humanity to this lofty condition through his wise interaction with heaven.

The Song capital, which evolved into present-day Hangzhou, was the most advanced and prosperous city in medieval China, serving as an intellectual center where literature and woodblock printing thrived, various painting genres developed, and art was discussed in countless biographical, theoretical, and investigative texts. Representations of the cosmological order, landscape paintings were understood to record the principles that organized the Chinese garden. In his encyclopedic *Brush Talks From Dream Brook*, the Song polymath Shen Guo (1031–1095) wrote, "All landscapes have to be viewed from the angle of totality to behold the part, much in the manner in which we look at an artificial rockery in our gardens."[9] In their design for the Hangzhou National Archives, Wang Shu and Lu Wenyu sought to mine classical Chinese history in search of a form of expression that is both new and timeless. Using Li's *A Solitary Temple Amid Clearing Peaks* as a blueprint, they produced a building that mirrors the painting's spatial composition, forming a cosmological sum of parts that reflects the ethos of the institution it houses. The distant past of Chinese civilization, as it existed in the

---

9. Michael Sullivan, *The Art of China* (Berkeley: University of California Press, 1984), 178.

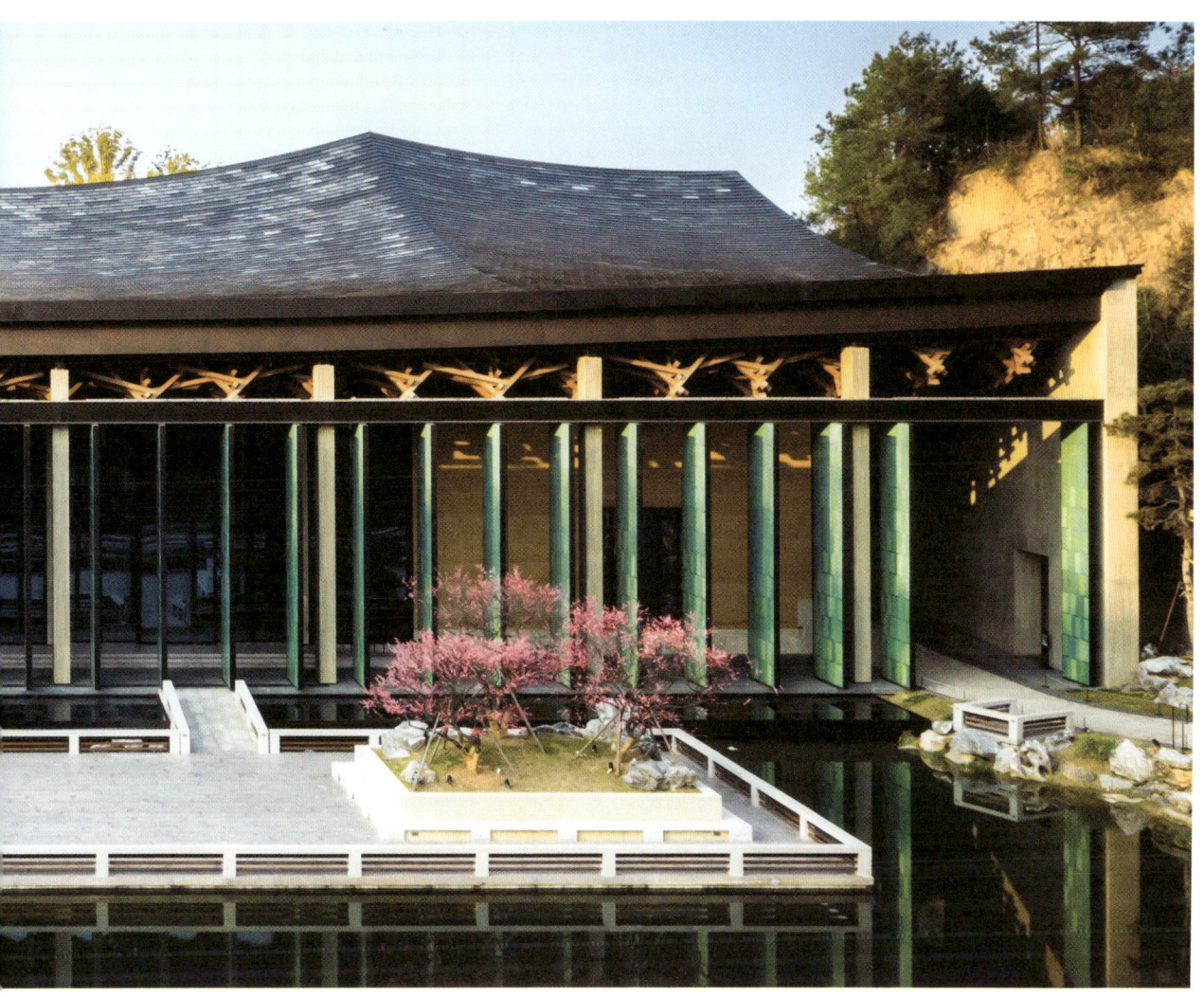

prosperous Song era—one of the most revered ancient dynasties, which unified China for three centuries—is brought to the foreground, enduring in the present through this contemporary architectural masterpiece.

Previous pages: Seen from the highest viewing point, the campus offers yet another sensation and experience. The roof tiles reflect light at different times of day and across the varying seasons, highlighting the organic materiality of the architecture.

Above: The tall celadon panels allow for the pavilions to entertain a fluid relation with the garden. They can be closed when the gallery space hosts exhibitions that require less natural light.

Following pages: The Grand Egyptian Museum, designed by Heneghan Peng, is a monumental structure meant to house, among other things, the 3,200-year-old Statue of Ramesses II that was relocated from Ramses Square in Cairo to the Museum's atrium. The entrance facade is adorned with pyramid motifs, in a maximalist evocation of the nation's icon, the Giza Pyramids.

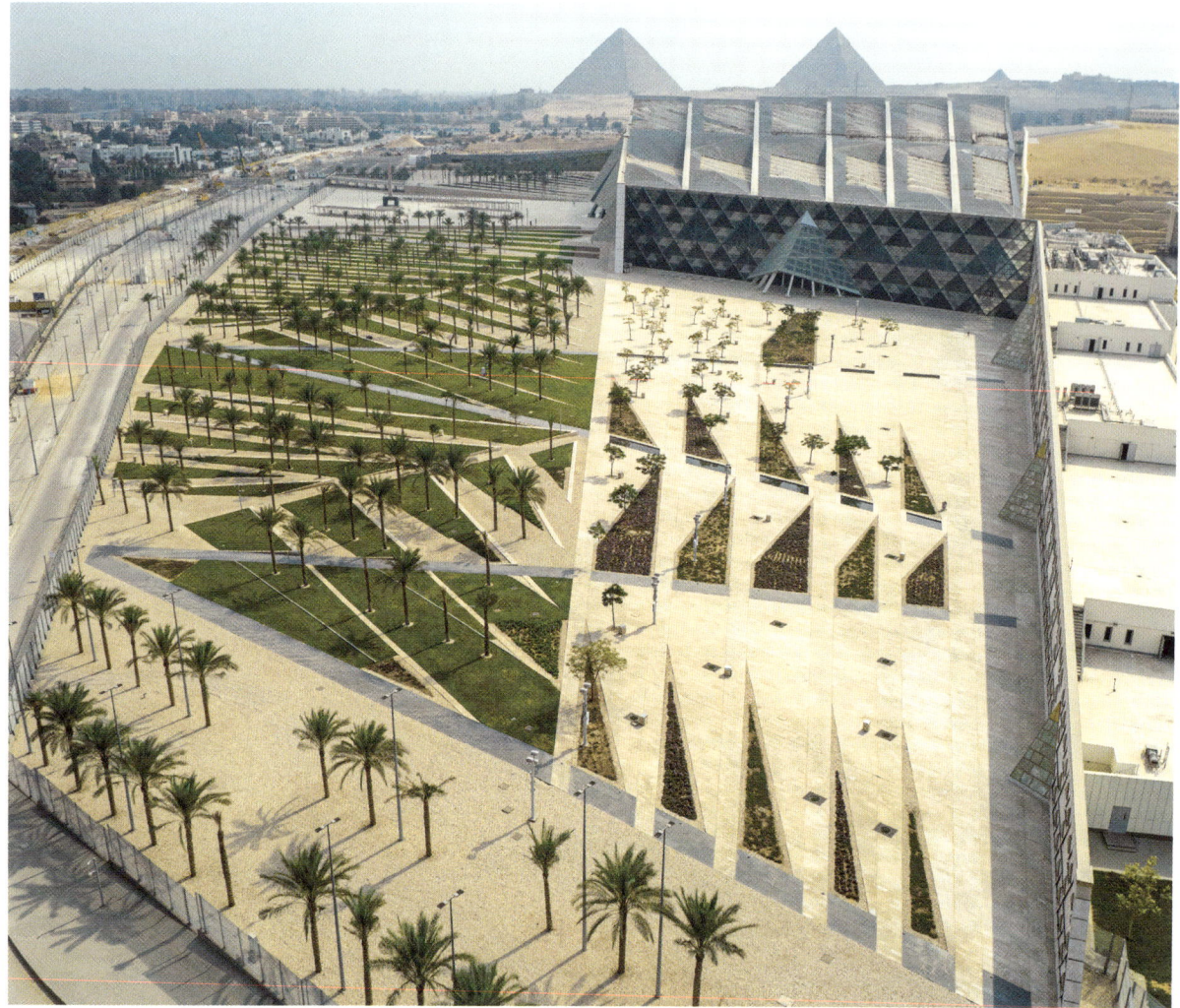

In other countries, a related museum phenomenon can be observed, where museum architecture is driven by the imperative of recontextualizing and reappropriating a historical narrative on a civilizational timeline. The Grand Egyptian Museum—its name states its ambition to be physically all-encompassing, and indeed it delivers on this promise with some 124 acres of space open to the public. It partially opened to the public in 2025.[10] Designed by Heneghan Peng Architects, the museum is an homage and an ambitious attempt to reclaim the heritage of Egyptology, which has been scattered across the globe since the eighteenth century, following excavations of archaeological sites by European powers over nearly two centuries. The landscape in front of the museum (designed by West 8), its shape, and the decorative motifs on the facade, evoke one of Egypt's most famous monuments, the Giza Pyramids, only 1.3 miles away. A walkway under construction will soon link the two. This physical affirmation that Egyptology belongs to Egypt, at the very site of the Pyramids of Giza, positions the museum as both a temple to them and an extension of their experience, in offering a resting place for all other objects related to Egyptian civilization.

---

10. At the time of writing, the remainder of the galleries have yet to be assigned a set opening date.

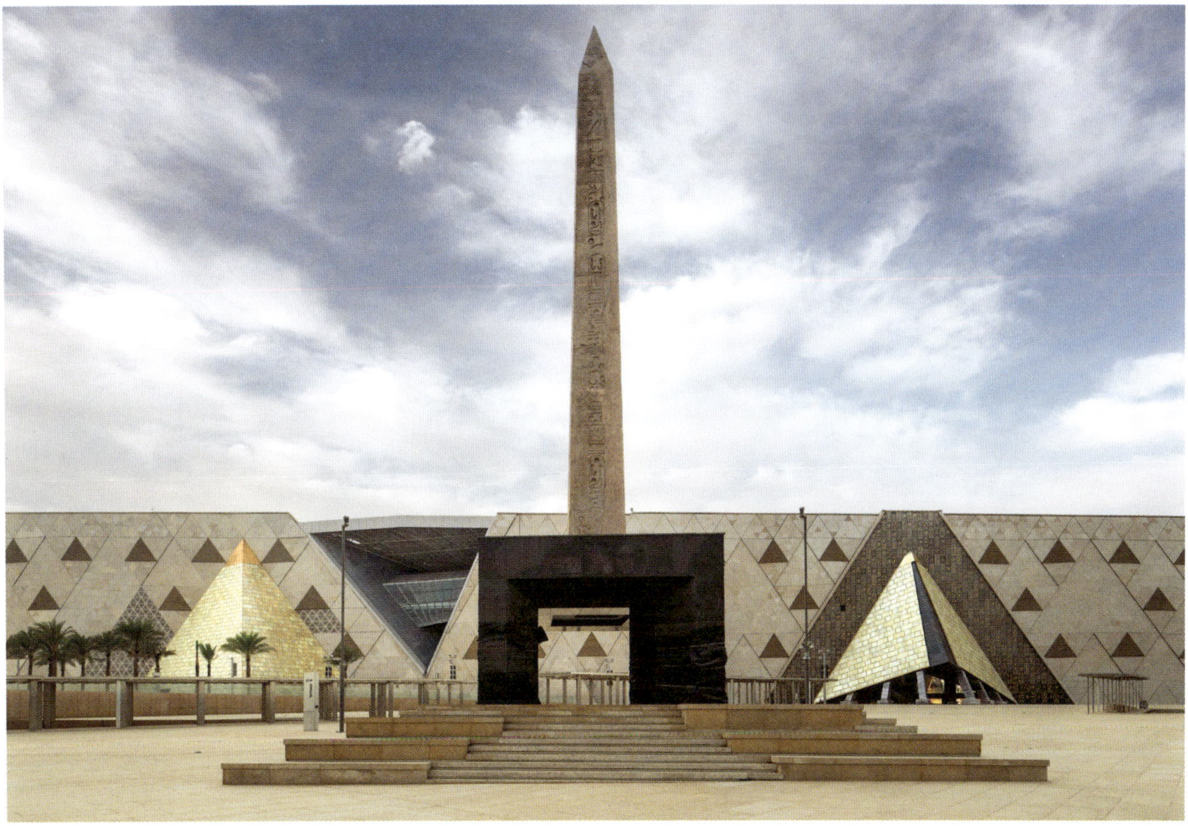

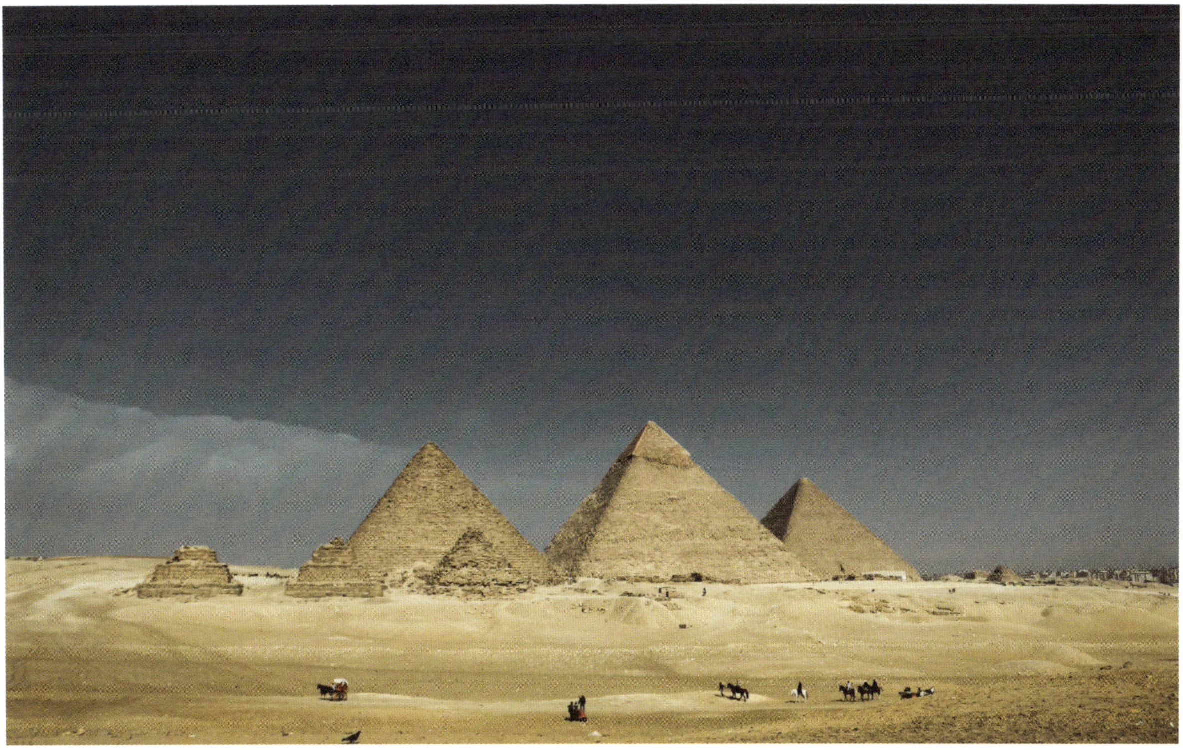

THE MUSEUM IS SCROLL PAINTING

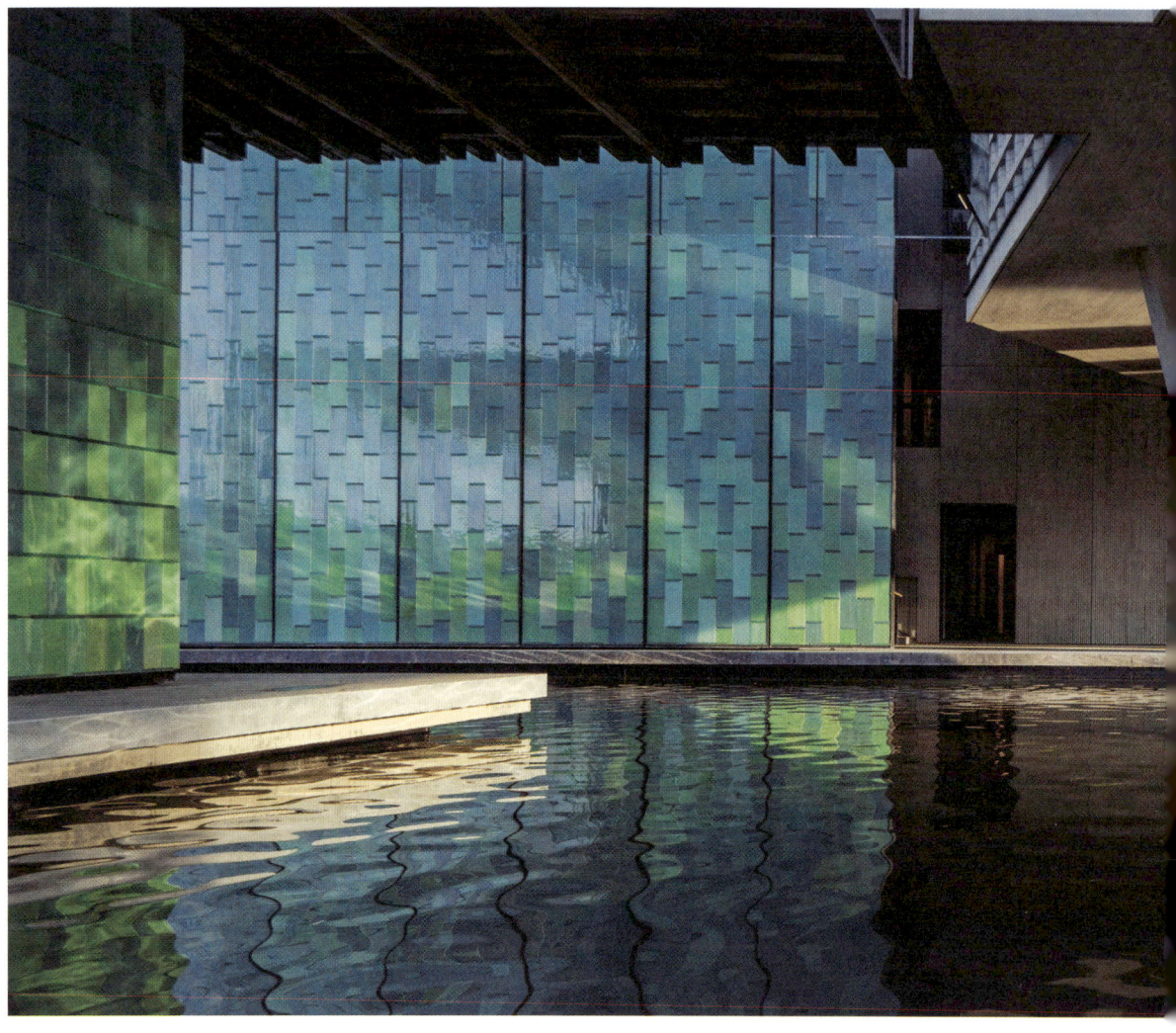

Conversely, the Chinese government's approach offers a new cultural typology that lies between a museum and a library. Deployed on a national level, the Chinese government seeks to establish a narrative in which the country's past civilizations serve as the overarching thread of continuity. With the distant past and the most recent present of the twentieth century reunited in these significant cultural sites, the ruptures of the twentieth century can be understood as nothing but a hiatus in the continuous arc of Chinese civilization. In this context, periods of history that could potentially be read as breaks in the unity of Chinese history—such as the iconoclastic New Culture Movement of the 1920s and the Cultural Revolution of the 1960s and 1970s—are, thanks to the national scale of the National Archives, recontextualized within a more distant past. The museum-library, where past and present coexist as an architectural fact, illustrates how today's triumphant modernity was always inherently possible and latent within Chinese tradition.

A significant shift in reclaiming the history of revolutionary China has been taking place, and the National Archives can be interpreted as a culmination of this effort to redraw a narrative that links the ancient past in continuous narration with the twentieth century. In July 2023, to mark its sixtieth anniversary, Beijing's National Art Museum of China (NAMOC) organized a

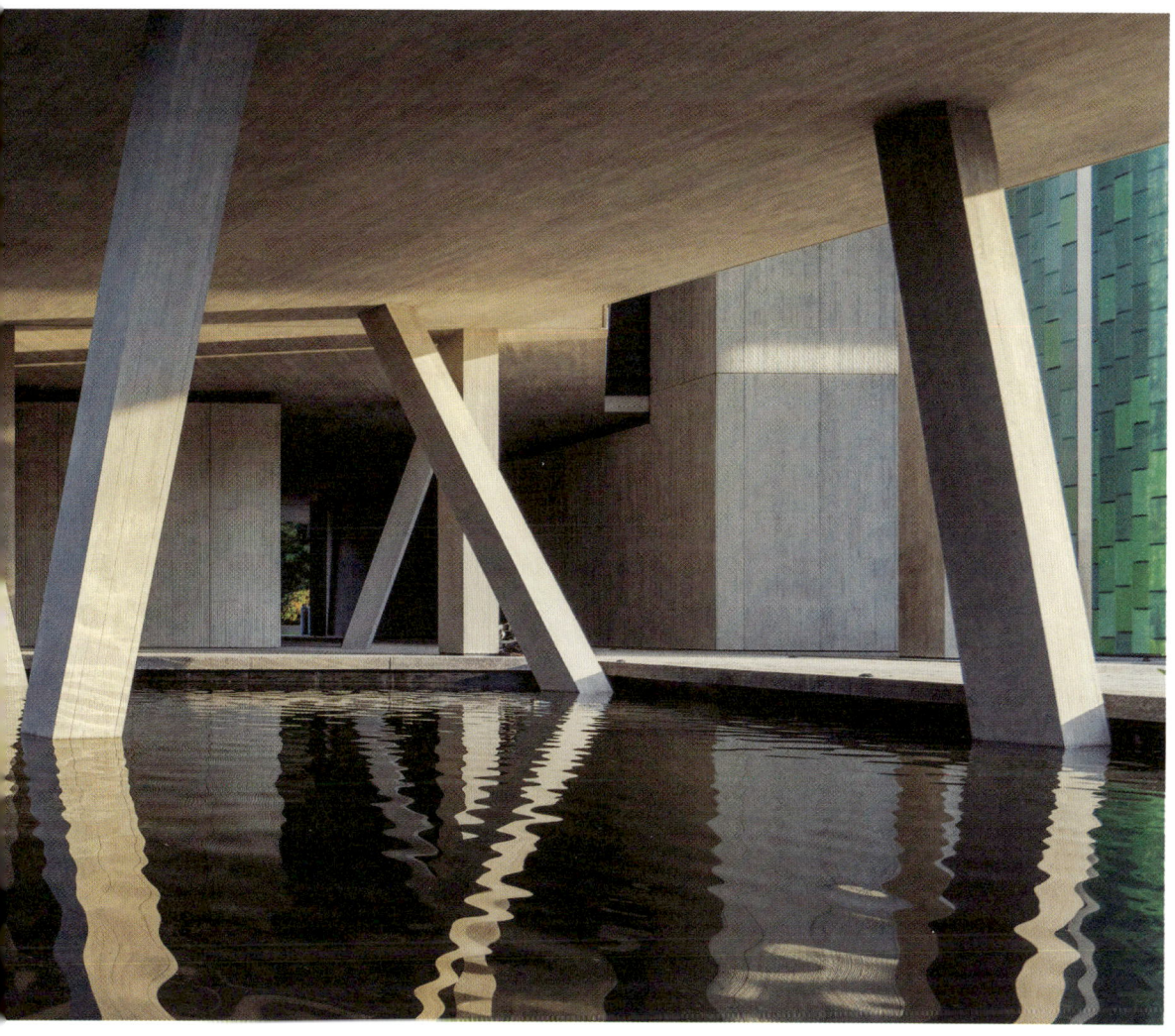

A view beneath the suspended walkways that surround trees and rocks and allow for multiple pathways and perspectives, and in turn re-creates the physical experience of viewing a landscape painting.

series of shows around the various media that served different ideologies in twentieth century China. Displayed side by side, like parallel timelines in art history, were calligraphy, ink painting, and revolutionary art. In conjunction with this celebration, an exhibition of socialist-realist sculptures depicting important battles in the Long March (the Red Army's 1934–1935 retreat and regrouping during the civil war) also opened. Commissioned in 2021 by NAMOC director Wu Weishan, these sculptures were intended to celebrate and prolong the "spiritual values" of the Long March, a seminal moment in the history of Chinese communism that "deeply influenced China and impressed the world." As the exhibition's wall text put it, "... it is the

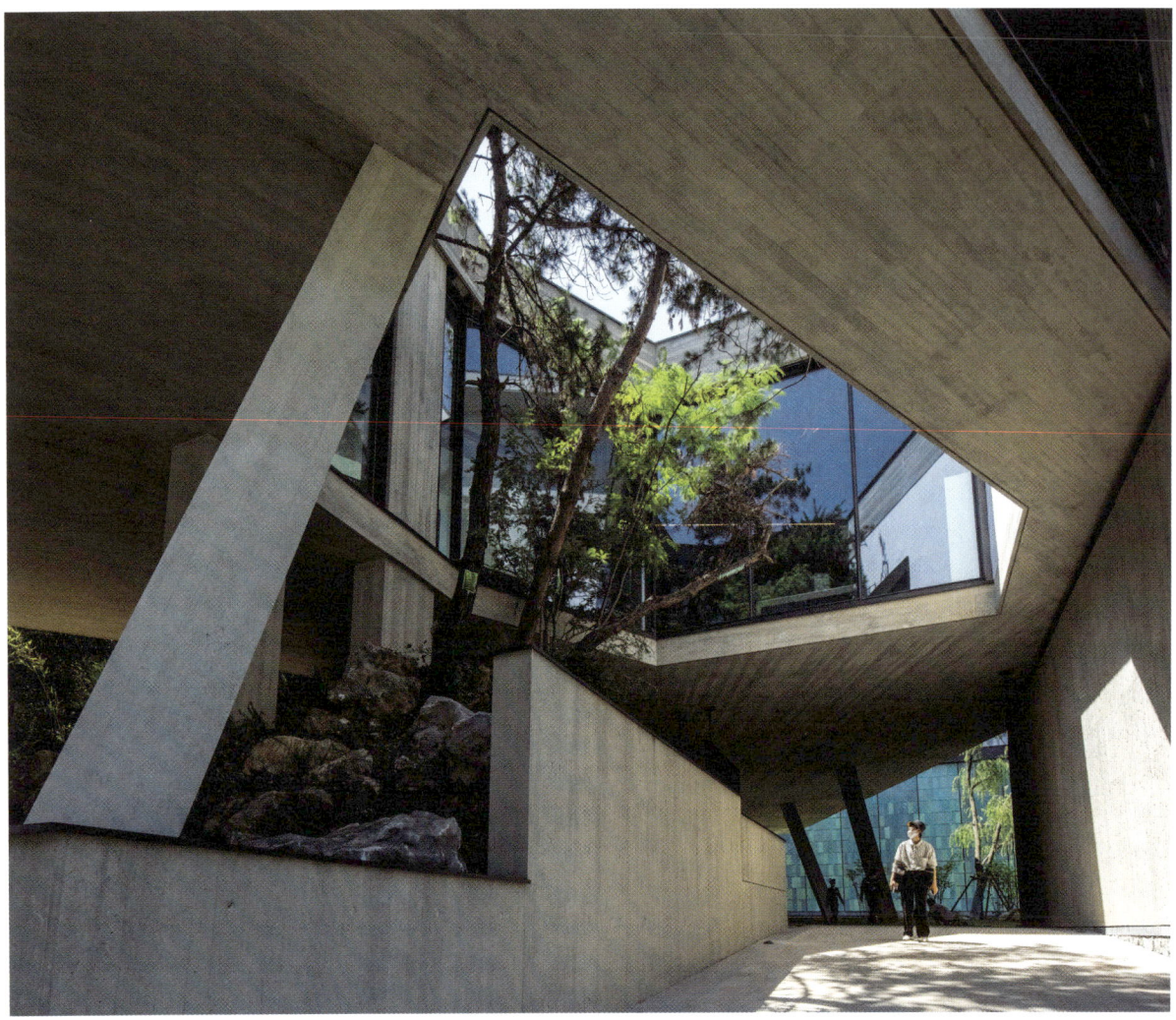

responsibility of artists in the new era to vigorously promote the great spirit of the Long March in an artistic form. To inherit the revolutionary culture, practice the spirit of the Long March in an artistic way ..." What the National Archives have achieved in architectural symbolism and institutional mandate is what this exhibition attempted to do: to join together the revolutionary twentieth century with the classical history of China and its imperial past.

This process of rewriting history arguably began when Harald Szeemann invited Cai Guo-Qiang to present *Rent Collection Courtyard* (*Shouzhouyuan* 受阻院) at the 1999 Venice Art Biennale. Cai's work recreated in situ an iconic socialist-realist sculpture of the same name, made in 1965 by a group of artists at the Sichuan Academy of Fine Arts. It depicted 114 life-size clay figures in various situations of oppression by their landlords. In Venice, Cai invited Long Xu Li, who directed the original work's production, along with nine guest artisans, to recreate the scene, imagining the new work as a performance that would reclaim the political in art:

> In addition to the experiments with artistic form, I was actually consciously trying to use the exhibition of Venice's Rent Collection Courtyard in this last biennale of the century to call attention to socialist art that has been quickly forgotten in contemporary culture, and to remind people

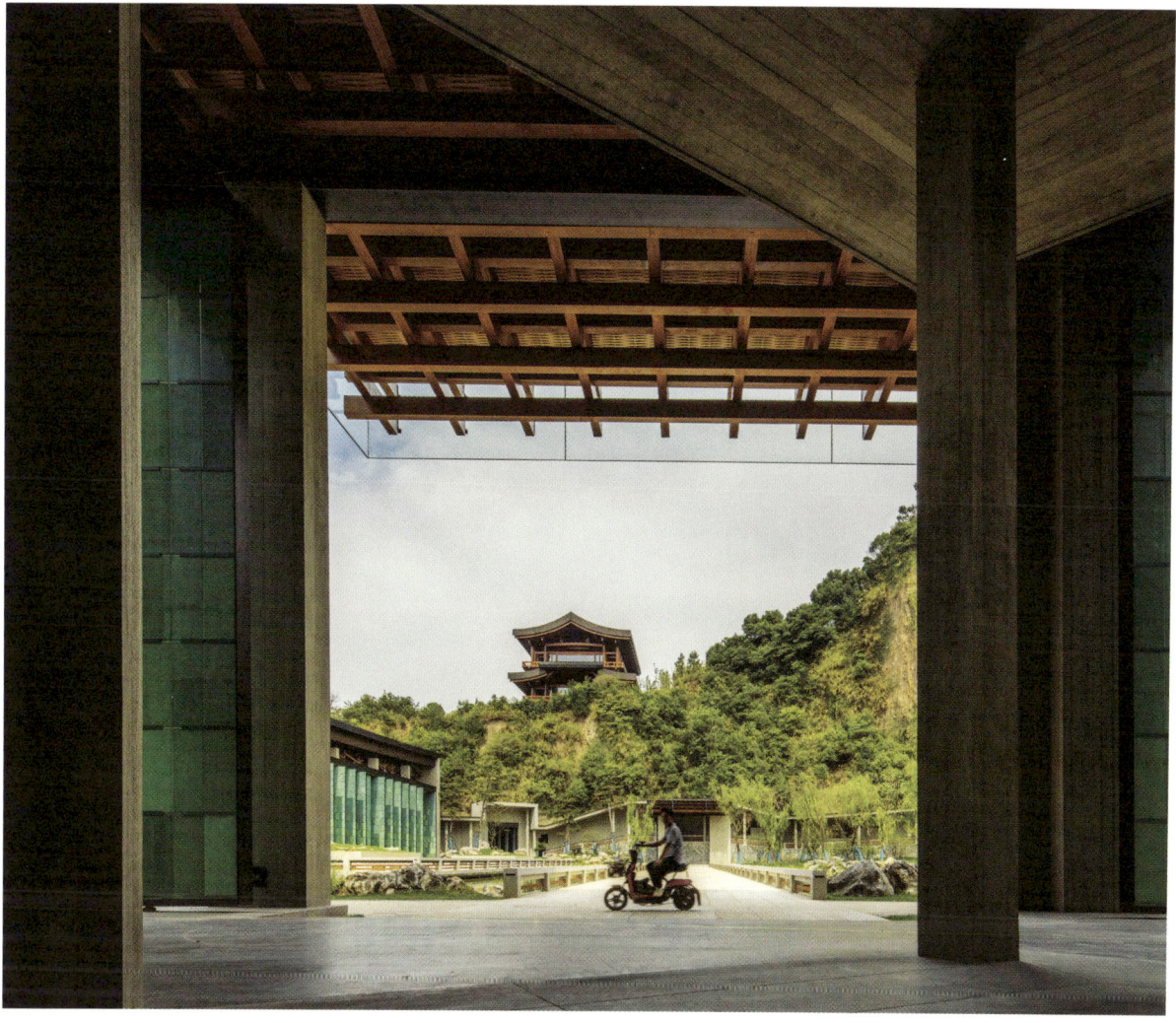

of the relationship between art and politics and special artistic features of this art.[11]

At the time, the Chinese government did not fully grasp the significance of foregrounding history in one of the world's most

11. Cai Guo-Qiang, "Guanyu Weinisi Shouzuyuan," [Concerning Venice's Rent Collection Courtyard] *Jinri xianfeng (Avant-Garde Today)*, no. 9 (2000). See also Zhu Qi, "We are all too sensitive when it comes to Awards! Cai Guo-Qiang and the copyright infringement problems surrounding Venice's Rent Collection Courtyard," in *Chinese Art at the Crossroads: Between Past and Future, Between East and West,* ed. Wu Hung (Hong Kong: New Art Media; London: Institute of International Visual Arts, 2001), 56–65. Trans. Krista Van Fleit. The work was part of the seminal restrospective of the artist at the Guggenheim Museum in New York a decade later. See Cai Guo-Qiang, *I Want to Believe* (New York: Guggenheim, 2008).

Opposite: Throughout the campus, the architecture structures striking views of elements of nature that invite contemplation and symbolically evoke architecture's role in bridging our relationship with nature.

Above: Different frames of perspectives anchor the view in a manner reminiscent of the experience of reading a scroll painting: architecture is both framing as well as within the landscape.

THE MUSEUM IS SCROLL PAINTING

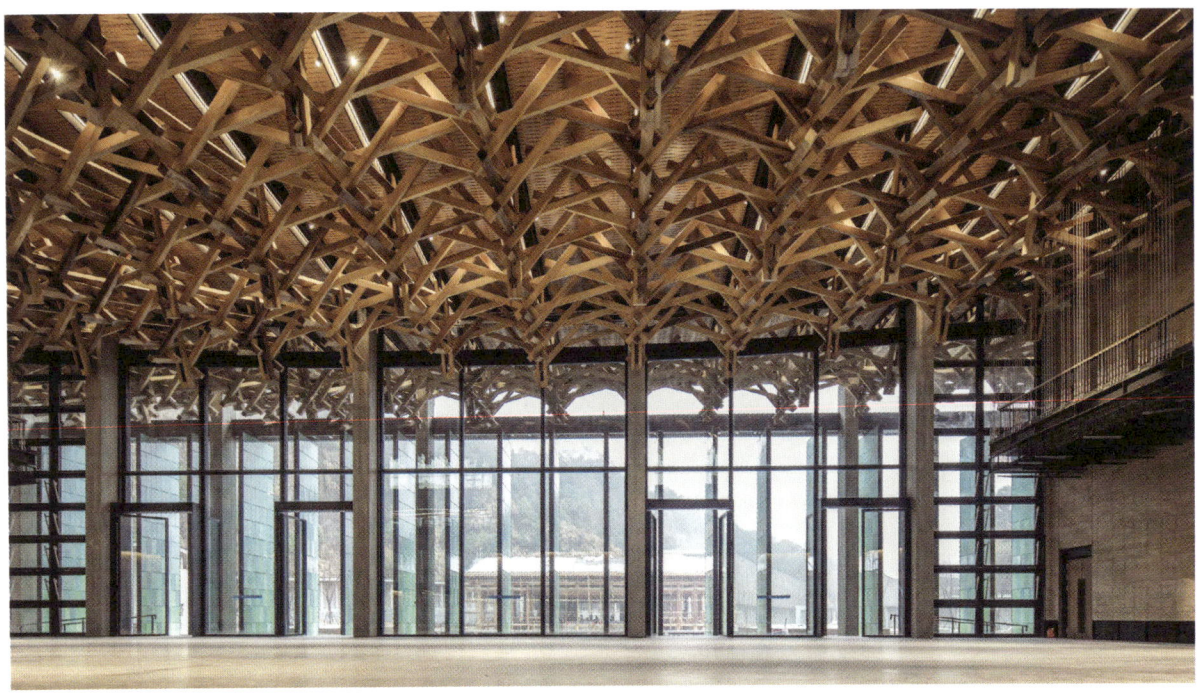

contemporary art forums. Although officials recognized the radical nature of this approach, they reacted strongly after Cai won the Golden Lion, suing him for copyright infringement despite his careful crediting of the original piece and framing his work as a performance. He also involved the chief artisan who contributed to the original work. What was radical and concerning for the Chinese government was the idea of ownership of history and its right to exist in the present, which they believed was their sole prerogative. Cai's performance, as an expression of an unofficial voice, was unacceptable because it held the potential for irony within the context of the Venice Biennale.[12]

Today, however, through initiatives such as the National Archives of Publications and Culture and the 2023 NAMOC exhibitions, the Chinese Communist Party is arguably engaging in the same maneuvers as Cai. In both cases, the museum serves as a tool to achieve a cross-temporal reunification of Chinese culture, aiming to nullify and erase the iconoclastic, modernizing extremes of Maoism and its consequences throughout the twentieth century. In this contemporary context, such initiatives express a political will to rearticulate the history of the twentieth century in continuity with the nation's pre-communist past.[13] On an unprecedented scale and with unprecedented speed, the Chinese government is rewriting the country's history through its reenactment in museum settings.

The result of this national project is a reinvention of the concepts of museum and library as being distinct, provoking the emergence of a new visitor experience. In the European history of museums, since the time of Vivant Denon, the first director of the Musée Napoléon (now the Musée du Louvre), museums have mostly

---

12. By 2008, however, Cai had been integrated into official discourse and was invited to join the Special Effects Committee for the opening ceremony of that year's Beijing Olympics.
13. From 1966 until Mao's death a decade later, China underwent an acceleration of the destructive impulse that had begun with the New Culture Movement. Mao did not invent the term "cultural revolution": half a century earlier, the Western-oriented Chinese intellectuals associated with the New Culture Movement—particularly those writing in the *New Youth* magazine founded by Lu Xun—had called for a "cultural revolution" to bring about a fundamental national transformation. As used by China's radical democratic intellectuals in the second decade of the twentieth century, the term conveyed two notions that are enduring significance in contemporary Chinese thought: first, a wholesale rejection of traditional Chinese cultural heritage; second, an extraordinary emphasis on the role of human consciousness in shaping history. These ideas deeply influenced the young Mao Zedong and were crucial to the Maoist version of Marxism-Leninism.

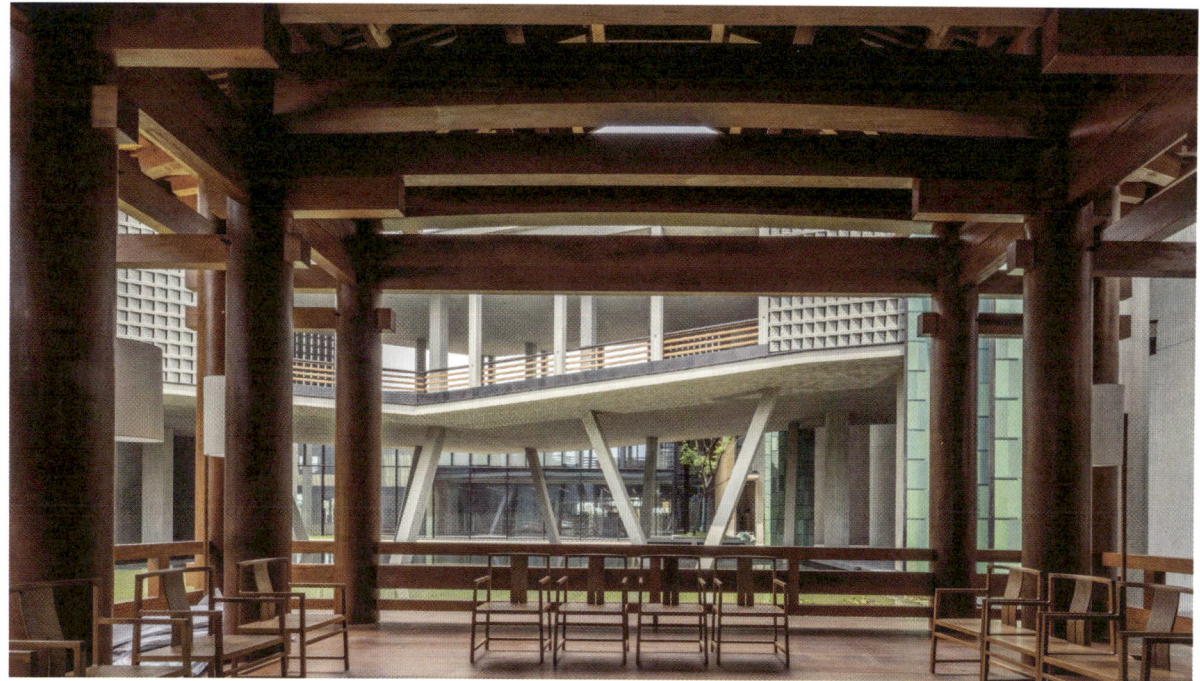

metamorphosed from a library-like form—exhibiting fragments of the past without a linear narrative—into spaces where history is materialized through chronological display organized by national schools of art history.[14] China's National Archives lie somewhere between a museum and a library, focusing on the experience of reading due to the nature of their collections and the unique status of Chinese painting as a potential record of Chinese history. In the Louvre, visitors move through galleries, viewing paintings alongside texts written by the museum's curatorial staff. In contrast, the National Archives exhibit texts, books, and objects related to the written word as works of art, displayed in a way that allows their content to be read—they serve as both objects and evidence, records, and repositories of culture.

The "viewer-reader" is invited to participate in "performing" the "record of heritage" through the act of reading. At China's National Archives, the new museum experience fosters

Opposite and above: The architecture presents visitors with an impression of abundance and variety, its multifarious materials having been chosen for both their intrinsic properties and their historical symbolism. Wood was a predominant material in the finest examples of Song dynasty constructions.

Following pages: Some galleries function as modular reading rooms and other as exhibition galleries, recalling the scholar's study in classical Chinese culture.

Destruction was Mao's injunction in 1966, taking the New Culture Movement's ideas to a violent extreme. At its core, the uld be created ex-nihilo. For more on this period, see Peter Zarrow, *China in War and Revolution, 1895–1949* (London: Routledge, 2005). And Jonathan Spence, *The Search for Modern China* (New York: W. W. Norton, 1990).
14. For a comprehensive account of this history, see Krzystof Pomian, *Le musée, une histoire mondiale, tome II, L'ancrage européen, 1789–1850* (Paris: Gallimard, 2021).

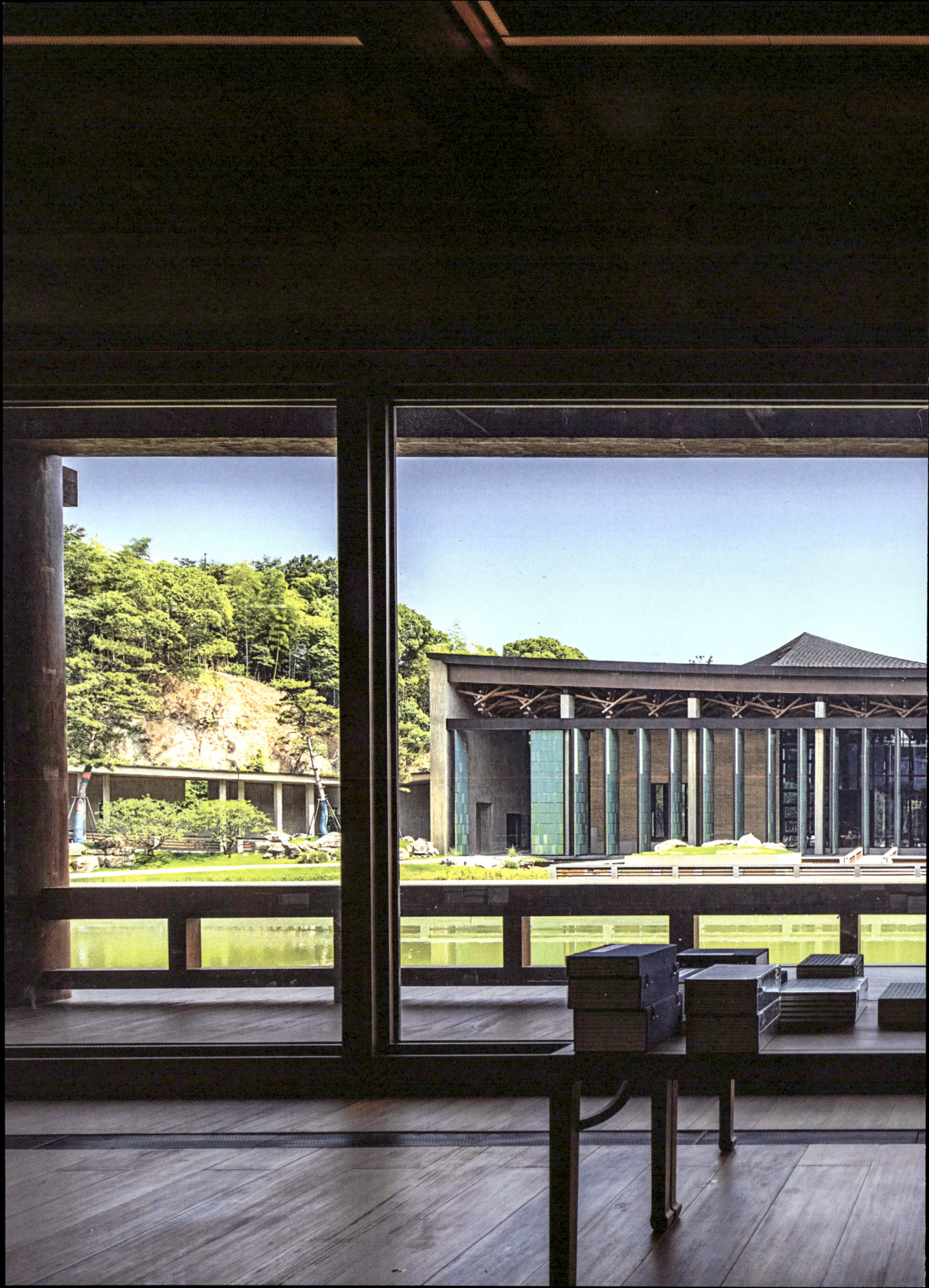

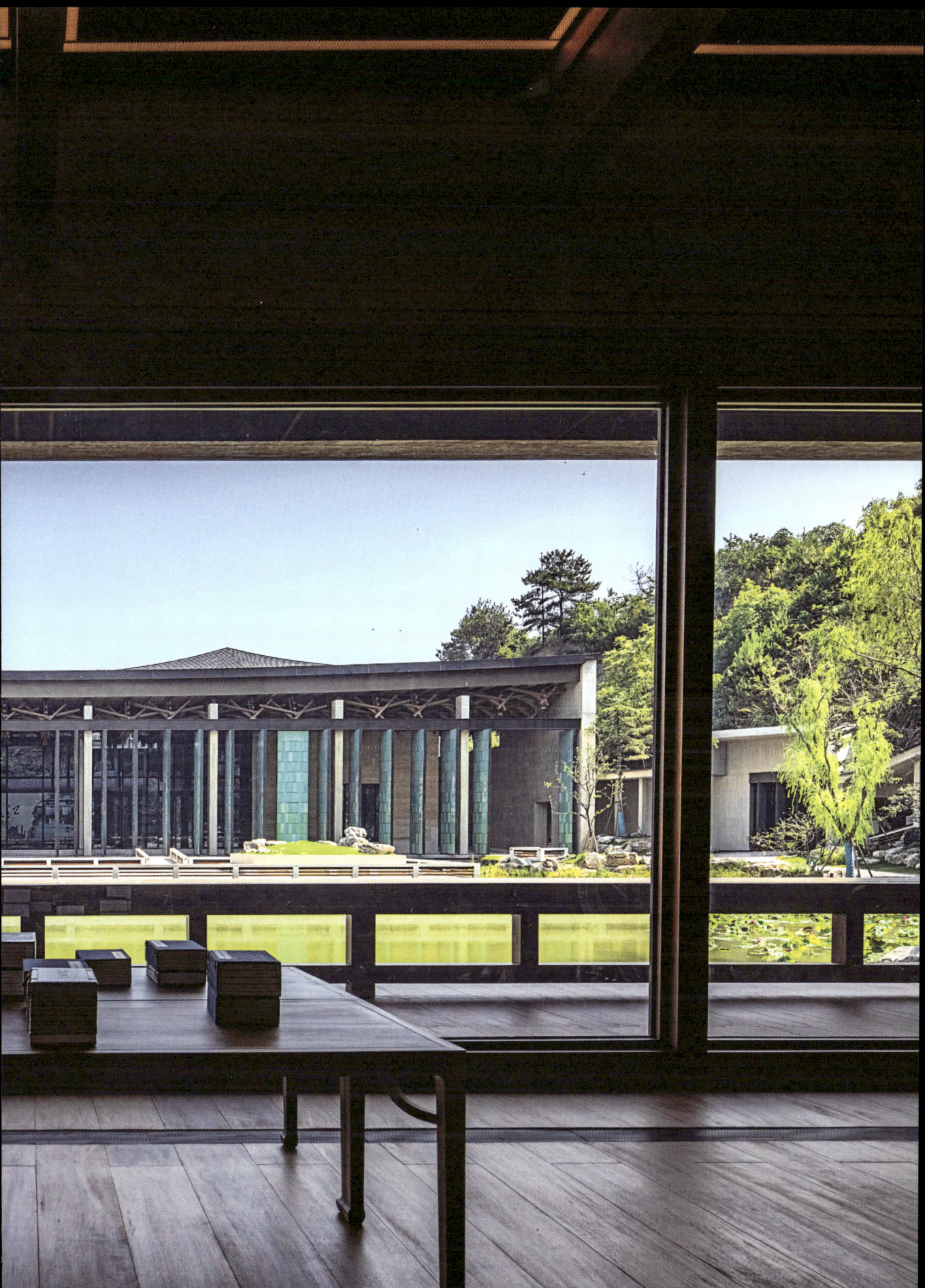

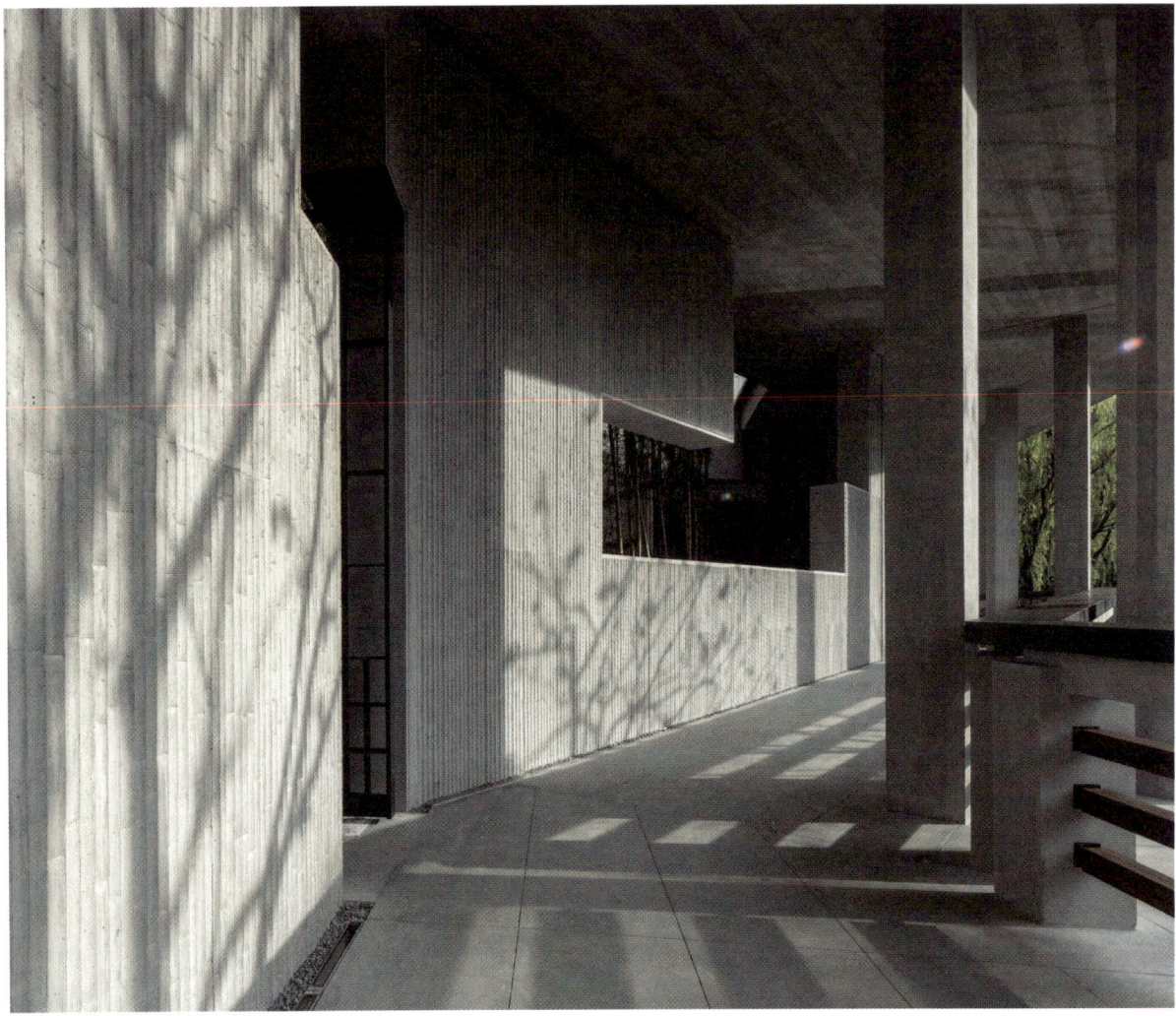

a form of participation centered on readership; in an almost ritualistic sense, visitors interact with objects that possess an eternal potential to be read, voicing the histories they record and embody in the present. The Centre Pompidou's program was not entirely unlike that of the National Archives, but the latter has the potential—due to its display methods and collections and the specific status of writing in Chinese culture—to encourage an almost ritualistic dimension of the museum space as a site of historical reenactment. Its "viewer-readers" partake in the performed prolongation of ancient Chinese civilizations, subsuming the iconoclastic break of twentieth-century Maoist China. Both modernity and tradition have always been located in the past, just as they are simultaneously located in the future.

The performative dimension of the building itself—the blueprint being Li Cheng's masterpiece—represents an architectural reenactment of history, where all periods from the past find themselves on the same plane as contemporaneity. This historicity of time which makes the past and present simultaneous, aligns with what André Malraux proposed in his 1947 concept *Le Musée imaginaire* ("Museum Without Walls"),[15] published nineteen years before Mao launched the Great Proletarian Cultural Revolution. For Malraux, photography allowed for the joining of artifacts from any civilization into a kind of supramuseum that would place

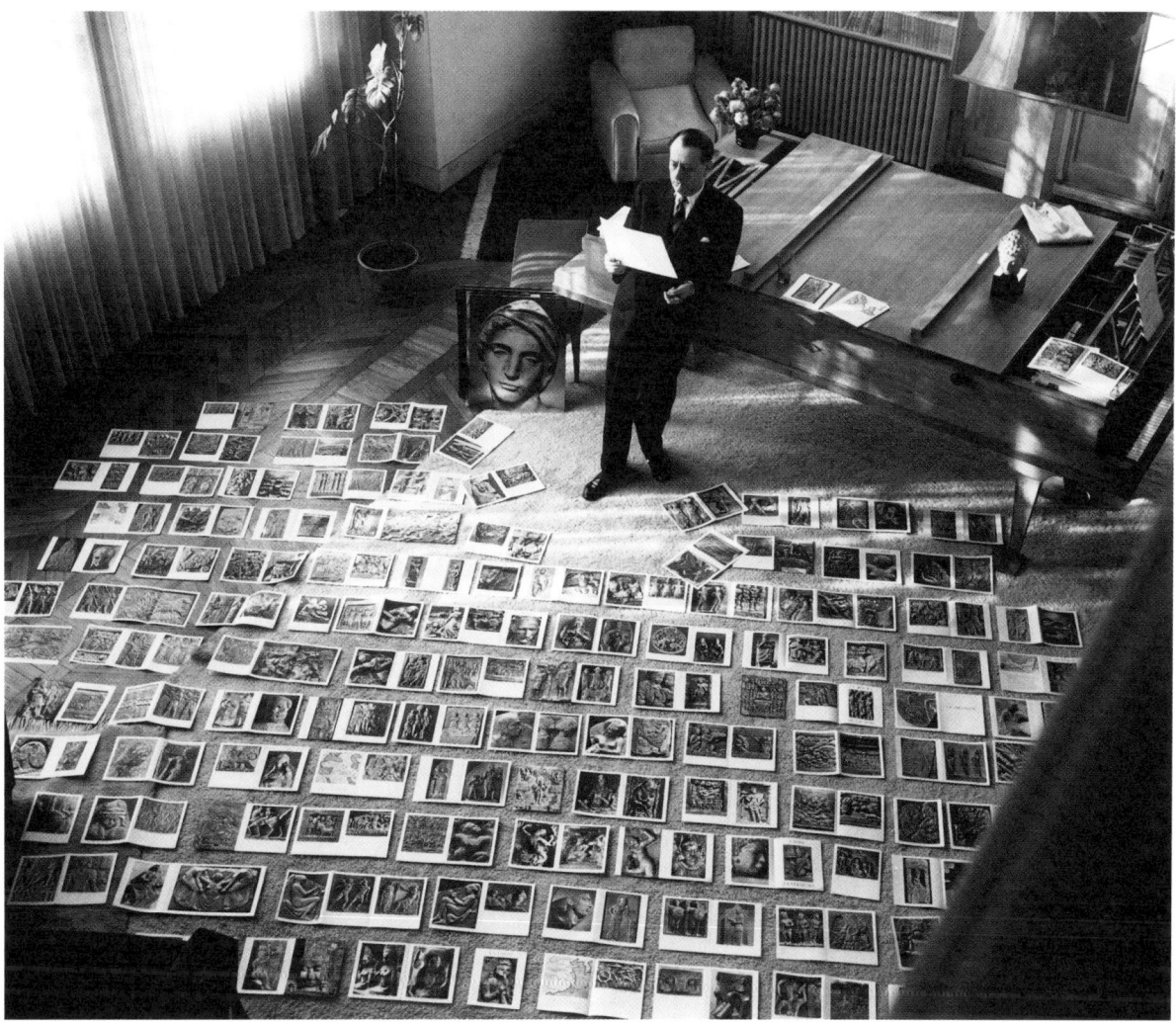

any artwork from any culture on the same level of importance. But of course this could only be possible in the form of a book or, today, in a digital museum.[16]

Wang Shu and Lu Wenyu's National Archives of Publications and Culture actualize the hypothesis of the "Museum Without Walls," both as architecture and as a spatial and material experience of history. Did Malraux simply underestimate architecture's potential performative power? Was he unconvinced by the attempts

Opposite: A motif of bamboo-pressed concrete is the backdrop of the corridors of the walkways.

Above: André Malraux gazing on a selection of images of works of art. His concept, the *Musée imaginaire*, reflected his belief that the reproducibility of the work of art in publication forms allowed for a new experience of the museum, which could finally surpass the linear narratives of classical museum architecture.

Following pages: Exhibition halls and circulation leading to the archival sections of the architectural program are as intensely punctuated by rhythm as the experience of the landscape outside the museum.

---

15. As Rosalind Krauss has pointed out, the English translation is both productive and also lacking. See "Le Musée sans murs du postmodernisme," in *L'Œuvre et son accrochage*, special issue of *Cahiers du Musée nationale d'art moderne*, 17/18 (1986), 152–58.
16. See Douglas Crimp, "On the Museum's Ruins" and "The Museum's Old, The Library's New Subject," in *On the Museums Ruins* (Cambridge, MA: MIT Press, 1993), 43–84.

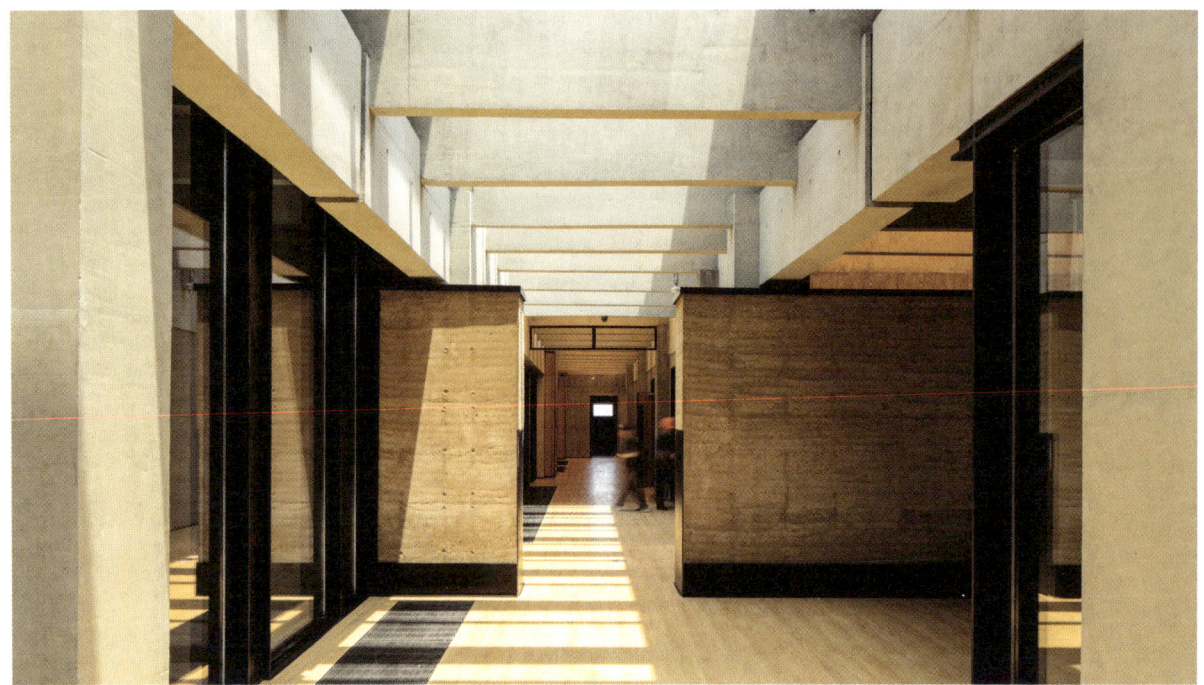

during his lifetime to rewrite the terms of the museum, such as Ludwig Mies van der Rohe's "universal space," Le Corbusier's ramps, or Frank Lloyd Wright's spiral?[17] He did not live to see the architectural interpretation of his own idea of the Maison de la Culture, for, as Renzo Piano, Richard Rogers, and Gianfranco Franchini's early description of the initial inspiration for the Centre Pompidou makes clear, it owed a big debt to Malraux's concept.[18]

The history of twentieth-century art is a complex superimposition of timelines representing an extraordinary hybridization of cultures.[19] Today, the Chinese government is actively trying to rearticulate this history in continuity with its ancient past. In writing his definition of the museum, Malraux did not think that this cross-temporal and cross-cultural juxtaposition was possible in physical space. Indeed, the museum archetypes he had in mind were the Renaissance palaces or its modern equivalents, such as New York's Metropolitan Museum of Art or Washington's National Gallery, characterized by their enfilades of classically proportioned galleries—architecture that mandates a linear trajectory within the museum. For Malraux, the museum had to transcend its physical confines to surpass its accepted meaning, one in which art history and display function together as tools for remembering the past. Yet, Amateur Architecture Studio's Hangzhou project for the National Archives suggests that the answer may lie in architectural form.

---

17. Examples are discussed later in the book. For Frank Lloyd Wright, see pp. 81–83, for Ludwig Mies van der Rohe see pp. 149–50, and for Le Corbusier, see pp. 174 and 184.
18. The Musée d'Art Moderne is just one of several institutions housed on the site, it also includes the Bibliothèque Nationale and the IRCAM. For Donald Kuspit on Theodor W. Adorno's, "Valéry Proust Museum" (1967), see "The Magic Kingdom of the Museum," *Artforum*, vol. 30, no. 8 (April 1992).
19. This was especially the case in China after the death of Mao. The generation that came of age during the Cultural Revolution became the chief protagonist of the '85 New Wave, and drove the "reading fever" that characterized this avant-garde art movement. International book fairs held in China in the early 1980s were hubs for the dissemination of reproductions of modern and exhibition catalogs from the West. China's cultural and artistic world was receiving a vast and heterogeneous array of cultural images and artifacts that, uprooted from their original contexts via reproduction, were reconstituted as fictional collections of objects free of any geographical mooring.

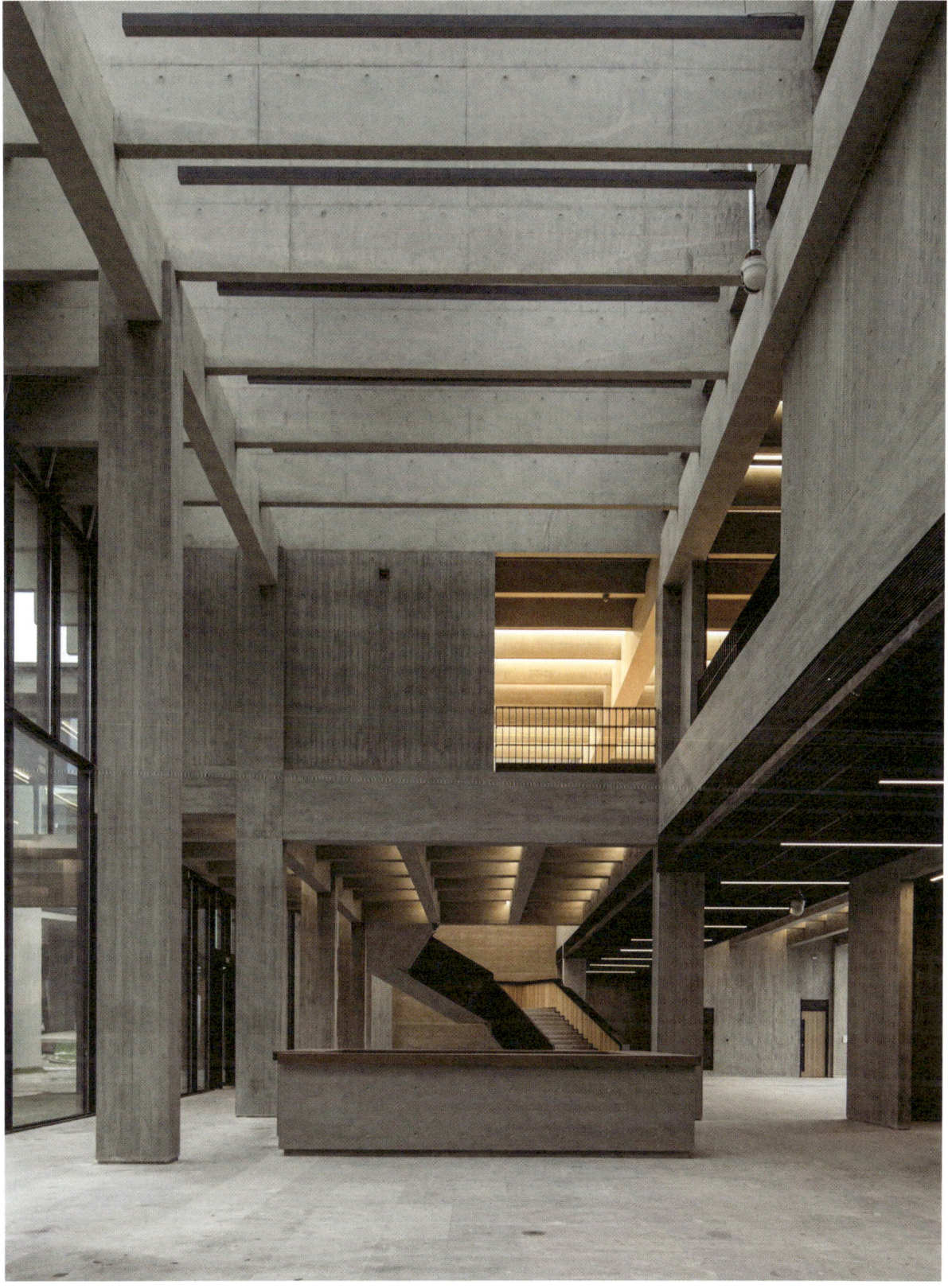

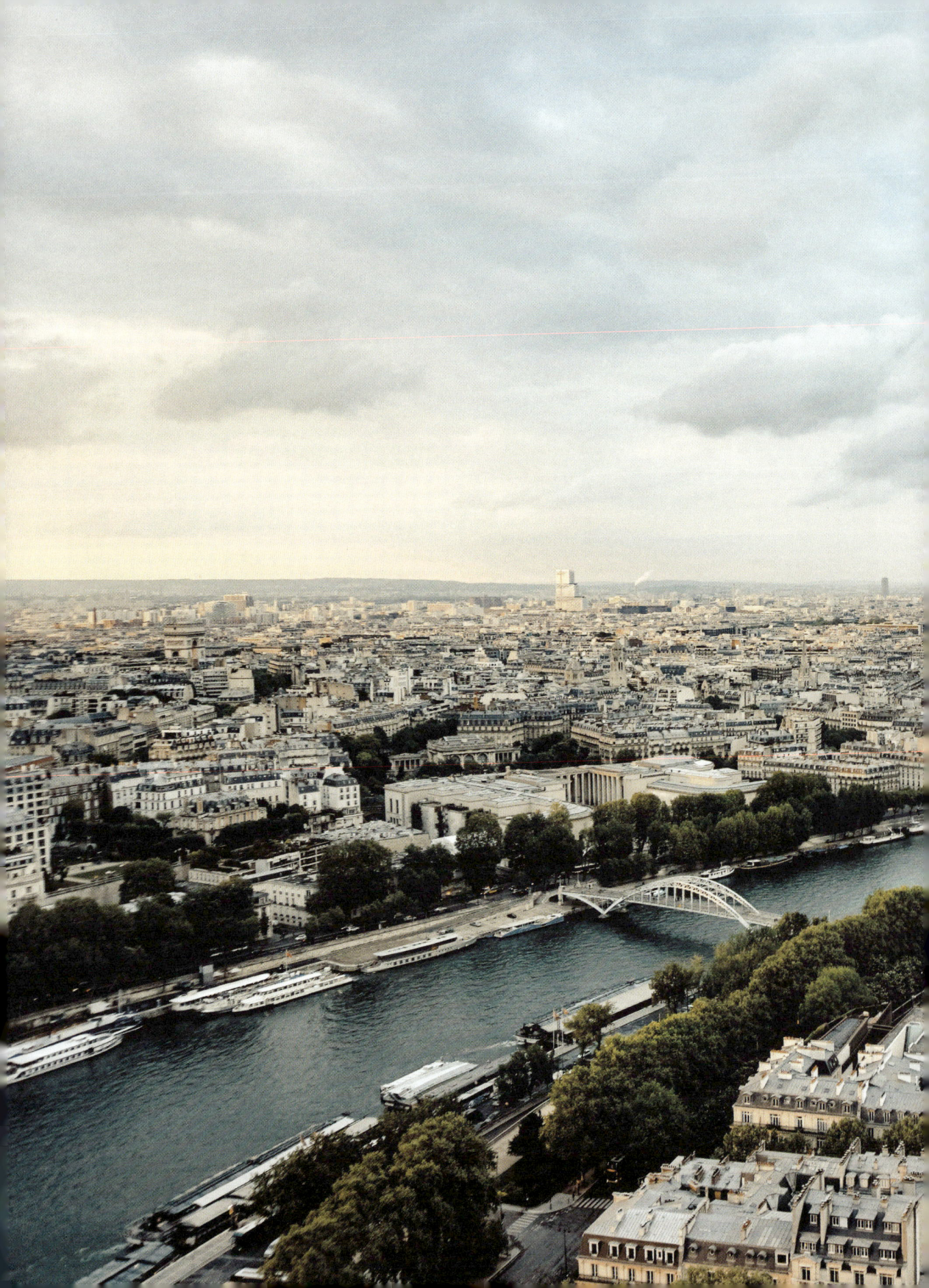

The *museum is* CITY

In Paris, the city is an encyclopedic museum; in Abu Dhabi, the museum is a universal city

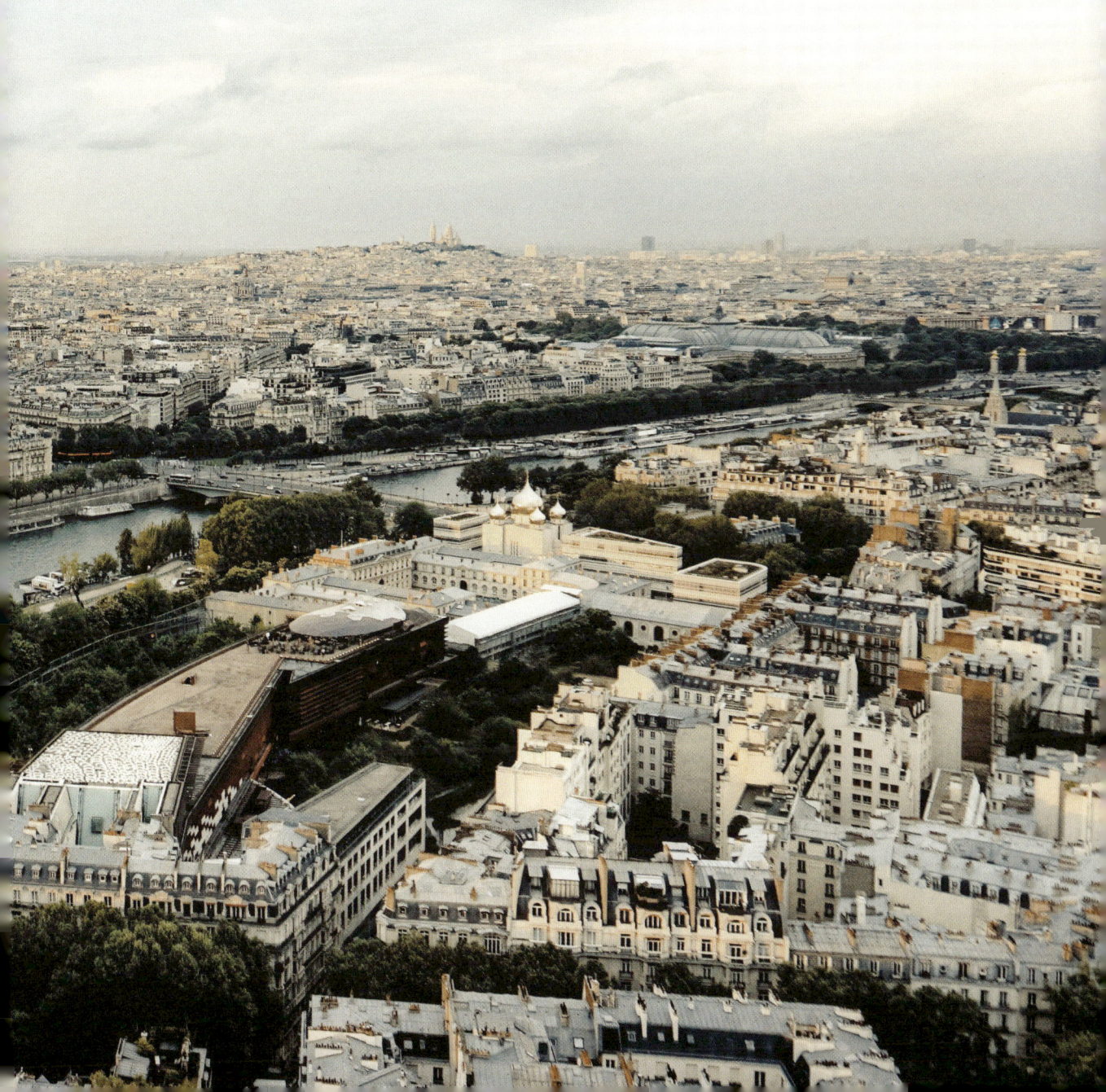

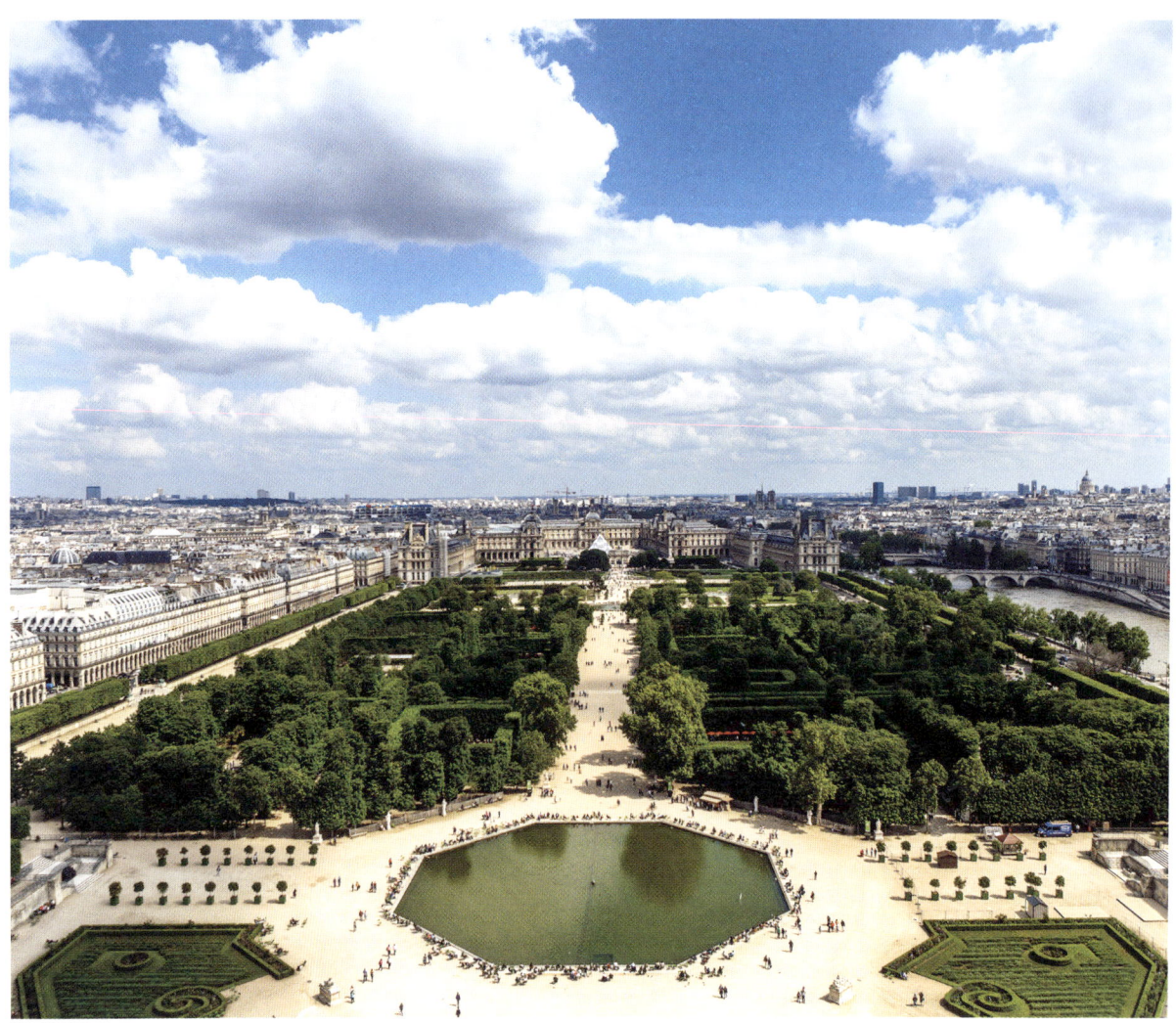

The most compact of all of Europe's global cities—assuming we restrict ourselves to its municipal rather than metropolitan boundaries—Paris in the twenty-first century presents a cityscape that seems forever fixed in time. For twelve euros, you can enjoy its essence from the Ferris wheel in the Jardin des Tuileries, a ten-minute ride during which all the prestige of the historic center offers itself up to the beholder. Looking left and then right, we see, roughly following the Paris Meridian, Montmartre, Opéra, the Place de la Concorde, the Rue de Rivoli, the Musée d'Orsay, and Les Invalides. Looking ahead or behind, along the city's east–west axis, our gaze devours, following the course of the Seine, the world-famous monuments that are Notre Dame de Paris, the Grand Palais, and the Eiffel Tower.

The Middle Ages, the classical period, and modernity all engage in an eclectic game of architectural flirtation. As we reach the highest point of the wheel's rotation, the machine pauses: hanging above the Tuileries, we enjoy a plunging view into the heart of the Louvre, where a giant postmodern lantern, in steel and glass, swarms with visitors. Is it a pyramid or an hourglass? A reminder of time past and of the ambitions that once emanated from within this venerable palace? Here, in the 1980s, the vestiges of the original twelfth-century fortress, built to defend the capital of Philip II's France,

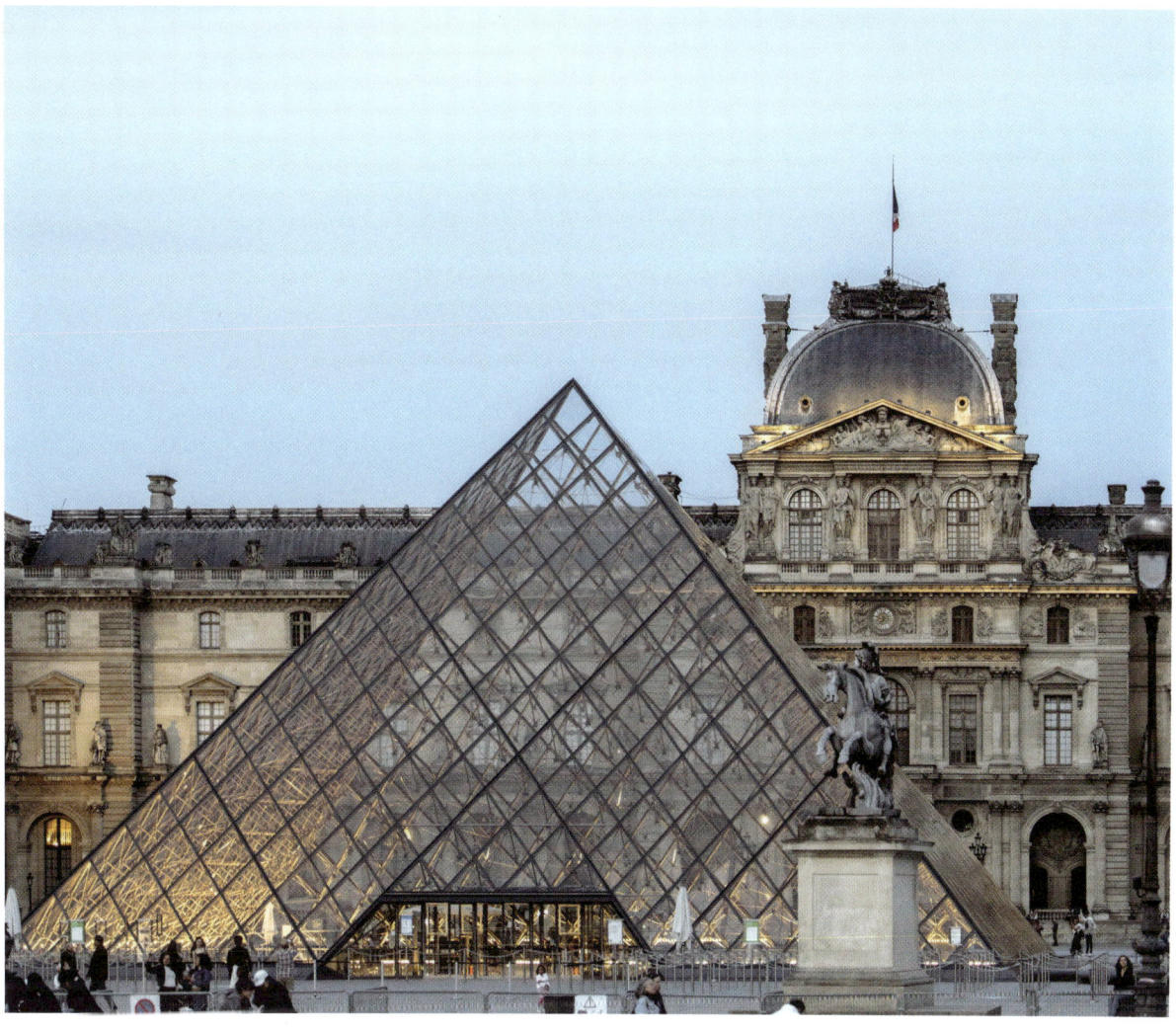

were brought to light during the enormous remodeling project that saw I.M. Pei seek, in an admirable spirit of utility, to endow the Musée du Louvre with a modern symbol of the Republican ideals under which it was founded; below ground, invisible from our vantage point, older patterns of occupation are traced out in moats and ditches lined with stone, reminding us of the violence, aspiration, and dreams that built an entire metropolis. A place of memory, the Louvre today has come to find itself at the epicenter of a status quo, the museum-city that is Paris today.

Previous pages: The east-west axis of the Seine is punctuated by a dense concentration of museums.

Opposite: An aerial view of the Jardin des Tuileries, framed within the fortress of the Louvre.

Above: I. M. Pei's pyramid, a postmodernist attraction of steel and glass, swarming with visitors, offers itself as a monument within the inner walls of the ancient city. Is it a pyramid or an hourglass—a reminder of time past and the former ambitions that animated the walls of this ancient palace?

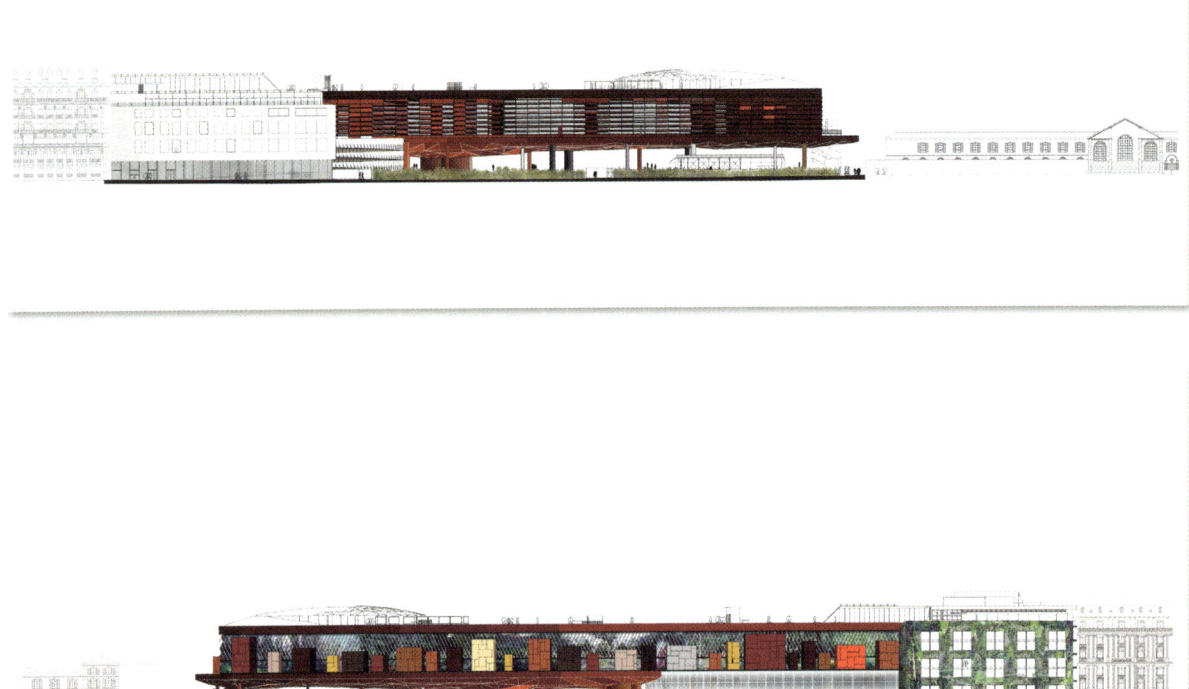

Both a city preserved as a museum and a city filled with museums, Paris contains countless institutions of culture and memory. Among them, the Musée du Quai Branly—Jacques Chirac deliberately seeks to set itself apart. Located on the Left Bank, in the shadow of the Eiffel Tower, Jean Nouvel's building, which was completed in 2006, raises tall glass palisades along the street, which contrast with the stone architecture of the surrounding Haussmannian fabric. Between these glass screens and the museum building itself, a lush garden grows, evoking a sacred forest, a space of transition intended to displace the visitor from the Paris of today to other, non-Western times and places. Looking up at the building's river facade, we see different-colored projecting masses—red, purple, yellow, orange, etc.—which, as we will discover, house a display circuit divided geographically between Africa, the Americas, Asia, and Oceania.

Entering the Quai Branly is like entering the "heart of darkness in the city of light," wrote influential architectural critic Michael Kimmelmann in a widely visible review published in *The New York Times* on the inauguration of the Quai Branly.[1] So low are the lighting levels that time seems limitless: it could be noon or midnight in this disorienting space,

---

1. Michael Kimmelman, "Heart of Darkness in the City of Light," *New York Times*, July 2, 2006.

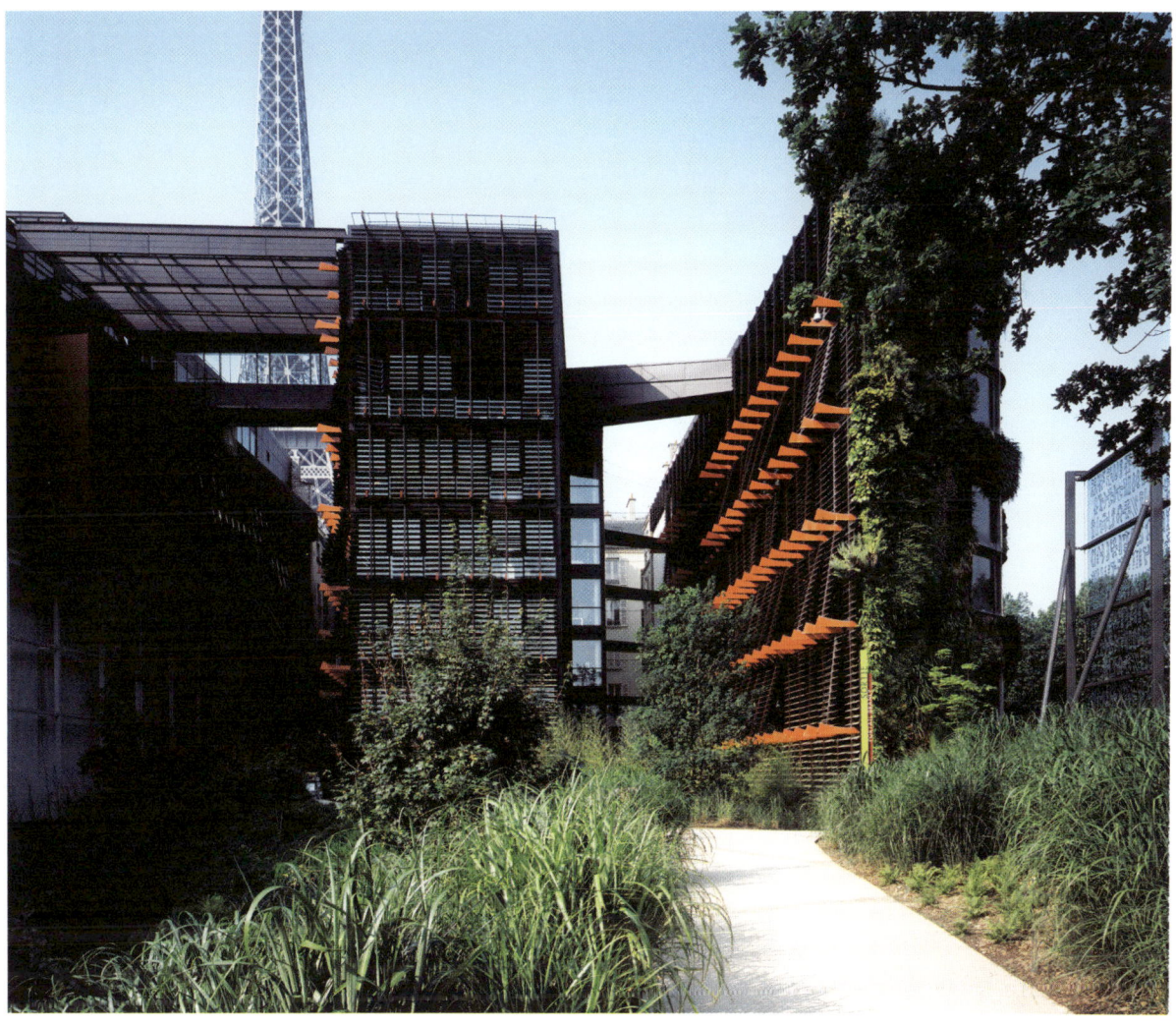

whose boundaries are obscured rather than defined by what little artificial light there is. Just like the architecture of casinos, Nouvel's building cuts us off from time and from history. This disorientation is amplified by the display of the permanent collections, with glass cases that create multiple reflections, glare, and superimposition, and are themselves reflected in the glass facades, while within the displays objects are reflected in other objects. If this blurring and mystification were not enough, explanation is kept at a distance, the labels deliberately discreet so as not to interrupt the visual impact of the objects, artfully lit in isolation or in dramatic clusters. The concept of the legible museum is challenged, with contextual

Opposite: Section cuts of the Musée du Quai Branly demonstrate the maze-like layout of the exhibition galleries.

Above: Beyond the gate, the museum's garden contrasts with the experience of the streets: a sort of sacred forest, a rite of passage, announcing a departure from the pace of Paris. Looking around, red, purple, yellow, and orange colorful projecting masses on the facade signal the spaces according to which the museum's collections are divided, corresponding with major geographical areas, Oceania, Asia, Africa, and the Americas, that one is about to discover.

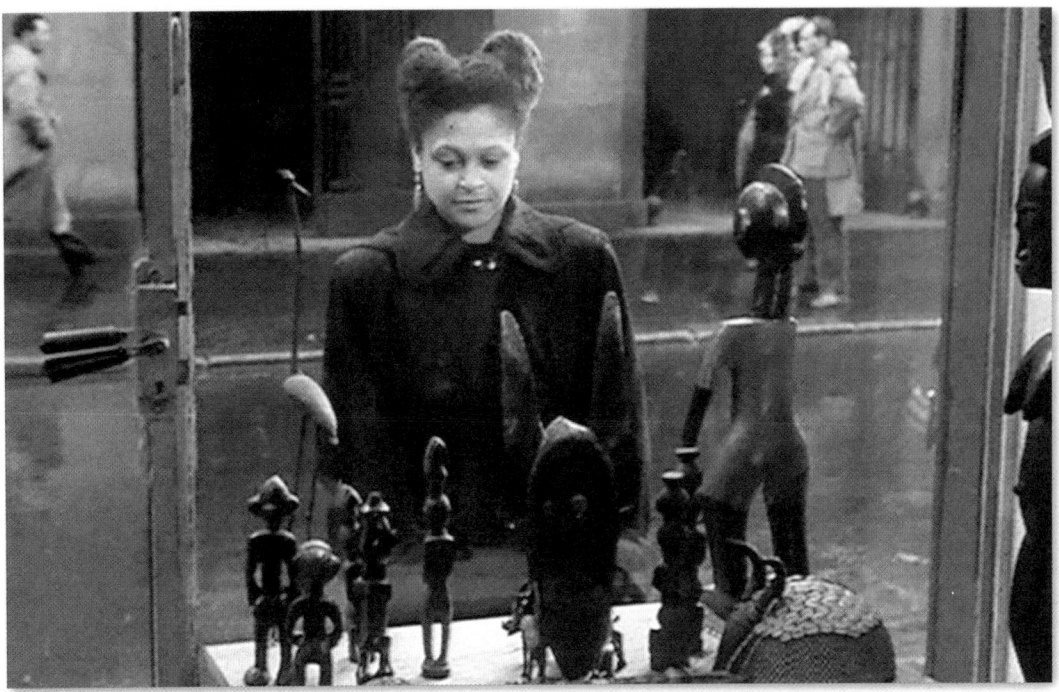

data—photographs, films, maps, descriptions, living people—being provided only on the monitors and screens installed in various places along the visitor's route. This choice serves to create a distance between information and historical data and the artifacts themselves.[2]

Just over half a century earlier, the film *Les Statues Meurent Aussi* (*Statues Die Too*, Alain Resnais, Chris Marker, and Ghislain Cloquet, 1953), which was partly shot in the galleries of Paris's Musée de l'Homme (Museum of Mankind, whose collections have since joined the Quai Branly), captured exactly this kind of atemporality. Commissioned by the periodical *Présence africaine*, the 30-minute short takes traditional African art as its subject, with a point of view based in "the scandal" that "in Paris, African sculpture is not found in the Louvre but in the Musée de l'Homme," as Resnais would later explain. Marker's recognizable voiceover in the film seems to mock that of Apollinaire and Picasso's which implored Malraux to elevate African objects to works of art and liberate their beauty from ethnographic curiosity. In some sequences, the film dwells on visitors' expressions of discovery and awe, the camera positioned next to the artworks to capture their reactions. Other sequences show dramatically lit statues in a theater of forms that, like the Quai Branly today, present the works outside of time in an imaginary, autonomous world. "When men die, they enter into history. When statues die, they enter into art," the voiceover intones as the film begins.

Seven years later, in 1960, in an evolving post-colonial context, control of the Musée de la France d'Outre Mer (Museum of Overseas France, which had been founded by the Ministry of Colonies in 1935) was transferred to the Ministry of Cultural Affairs, then headed by André Malraux, who renamed it the Musée des arts d'Afrique et d'Océanie and reoriented it as an art rather than an ethnographic museum. At the end of the millennium, its collections were united with those of the Musée de l'Homme to form the basis of today's Musée du Quai Branly, which, despite attempts at contextualization, still has a tendency to aestheticize its holdings. "Of course we could just be content to enjoy the beauty of a great piece, that's an approach to art on the level of sensibility and aesthetic emotion, but we can enrich the pleasure by learning about who produced it, which societies, which traditions, and what the exchanges were between the individuals

---

2. At the British Museum, historical information guides the visit to the Sainsbury African Galleries, which are evenly and brightly lit.

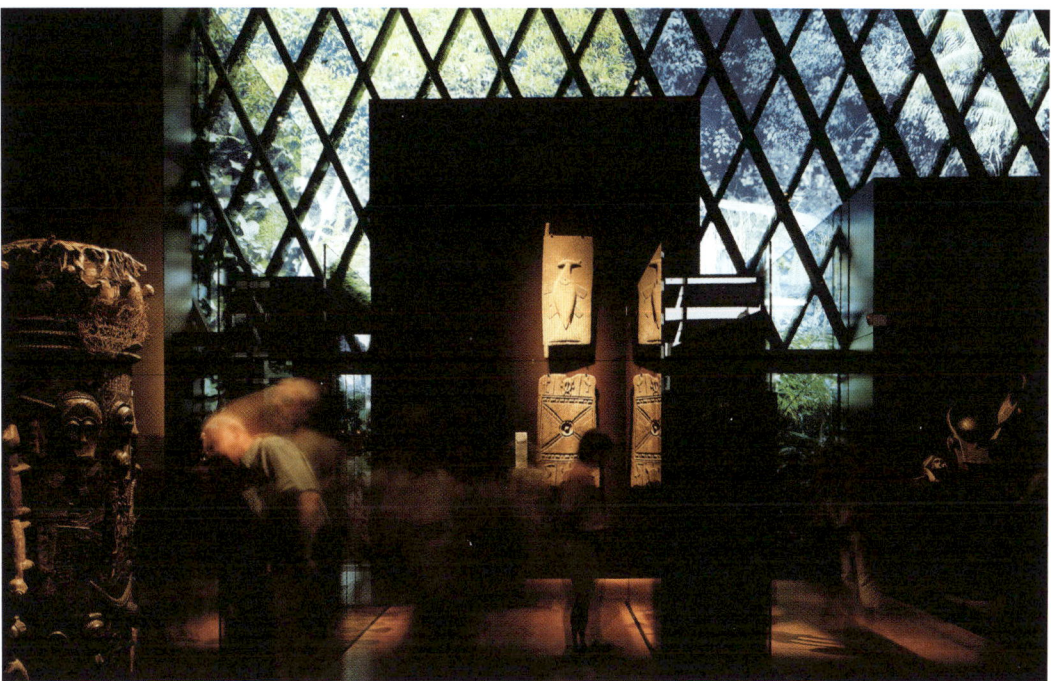

who made up those communities," declared Maurice Godelier, the museum's scientific director from 1997 to 2000, to the newspaper *Libération* in 1999.[3]

Despite the scientific statement, architecture accomplished something different, and the project realized by Ateliers Jean Nouvel was more in line with the dreams of Picasso and Apollinaire, who saw it as the role of museums to attribute to objects of African provenance their aesthetic worth, their beauty. The international museum community interpreted Nouvel's museography as a sign that the Quai Branly was ignoring ideas circulating internationally about how non-Western cultures should be historicized in Europe and America, outside the geographies in which they were created.[4] More specifically, the architecture of the Quai Branly planted a flag that affirmed the rejection of post-colonial theory and

Opposite: Film still of Chris Marker, Alain Resnais, and Ghislain Cloquet *Les Statues Meurent aussi* (1953), which critiques the ethnographic gaze cast on African objects in ethnographic museums.

Above: Spaces of the Quai Branly are dark and dramatically lit, creating an atmosphere of mystery, as James Clifford, influential scholar, had critiqued at the time of the opening of the museum in 2007.

---

3. Alain Leauthier, interview with Maurice Godelier, "Comment construire un musée post-colonial," *Libération*, April 20, 1999.
4. One of the most important criticism was published in the influential art historical journal *October*. James Clifford, "Quai Branly in Process," *October*, vol. 120, (Winter 2007). See also, the most widely read book on the topic in euro-American Academic circles, Sally Price, *Paris Primitive: Jacques Chirac's Museum on the Quai Branly* (Chicago: University of Chicago Press), 2007.

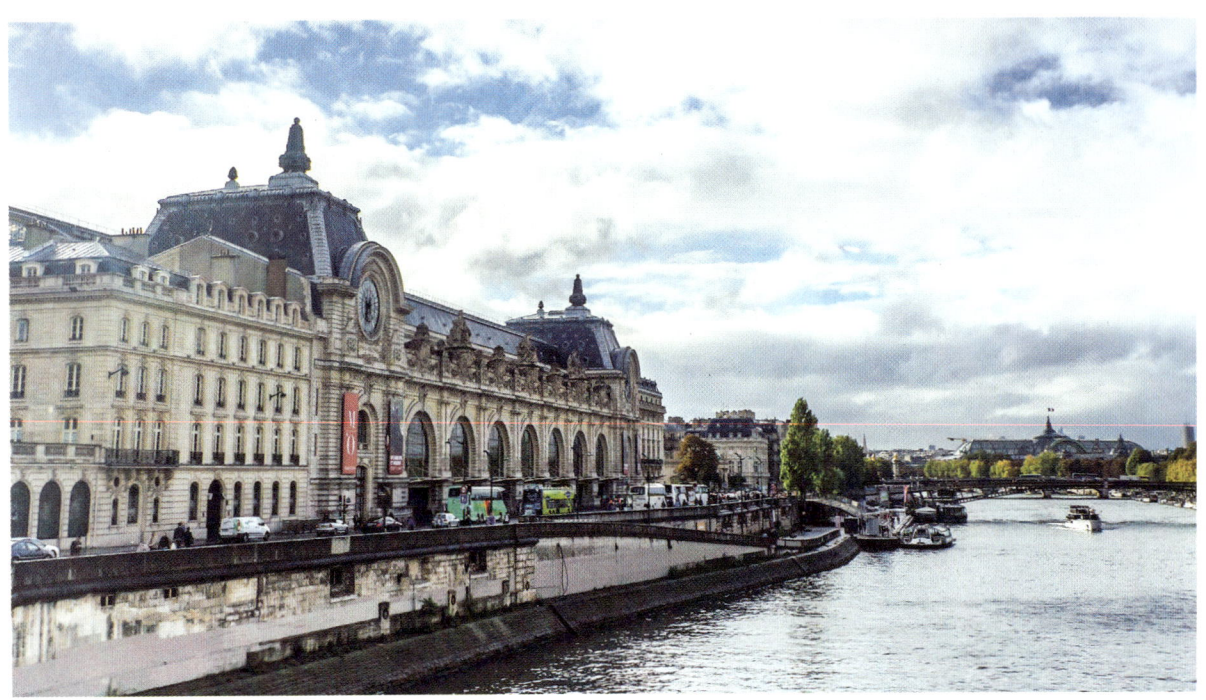

North American models that, since their advent in the 1980s, seek to acknowledge indigenous voices and rights (e.g., the Smithsonian's National Museum of the American Indian in Washington, DC). Instead, as unveiled in 2006, the Quai Branly shamelessly upheld ideas of "primitive authenticity." This was accomplished by clearly separating the contemporary commissions to artists from Oceania and Africa, who were attributed functional spaces of the museum (such as the hallways and offices), whereas the more distant past of cultures associated with these geographies is reserved for the permanent spaces dedicated to the collection.[5] Another example of the persisting ambiguous treatment of the collections is the recent addition of "aura" vitrines, commissioned to Jean Nouvel and designed specifically for thirty-six artworks donated by a private collector.[6] Of African and Oceanic provenance, these artifacts are now exposed in curvy plexiglass cases that create infinite reflections. Upon their installation, they were advertised for the possibility of "contemplation" that they allow for. Relegating access to information to the scan of a QR code, this new display takes to the extreme the notion that beauty should be the means by which audiences apprehend culture.

With the Quai Branly, the trouble was clear right from the start with the controversy over what to call the new museum: the initial idea, "Musée des Arts Premiers" (Museum of the First Arts) was soon rejected as being too close to the pejorative "arts primitifs" (primitive arts), and, after other options fell by the wayside, it was decided, perhaps to circumvent the problematic museographic stance of the museum, to simply use the building's address (to which was later appended the name of Jacques Chirac, the president whose pet project this was). The subtitle "Là où dialoguent les cultures" ("Where cultures enter into dialogue") served as a hint at what the institution sought to achieve.

In 1986, another museum that had a difficult naming process, and that also ended up being called after its own address—the Musée d'Orsay—abruptly deprived the Louvre of post-1848 art, forever cutting it off from modernity. Over the years, there have been many controversies over which objects—from when? from where?—the Louvre should show, a process that has seen collections come and go.

---

5. In contrast again, at the British Museum, contemporary works are exhibited alongside more traditional pieces.
6. Marc de Lacharrière donated these works to the Quai Branly in 2018.

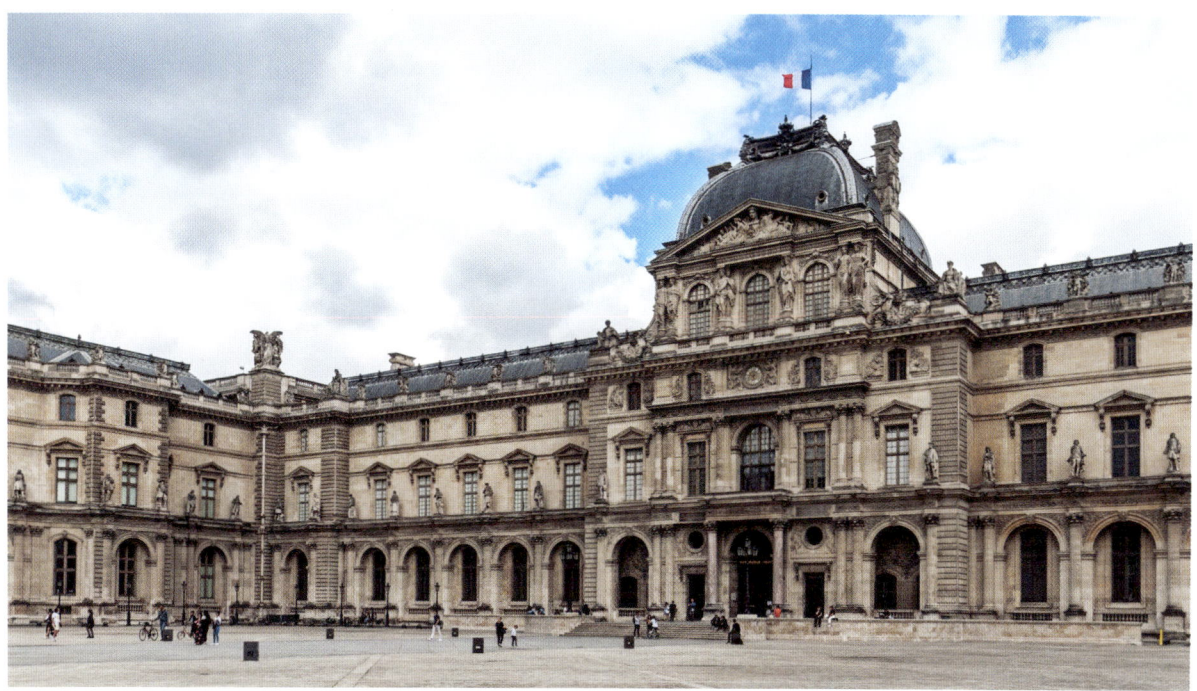

For example, in 1827, Charles X established the Musée de Marine et d'Ethnographie within the palace's walls, but, still not recognized as works of art, its collections were dispersed in 1905. This process, which has spawned new Parisian museums that receive what the Louvre is no longer allowed to display, has created a condition of center and periphery, with the "imperial body" of the Louvre at the heart of the system. This, in turn, reinforces the bond between the Louvre and Paris itself, the city and museum having become inseparable in their universalizing ambitions. At the Louvre, this tendency was confirmed when, in 2000, one hundred of the most striking works from the Quai Branly's collections took up permanent residence in the palace's Pavillon des Sessions. "Nous sommes au Louvre!" ("We're in the Louvre!") triumphantly proclaimed the posters announcing the reinstatement of works from Africa, Oceania, and the Americas in France's oldest, biggest, and most prestigious museum, half a century after Resnais and Marker's anticolonial movie, and almost a century following the poet Guillaume Apollinaire's 1909 call for their display within the palace's walls on the basis that, as artworks, they are "no less moving than … the best examples of Western statuary."

Opposite and above: The Musée d'Orsay was created to house objects post-1848, establishing a temporality appropriate to both museums. This timeline is now challenged by the contemporary programs of the Louvre.

Following pages: The dome of the Louvre Abu Dhabi unites its different buildings, boxes, or houses. The fifty or so of them are a strong symbol of the institution and an architectural proposal for universality.

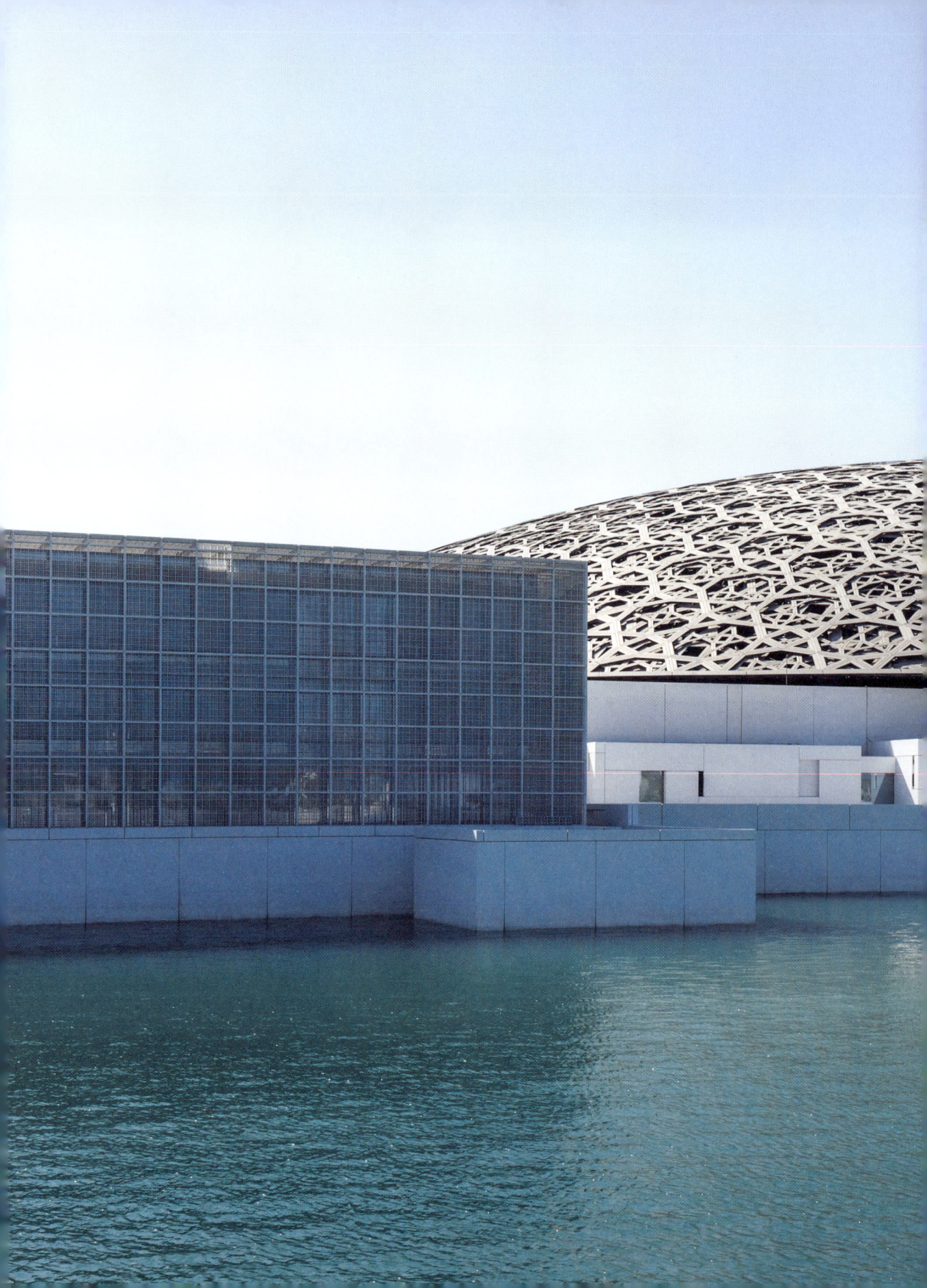

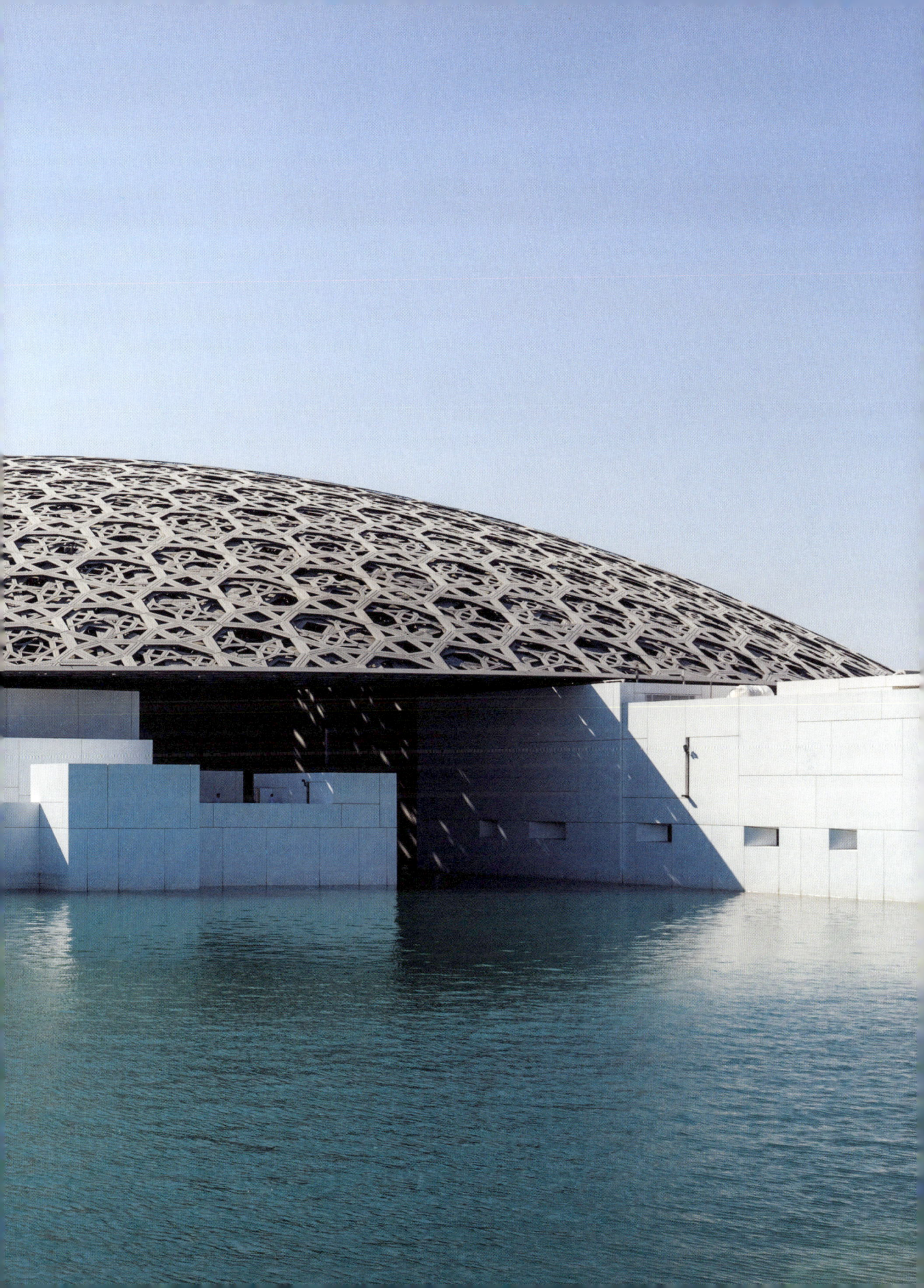

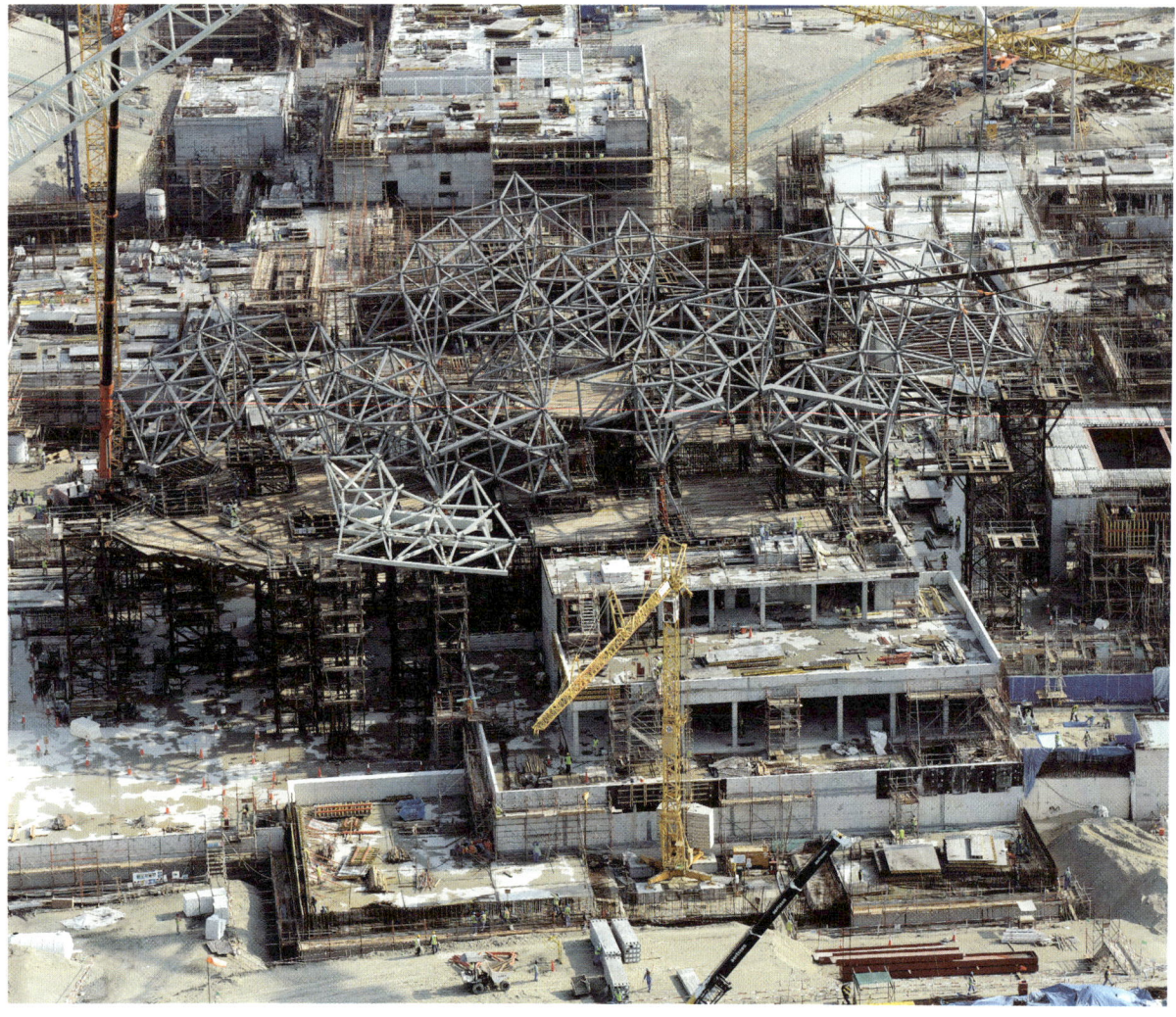

It took five long years to add a small pocket of land to Saadiyat Island, just off the coast of Abu Dhabi. Once the water was gone and the infill complete, a strange new city began to take shape on the reclaimed terrain. Inscribed within a circle that is 354 feet in diameter, its channel-like thoroughfares frame carefully studied views—glimpses of the ocean, patterns of light and shade, a distant facade—and provide access to various districts, organized by time: ancient worlds, medieval periods, first globalizations, and modern times. At the points where these districts meet, benches invite pause, offering moments of contemplation, as visitors decide which direction to take next. Landmarks orient the eye as visitors pursue their *flânerie*: here a sculpture, there a facade inscription, further along a mosaic, and not to mention the plaza that affords panoramic views over Khor Laffan Bay.

Unlike Paris, ringed by an orbital freeway, this city is encircled by a giant dome. At Jean Nouvel's Louvre Abu Dhabi (2017), a shallow cupola of superimposed metal mesh, designed to let countless narrow beams of sunlight filter through its interstices, unites about fifty structures—buildings, boxes, houses—within a play of light that contributes to a unique aesthetic experience. Materials, colors, and patterns are crafted to impress, with granite, marble, leather, and light combining to create a legible experience of this complex building, all

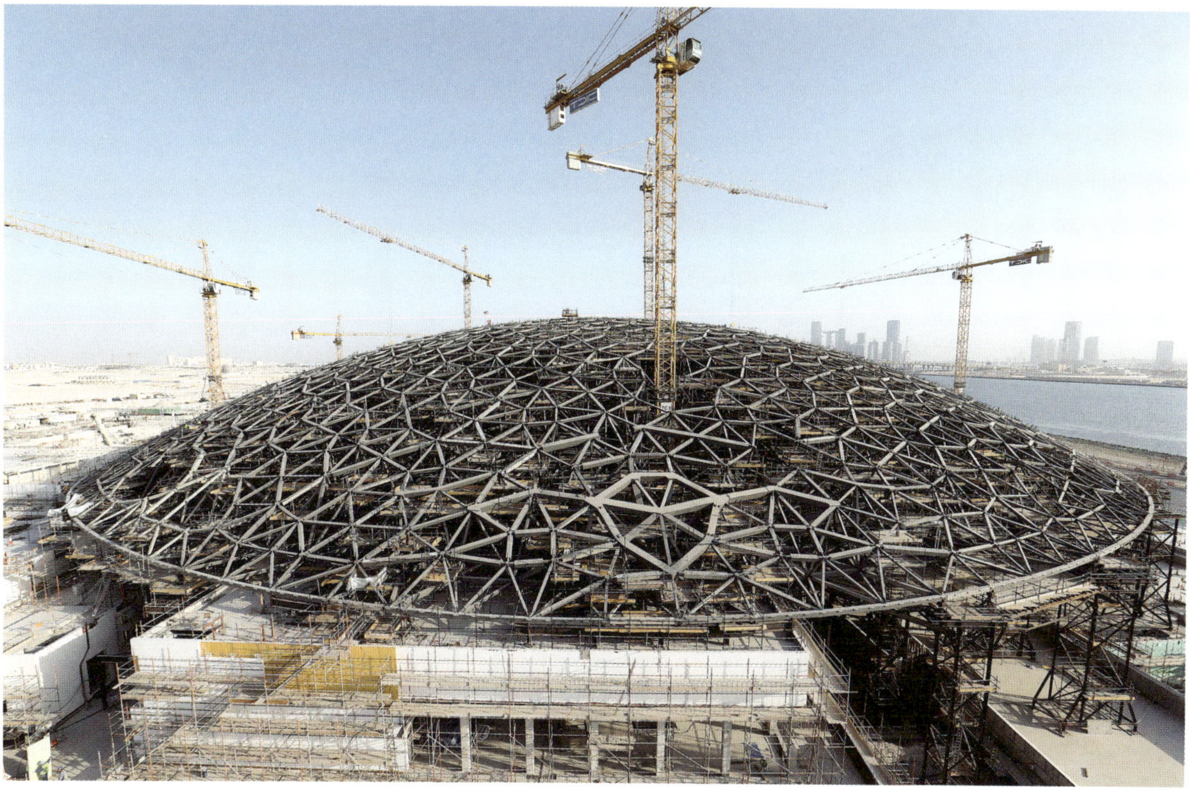

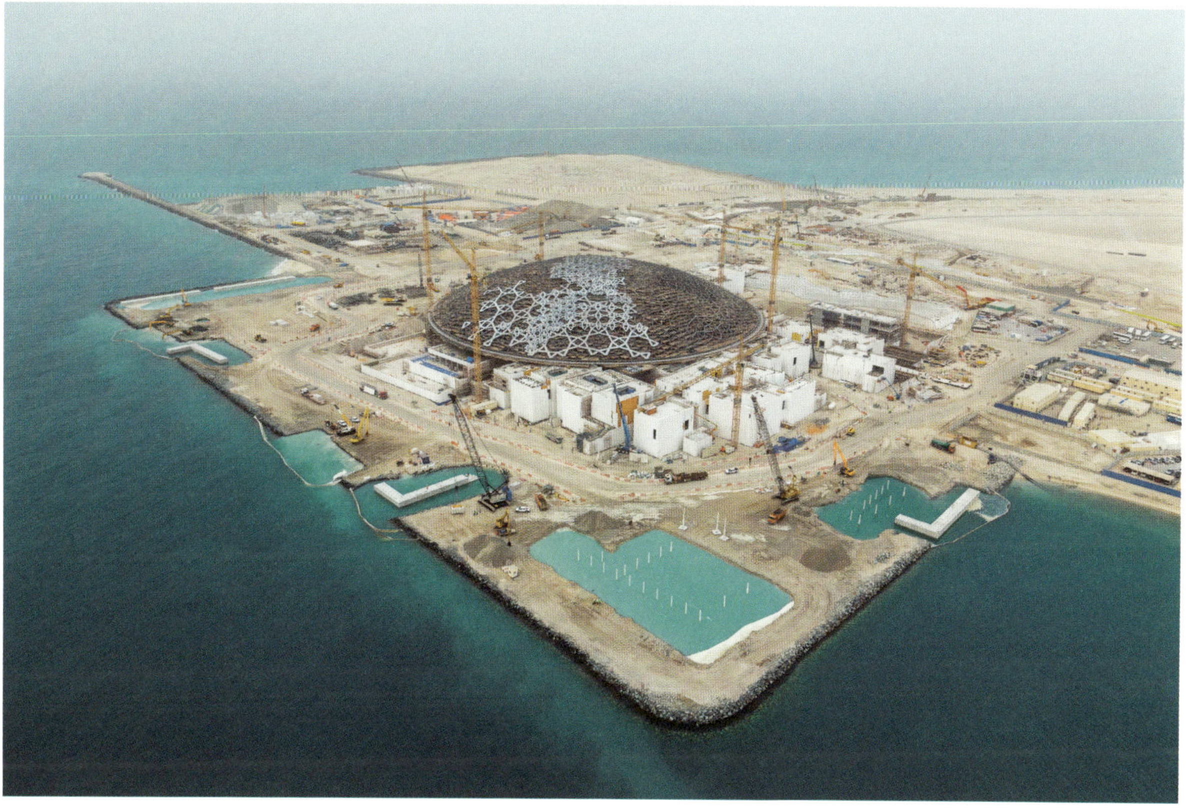

THE MUSEUM IS CITY

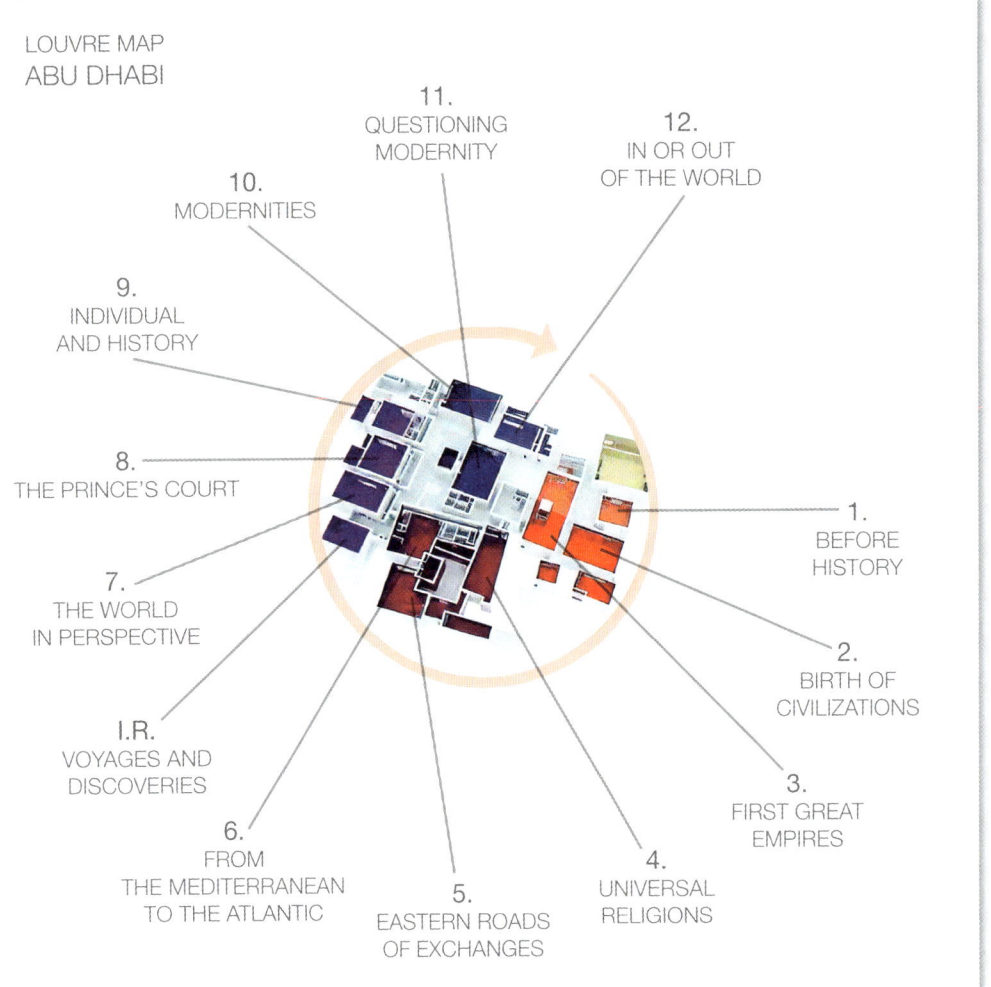

LOUVRE MAP
ABU DHABI

1. BEFORE HISTORY
2. BIRTH OF CIVILIZATIONS
3. FIRST GREAT EMPIRES
4. UNIVERSAL RELIGIONS
5. EASTERN ROADS OF EXCHANGES
6. FROM THE MEDITERRANEAN TO THE ATLANTIC
I.R. VOYAGES AND DISCOVERIES
7. THE WORLD IN PERSPECTIVE
8. THE PRINCE'S COURT
9. INDIVIDUAL AND HISTORY
10. MODERNITIES
11. QUESTIONING MODERNITY
12. IN OR OUT OF THE WORLD

brought together under the dome, a classic representation of the heavens and a metaphor for universality. The city of which this building is a symbolic representation is, of course, Paris—a condensed version at a scale of 1:55.[7]

At the Louvre Abu Dhabi, the Grand Vestibule is the first gallery visitors enter in the permanent collection display galleries. It is the portal to this "city," whose overall architecture, encompassed under the dome, sustains the fiction of a coherent representational universe, much like the urban condition of Paris does throughout its logic of museum nomenclature as urban place. In the Grand Vestibule, a thematic presentation of works highlights formal similarities and particularities across time and space: the Egyptian goddess Iris nursing her son Horus (800–400 BCE), an ivory Virgin and Child (1300–1400 CE), and a nineteenth-century Congolese maternity figure stand together in a glass case, setting the tone for the curatorial approach to come. This program, as outlined in the 2007 agreement signed by France and Abu Dhabi, was defined as:

> *A universal museum showing major works from the fields of archaeology and the fine and decorative arts, open to every period, including the contemporary ... to every geographic region, and to every field of art history,*

---

[7]. Figure disclosed by Hala Wardé, chief architect at the time, working with Ateliers Jean Nouvel.

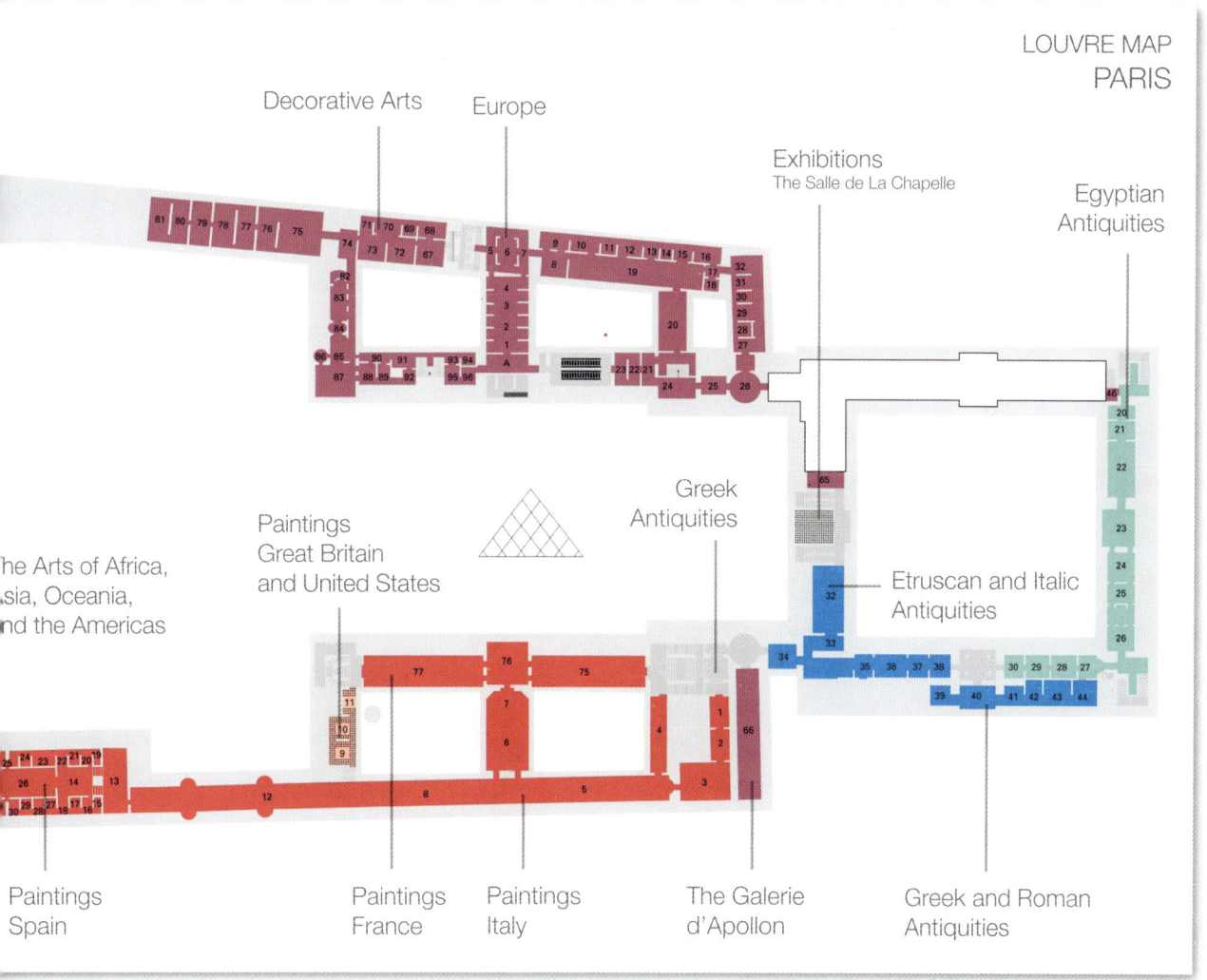

fulfilling at all times the Musée du Louvre's criteria of quality and scholarly and museological ambitions, and intended to foster a dialogue between East and West…[8]

At the mother institution, Pei's pyramid acts as the museum's main vestibule—a gesture of light, monumentality, and a certain populism that responds to the functional requirements of demographics and tourism rather than

---

8. Agreement between the Government of the Republic of France and the Government of the United Arab Emirates relating to the Abu Dhabi Universal Museum (March 6, 2007), author's translation, accessed at https://docs.pca-cpa.org/2016/01/Agreement-between-the-Government-of-the-Republic-of-France-and-the-Government-of-the-United-Arab-Emirates-relating-to-the-Abu-Dhabi-Universal-Museum-Mar.-6-2007-2007-J.O.-17170.pdf.

Previous pages: The Louvre Abu Dhabi was built on reclaimed land, Saadiyat Island, off the coast of Abu Dhabi.

Opposite and above: Floor plans of the Louvre Abu Dhabi and the Louvre in Paris demonstrate the different organizational principles of the collections. The former being circular allows for different juxtapositions across time and geography, while the latter, constrained by architecture, is necessarily linear in its representation of time.

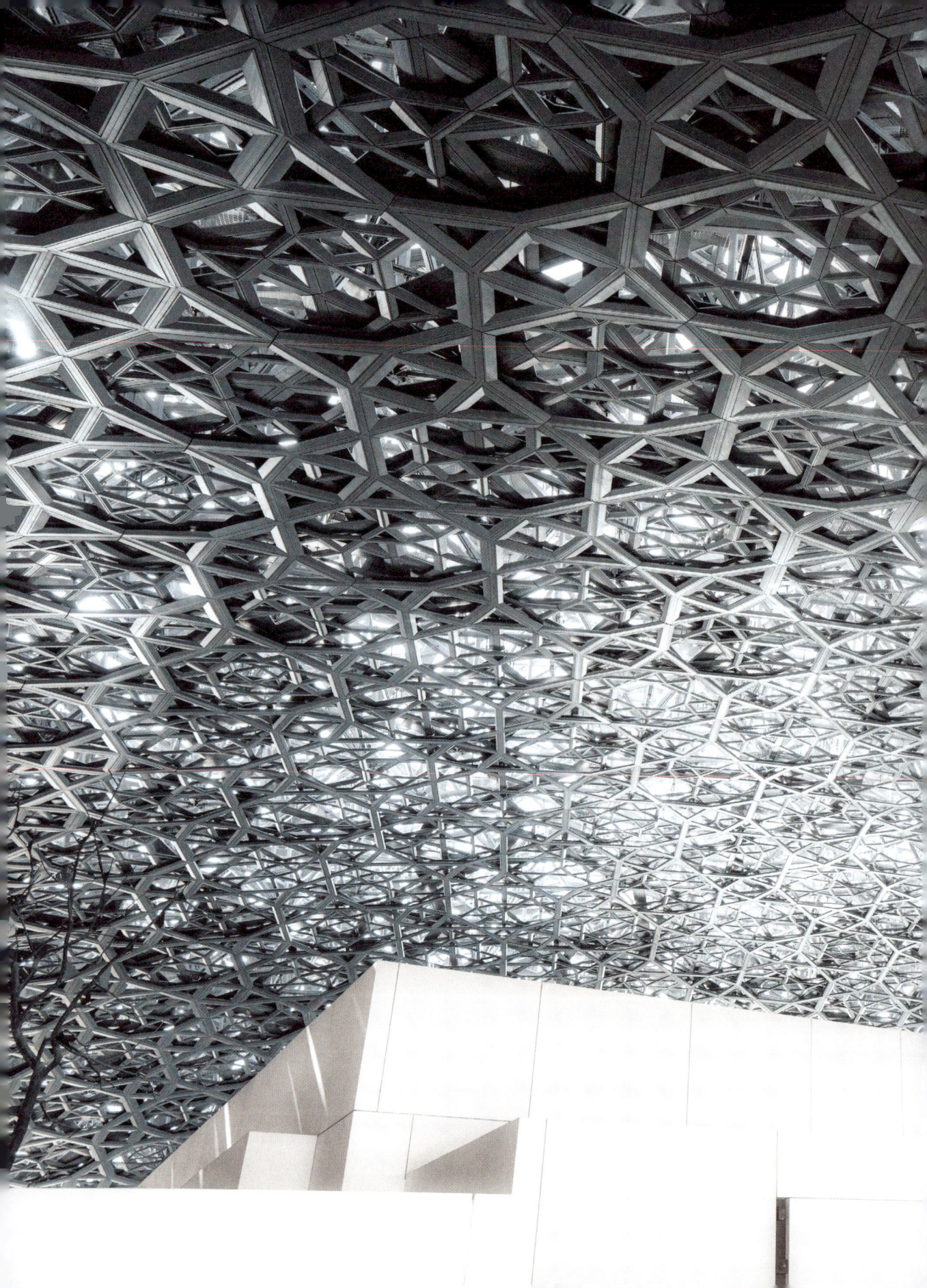

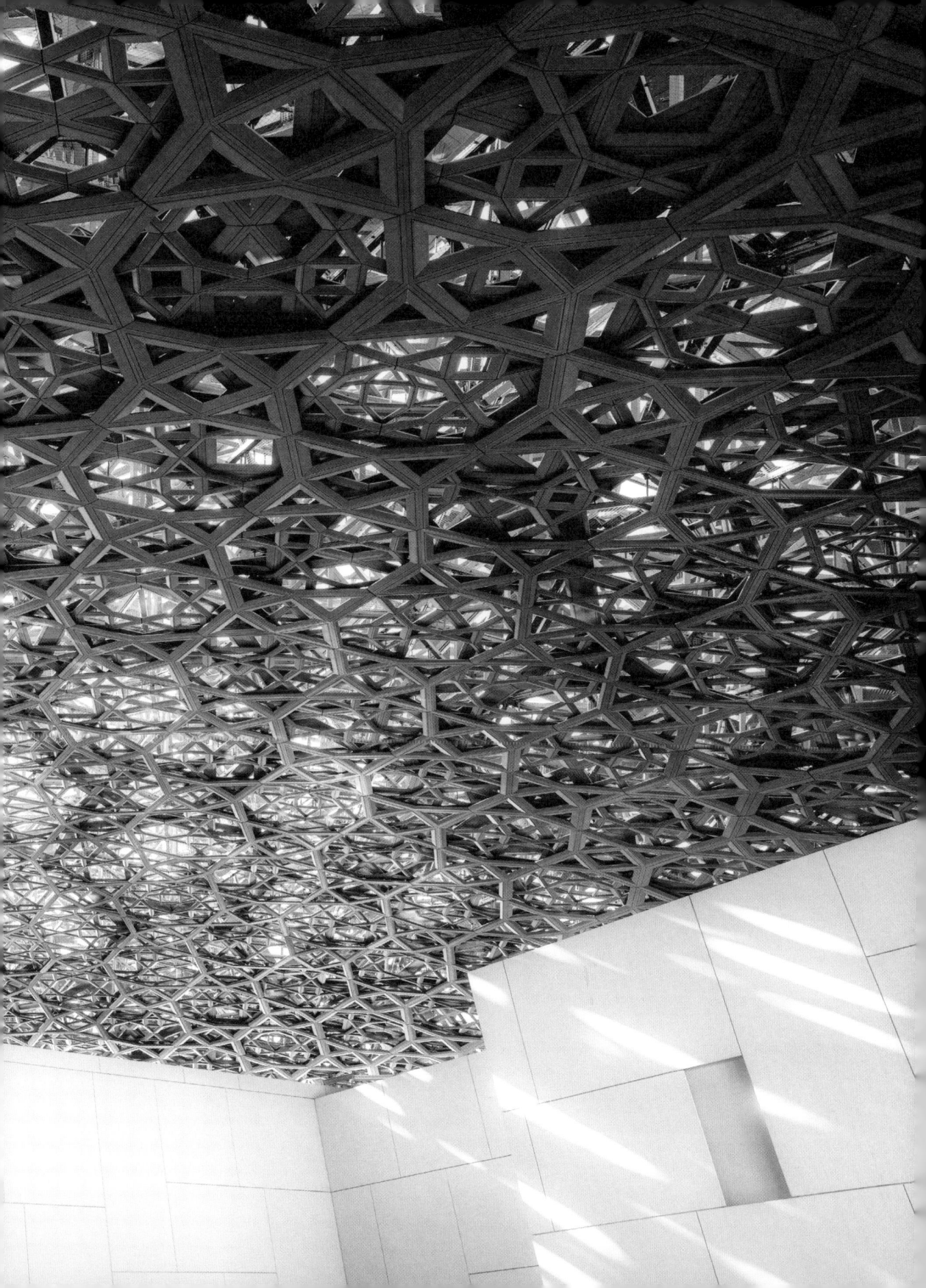

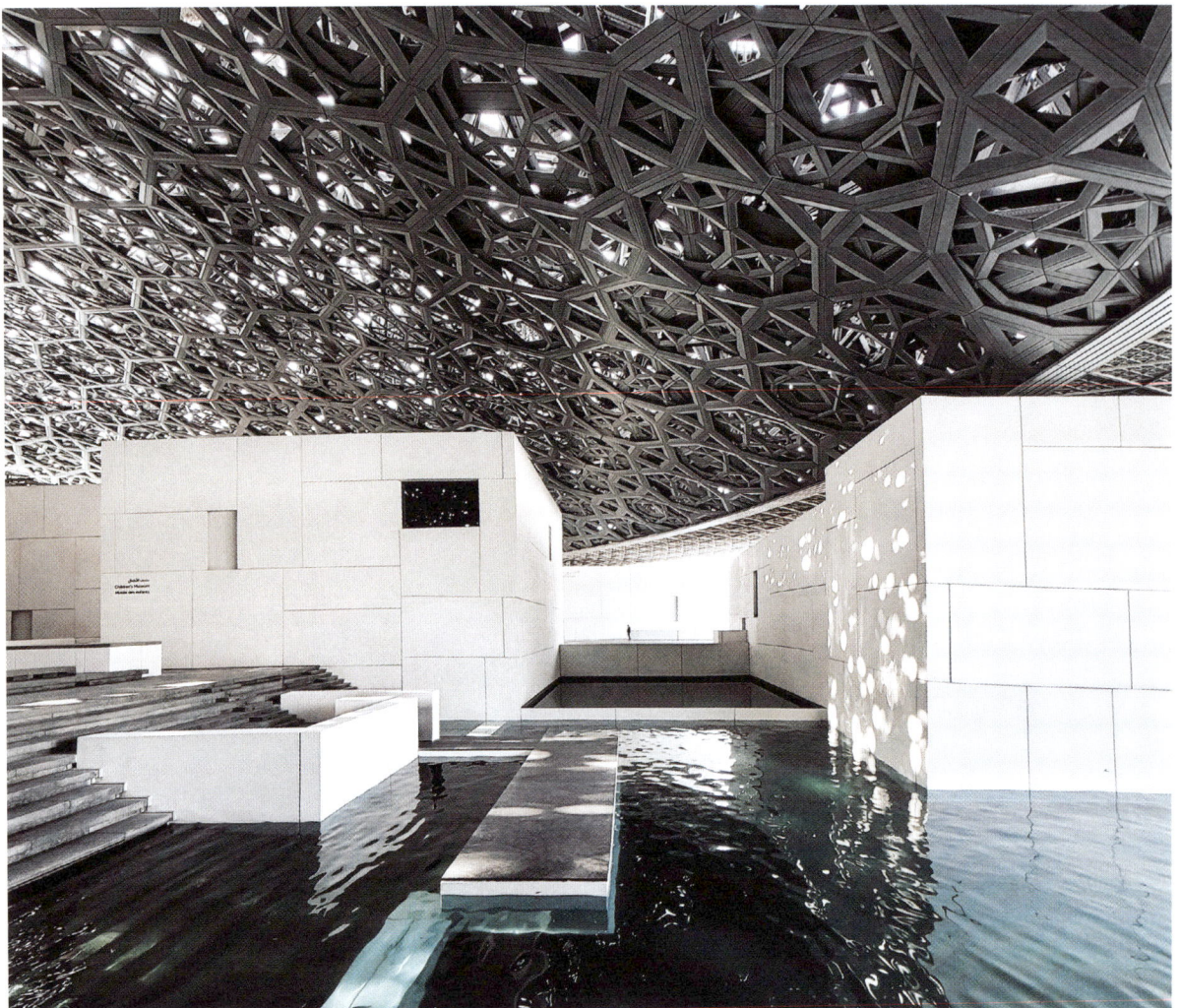

conceptually to what the architecture of the palace fundamentally embodies and how it operates as a representational universe displaying objects grouped according to a perceived logic. The classical museum par excellence, first opened to the public in 1793, the Louvre presents a spatial juxtaposition of fragments of the world, whose underlying narrative is a vestige of the Napoleonic order. The museum's expansion in the 1980s, of which Pei's pyramid was part, also heightened the continuity between the Louvre and Paris, not only by entirely opening its passages and courtyards to pedestrians, but also by connecting the pyramid directly to line no. 1 of the subway via a short tunnel.[9] A universalizing institution at one with the city, it is complemented by outposts elsewhere in Paris— the Quai Branly, for example, or the Musée National des Arts Asiatiques Guimet—that hold all that was denied a place in the main palace.

Built on a non-place, a tabula rasa of sand, the Gulf iteration of these universalizing ambitions reimagines the spatial idea of the Louvre and its Paris satellites, bringing times,

---

9. A contextual plan drawn by Pei clearly outlines the ambition to connect between the museum with the city's transportation infrastructure.
10. As outlined, the Louvre Abu Dhabi embodies France's vision of "universalism," articulated and made tangible throughout the city of Paris—realizing this vision is at once the powerful consecration in architectural form of this very idea and, moreover, its perfect expression.

ARCHITECTURE FOR CULTURE

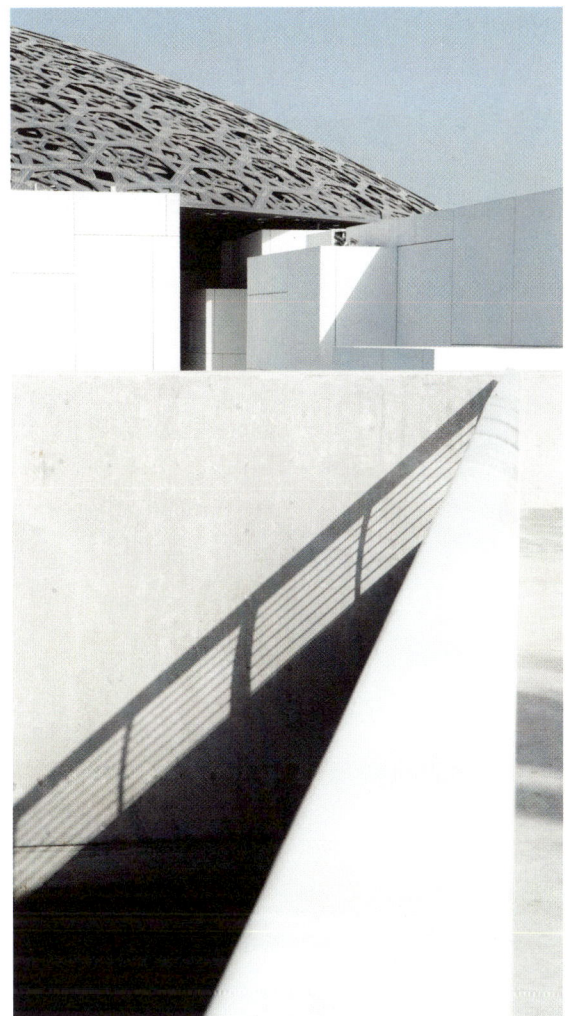
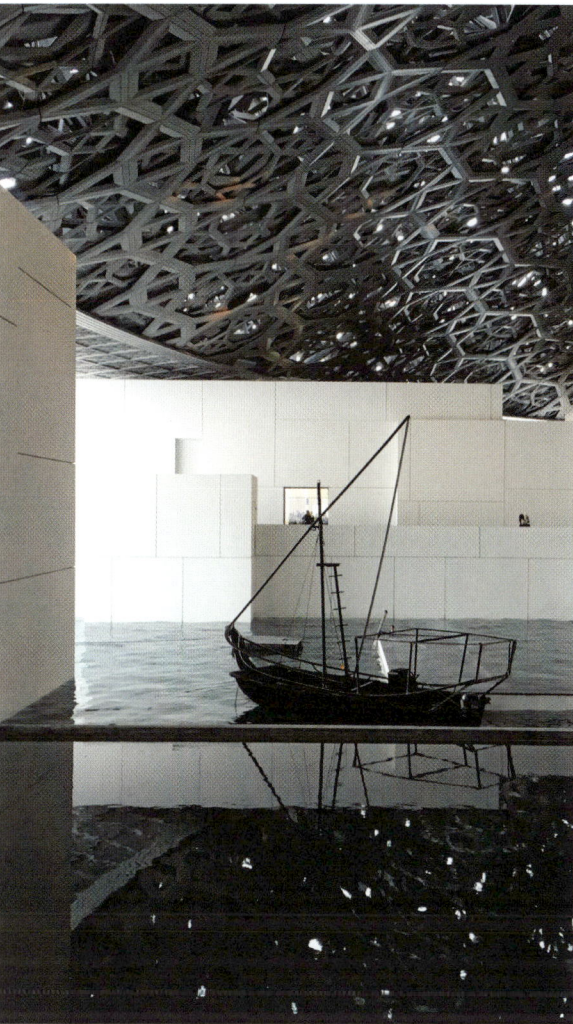

places, and ideas together with far greater efficiency than in France's capital. For example, to explore the themes tackled in the gallery titled "Mediterranean to the Atlantic," a visitor to Paris would need to go to both the Louvre and the Quai Branly; those evoked in the gallery "The Prince's Court to Modernity" would require a trip across the Seine to the Musée d'Orsay. In this way, the Louvre Abu Dhabi acts as a microcosm of the museum-city that is Paris, a concentrated outpost of French ideas of universalism.[10]

Previous pages: The dome of the Louvre Abu Dhabi is a remarkable architectural feature that creates an infinite variety of light underneath. It acts as an immense roof to a "public plaza" beneath it.

Opposite and above: The reflecting light on the dome and on the surface of the water offers an infinite variety of aesthetic experiences. Jean Nouvel considers the scenography of "light" an integral element of his architecture.

Following pages: Beyond the dome lies the horizon of the bay and the city of Abu Dhabi.

Its export to Abu Dhabi in a more radical and synthesized form that seeks to accomplish what the Louvre cannot, architecturally speaking, achieve in the Parisian palace. Paradoxically, this has in recent years created a strange new movement from the city back to the museum – one that manifests itself in new initiatives whereby the Louvre seeks to further include new geographies or other temporalities historically rejected or heretofore excluded: contemporary art, the Byzantine Pavilion, and the arts of Islam.

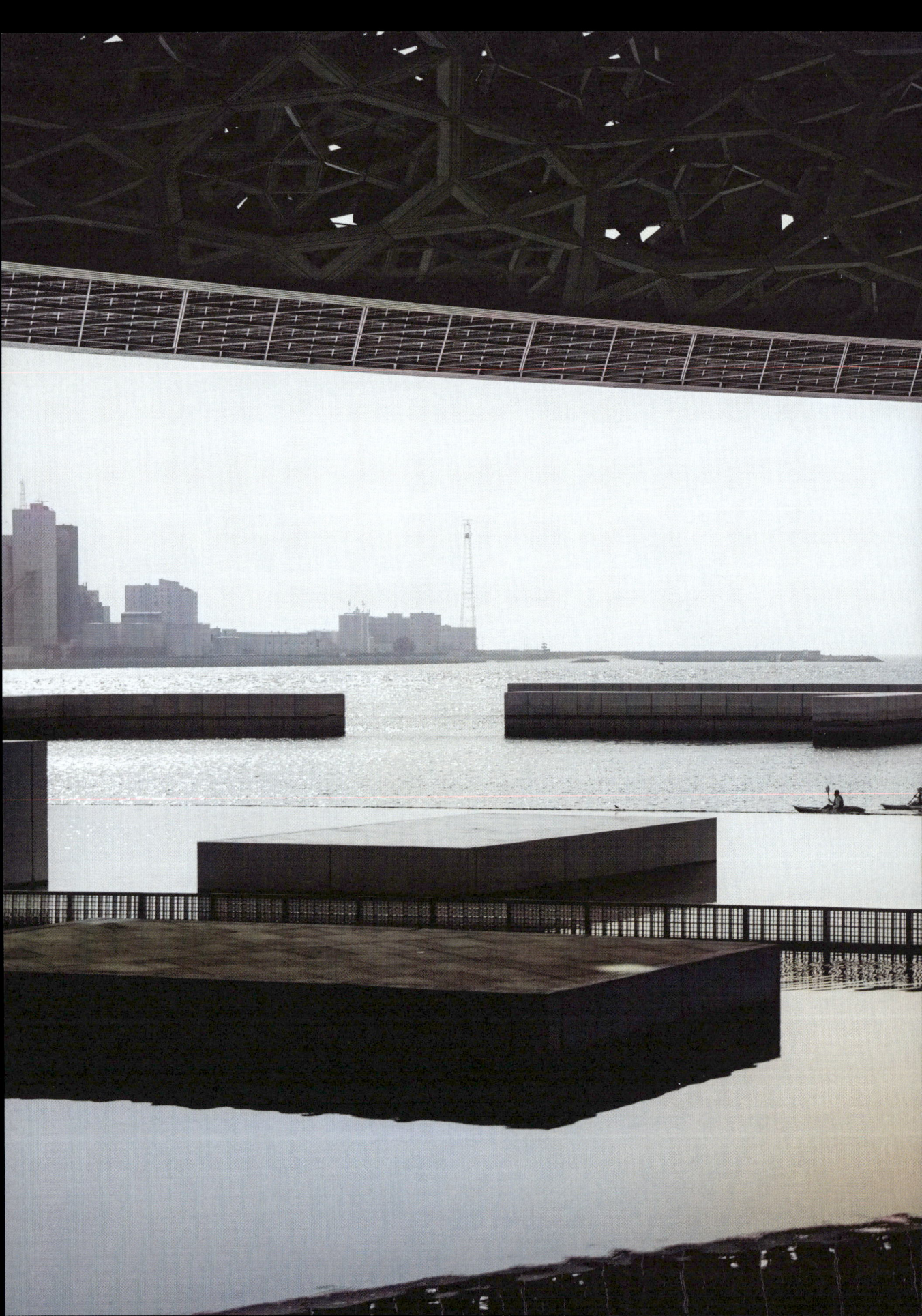

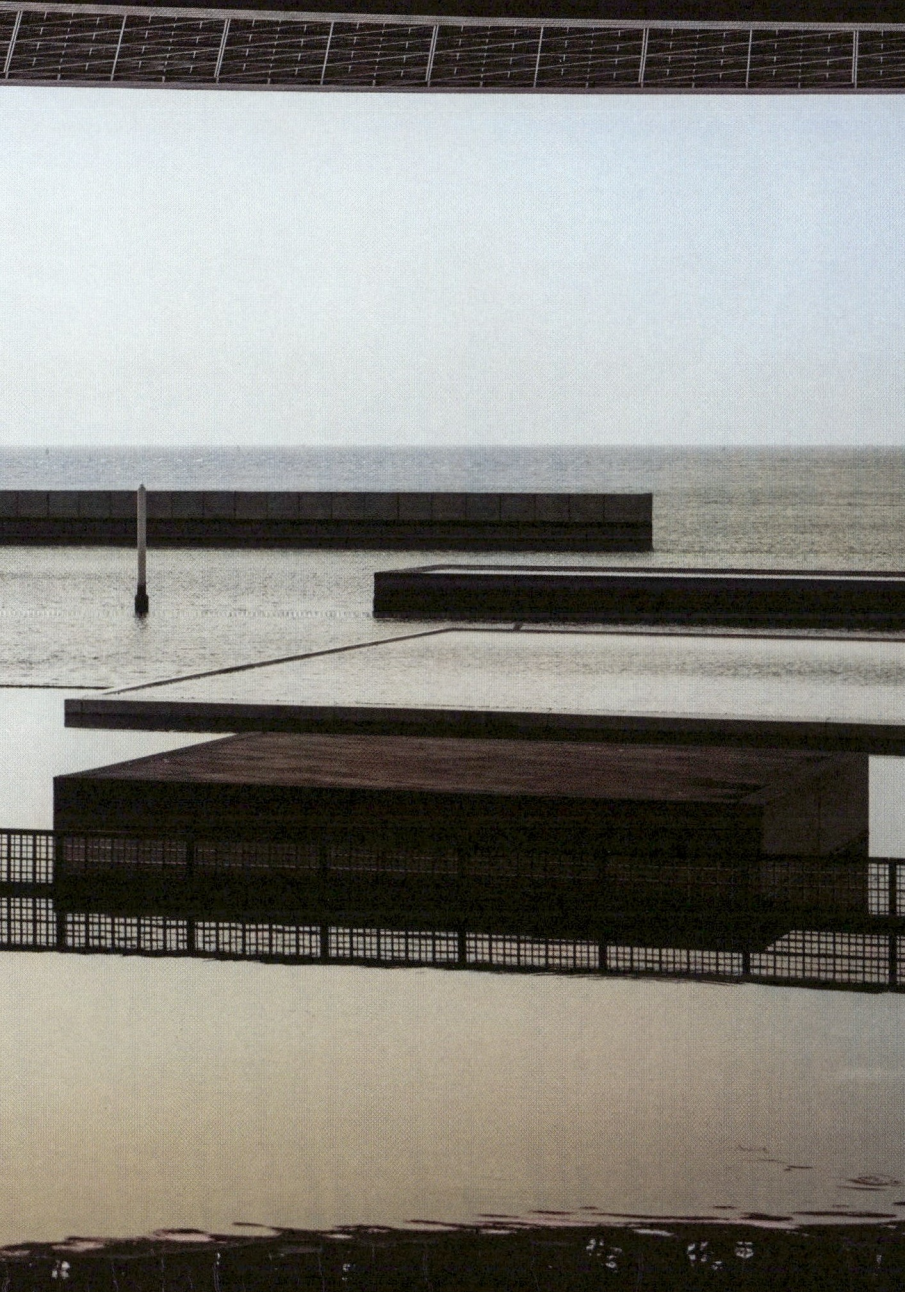

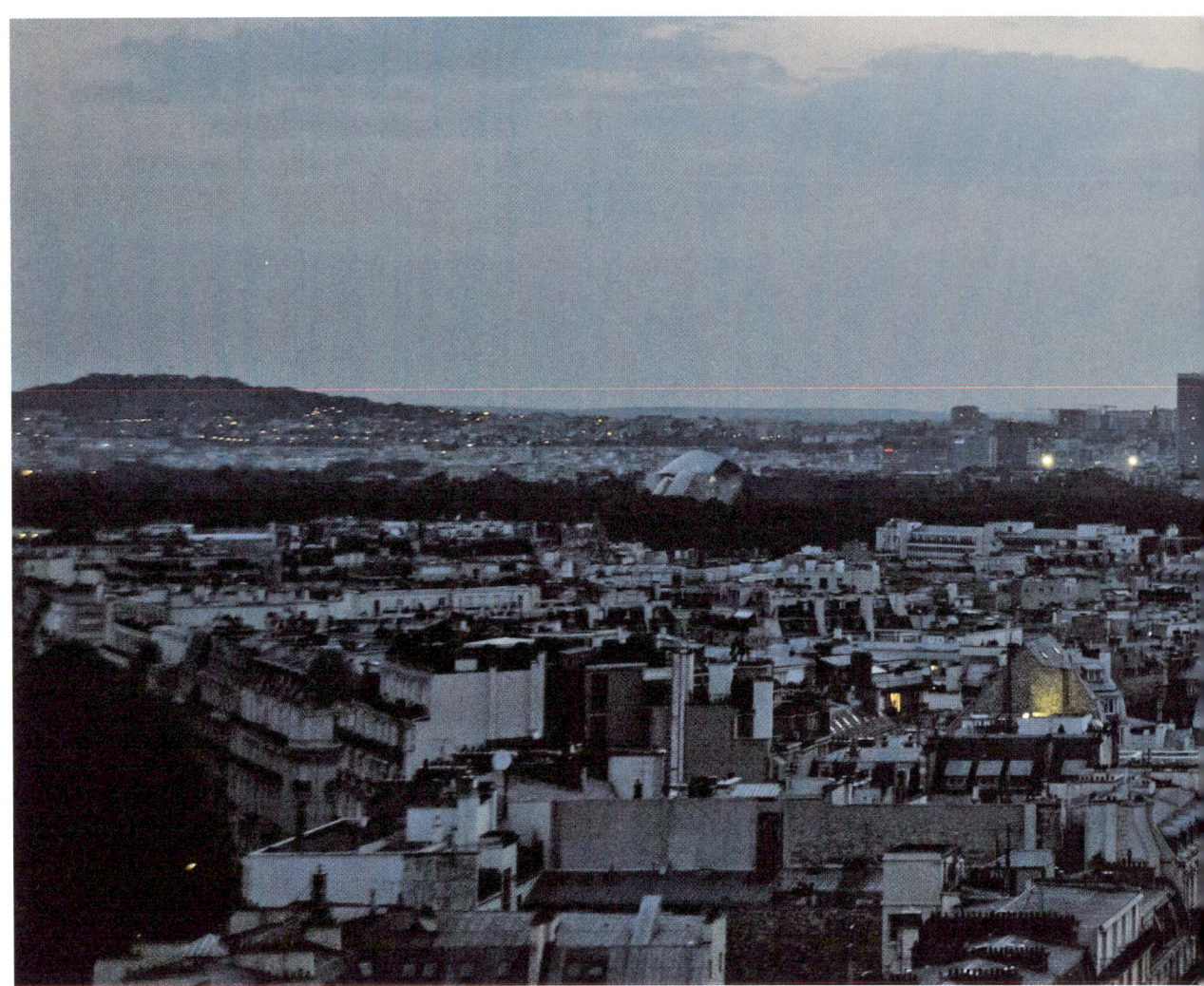

At the Window of the World, a theme park in the Chinese city of Shenzhen, tourists can file past one-third-scale reproductions of over one hundred well-known monuments from around the globe. Among them is the Louvre, reproduced synecdochally in the form of Pei's pyramid, serving, like the original, as the entrance. Beyond it lies a fantasyland filled with the Eiffel Tower, the Taj Mahal, Big Ben, the Leaning Tower of Pisa, various well-known statues, and pleasant gardens of different styles. The park's neon slogan could serve as a stand-in for Paris's museum-city ambitions: "Give me a day and I will give you the world." Back up in the Tuileries Ferris wheel, if you look west, in the opposite direction from the Louvre, you will see, far away on the horizon, beyond the city limits, the business district of La Défense. Its towers are located at the end of the "Triumphal Way," which starts at the Tuileries and continues up the Champs-Élysées, past the Arc de Triomphe. Straddling the far end of the Triumphal Way, Johan Otto von Spreckelsen's monumental Grande Arche de La Défense (1989) appears as a gateway to the business district, marking the entrance to Paris's "Shenzhen," a concentration of all that does not belong in the amusement park that is historic Paris.[11]

Since the late 1950s, with the building of La Défense, Paris has become a spectator to

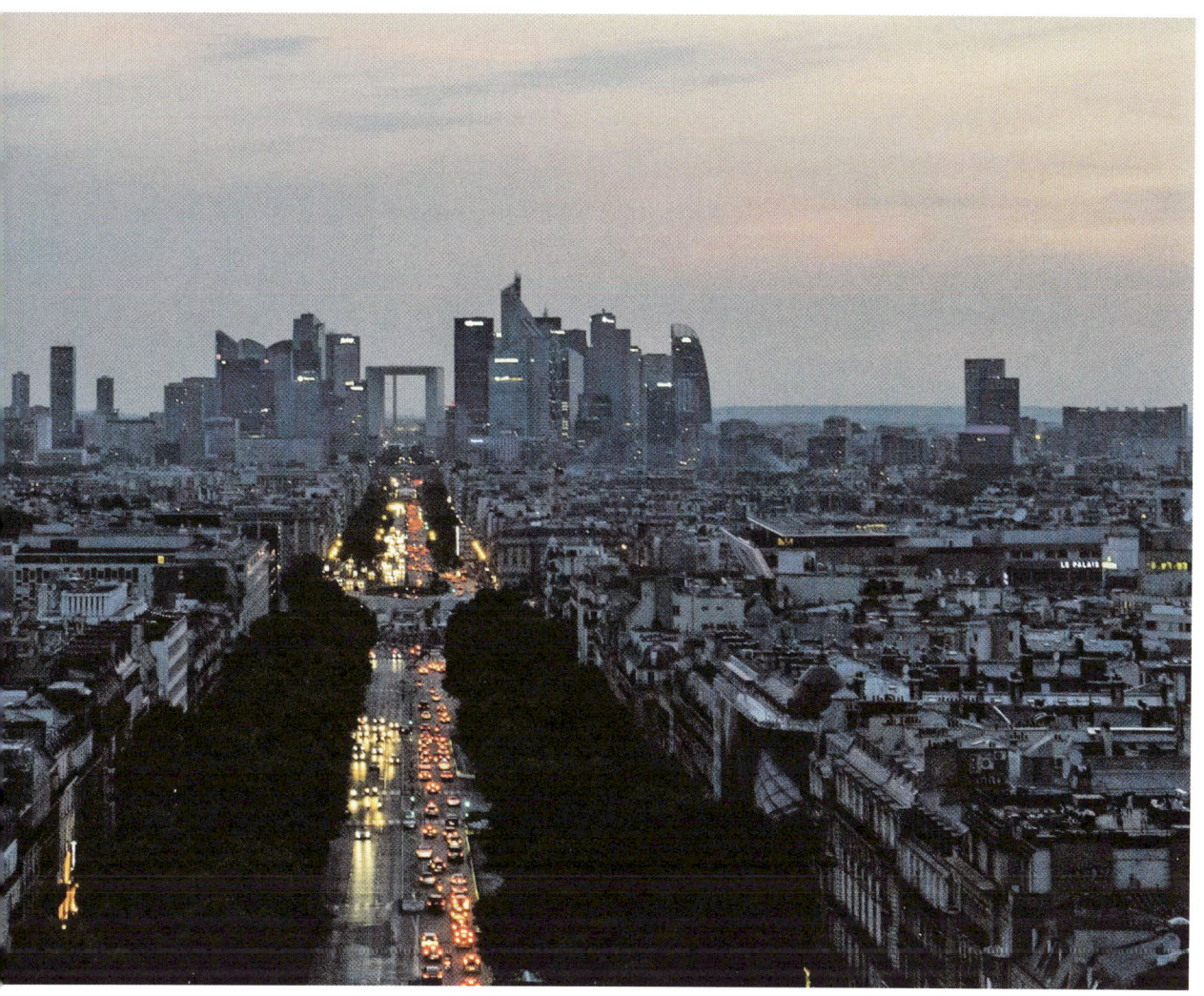

Since the late 1950s and the creation of La Défense, Paris has become a spectator to modernization, which it observes at a distance.

modernization, observing it from a distance. In the name of preservation, towers were pushed to the periphery so that the old city would retain its authentic identity. Although the historic fabric does not appear to have changed, at least on the outside, the process has rendered the city ersatz—a theme-park caricature of itself—where the museum stands as a relic of an outdated worldview. Despite all its sublime beauty, it may be that the Paris we see from atop the Ferris wheel in the Jardin des Tuileries is no more than a melancholic ruin.

---

11. The banishment of modernity to La Défense is clear from a symbolic standpoint in Spreckelsen's Grand Arche. Pei's unbuilt project for Tête de la Défense in 1970–1971 was slightly more nuanced and introduced notions of circulation and connectivity with the historical city, which ultimately became part of his project for the Grand Louvre.

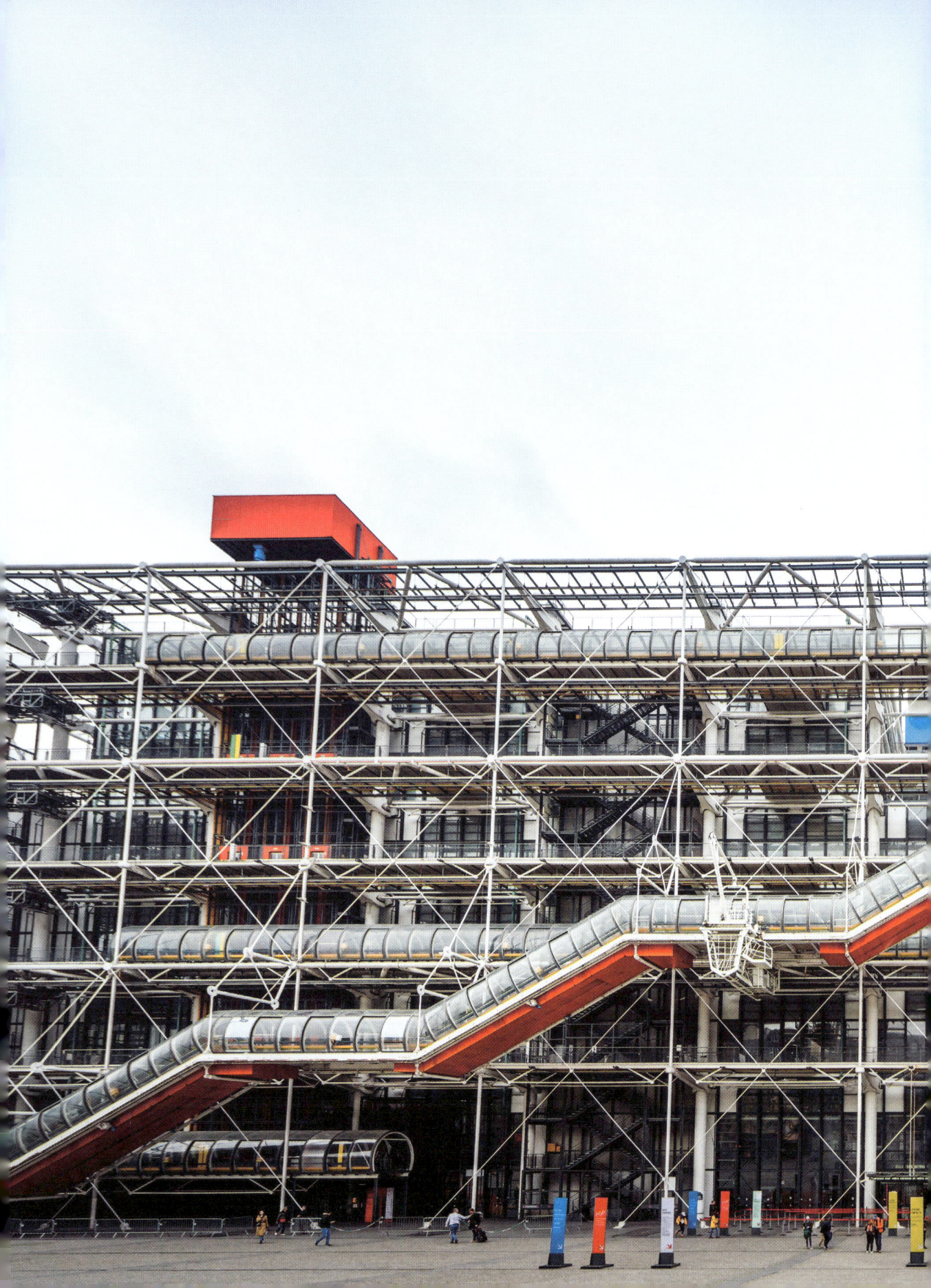

The museum is DRIVE-THROUGH

The museum as built infrastructure for the artifact of its time: the car

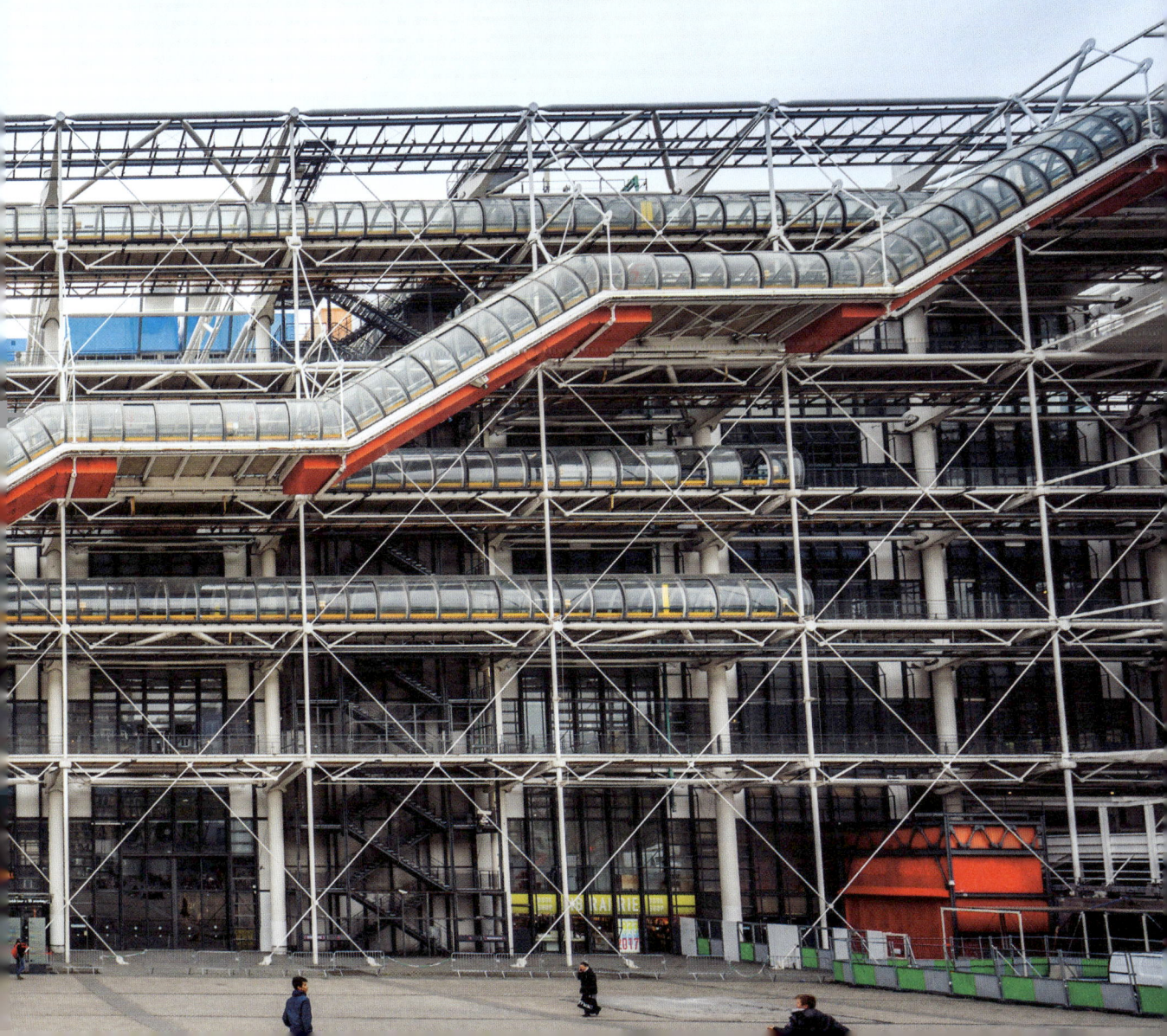

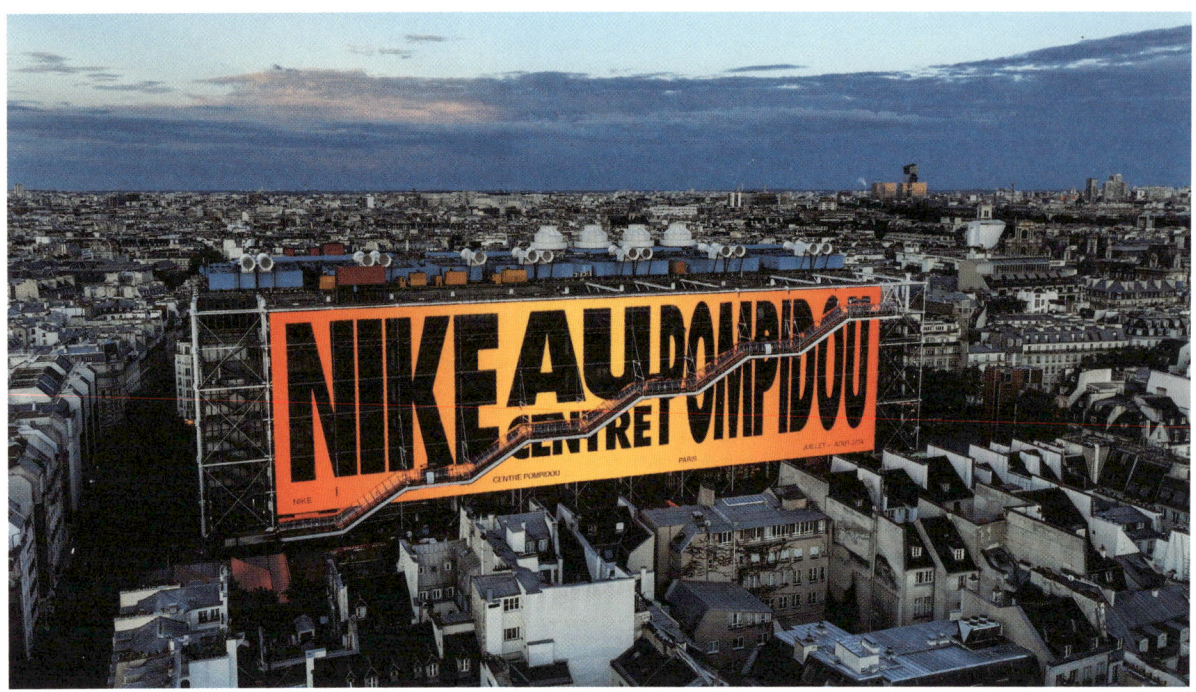

In the summer of 2024, a giant video billboard appeared in central Paris, covering the entire piazza facade of the Centre Pompidou with a luminous screen. For that year's Olympics, Nike used Piano's and Rogers's building—architecture that inspired Tim Hatfield to design the Air Max shoe in 1981[1]—to advertise its sporting culture. Featuring, among others, the recognizable silhouette of Eliud Kipchoge, the world-renowned Kenyan marathon runner, the museum's facade commanded attention at a time when all eyes were on Paris for the summer games, which the city had last hosted exactly a century earlier.[2] Reactions to the billboard ranged from enthusiasm to skepticism, echoeing the criticism of the Centre Pompidou faced when it first opened in 1977.

During the Olympics, advertisement—central to a heralded emblem of democratic culture—transformed the museum into a space open to all the arts: fashion, industrial design, technology, street culture, and more. This association with Nike allowed the museum to become a venue for the brand's followers and the fans of its ambassadors, where new forms and notions of culture are worthy of art historical attention, alongside the canon of modern art housed within the Centre Pompidou. Consequently, an audience member might visit to see the exhibition of Nike's Air Max shoe "Art of Victory" and decide to venture in the permanent collection galleries to contemplate the works of Paul Cézanne or Piet Mondrian. In turn, Nike's collaboration with the Centre Pompidou decentralized the institution's perception as a central actor in culture, welcoming new audiences that perhaps wouldn't have set foot in the museum without the brand's endorsement of the space as a cultural hub in the city.

Unbeknownst to the Centre Pompidou, the Nike campaign facilitated an incredible act of opening up to the city, perhaps better than any artist or exhibition in the institution's past programming, by utilizing the architecture as it was intended. Indeed, the initial dream of Richard Rogers and Renzo Piano was for the facade of the museum to act as a membrane that allows interactions between the contents of the museum

---

1. Tinker Hatfield, who designed the Air Max 1, joined Nike in 1981 as the architect for the brand's showrooms, and later that decade began designing shoes. Interviewed in Thibaut de Longeville's 2006 film *Respect the Architects*, he explained that it was the Centre Pompidou, with its exposed external HVAC, that inspired him to reveal the shoe's air bag, which had been hidden in previous Nike designs.
2. The first Paris Olympics took place in 1900; the city hosted the Games again in 1924.

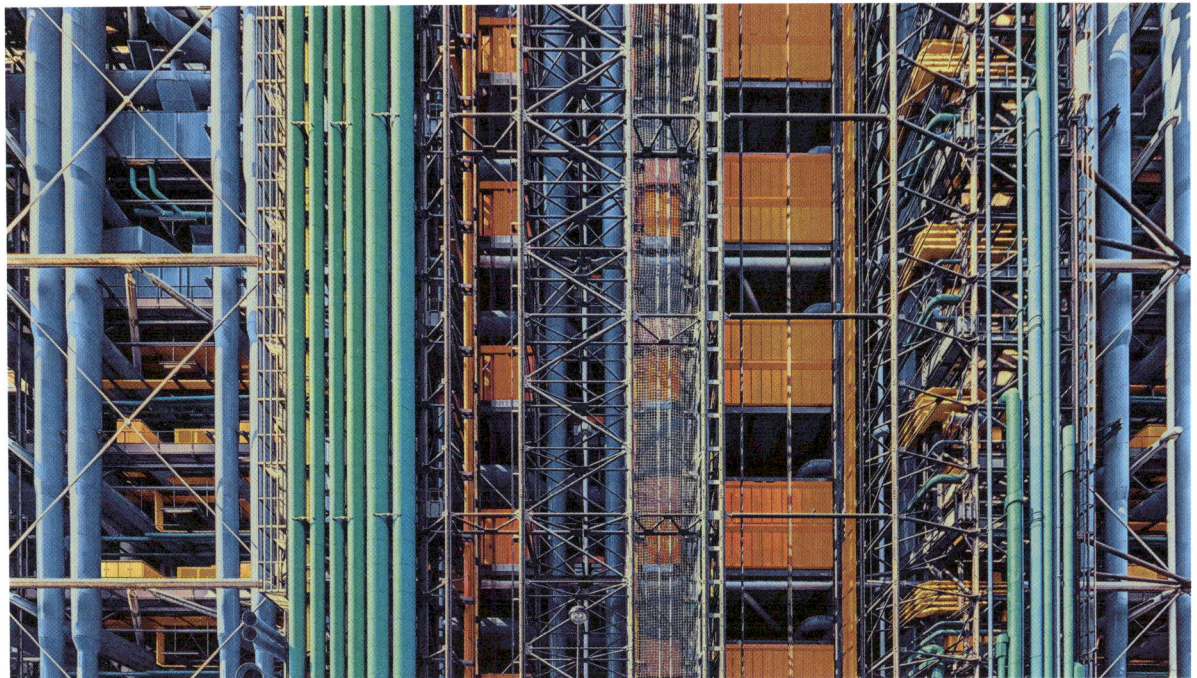

and the rest of the city: both reacting to and enacting its urban culture. This architecture of the billboard could only have emerged in an era when the automobile was the city's technological protagonist. Cultural infrastructure always reflects the prevailing technology of its time.

The result of 1930s slum clearance, the Plateau Beaubourg—a 7.4-acre hole in the urban fabric that would become home to the Centre Pompidou—had long served as a parking lot for Les Halles, Paris's central market several hundred feet to the west. In 1975, as Piano's and Rogers's building was being constructed, neighboring historic buildings to the north were falling to the wrecking ball to make way for the new Quartier de l'Horloge. Inspired by the site's charged history, American artist Gordon Matta-Clark chose to work with two of these structures for that year's Paris Biennale. As he wrote in *Flash Art International* in 1976, "The site was 27–29 Rue Beaubourg, two modest townhouses built in 1700 for Mr. and Mrs. Lesseville as what looks like his and her domiciles. Though these buildings are of little historical importance, they remain among the last structures to be torn down in a general Gaullist-Pompidou inspired 'modernization' of Les Halles and Plateau Beaubourg. These buildings are brought into full relief by an impressive backdrop of the

Previous pages: The iconic facade of the Centre Pompidou reveals the details of the escalator, which allows movement throughout the floors of the museum.

Opposite: The Nike campaign lasted for the duration of the Olympics featuring inventive graphic campaigns and collaborations with artists, which were chosen with input from the Pompidou curatorial staff.

Above: The Centre Georges Pompidou: this immense, futuristic building, covered with a tangle of blue, yellow, red, and green pipes and ducts is an act of vandalism and a masterpiece all at once.

THE MUSEUM IS DRIVE-THROUGH

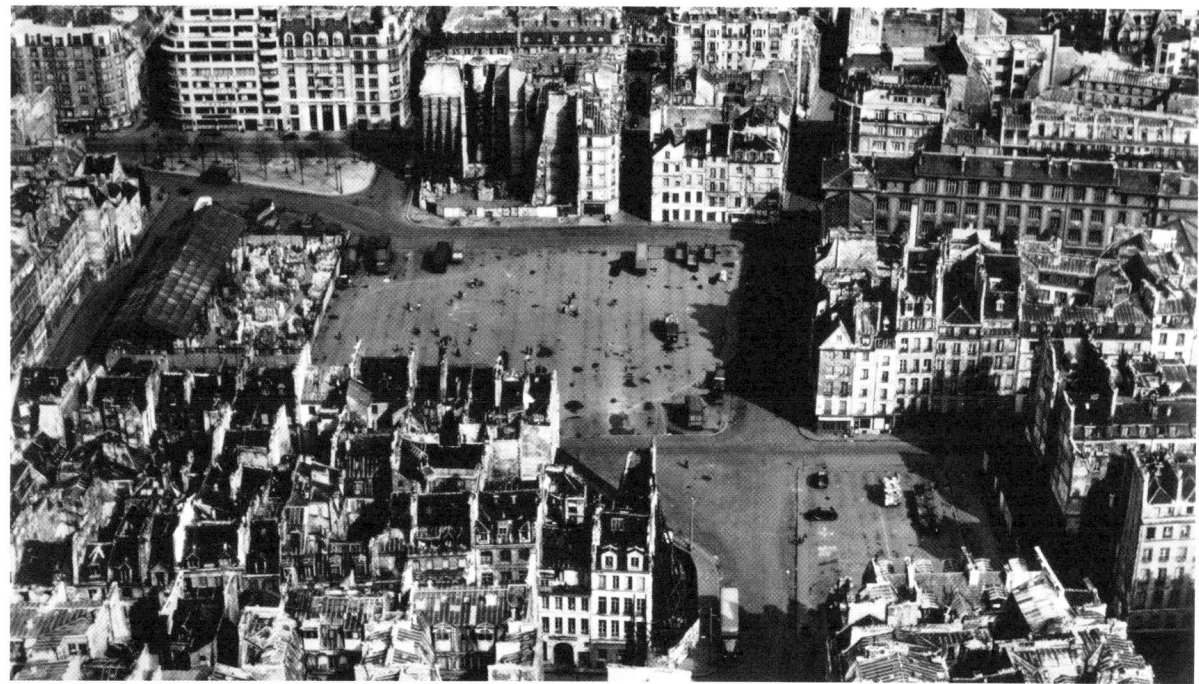

Centre Georges Pompidou's immense bridge-like structure..."³ Realized as part of his *Building Cuts* series, *Conical Intersect*, as he titled the work, involved "two plaster-dusty weeks ... cutting a conical void out of the upper halves of 27–29 Rue Beaubourg so that its base with the north facade was 13 feet in diameter, diminishing in circumference as it passed through walls, floors, and the attic-roof of the adjacent buildings. The central axis of the opening was set at an approximately 45° incline from the center of Rue Beaubourg." While working on *Conical Intersect*, Matta-Clark wrote to his family: "America has no forms on its own except distortions of European monumentality, the billboard, and the tragedy of an exterminated native population."⁴

With its tangle of blue, yellow, red, and green ducts, the immense, futuristic Centre Pompidou was criticized by many as an act of vandalism against one of the oldest quarters of Paris and variously compared to a battleship run aground or an oil refinery.⁵ Among other interpretations, Matta-Clark's intervention can be seen as a response to the uneasy reception of this new architecture—which emphasizes the violence of demolition and the pressures of rapid modernization—in a city deeply invested in preservation. Paradoxically, at the same time that the "Gaullist-Pompidolian" drive for technocratic "progress" was gathering momentum, Charles de Gaulle's culture minister, André Malraux, introduced a 1962 law to protect entire historic neighborhoods from destruction. In this climate, the Centre Pompidou's reception was bound to be controversial, the most scornful insult the French public hurled at it being that it resembled a "supermarket."⁶ This, however, is precisely what Rogers and Piano had in mind, a kind of emporium of intellectual services advertising itself through its architecture. Like a department store, their building is a microcosm of the city at large, its escalators, spectacularly hung off the facade, forming boulevards from which visitors can choose to turn onto smaller streets leading to different "neighborhoods," thereby mimicking life in the modern metropolis.

---

3. Gordon Matta-Clark, "(Etant-d'art pour locataire) – *Conical Intersect*, Paris, 1975," *Flash Art*, no. 349 (Winter 2024–2025).
4. Gordon Matta-Clark, Notebook GM CT 1260, estate of Gordon Matta-Clark on deposit at the Canadian Centre for Architecture, Montreal, 113.
5. As recounted by Renzo Piano. See also Reyner Banham "Pompidou cannot be perceived as anything else than a monument," *Architectural Review*, May 11, 1977.
6. See ibid. and Ada Louise Huxtable, "Architecture View," *New York Times*, December 25, 1977.

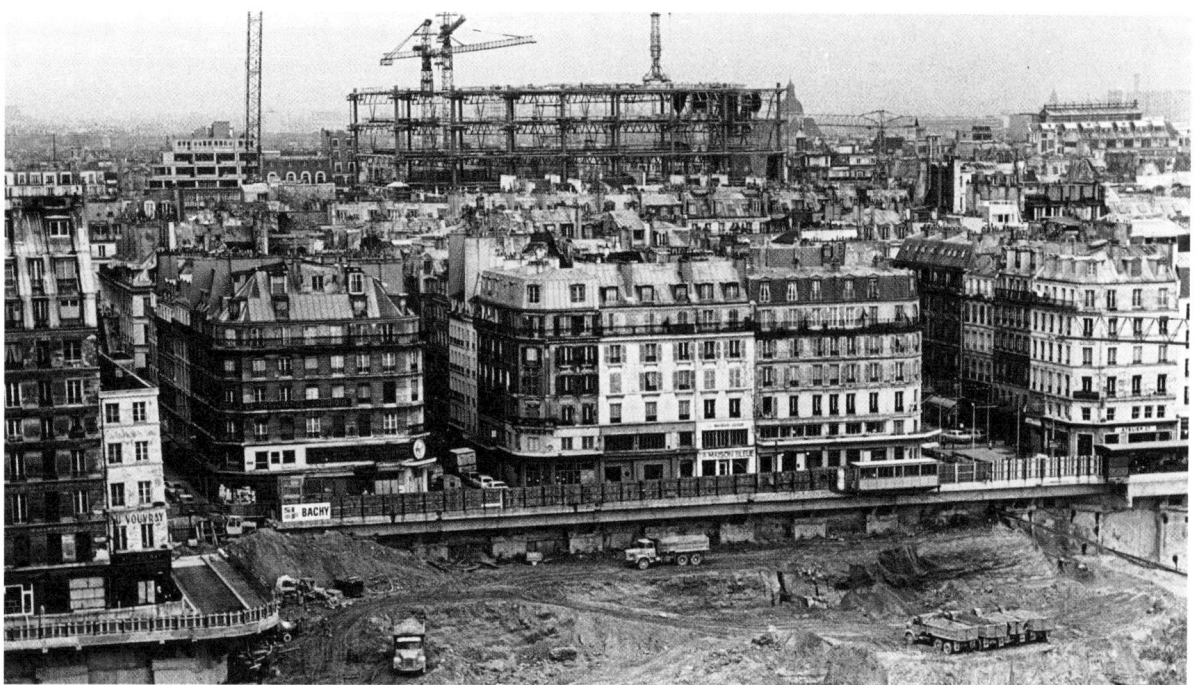

Instead of situating their monument at the center of the Plateau Beaubourg with public space at its periphery, Piano and Rogers positioned it adjacent to the busy Rue du Renard, thereby creating a vast piazza on the building's western side. Just as the billboard functions in relation to the freeway, so the Centre Pompidou's piazza-facing elevation functions in relation to the pedestrian—the automobile that once parked there having been banished in favor of a much older idea of urban social space and the kind of activities it can accommodate. Approaching the building from the eastern side, the sudden appearance of its mad jumble of pipes, breaks up the neighborhood's monochromatic monotony in striking Hi-Tech contrast. The elevation is uncannily reminiscent of future Archigram member Michael Webb's 1958 student project for the Furniture Manufacturers Association HQ, in which the articulation of tubular passageways and elevator shafts celebrates the mobility and vitality of city life.[7] As we have seen, in Piano and Rogers's

Opposite and above:
The Plateau Beaubourg—before the construction of the Centre Pompidou—was deemed a slum, which motivated the modernization of this area. Rogers's and Piano's project positioned the Centre Pompidou thusly, recessed from the center of the Plaza, in order to create a public square in front of the building. This was crucial to the architectural project and its ability to in dialogue with the city.

---

7. Archigram was formed in 1961 by a group of young British architects—Warren Chalk, Peter Cook, Dennis Crompton, David Greene, Ron Herron, and Mike Webb who joined forces to produce an alternative architectural magazine as a venue for their drawings and collages. In keeping with their enthusiasm for the immediacy of information-age electronics, they called the new publication *Archigram*, liking the title's association with "telegram" and "aerogram." When critics like Reyner Banham began referring to the work of the Archigram Group, the name stuck and this architectural collaboration was born.

THE MUSEUM IS DRIVE-THROUGH

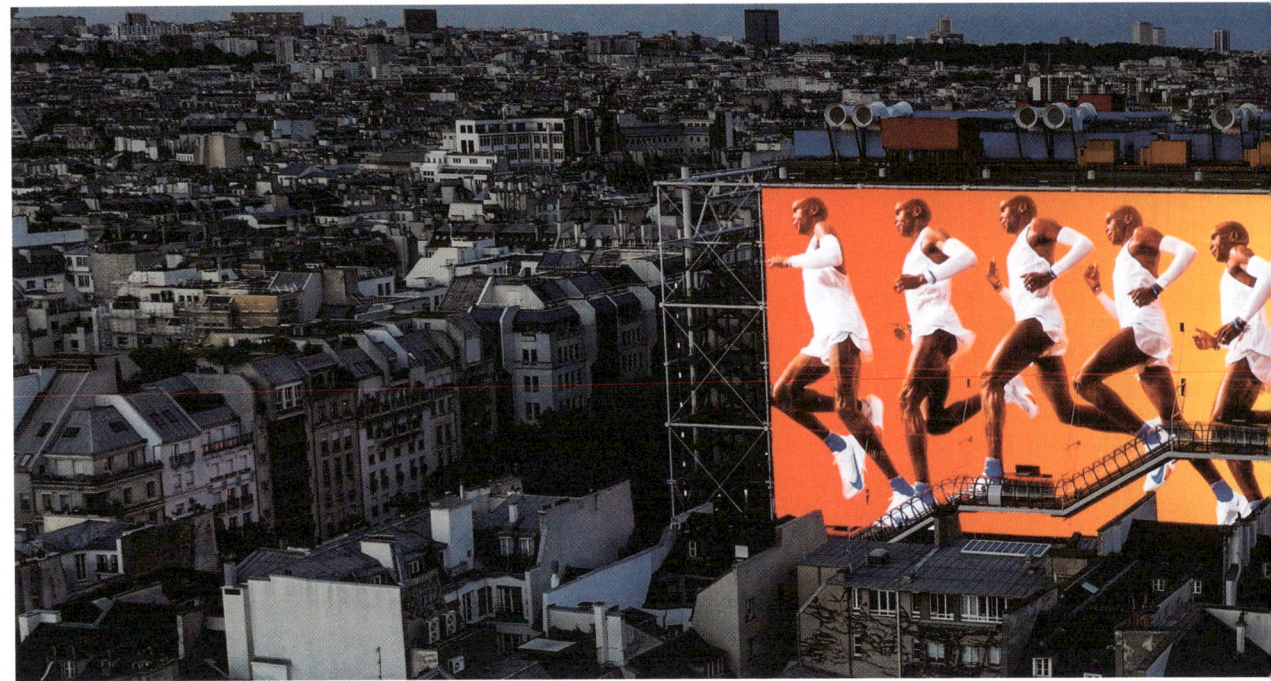

competition proposal, the Pompidou was envisioned as a "live center of information," its exterior animated by changing images and political and cultural slogans proclaiming its content, while its architecture hid nothing, fully expressing all the technology that went into its creation. In the end, however, some of these proposals were dropped after Valéry Giscard d'Estaing's election to the French presidency in 1974: the facade would no longer serve as an augmented billboard, nor would the open-plan floors allow for total flexibility, and, perhaps more importantly, visitors would no longer be able to move freely between the building's various institutions without a ticket.

Ultimately, Piano's and Rogers's building is a formulation of the postmodern condition that considers the city its terrain of expression par excellence. In some respects, it resembles a "decorated shed," as defined by Robert Venturi, Denise Scott Brown, and Steven Izenour in their influential 1977 manifesto *Learning from Las Vegas*—a building whose "space and structure are directly at the service of program," but whose form says nothing about its function, which must be indicated to the visitor through the use of a sign.[8] The Pompidou is both a blank billboard and a formally expressive modernist monument. This hypothesis of the postmodern condition crystallized in the 1985 exhibition *Les Immatériaux*, the largest and most expansive project presented by the Pompidou since its opening in 1977. Curated by philosopher Jean-François Lyotard and design theorist Thierry Chaput, the show took the form of a labyrinthine theater of the new, divided into different "zones," which together conjured an urban condition linking technology to the city. Liberating itself from the representation of knowledge, the exhibition sought to explore the physical landscape of globalization and demonstrate how this phenomenon was altering ways of thinking and being in the city.

For Lyotard, the concept of the "zone" evoked the intermediate space that long existed between Paris and its suburbs—a wide, blank glacis surrounding the city's nineteenth-century fortifications, which became the site of an infamous shantytown.[9] In the early 1970s Paris, fifty years after World War I had made the fortifications redundant and spurred their demolition, the last remnants of the zone were disappearing under

---

8. Robert Venturi, Denise Scott Brown, and Steven Izenour, *Learning from Las Vegas* (Cambridge, MA: MIT Press, 1977).

9. See Jean-François Lyotard, *Postmodern Fables* (Minneapolis: University of Minnesota Press, 1997).

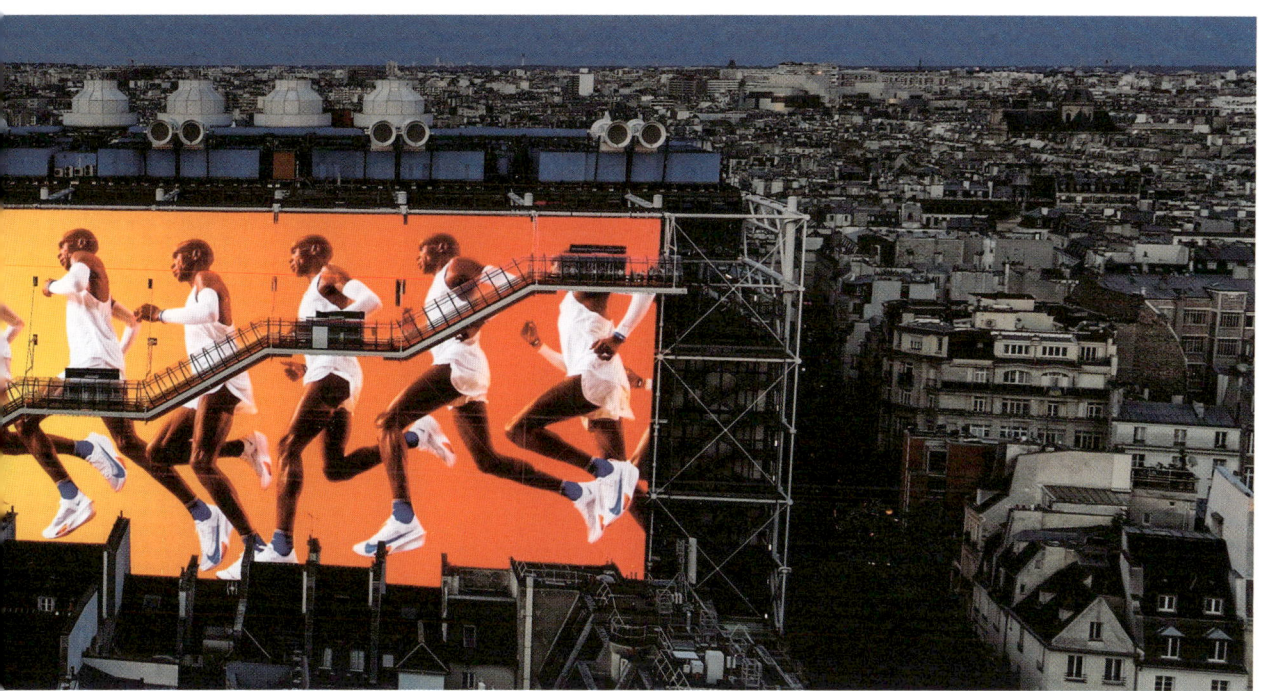

Nike's Olympics campaign demonstrates the use of the architecture of the building as it was intended: a billboard that speaks to the city.

the concrete and asphalt of the *boulevard périphérique*, Paris's orbital freeway. In this context, the nineteenth-century modernity of the flaneur and the situationist modernity of the *dérive* found themselves clashing with the very different modernity of the automobile city, while another form of modernity emerged in the zonal conditions that were Les Halles and Plateau Beaubourg—uninhabited spaces of waiting, "in-betweens," and parking lots as museums-to-be.

In *Les Immatériaux*, the curators made the "zone" physically manifest through the different spaces in such a way that the museum became the illustration of the city as a thought incubator, a place with no inside or outside, since in the postmodern metropolis everything is simultaneously interconnected thanks to technology. *Les Immatériaux* replicated the relationship between the museum and the city at the scale of the exhibition. By using and displaying computers and radios, visitors were equipped with headsets that communicated information via infrared signals as they moved through the space. As an urban simulacrum, *Les Immatériaux* suggested complete continuity between the city and its suburbs, with technology having abolished urbanity's "outside" and the idea of entering or exiting it—thanks to the instantaneity of information, the city is

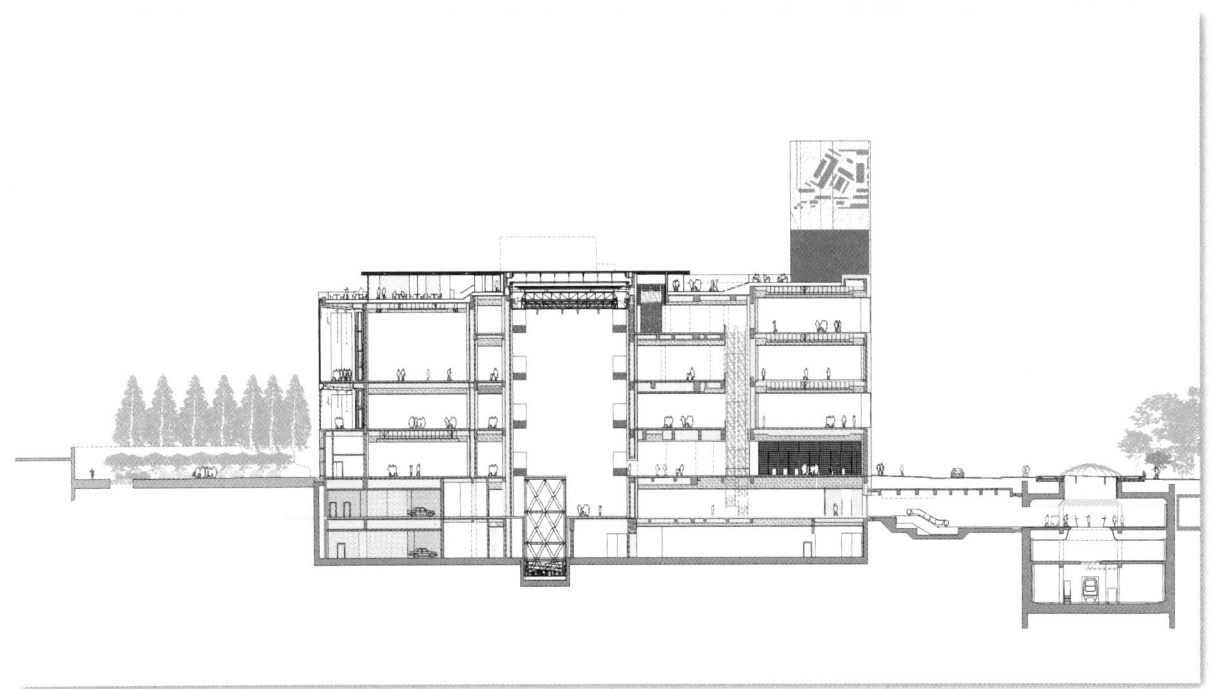

everywhere at once. This is what the Pompidou, as an architecture of connectivity with its urban context, sought to accomplish at the scale of the city.

By integrating information technology into the exhibition, Lyotard further pushed the formlessness of Malraux's "Museum Without Walls," allowing non-aesthetic objects—both scientific and technical—to coexist in the same space as artworks. Consequently, the experience of the metropolis is one that disrupts the book, the museum, and the encyclopedia. *Les Immatériaux* embodied the ambitions of the Centre Pompidou's architecture, at once the incarnation of a commitment to futurist technology and its extroverted display, serving as a *sign* and *billboard* for the specific postmodern condition described by Lyotard and embodied in the notion of the *zone*. At the Pompidou, the rejection of using the facade as a surface for projection, along with its exploitation as a simultaneous embodiment of the city, can be read as the abandonment of Archigram's dream of imaging the technology of the city; *Les Immatériaux* was its last incarnation.

This same condition resurfaced fifty years later in Jean Nouvel's Pudong Museum of Art in Shanghai and Herzog & de Meuron's M+ in Hong Kong (both 2021),[10] with both buildings striving to embody the city's technology with facades in the form of giant screens. Visible from miles away, these waterfront museums manifest the possibility, at any given moment, of capturing and embodying the city itself in the most contemporary form. The quintessential expression of European avant-garde modernity found its ultimate triumph in the metropolises of China.

In 1964, the influential American urban planner Kevin Lynch fixed a camera to his car to document movement through the city at accelerated speed. In the resulting three-minute sequence, we see an apparently generic cityscape—parks bordered by concrete

---

10. This project is discussed at greater length in the chapter "Fiction," p. 129.
11. Kevin Lynch, *The View from the Road* (Cambridge, MA: MIT Press, 1965). Urban planning in the postwar United States. is inseparable from the history of cars: the experience of Los Angeles, the freeway city, is entirely different from that of Paris or New York, where drive-by continuity makes up an added layer (whether on the street or in *Les Immatériaux*). See, for example, Eric Avila, "All Freeways Lead to East Los Angeles: Rethinking the LA Freeway and Its Meanings," in *Overdrive: LA Constructs the Future 1940–1990* (Los Angeles: Getty Research Institute, 2013).

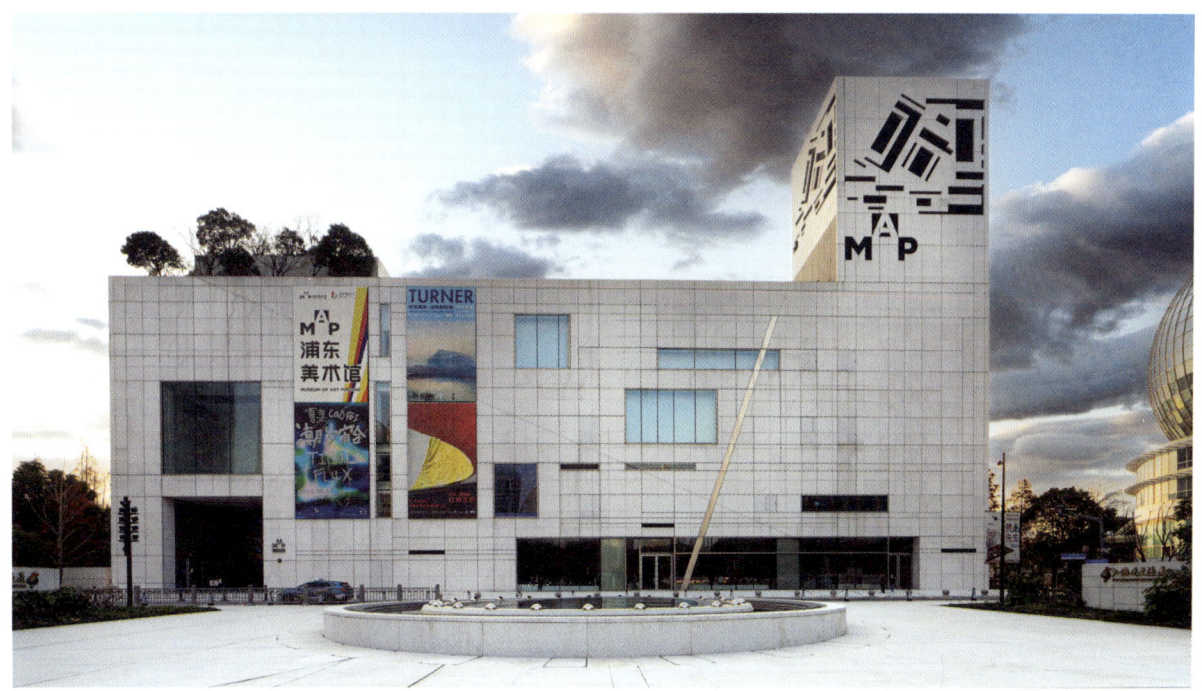

sidewalks, one-way streets, billboards, gas stations, bungalows, and occasionally an intersection or a bridge.[11] A split-second glimpse of St. Stephen's unmistakable clocktower tells us we are in Boston, allowing us to deduce that we are following the tree-lined parkways designed by Frederick Law Olmsted (1822–1903), widely regarded as the founding father of landscape architecture in America, which connect Boston Common to Franklin Park. With an audience of engineers and urbanists in mind, Lynch showed how, if well conceived, the road can produce a sequence of visual delight akin to a cinematic experience—his record of drive-by perception constituted a manifesto on how to design the American highway.

Two years later, in Los Angeles, artist Ed Ruscha tried something similar with a Nikon mounted on the back of a pickup truck: with 35mm film wound around cassettes inserted into a motor drive, the camera automatically advanced the frames at predetermined intervals, with Ruscha monitoring the camera and turning off the drive when the truck stopped. A diagram from his record book shows the Nikon affixed to a tripod and weighed down with sandbags. According to his notes, Ruscha tilted the camera slightly upward and set its focal range to infinity, making everything appear rather

Opposite: The section cut of the museum plan reveals the internal volumes. At the center of the plan is a gallery that spans four stories of the building.

Above: Jean Nouvel's Pudong Museum of Art, which faces the Bund in Shanghai.

Following pages: The museum facades display a large screen that allows for programs to be broadcast and addressed to the cityscape. Experiencing the museum begins outside, before one even enters.

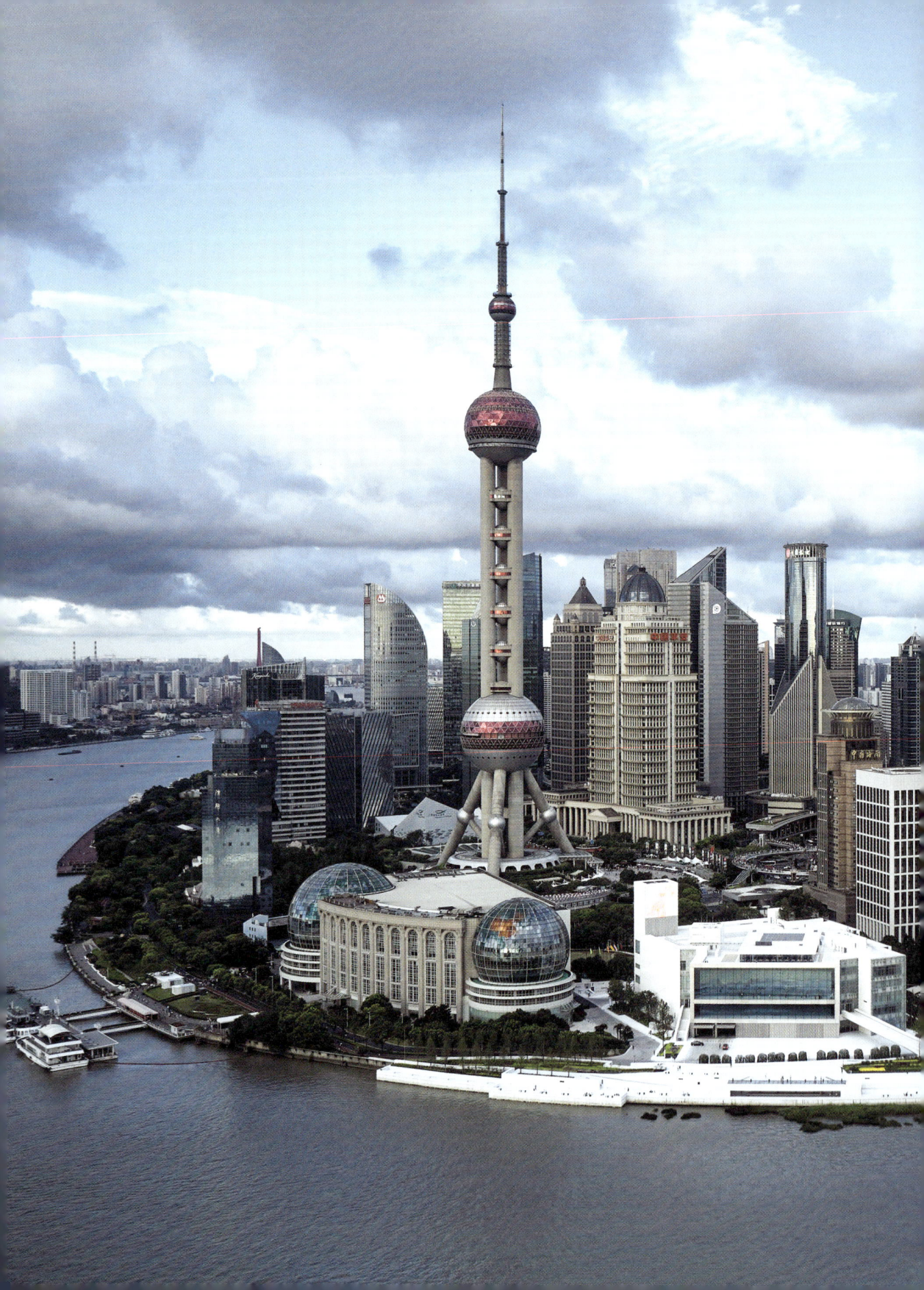

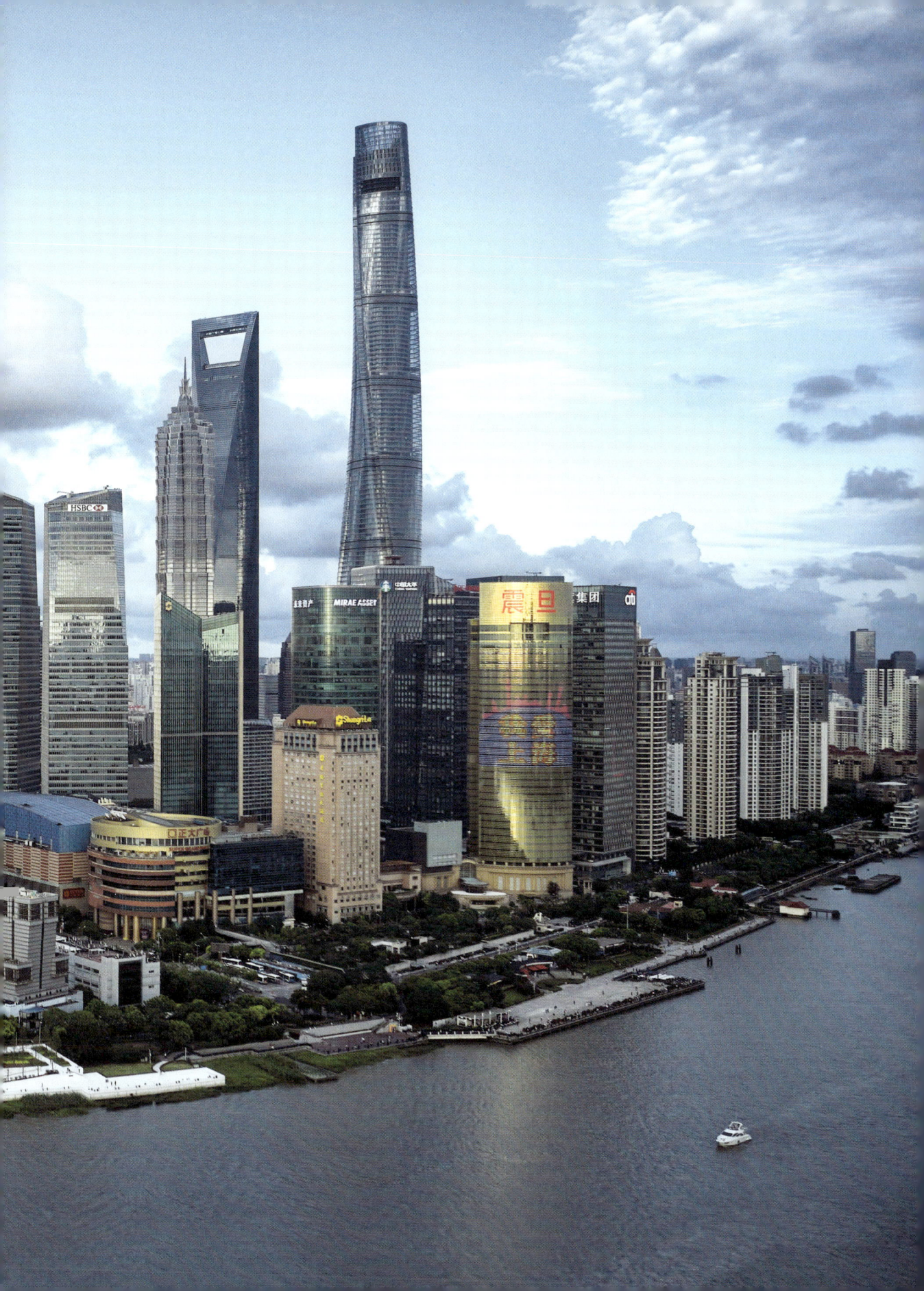

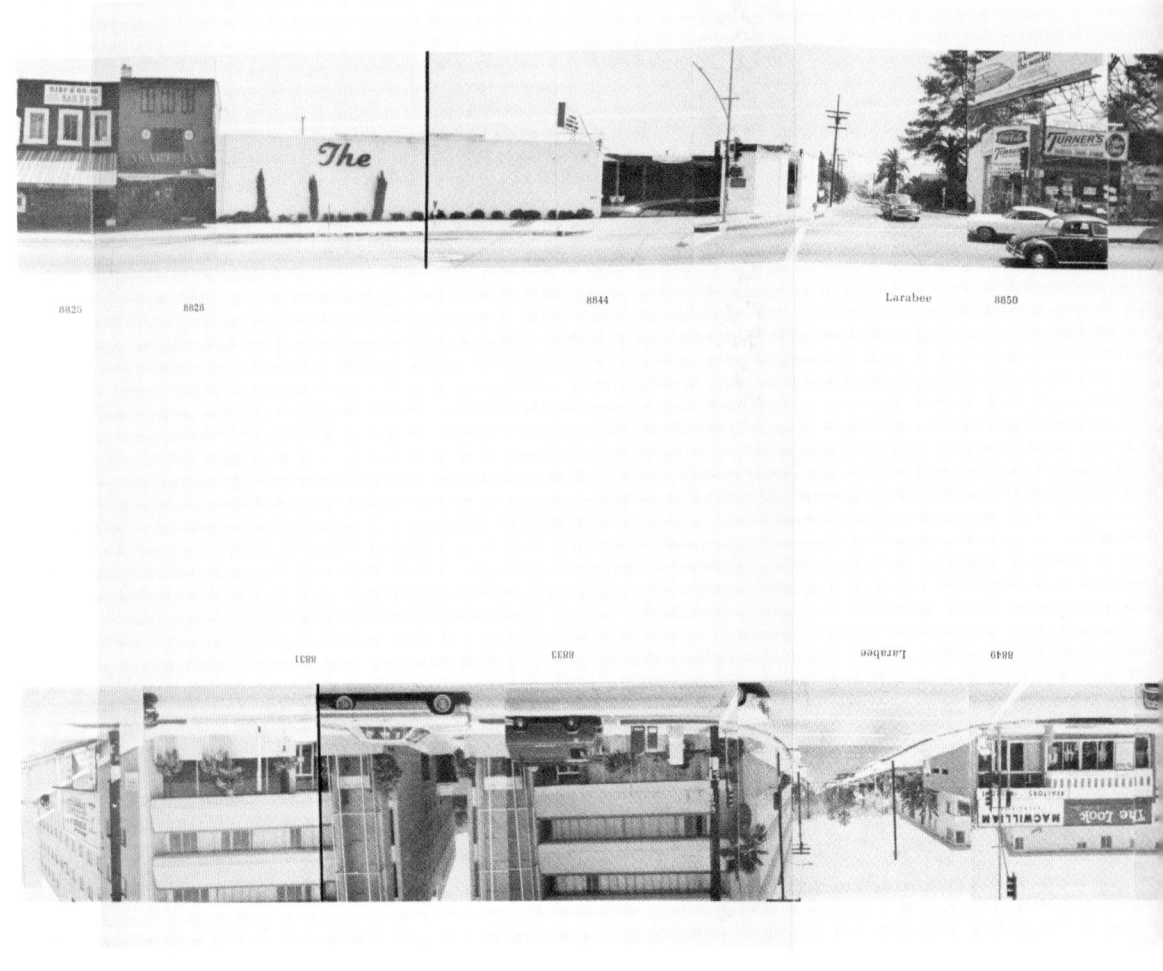

flattened, with no divergence in depth of field. In this way, he produced a collection of black-and-white photographs of mini-malls and low-rent apartments, seemingly unimportant and indistinguishable from one another. Isolated against a white background, they formed a nullified landscape, devoid of people. For the 1966 accordion-format book *Every Building on the Sunset Strip*, Ruscha printed two friezes of these photographs, each approximately 26 feet long, documenting both sides of the iconic Sunset Boulevard.[12] Characterized by an indexical aesthetic, his simple enumeration of forms revealed the vocabulary of forgettable typologies of commercial architecture.[13] The result of Ruscha's use of the car to generate the artifact of its time, the book was later hailed as a visionary engagement with the city's vernacular.

For Lyotard, the automobile itself—the ultimate symbol of technological mobility—was

---

12. Unlike Lynch's, Ruscha's expanded view from the road is one the driver could never experience sitting at the wheel.
13. Denise Scott Brown would later describe her art as a process of "deadpanning," encouraging her students to adopt his indexical methodology in their retroactive study of Las Vegas. Ruscha had already mastered this technique in his first book, *Twentysix Gasoline Stations* (1963), compiled during trips from Oklahoma to Los Angeles and back. See Robert Venturi, Denise Scott Brown, and Steven Izenour, *Learning from Las Vegas* (Cambridge, MA: MIT Press, 1977), and *Reyner Banham Loves Los Angeles* (1972),

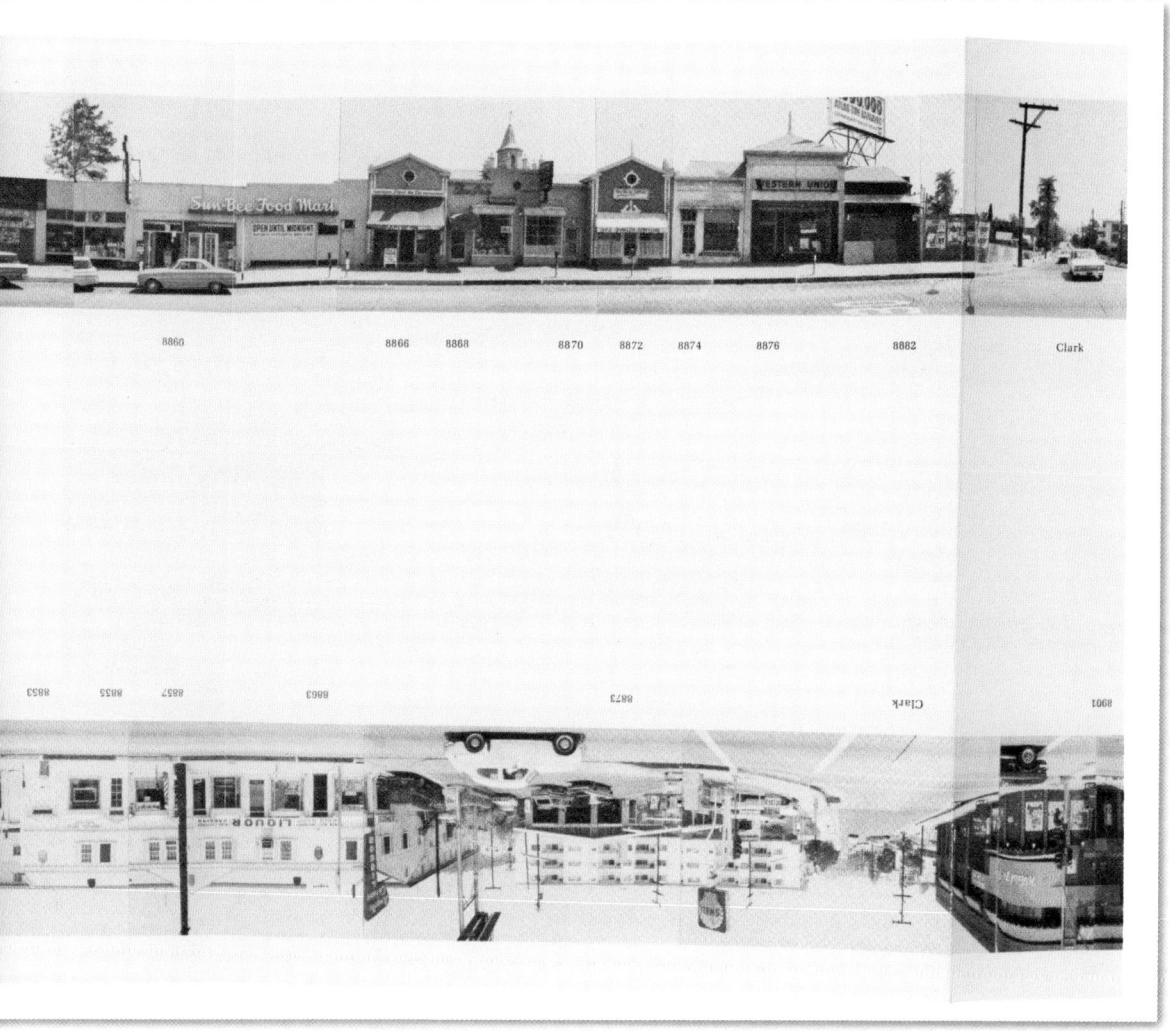

the artifact of the time, helping to abolish, as it did, the divide between the city and the rest of the globe. Perhaps he understood this most viscerally in California, with his car radio tuned into the latest news from Asia.[14] Fifty years earlier, in his 1932 Broadacre City scheme, Frank Lloyd Wright had foreseen the acceleration of this condition: "When a man sits in his car and turns a knob, the modern newspaper opens up to him by sight and sound. He is informed as he drives …"[15] For Wright, the

The accordion-format book, *Every Building on the Sunset Strip*, is artist Ed Ruscha's documentation of American vernacular architecture. It appeared in 1966 and is acknowledged as having inspired the methodology behind Denise Scott Brown's and Robert Venturi's *Learning from Las Vegas*.

a BBC documentary shot in the manner of a European travelogue that takes a cheeky but almost reverent look at Los Angeles, in which Ruscha makes a guest appearance.
14. From 1987 to 1994, Lyotard taught at the University of California, Irvine, in a joint position with Jacques Derrida.
15. Frank Lloyd Wright, "America of Tomorrow," *American Architect*, vol. 141, no. 2607 (May 1932).

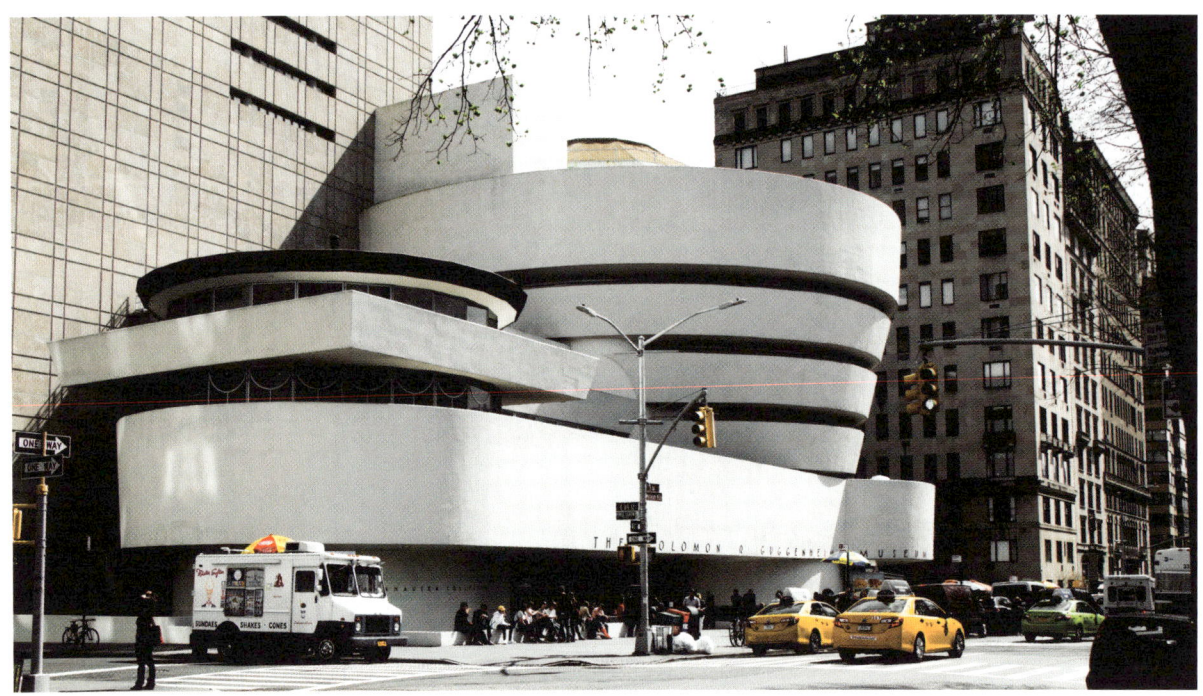

automobile would abolish the boundary between city and countryside, which is to say the car displaces the city to the countryside.[16] At the time of his first writings on Broadacre City, Wright thought that humankind had yet to liberate itself from the shackles of urban density, and that the internal-combustion engine, once fully exploited, would allow us to realize that humans embody the city, which is therefore displaced wherever we go. In this way, nineteenth-century urbanism would burst apart and redistribute itself across the American agrarian grid—indeed, Wright proposed that the city should be an ever-extending continuous line. "It's not hard to imagine the architectural high road with its sidewalk markets, super service stations, beautiful schools and playgrounds, integrated and intensive small farms, great automobile objectives, and pretty homes that follow the curves of the natural landscape in tomorrow's Broadacre City," he wrote.[17]

Wright's Guggenheim Museum in New York traces its origins to one of these "automobile objectives," a 1924 proposal for a commercial tourist attraction atop Sugarloaf Mountain in Maryland. With natural history exhibitions on the ground floor and a planetarium above, which evoked the vault of the sky, the facility aimed to attract the large motoring public that had developed in post-World War I America, and to that end featured automobile ramps spiraling up and down its exterior. With this project, Wright's primary concern was to accommodate the car and provide a new and different scenic experience for drivers and passengers, the spirals forming dynamic paths of movement capable of generating visual and kinesthetic sensations comparable to amusement-park rides. Where the Sugarloaf Automobile Objective narrowed as its spiraled upward, the Guggenheim—designed about twenty years later—starts wide at the top and constricts as it descends, its scale adapted to pedestrians: here, visitors take the elevator to the top and, following the pull of gravity, leisurely descend the ramp, observing the cumulative experience of artworks on the left and the view across the cavernous atrium on the right. Like Ed Ruscha's books—*Twentysix Gasoline Stations*, *Every Building on the Sunset Strip*, and *Thirtyfour Parking Lots in Los Angeles*—the Guggenheim condenses the American landscape; a continuous expanse punctuated by beacons of visual culture, it

---

16. Ibid.
17. Frank Lloyd Wright, *The Disappearing City* (New York: W. F. Payson, 1932).

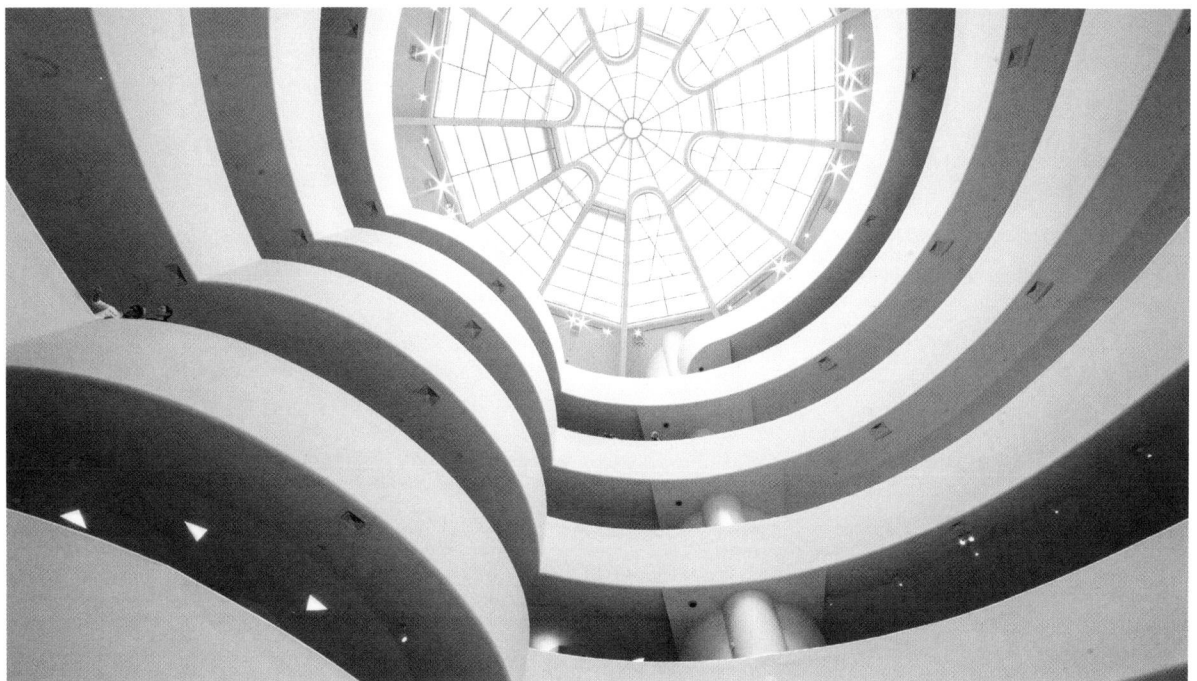

celebrates the automobile age by lining up artworks for drive-by perception.

If we follow Rem Koolhaas—who famously conceptualized in *Delirious New York* the notion that Manhattan is a collection of different forms of modern urbanization, with every block symbolizing an idea of metropolitan consciousness as imagined by the canonical avant-garde movements of the twentieth century—we can understand Fifth Avenue between 89th and 90th Streets as a manifesto of the urban sprawl, a microcosm of Broadacre City.[18] Since, for Wright, the city should be everywhere and nowhere thanks to the automobile, a museum for Broadacre should be articulated around its most important component. It comes as no surprise that Wright's design for New York's new modern art museum—a response to director Hilla Rebay's request for "a temple of spirit, a monument"[19]—is a sculpture of a parking ramp. Much like the Centre Pompidou in Paris, which it preceded by two decades, the Guggenheim is a sign for and of the city.

Opposite: Wright's Guggenheim New York can trace its origins to a previous project "Automobile Objective," a new scenic experience for drivers and passengers, hence the spiral.

Above: View of the iconic rotunda of the Guggenheim. Today the building, on Fifth Avenue and 89th Street stands as a monument and testament to the protagonist of the age—the car—as Wright had theorized in his Broadacre manifesto.

---

18. The Guggenheim Museum—much like El Lissitzky's Lenin Tribune, Superstudio's Isograms, or Mies van der Rohe's typical American building complex—could have sat on top of a base in Rem Koolhaas's *City of the Captive Globe* illustration. For discussion, see Rem Koolhaas, *Delirious New York: A Retroactive Manifesto for Manhattan* (New York: Oxford University Press, 1978). Further analysis appears in chapter "The In-Between," pp. 148–51.
19. Rebay to Wright, June 3, 1943, in *Frank Lloyd Wright: The Guggenheim Correspondence* (Southern Illinois University Press, 1986), 4.

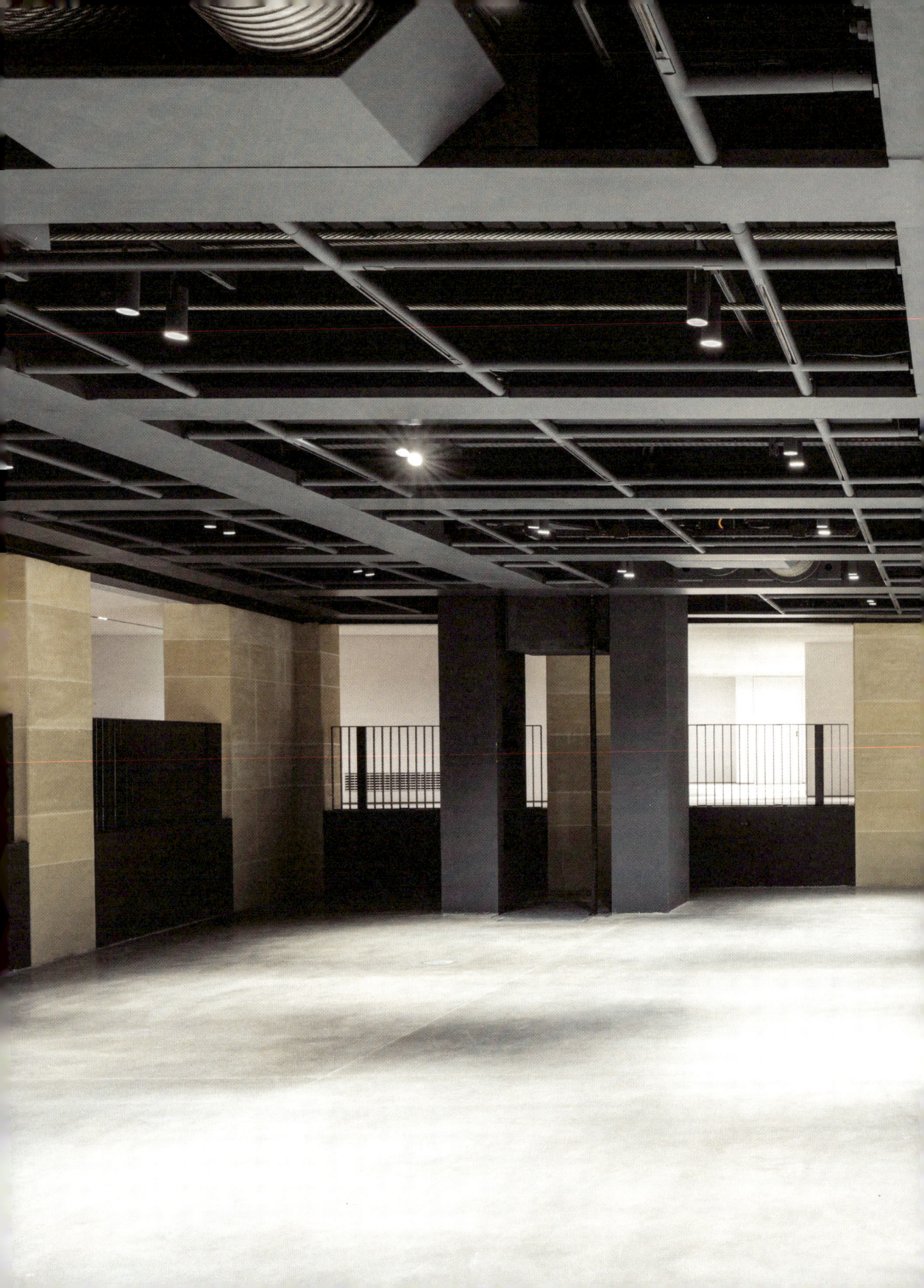

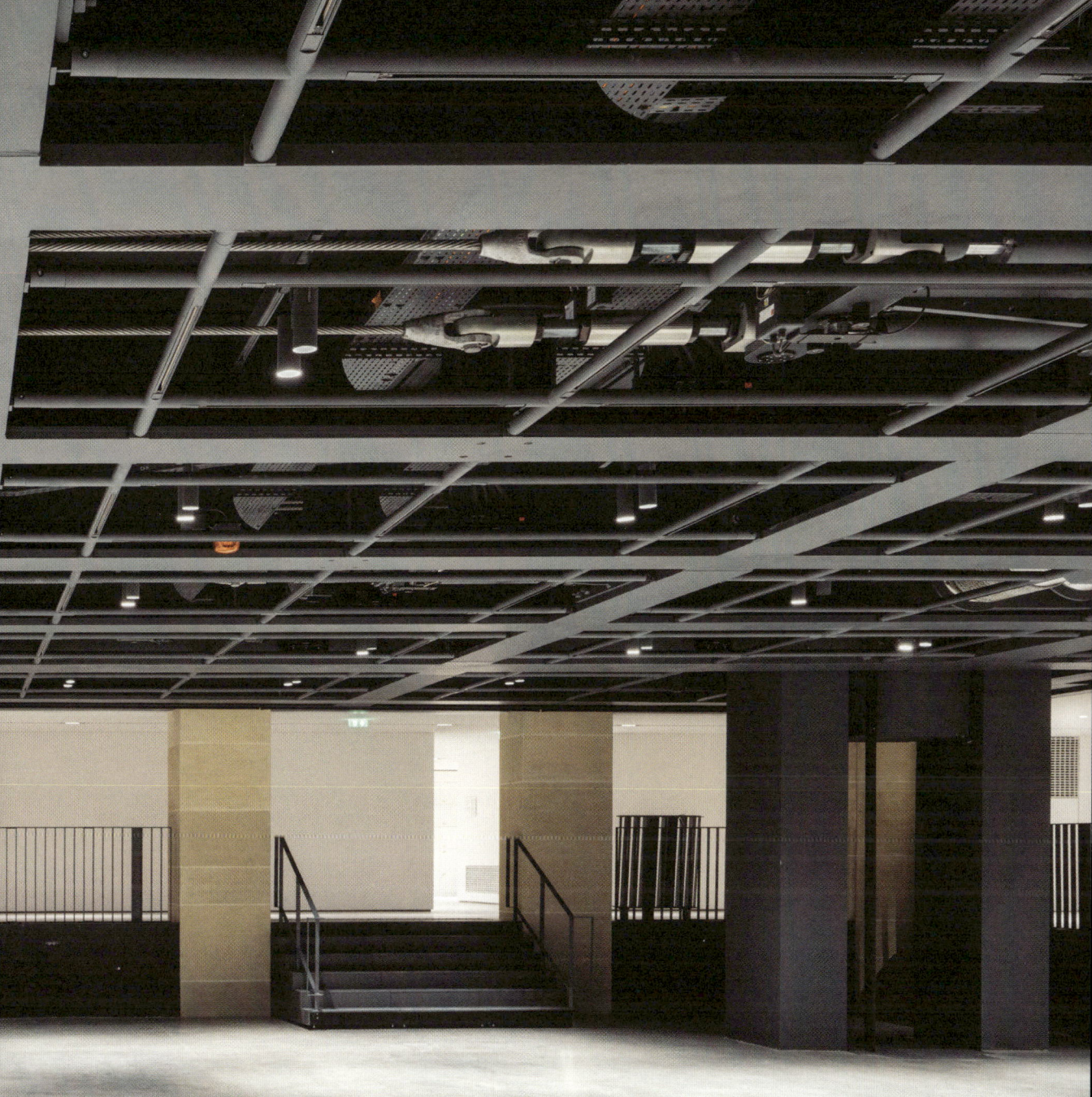

The museum is MACHINE

The museum needs dynamic architecture to be the site of cultural invention

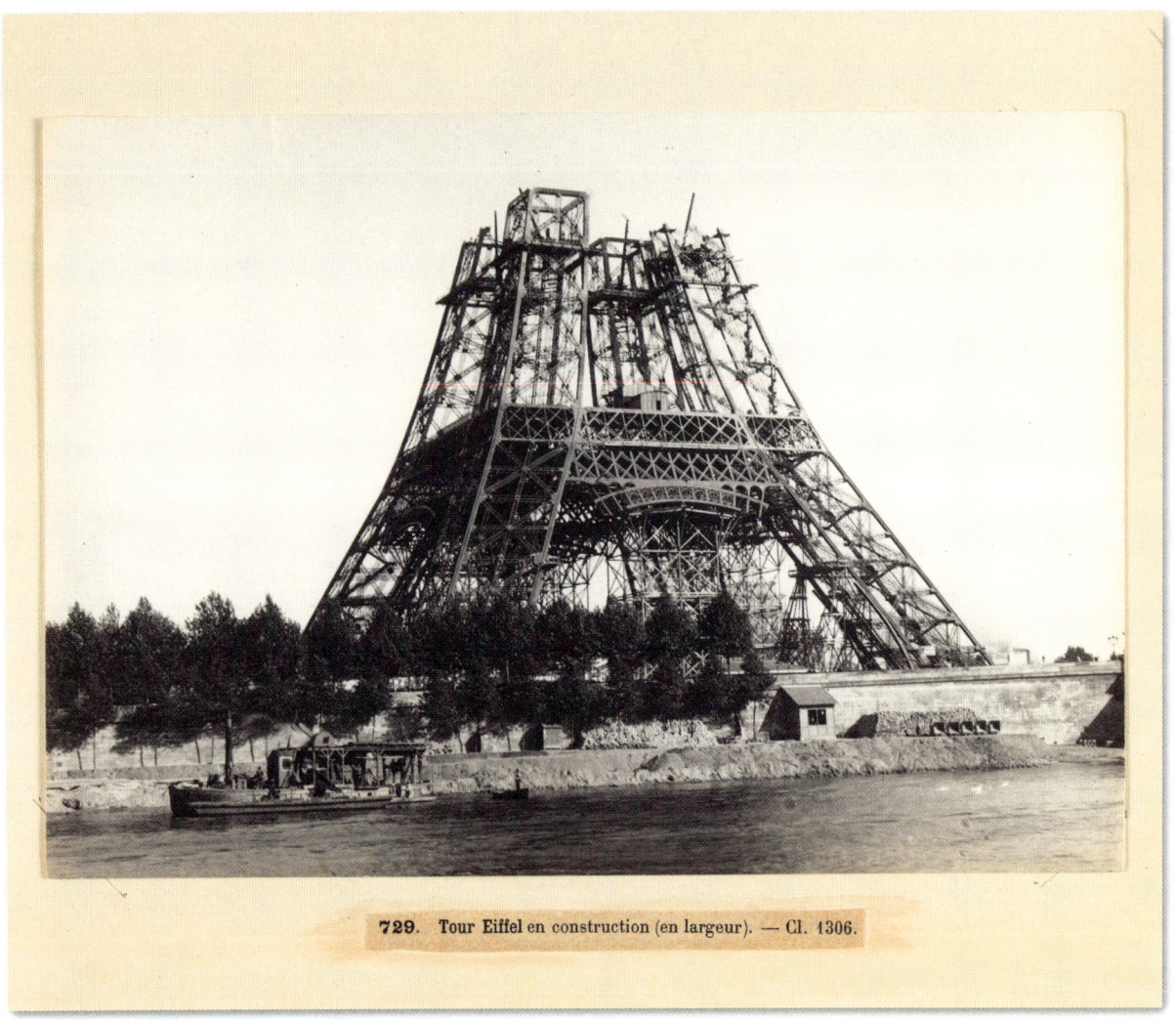

729. Tour Eiffel en construction (en largeur). — Cl. 1306.

On the banks of Australia's Parramatta River, the Powerhouse, Sydney's Museum of Design, Technology, and Science, is building a new home. Designed by the Franco-Japanese firm Moreau Kusunoki, it aims to offer ultimate flexibility in programming. Zigzagging around the facade, a monumental exoskeleton of white-painted steel allows for column-free galleries with ceiling heights of 59 feet.

If this "instant icon" of exhibition architecture elicits a sense of déjà vu, it is likely the memory of Paris's 1889 Exposition Universelle stirring in our minds. That year, to mark the centenary of the French Revolution, two record-breaking structures left their mark on collective memory: the Eiffel Tower, a pure exoskeleton with no interior, whose 984 feet made it the tallest building yet erected; and the Galerie des Machines (designed by Ferdinand Dutert and Stephen Sauvestre), the most visited exhibition hall of the event, whose steel-truss vault spanned 377 feet without intermediate support, making it the widest ever achieved at the time. "Never before, in the opinion of engineers of all countries who have visited it, has a building, proportionately to its vast dimensions, been constructed with such a wondrous combination of solidity, lightness, and grace, the general effect being enhanced by the flood of light freely admitted to all parts of the palace," wrote the American

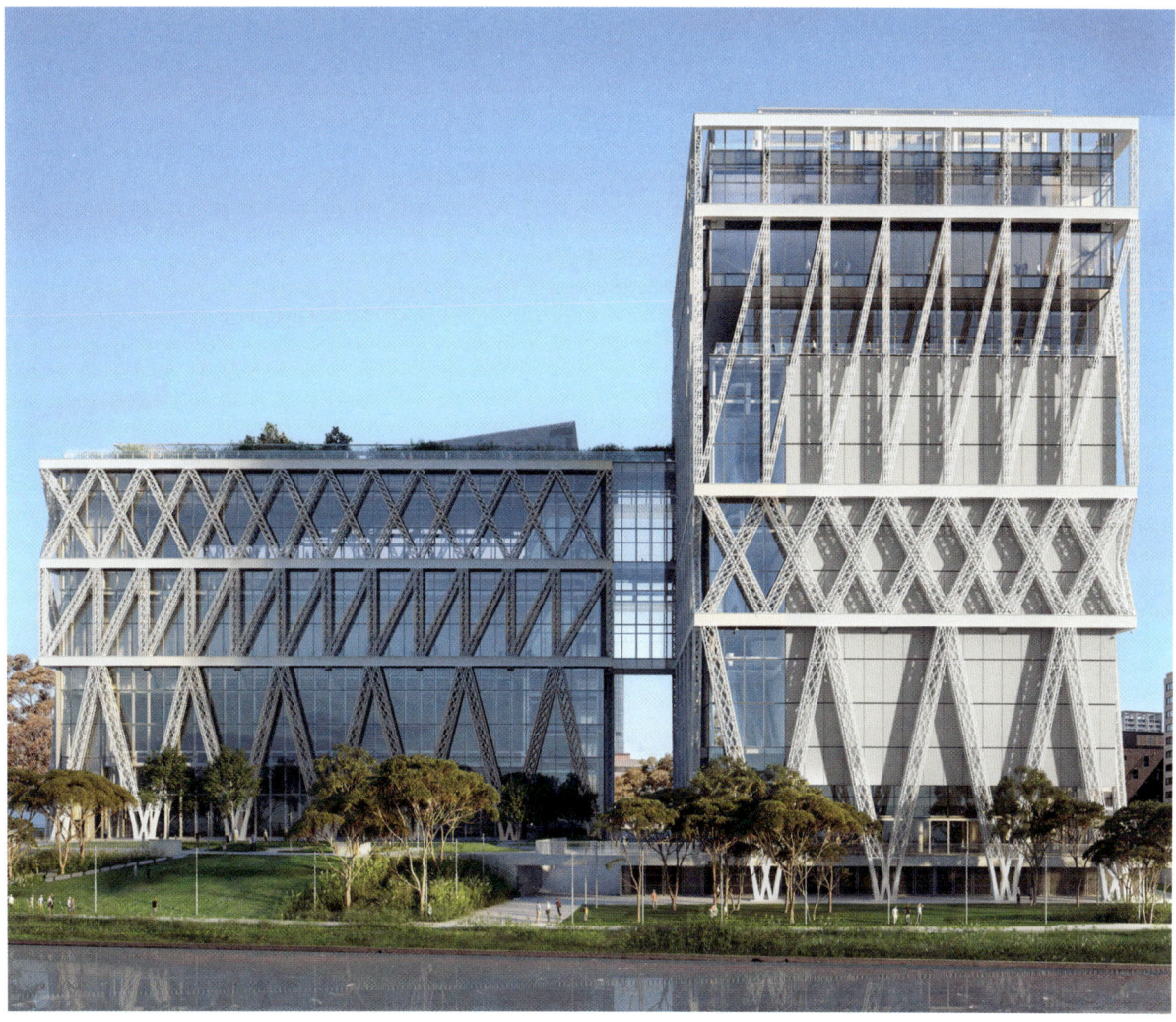

engineer William Watson.[1] With the Galerie des Machines and the Eiffel Tower facing each other at either end of the Champ de Mars, the 1889 Exposition crystallized one of those moments of technological acceleration when everything seemed possible. For the whole world to see, Dutert and Sauvestre's building displayed the machines that built the metropolis: atmospheric forge hammers, planing machines, Dayex voting machines, a Tissot watch factory, and Découflé & Charneroy's cigarette-making machine all featured among

---

1. William Watson, *Paris Universal Exposition, 1889, Civil Engineering, Public Works, and Architecture* (Washington, DC, 1892), 833.

Previous pages: In the Fondation Cartier's new exhibition spaces, dynamic architecture is composed of five platforms that can be adjusted to different heights: the floors are also the ceilings of the exhibition galleries and display an aesthetic of machinery.

Opposite: The Eiffel Tower is an iconic example or monument to architecture of the Universal Expositions, which later influenced the aesthetic of museums and exhibition halls.

Above: A rendering of the Powerhouse Paramatta. The monumental skeleton of white painted steel is poised to become the new symbol of Sydney's museum of design, science, and technology.

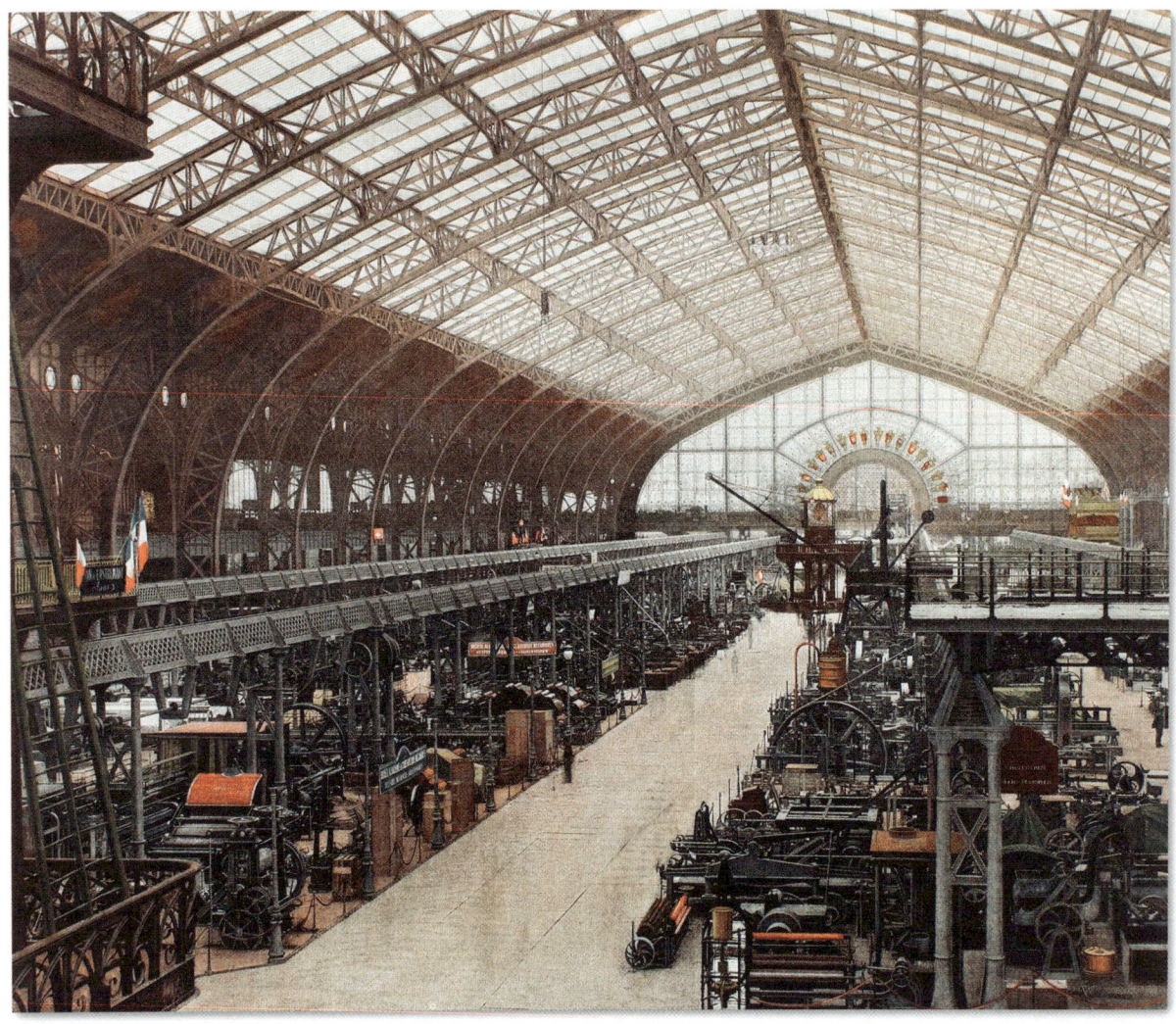

the eclectic collection of expressive kinetic objects. As well as representing new forms and functions, this spectacular show of industrial might affirmed the marvel of modern life.

One hundred thirty-six years later, Powerhouse Parramatta recalls the mighty metal tectonics of the Galerie des Machines, but instead of steam-powered engines, it will showcase space-age machinery.

Seventy-five years after the opening of the Galerie des Machines, the second machine age was gaining momentum as computers and cybernetics began to transition from theory to the physical world. In 1964, British architect Cedric Price announced plans for the Fun Palace, a now-legendary collaboration with radical theater director Joan Littlewood that would forever remain on the drawing board. A building whose form could adapt to its users' needs and desires, the Fun Palace was to be fitted with computer systems that could collect data about its usage and provide suggestions for future modifications. In another unbuilt design, the Oxford Corner House (1965–1966), Price proposed a twenty-four seven public "information hive" with floors that could move up and down and countless screens showing news and educational content. His Generator Project (c. 1976–1980) pushed these ideas further by proposing a system of 150 twelve-foot cubes that, thanks to computer-controlled cranes, could be

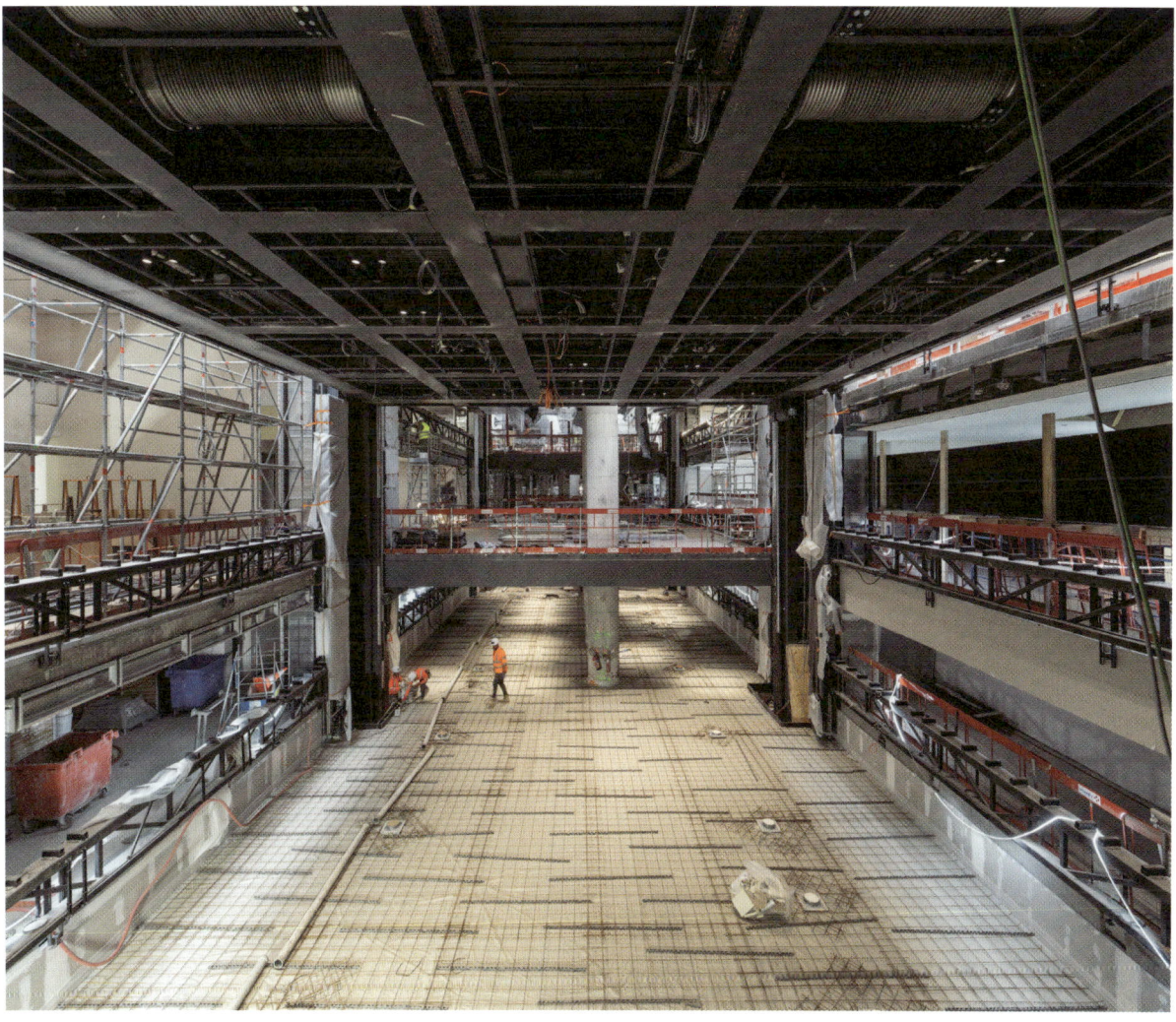

recombined into different structures according to users' desires, with programming that gave prompts for improving the combinations. Exploring the ecology of architecture and cybernetics, Price proposed new relationships between technology and culture.

Opposite: The Galerie des Machines, built for the 1889 Exposition Universelle in Paris, displayed machinery that enabled the modernization of city life.

Above: Jean Nouvel's contextualist approach stipulates that architecture must rely on the existing to build its future as a discipline. This is perhaps most evident in his Parisian project, the Fondation Cartier, where modernity's past selves are brought into the future.

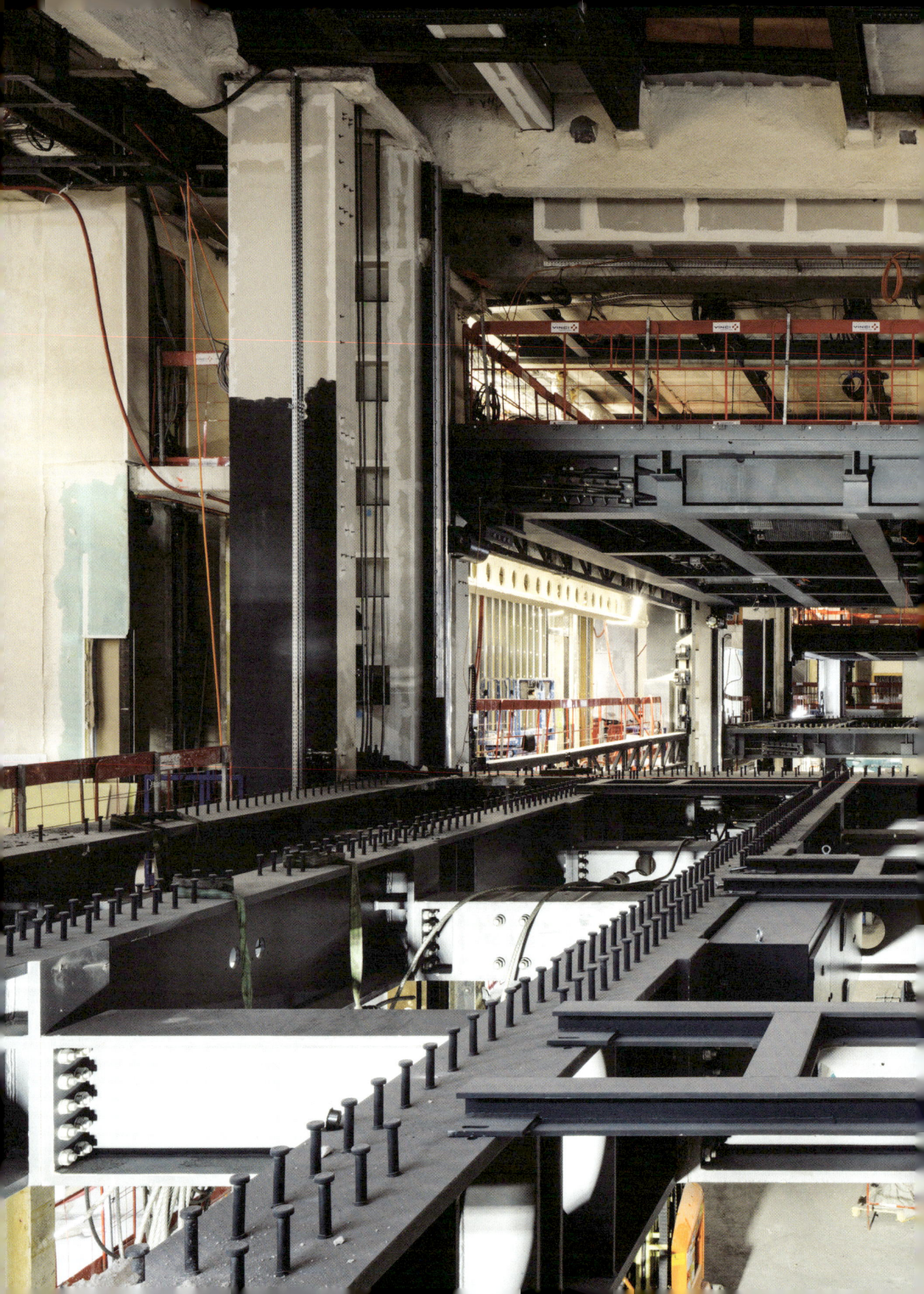

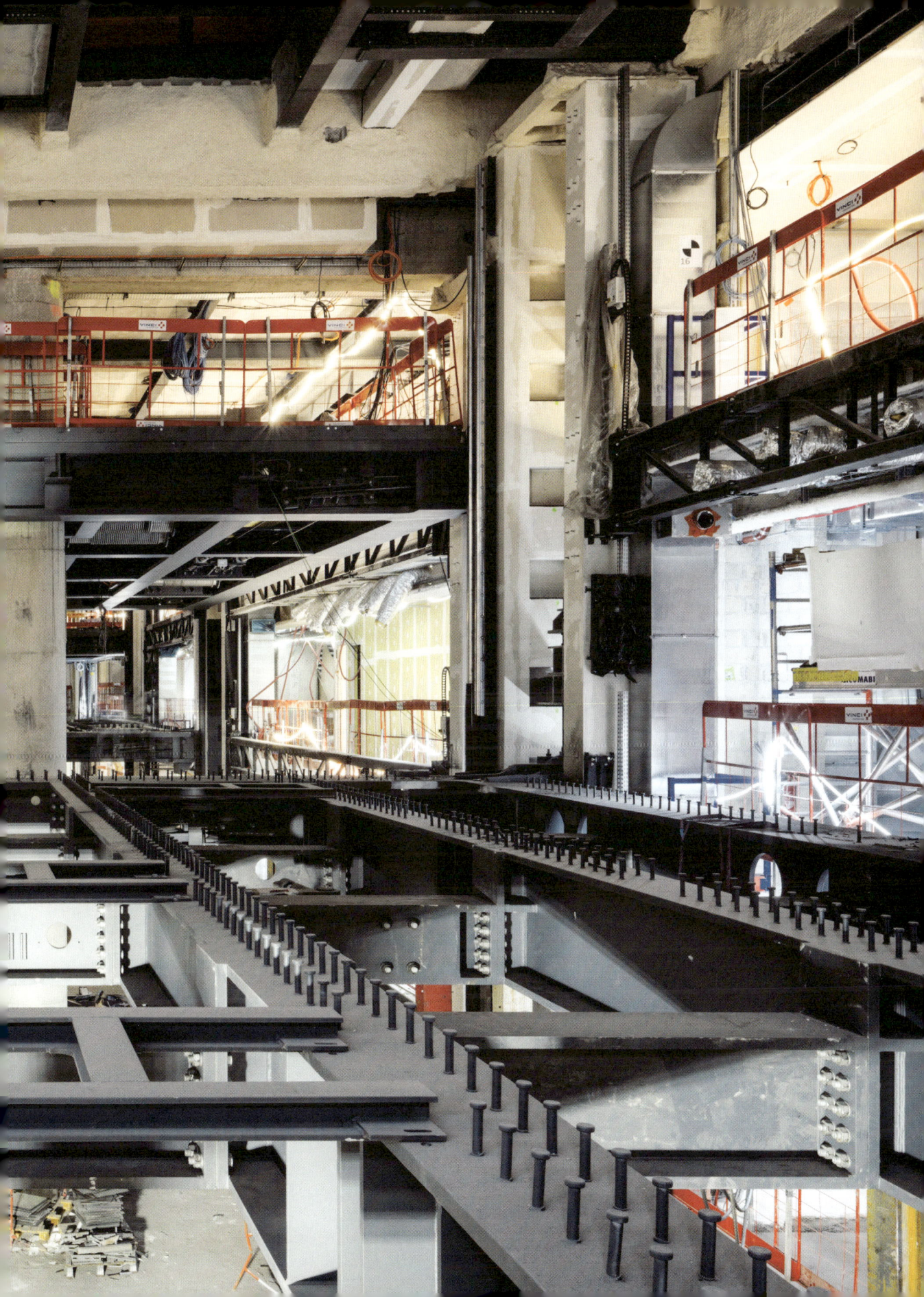

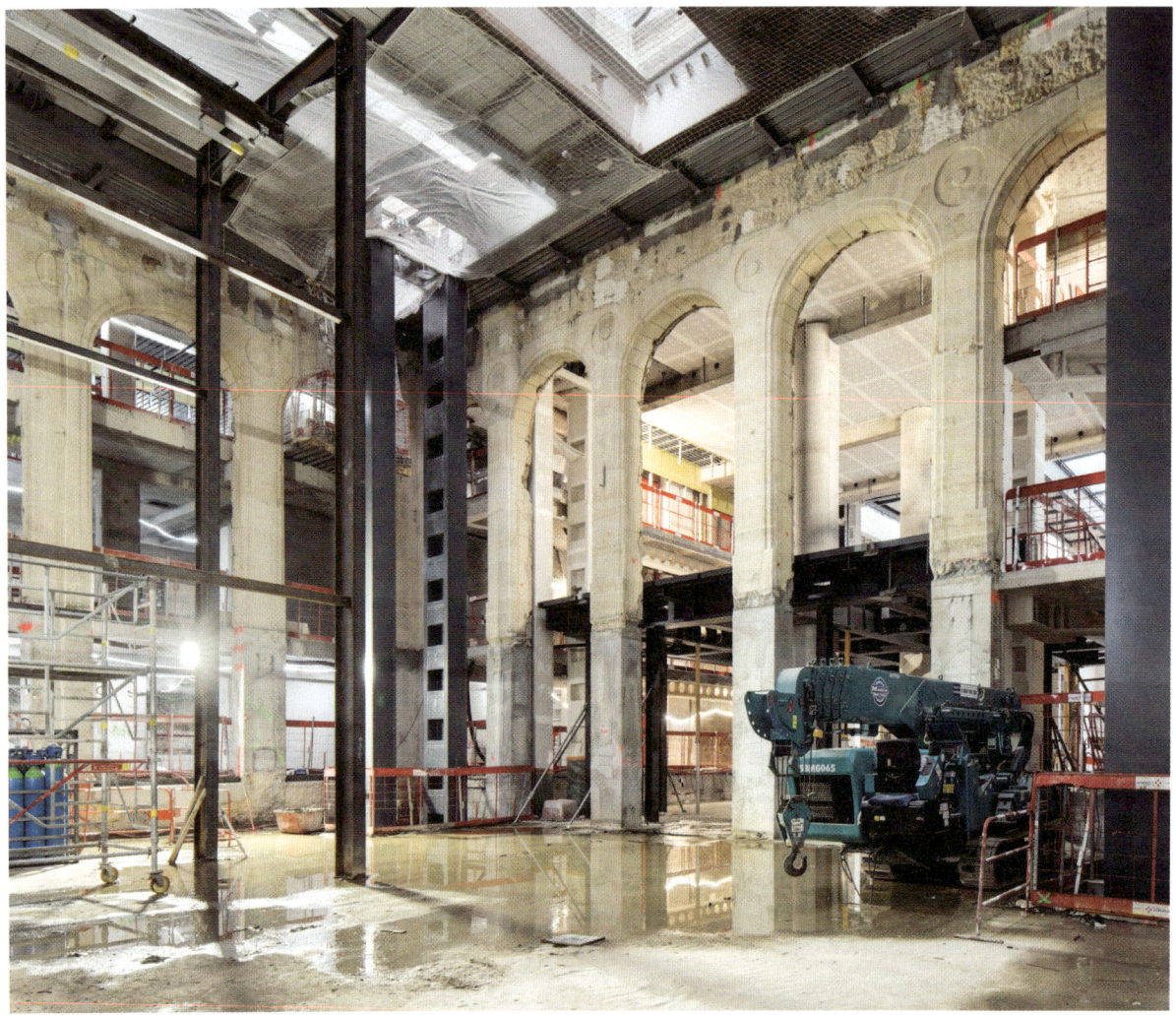

Jean Nouvel's most recent project in Paris—the new home of the Fondation Cartier, located in the heart of the city between the Louvre and the Palais-Royal—pushes the investigation of dynamic architecture further, building upon the long history of integrating technology within architecture. Nouvel envisions it as a dynamic machine. Rather than constructing a new building, the commission requires transforming an 1855 structure that initially housed the Grand Hôtel du Louvre, which opened for that year's Exposition Universelle, the first of its kind in the French capital. Within the Haussmannian shell, Nouvel's design hollows out the lower floors and basement to create a gigantic void in which he has inserted five enormous platforms, each measuring around 2,150 square feet and all mobile, capable of ascending and descending to any desired height. The result is an arts space without a fixed section or plan, where new spaces and volumes are continuously created—an architecture of a perpetual possibility and opportunity. Turning their backs to the Place du Palais-Royal, visitors pass through glass doors that reflect the historic city behind them, confronting a new experience each time they enter. They might find themselves facing a void, an immense volume framed by the arcades of the street outside, or a three-dimensional maze of platforms, with different routes opening through

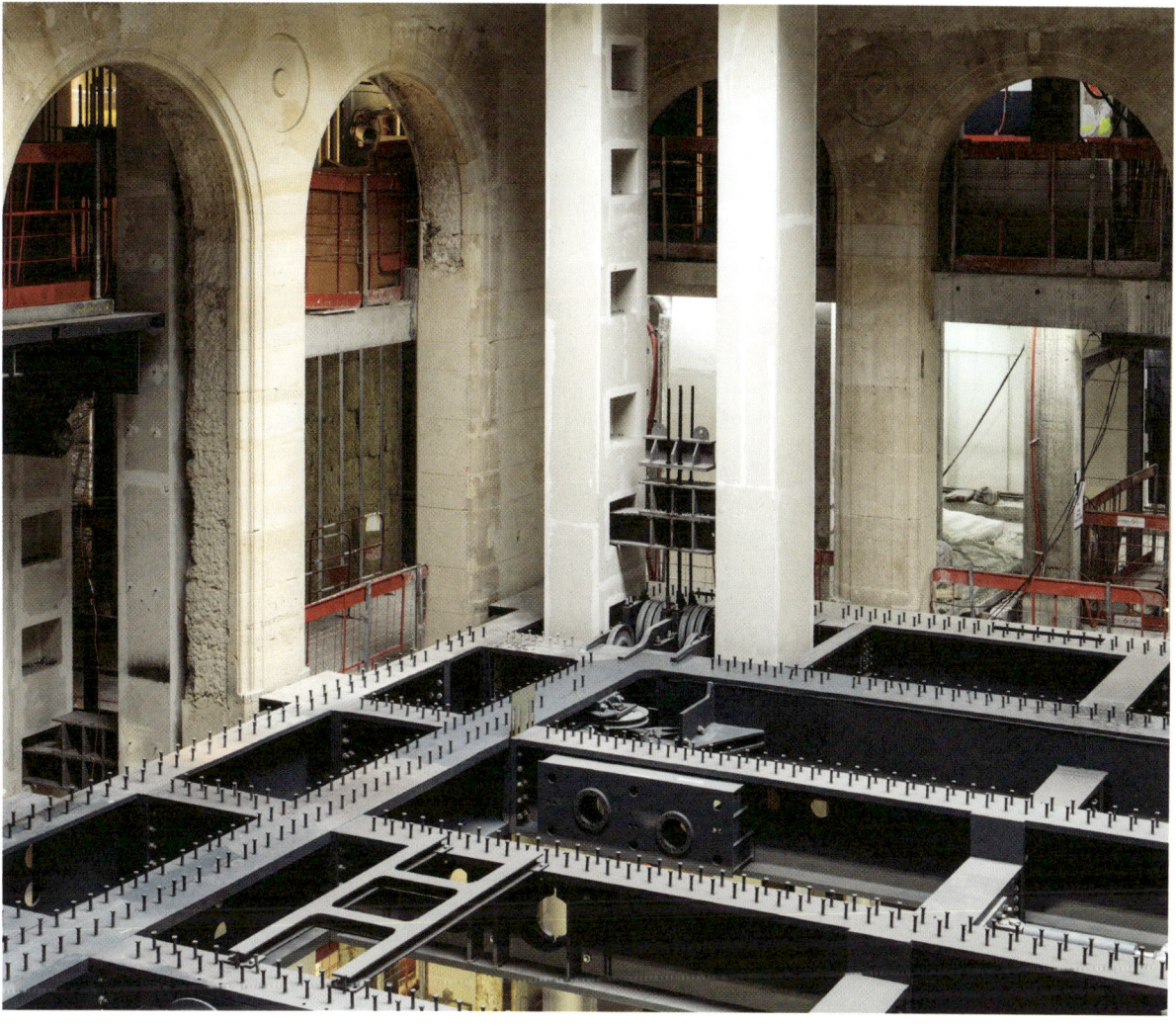

the building depending on the platforms' configurations. Here, there is no predetermined narrative; the architecture allows the cultural institution to shape what might happen in this space of anticipation. Indeed, for Nouvel, the intervention at the Grand Hôtel du Louvre adds another layer to the narrative of historic Paris, which he believes is not a museum preserved in formaldehyde but "a healthy city whose heritage must always be in tension with modernity. Paris must constantly reach asymptotically toward its apogee."[2]

Previous pages, opposite, and above: Kinetic floors and ceilings punctuated by cables and pulleys evoke the specter of the industrial age that saw the birth of the original architecture of the Hôtel du Louvre. The possibility of perpetual mutation evoked by the dormant mobility of the exhibition armature with which Jean Nouvel has equipped the Fondation Cartier captures the ambition of a nascent modern Paris at the time of the first Universal Exposition the city hosted in 1855.

---

2. Jean Nouvel, interview with the author, June 6, 2024.

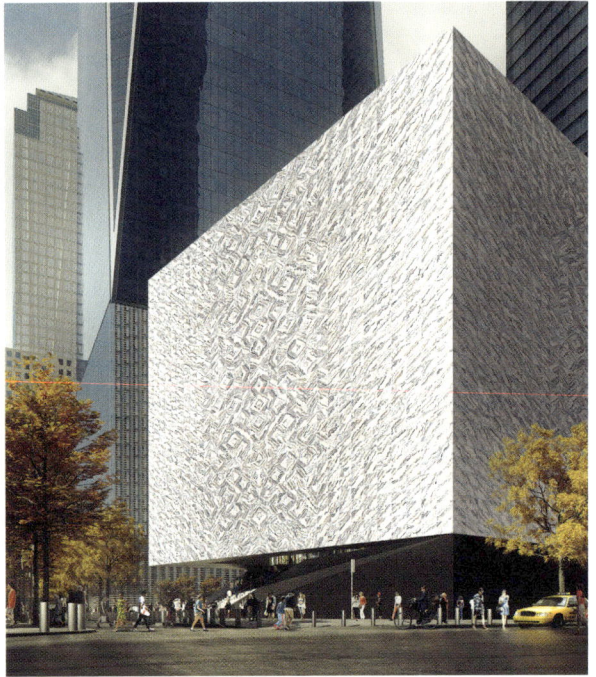 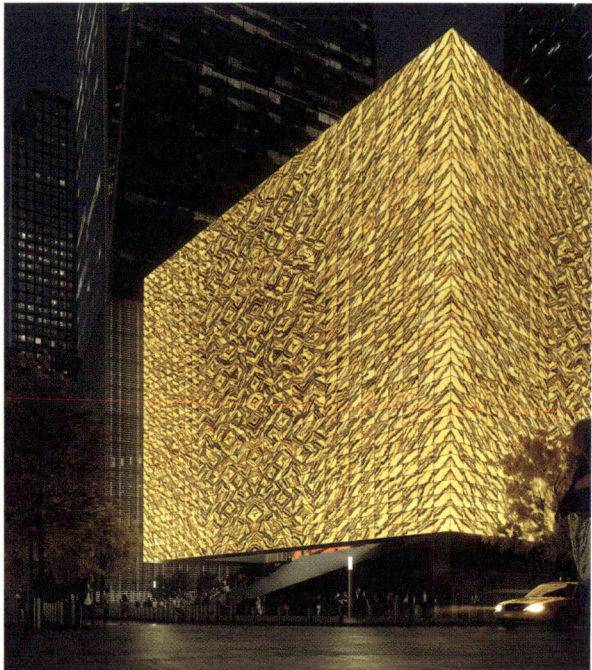

The idea that cultural infrastructure should feature dynamic architecture is not new; it harks back to the phenomenon of world fairs. In recent years, various cities have seen the introduction of kinetic elements to exhibition venues or performance centers. In New York, two recent cultural infrastructure projects from the past decade have sought to harness the potential of modular architecture—both Diller Scofidio + Renfro's The Shed in New York's Hudson Yards (2019) and REX's Perelman Art Center (PAC) at the World Trade Center (2023) allow varying configurations to accommodate different types of programming and audience sizes. The Shed, part performance venue and part exhibition hall, features a telescoping shell mounted on rails that can slide out onto the plaza in front to serve as an events pavilion.[3] Diller Scofidio + Renfro describes this building as "adaptive," meaning that it can "reconfigure and absorb technological or programmatic changes wrought by economic or social developments."[4] Meanwhile, the PAC's performance spaces can be arranged in sixty-two different configurations thanks to retractable walls that allow its three auditoria to interconnect. However, both projects fall short of realizing the visionary potential of adaptive architecture as articulated in Price's proposals, where information would be the driving force of movement. Instead, they echo a pre-computer-age model, reminiscent of Jean Prouvé's 1935 Maison du Peuple in Clichy, just outside Paris,[5] a community center whose retractable floor and roof allowed it to function as a market hall, a theater, and a cinema. The latter was reacting to the potential of mechanization in the automobile industry and integrated retractable floors that could function as additional surface for multiple programming to occur at once. The Shed and the PAC's novelty has more to do with the challenge that they pose with respect to programming—what kind of venues are these, and how might their architecture influence

---

3. For a detailed analysis of motion in Diller Scofidio + Renfro's work, see Maddalena Scimeni, "Motion: The Most Modern Experience," in Pippo Ciorra and Maddalena Scimemi, eds. *Restless Architecture: Diller Scofidio + Renfro* (Rome: MAXXI, 2024).
4. Ibid.
5. Prouvé sat on the jury of the competition for the Centre Pompidou, making Rogers and Piano likely aware of this project on the outskirts of Paris.

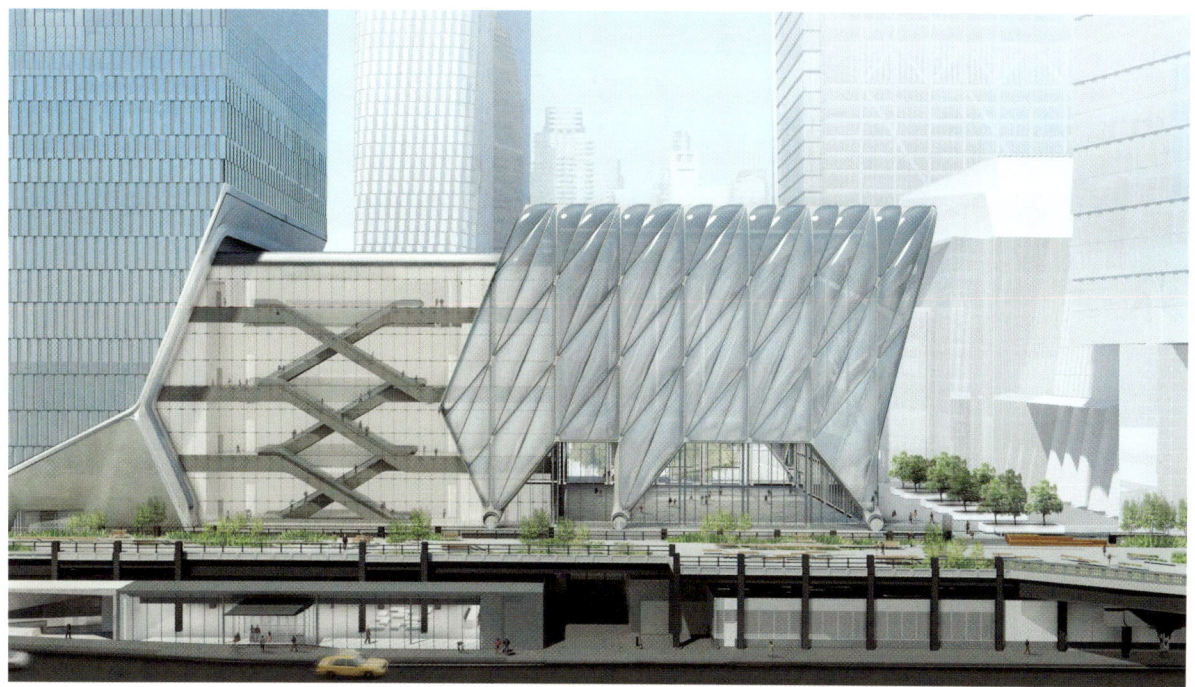

the way they are filled? Moreover, what kind of addition they propose to the cultural offering of a city filled with both museums and theaters? Both buildings offer the potential to create hybrid events in which the exhibition, the theater performance, the concert, and the immersive experience all merge into one, which in turn could foster a whole new kind of institution.[6]

Opposite: The Perelman Performing Arts Center is a beacon of light with its marble facade, at the foot of the Freedom Tower. Inside, the center boasts modular configurations for various sizes and formats of performing arts.

Above: The Shed, another innovative cultural venue in New York, is located at one end of the High Line. Its recognizable telescoping silver shell can be expanded or retracted to adapt to the desired programming.

Following pages: Unbeknownst to passersby, Lafayette Anticipations, in Paris's Le Marais neighborhood, features modular gallery spaces that can be configured differently depending on the positioning of platforms.

Pages 98–99: The architectural transformation that was designed by Jean Nouvel is not visible from the outside: the building, which first housed the Hôtel du Louvre (1855–1880), is historically an urban fragment that emerged on the city's map, with the extension of the Rue de Rivoli, during the first phase of Haussmann's work.

---

6. While the PAC's configuration can change to offer more than one performance to different audiences at the same time, it is nevertheless very costly to put on two small-scale productions simultaneously, an economic reality that compromises the potential to generate a new type of cultural program.

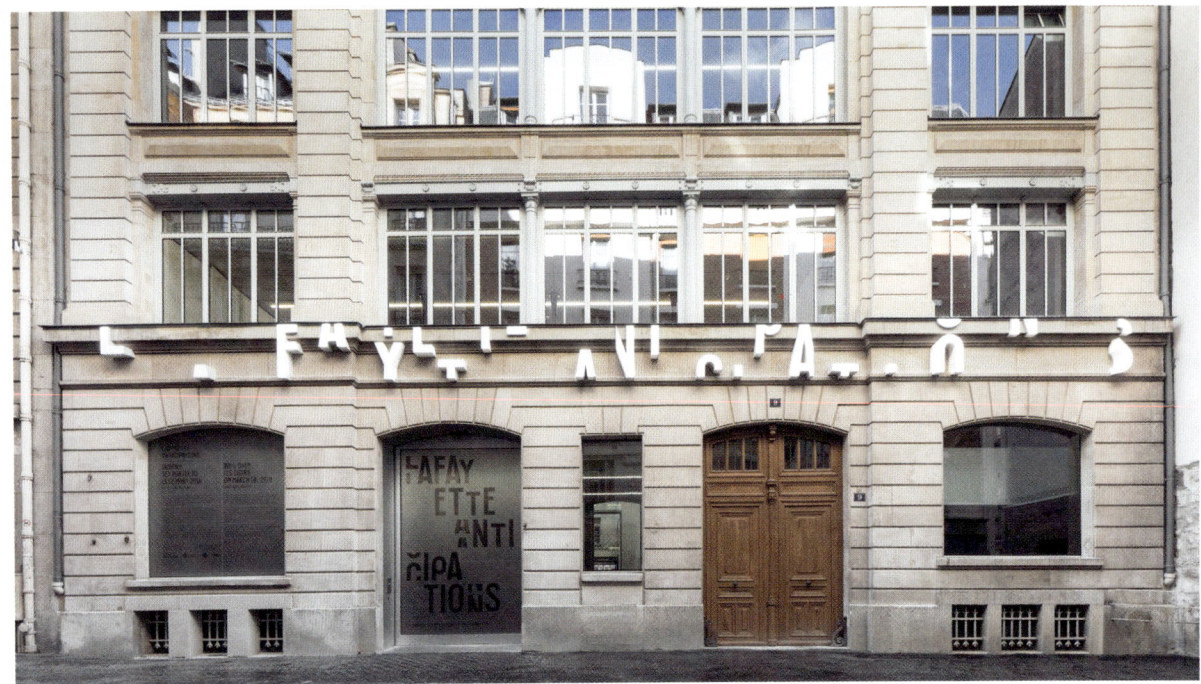

Closer to 2 Place du Palais-Royal—the Fondation Cartier's new home address—another Parisian example of dynamic architecture for exhibitions is Lafayette Anticipations designed by OMA/Rem Koolhaas. At the heart of a restored nineteenth-century building, OMA placed a giant platform that rises and falls. While both the most recent Nouvel and Koolhaas designs for the Lafayette group share the same basic architectural element—a kinetic floor—their references and programmatic outcomes are completely different. Koolhaas's architectural thinking, already evident in the early project House in Bordeaux, shares a similar plan with the Lafayette Anticipations space. Both have at their core a machine. In both cases, the dynamism creates a vertical storyboard where happenings or events can occur simultaneously as stacked scripts unfold independently. We can see in both the House in Bordeaux and the Lafayette spaces Koolhaas's thinking in terms of script-writing, where framing and sequence is used to theorize the design and use of space. Indeed, the movie script, structured around the idea of sequences in time, appears to be the literary medium best suited for this task, short of actually filming the building, which is what the owners' daughter of the House in Bordeaux ultimately did in 2008. Beka & Lemoine's *Koolhaas Houselife* went on to become one of the most popular films about architecture in recent decades.[7]

At Lafayette Anticipations, OMA's introduction of a kinetic floor allows for exhibition spaces with varying volumes. In this project, Koolhaas extends his exploration of architectural modernity in terms of the skyscraper—a vertical form of density—which he first demonstrated in *Delirious New York*.

In contrast, Nouvel lays this kinetic modernity flat and focuses on extending the horizontal Haussmannian city by creating a dynamic sequence of five kinetic floors, one succeeding after another. Indeed, there is no other possibility for the contextualist

---

7. This, in turn, has engendered criticism of their work in the form of narration, such as Beatriz Colomina and Blanca Lleó's 1999 appreciation of the Maison Lemoine in Bordeaux, completed by Koolhaas's firm OMA a year prior. Titled "A Machine Was Its Heart"—a reference to the giant platform that rises and falls at the center of the house's plan—their text attempts to restitute the meaning and experience of a major work of dynamic architecture through a narrative that segues into a dialogue. See Beatriz Colomina and Blanca Lleó, "'A Machine Was its Heart': A House in Floirac," *Domus* no. 811 (January 1999).

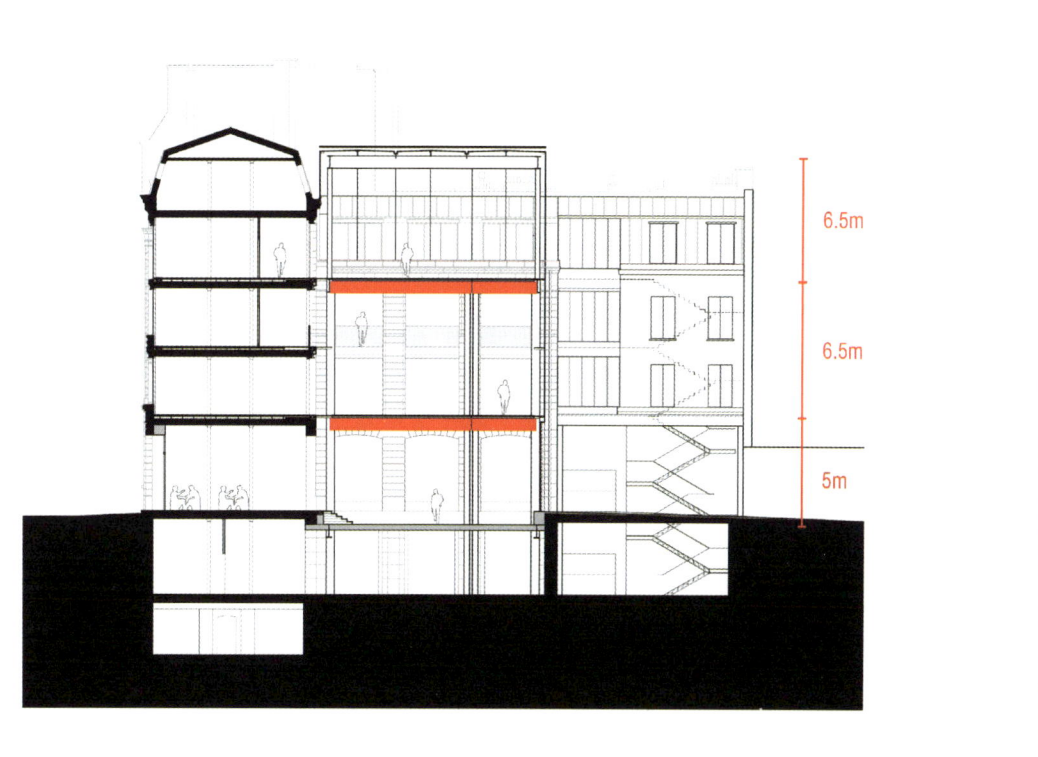

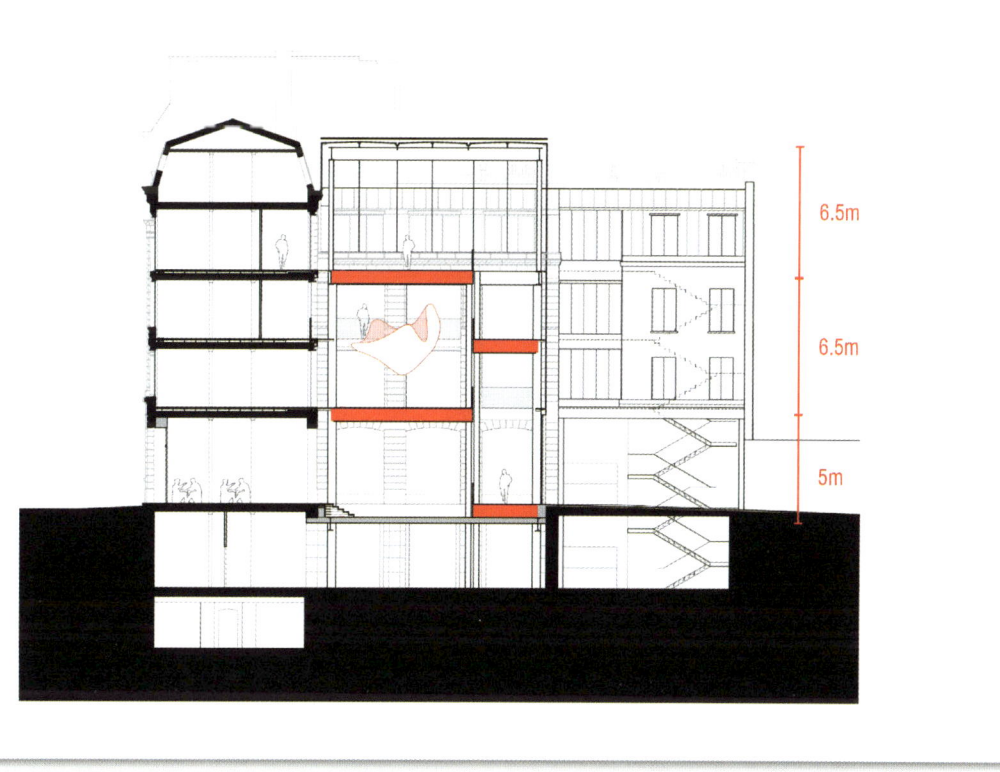

THE MUSEUM IS MACHINE

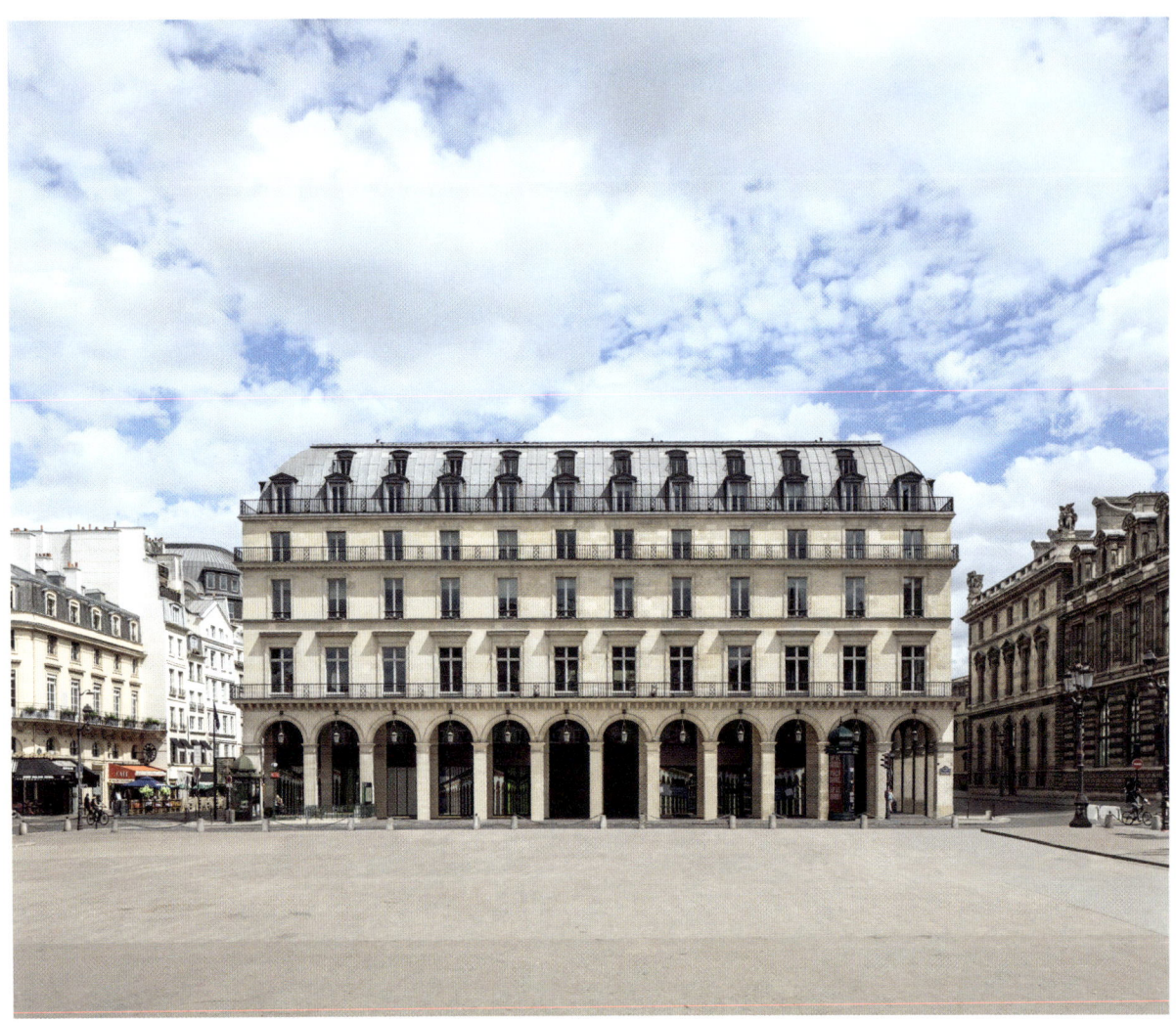

approach that Nouvel advocates than to seek modernization by extending history. As a result, the possible combinations of horizontality and verticality make for a nearly infinite number of potential spaces for programming exhibitions. Nouvel's architectural response to the technological innovations of our time is both aesthetic and philosophical. Indeed, it reimagines the museum in alignment with the evolving concept of "machine" in terms of technological progress. After the second machine age, this new notion is one that has made away with industrial might, and with information, and now bears infinite capacity of generating new combinations through the association of existing data.

Until the Fondation Cartier's Palais-Royal spaces, no cultural infrastructure with dynamic architecture had introduced such a radical departure from historical museographic conditions. In this project, Nouvel establishes a dialogue with the history of art, technology, and architecture like no other museum has done before. The specter of the Galerie des Machines and mechanical innovation looms large in these spaces, originally erected during the urban transformation of Paris in the mid-nineteenth century. However, unlike Price's desire to confront architecture with technology, Nouvel creates a spatial experience that engages in dialogue with the history of technology and puts it to use to invent a new museographic device.

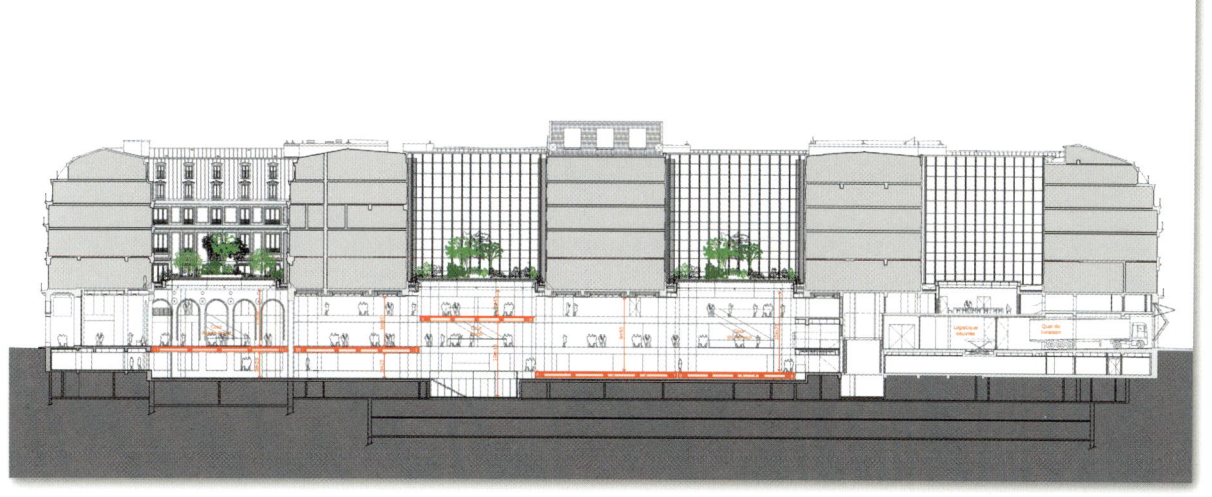
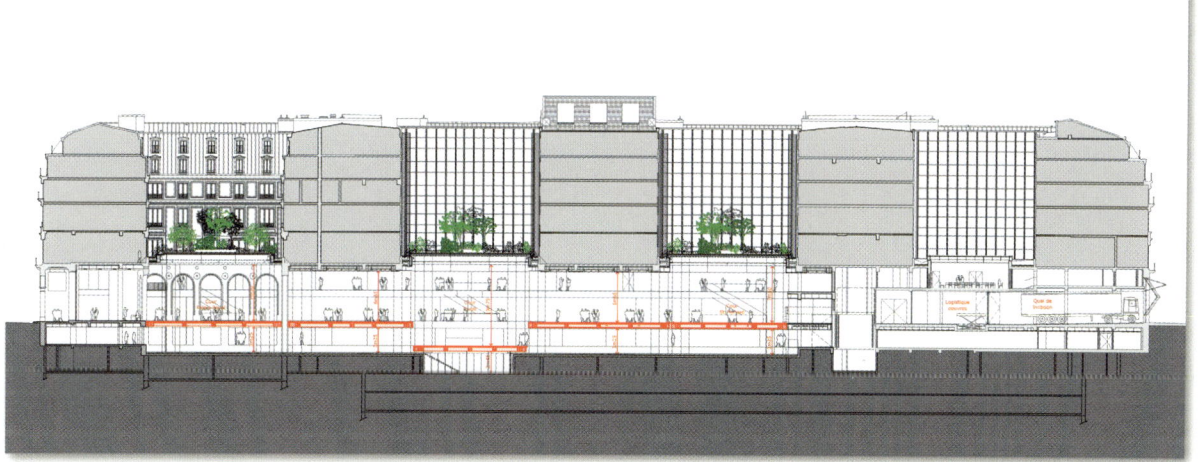
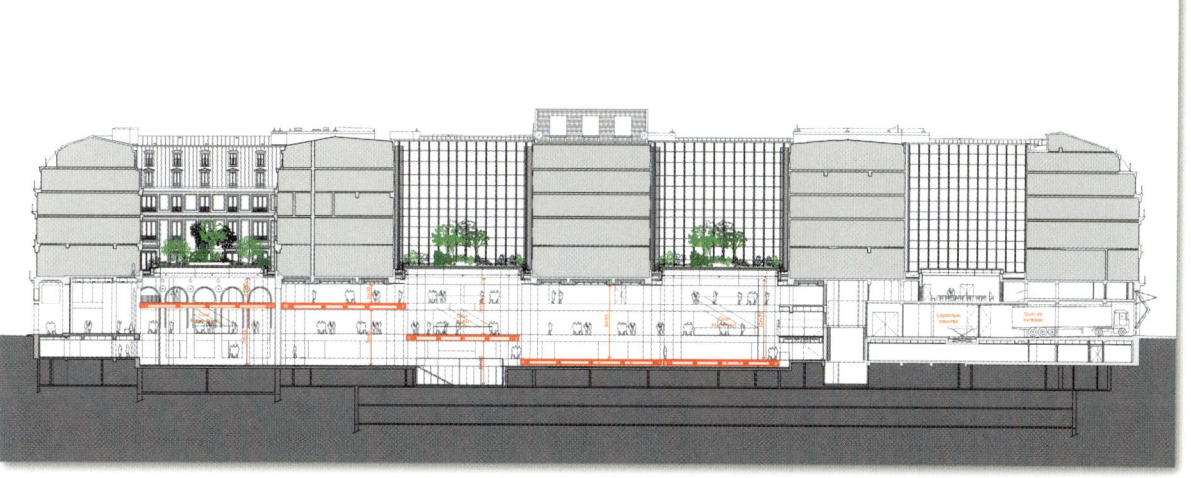

THE MUSEUM IS MACHINE

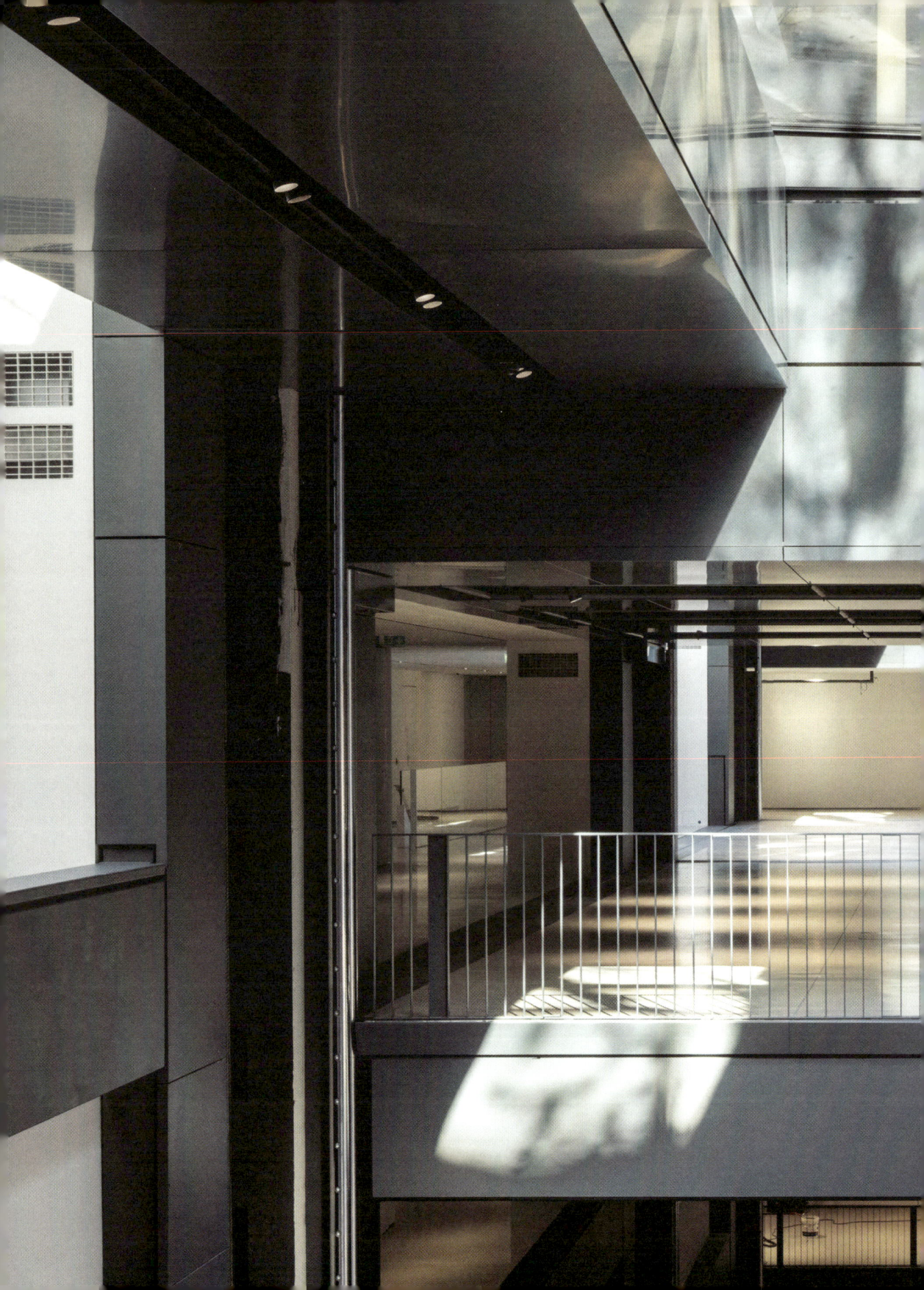

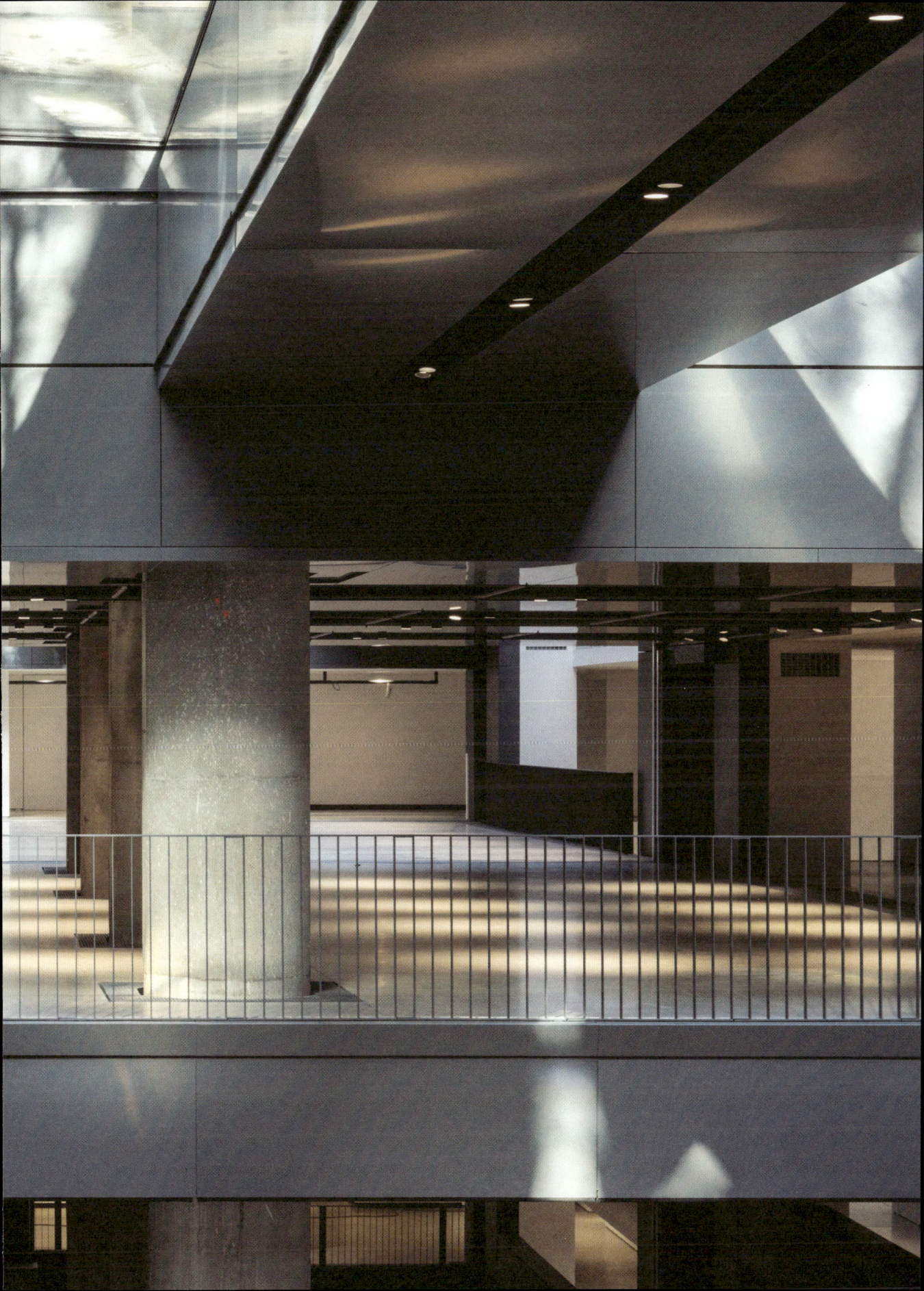

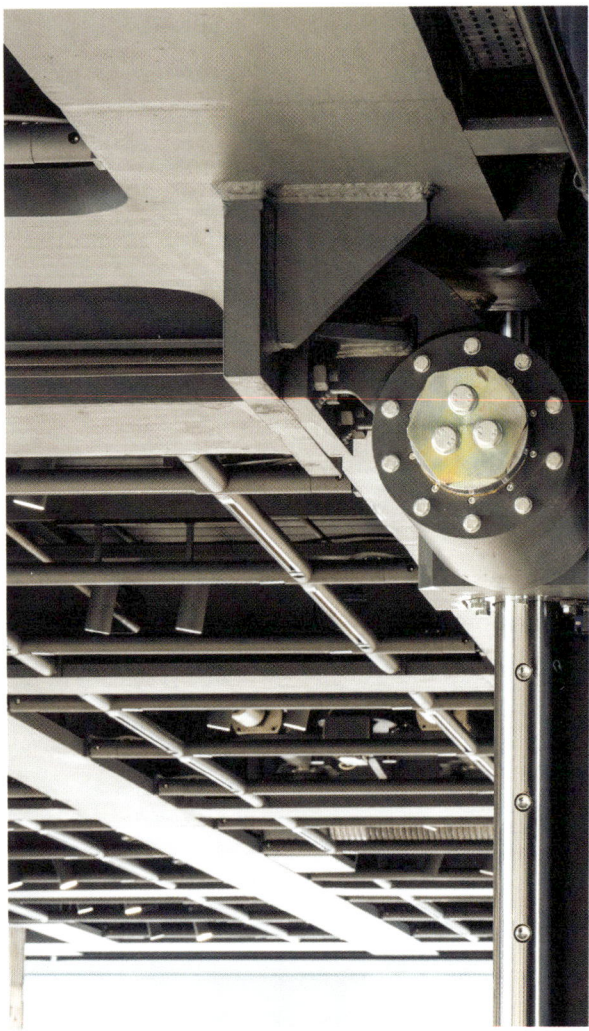

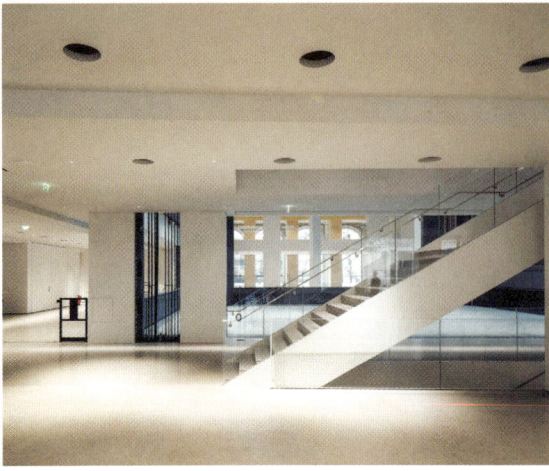

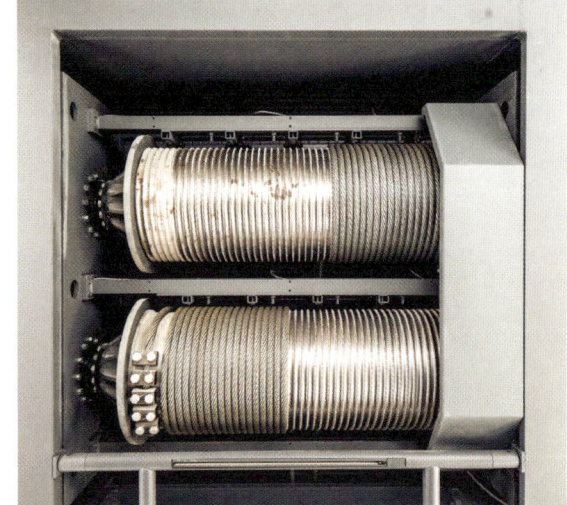

This device has yet to be fully understood and lacks a name to describe its aesthetic machinery. Nonetheless, it is clear that this new museographic device negates any previous form of display while suggesting possible formulations; it dismantles the white cube aesthetic that had previously sought to distance itself from the classical museography of successive galleries derived from palatial architectures. At the same time, Nouvel embeds a future within the museum-machine with its inherent perpetual mutability: beyond the platforms, retractable and expansive volumes, and the presence and absence of daylight, the visibility or invisibility of the surrounding urban environments integrates into the exhibition experience.

The dynamism made possible by the museum-machine introduces ambiguity regarding the medium of the exhibition, which prolongs contemporary art's engagement with this question in recent history. Long corridors that wrap around the central nave of the Fondation Cartier spaces offer visitors the possibility of a 360-degree perspective on the exhibition—which is to say that at any point, the viewer can attain a consciousness of the exhibition by stepping away from it (from its theater). The act of exhibition or display, the function of the museum, is thus put on view. The exhibition is the theatrical potential of viewing at the same time as the display device.

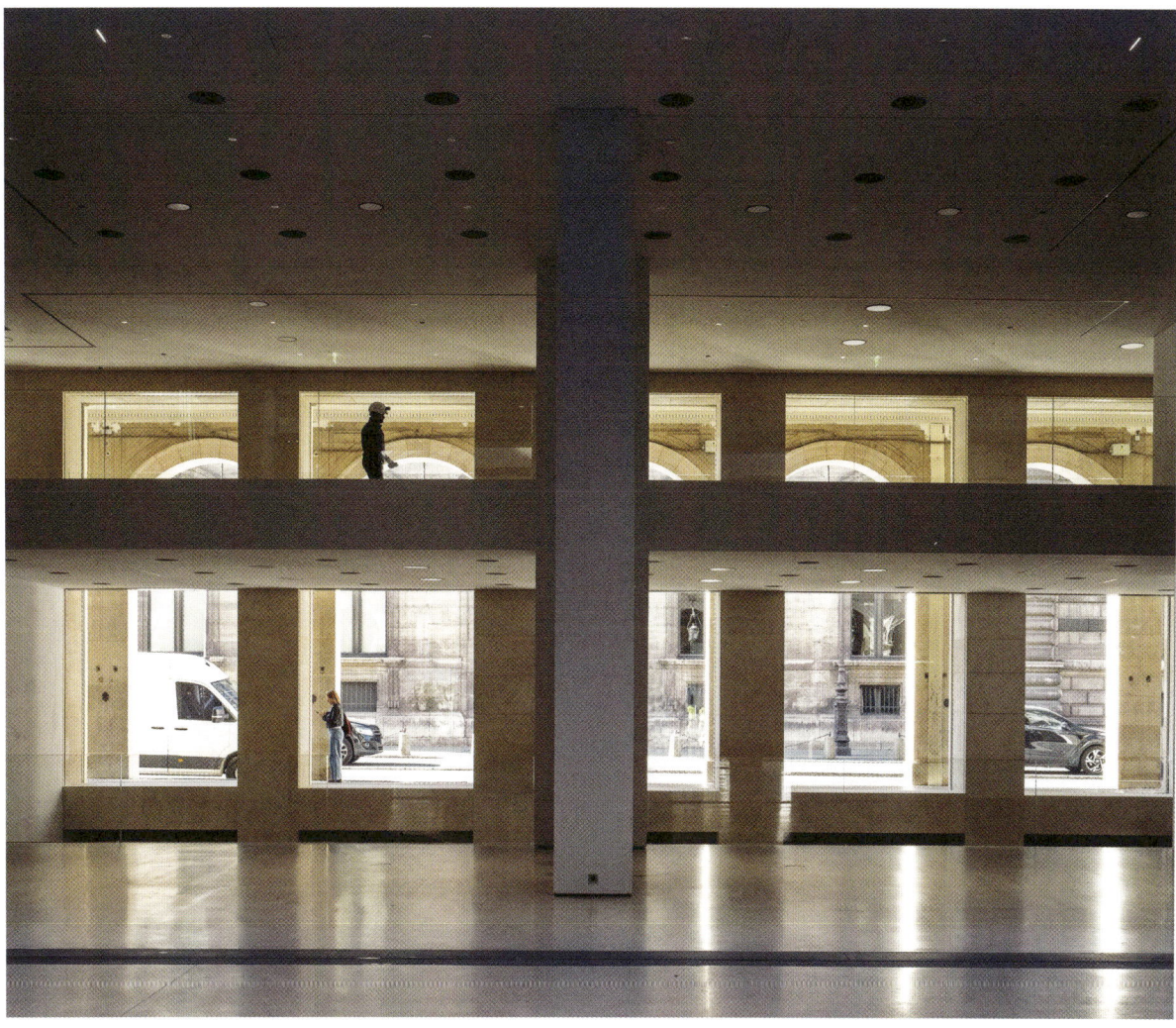

Nouvel was likely inspired in part by French artist Daniel Buren's concept of exhibiting the exhibition itself, which the painter developed in relation to large-scale events like *Documenta*, theorizing that the exhibition was the primary subject on display.[8] This notion was later embraced by artists such as Pierre Huyghe and Philippe Parreno in their early collaborative years, whose practices gave rise to a new role for artists as exhibition makers, and to the experience of the exhibition as a choreographed space. Their work contributed to enhancing the blurred boundaries between

---

8. Jean-François Lyotard, *Que peindre? Adami Arakawa Buren* (Paris: Éditions de la Différence, 1987), 108.

Previous pages: In its new headquarters, architecture is a dynamic exhibition-making tool, inserted into a nineteenth-century Haussmann building: five platforms create the possibility of a boundless combination of volumes, voids, and spaces.

Opposite: The mechanics of the platforms contrast with the limestone of the original Haussmann facade.

Above: At the Fondation Cartier, 2 Place du Palais-Royal, Jean Nouvel has made the city and the museum one and the same, sublimating any possible distinction between modernization and preservation. One enters to discover that the city is a collection of possibilities, and that its future hypothetical iterations might manifest on these speculative platforms.

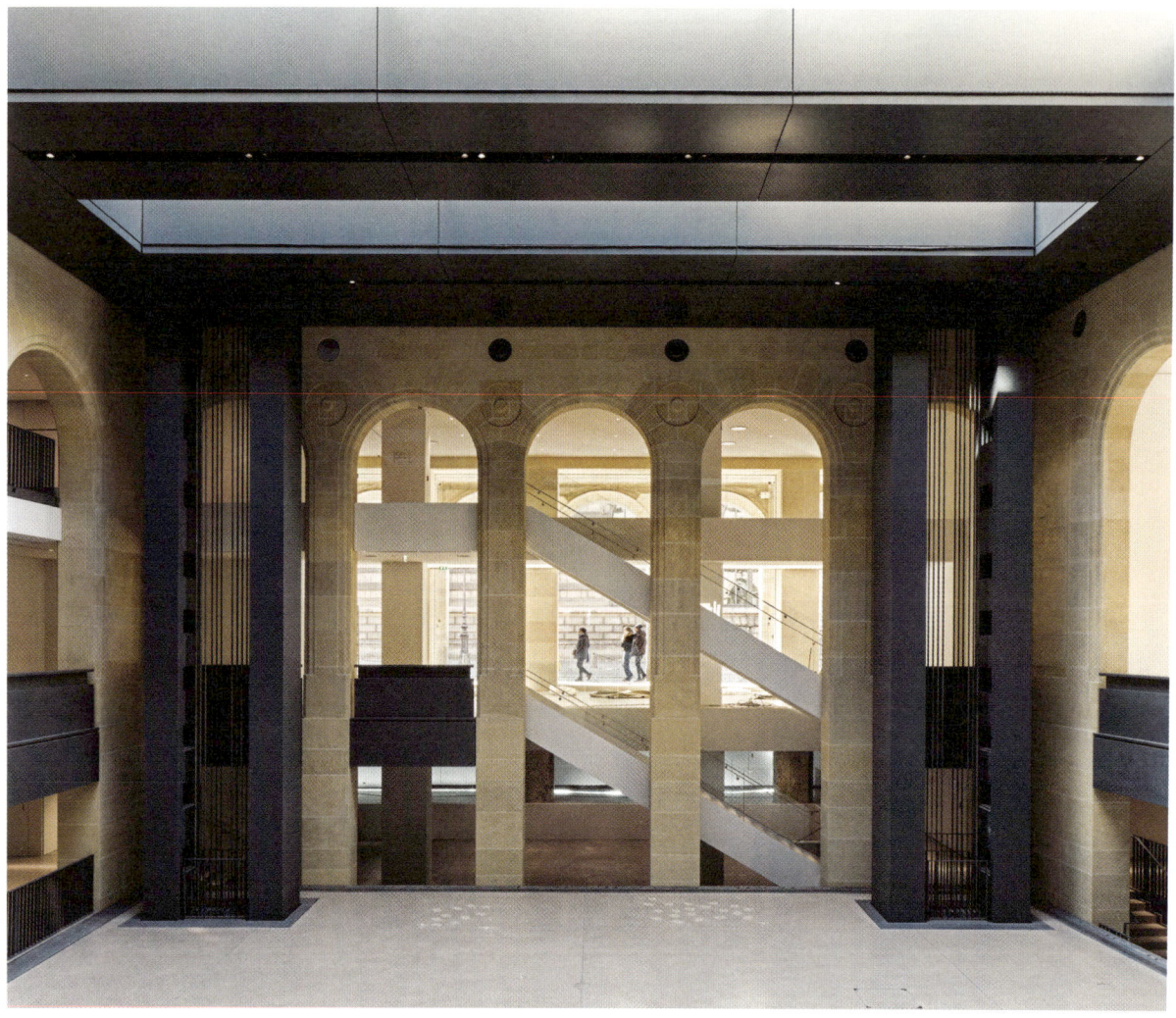

art and exhibition by involving the time-based work and viewer participation. Their contribution to contemporary art was a reflection of the philosophical status of the exhibition—an albeit fragile "environment"—for the enactment of ideas.

At the Fondation Cartier, the ability to enter and exit the exhibition space, and to view the exhibition from a distance or even a bird's-eye view, disrupts the linearity of museographic time that still remain untouched in the white cube, where one can only move forward or reverse course. In other dynamic architectures, this condition also remained unchallenged: at The Shed, the PAC, and Lafayette Anticipations, there is no opportunity to observe the path accomplished in the exhibition. Nouvel's architecture at the Fondation Cartier dismantles this sequential or narrative experience of the museum and makes it its infrastructural reality. Indeed, by making dynamism the central design principle of the space, Nouvel renders the linearity of time, so central to classical museum architecture and the cinematographic understanding of space, impossible. As a result, the museum has no choice but to reinvent itself for every exhibition, and thus be shaken to its ontological core with each architectural formulation.

If we expand the hypothesis formulated in Jean Nouvel's design into theoretical affirmations for the museum, it implies that dynamic

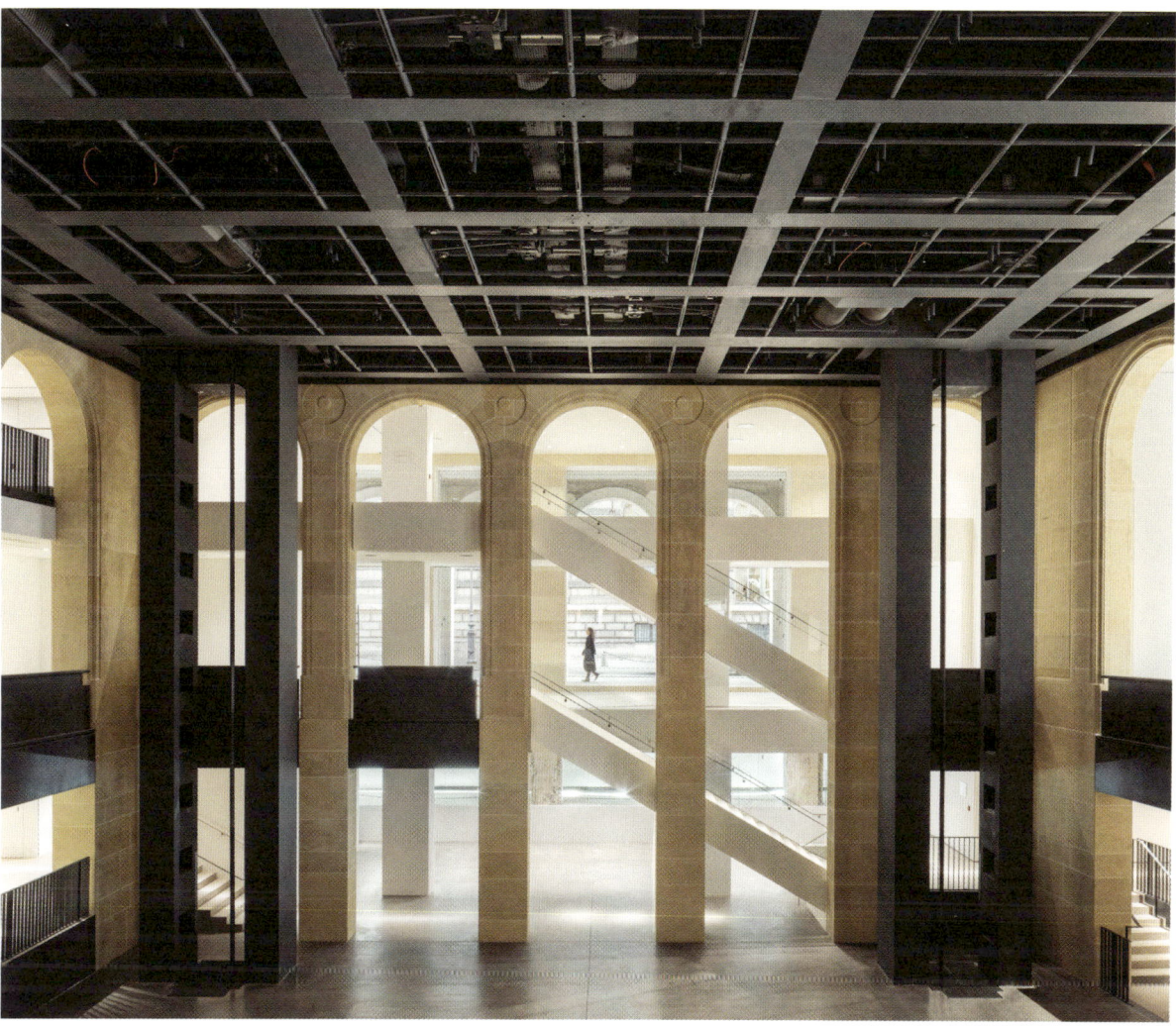

architecture for cultural infrastructure transforms the future of the museum into a machine for reinvention. Whereas Price's understanding of the relationship between architecture and technology was one where information would transform a building, Nouvel creates a device that allows us to see the dramaturgy of exhibitions, capturing the images and ideas of our time. In this sense, the new spaces of the Fondation Cartier pour l'art contemporain by Jean Nouvel serve as the ultimate allegory of the contemporary machine.

Opposite and above: The first courtyard of the Fondation Cartier's new exhibition spaces at 2 Place du Palais-Royal is an image of contradictions: the mechanic modernity that Jean Nouvel's architectural project adds to the historical context provocatively clashes with the iconic arcades that line the Rue de Rivoli, synonymous with Haussmann's city.

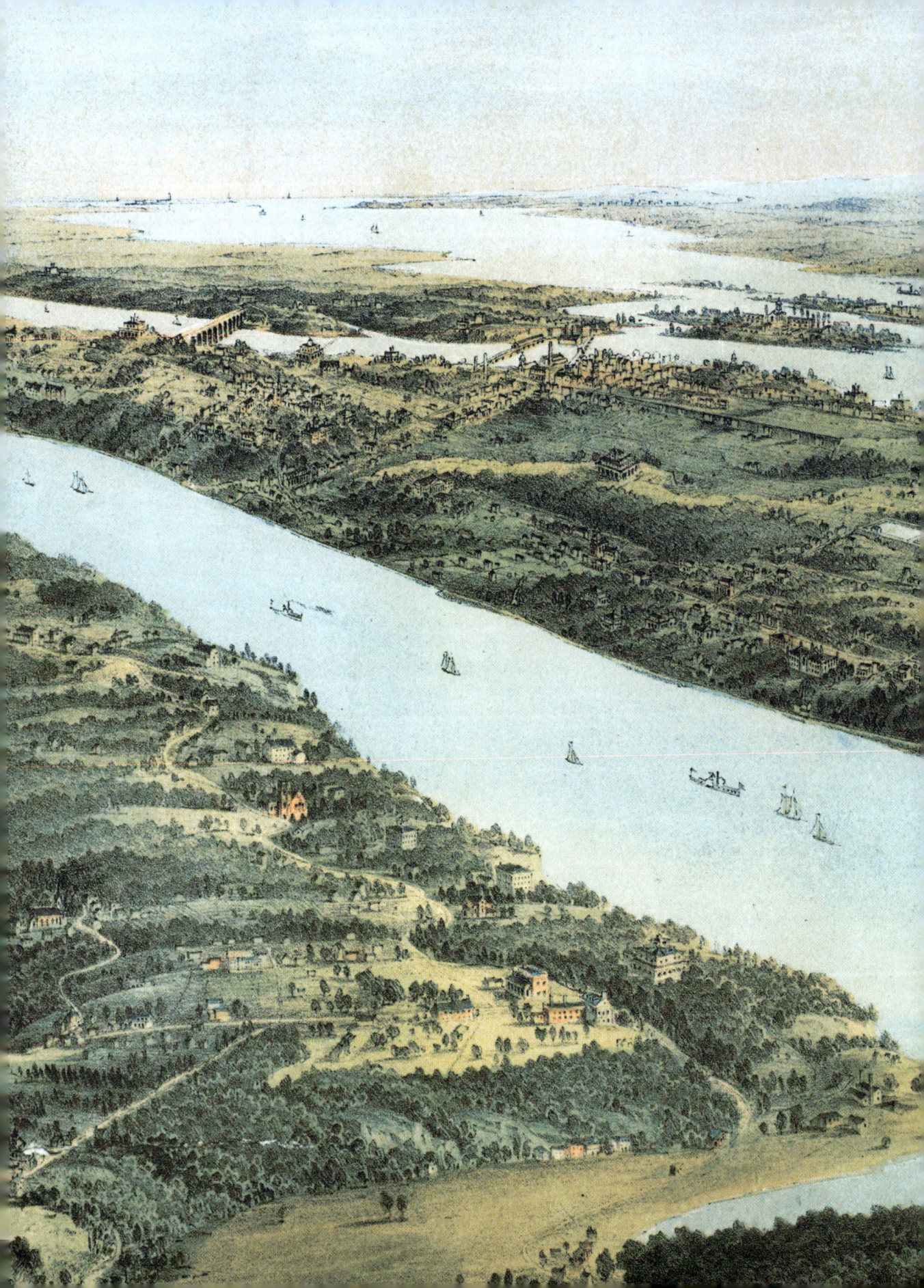

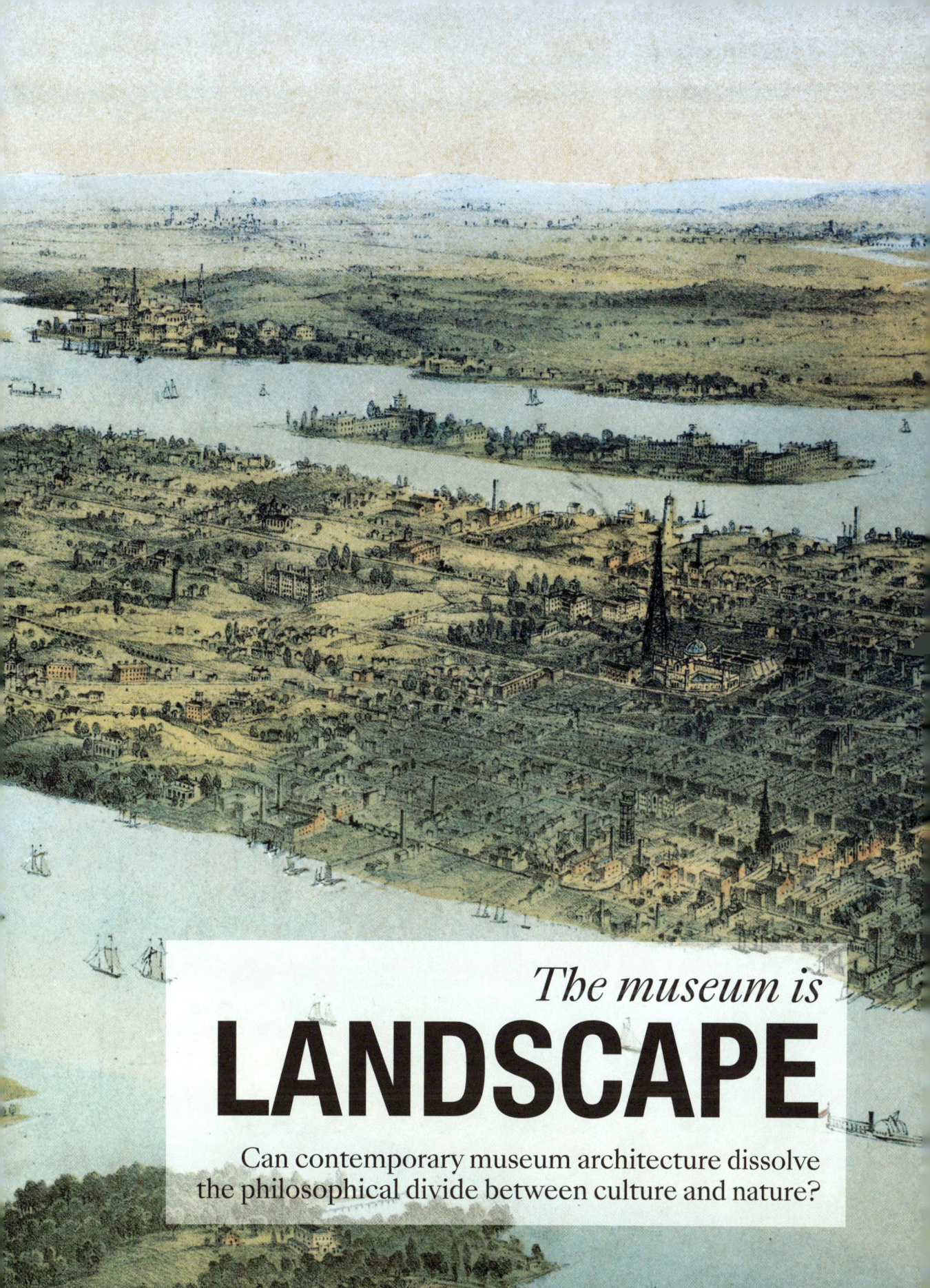

The museum is
LANDSCAPE

Can contemporary museum architecture dissolve the philosophical divide between culture and nature?

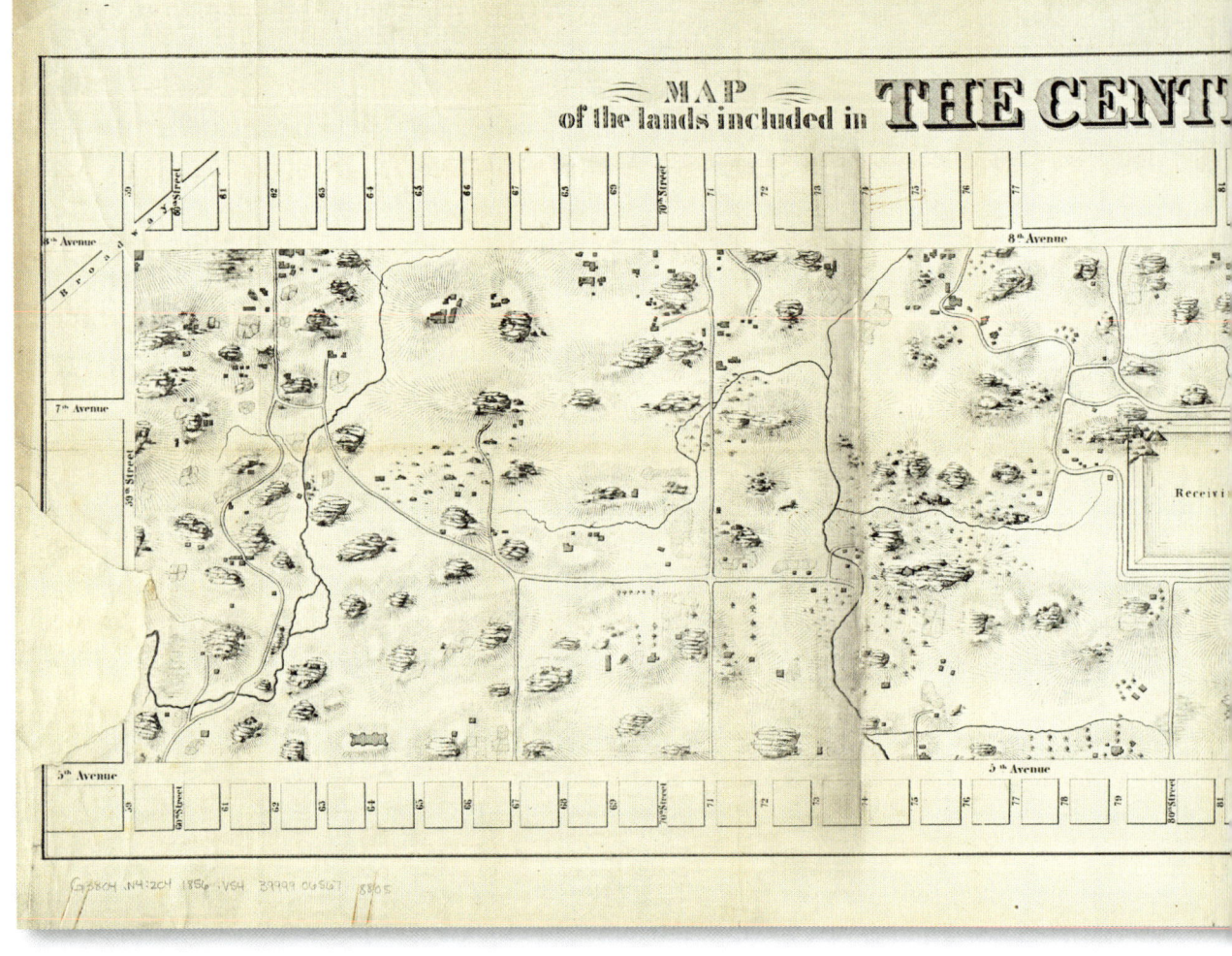

Central Park is Manhattan's first skyscraper. When viewed on a two-dimensional map, sketched from a bird's-eye view, it resembles the Empire State Building lying flat on one side. Carefully designed inclines and pathways create vistas and impressions of nature, shaping the relief of this skyscraper's facade. The traverses—think of them as tunnels within the park's architecture—are thick brick walls designed to hold and be filled with tons of dirt to support the weight of planted trees. From an urban standpoint, these traverses seamlessly connect the east and west, as well as the express elevator banks that eventually link to the island's edge and the waterfront. The walls around the edges act as the steel beams of the skyscraper, holding everything in place.

In their 1858 "Greensward" plan for Manhattan's Central Park, Frederick Law Olmsted and Calvert Vaux, the fathers of American landscape architecture, sought to exclude buildings as much as possible. Begrudging anything that disrupted the illusion of nature created by their design, they wrote, "The landscape is everything, the architecture nothing until you get to the terrace"[1] (a terrace that is invisible from most

---

1. Quoted by Morrison H. Heckscher in "Creating Central Park," *The Metropolitan Museum of Art Bulletin*, New Series, vol. 65, no. 3 (Winter 2008), 57.

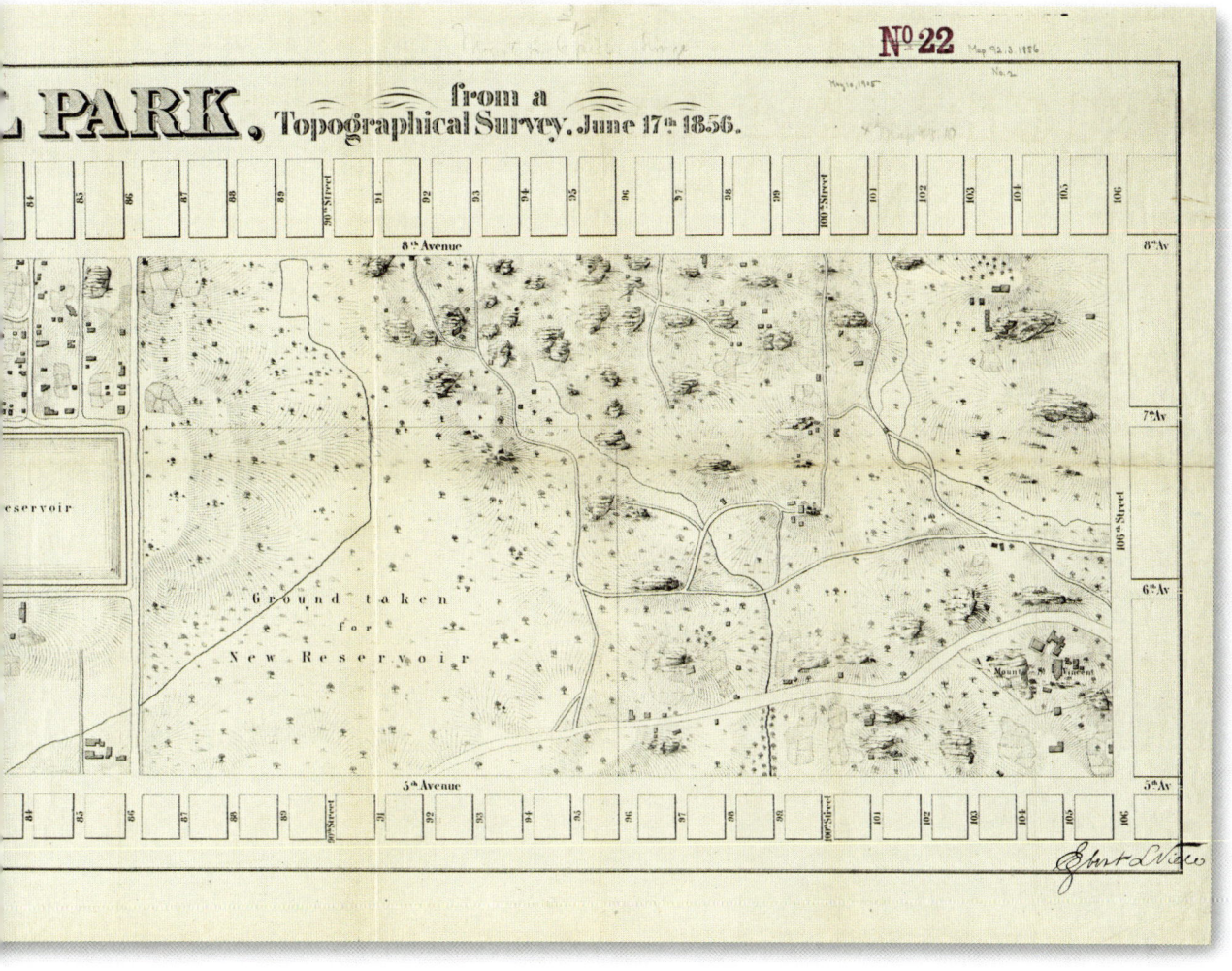

vantage points). Apart from the Metropolitan Museum of Art—a late arrival to the park, constructed years after its completion—New York's main temples of culture are located outside its limits, some of them looking onto its greenery from the road. In this way, the strict dichotomy between culture and nature is preserved—an antiquated philosophical divide that contemporary museum architecture has the potential to dissolve. Built over the course of the past three decades, the five following examples embody, both physically and metaphorically, current reflections on the cultural aesthetic, pedagogical, and architectural dimensions of landscape in the Anthropocene.

Previous pages: A panorama of Manhattan island before Central Park.

Above: An early topographical survey of Central Park shows the land before its redesign by architects Frederick Law Olmsted and Calvert Vaux.

Following page, left: A view of Manhattan from the south encapsulates the continuity between Central Park and the Museum of Natural History. An elevation plan drawn by Studio Gang reveals the contrasting facades that stand nearly a century apart. On the left, a view of the Manhanttanhenge phenomenon that inspired Jeanne Gang for the new Richard Gilder Center for Science, Education, and Innovation.

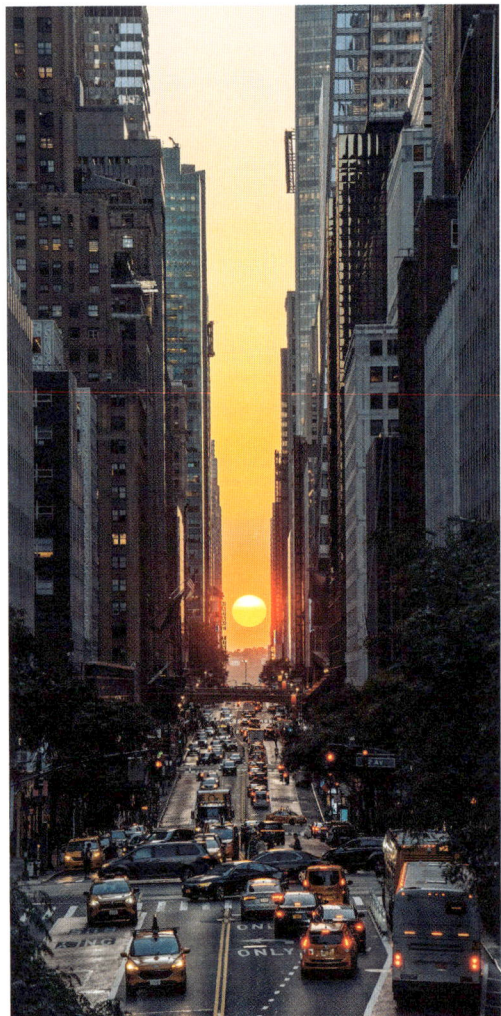
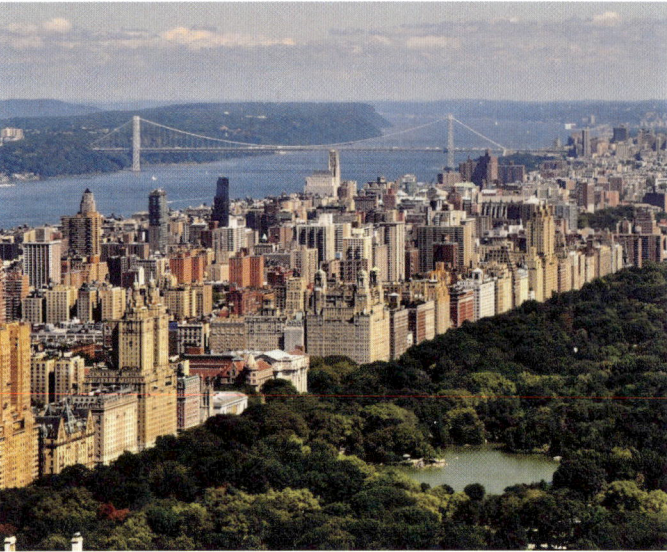
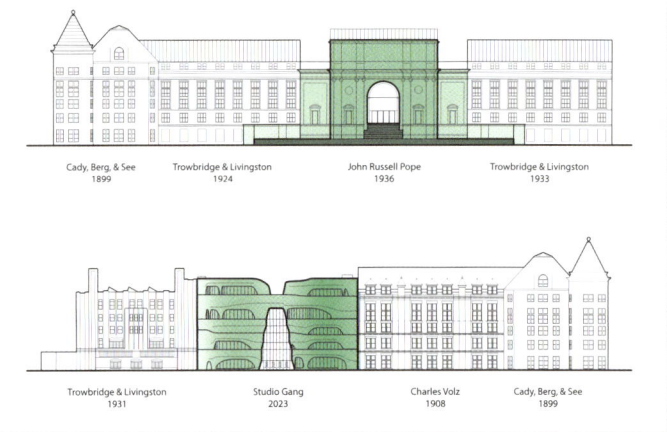

Located on Central Park West, the American Museum of Natural History (AMNH) opened its first building on this site in 1877. The monumental eastern entrance facing the park—part of an extension built between 1925 and 1936—takes the archetype of the Roman triumphal arch and enlarges to gigantic proportions, featuring 50-foot-high Ionic columns that dwarf visitors upon arrival. In the vestibule, human domination over nature is affirmed through William Andrew Mackay's three murals from 1935, depicting events from the life of Theodore Roosevelt. While two celebrate his achievements as America's 26th president—the construction of the Panama Canal, one of his imperial successes, and the signing of the 1905 Treaty of Portsmouth, which ended the conflict between Russia and Japan—the third glorifies the 1909–1910 Smithsonian–Roosevelt African expedition: broad-shouldered and dressed as an explorer, he stands assertively over a Nubian lion and lioness, flanked by his gun bearers.

The AMNH's new western entrance, on Columbus Avenue, is a powerful counter-statement to the original entrance and represents a major architectural evolution for the institution. Completed in 2023, the Richard Gilder Center for Science, Education, and Innovation is the most potent example to date of architect Jeanne Gang's philosophy of "architectural grafting," in which additions to existing buildings, parks, and urban contexts transfigure the originals so as to create

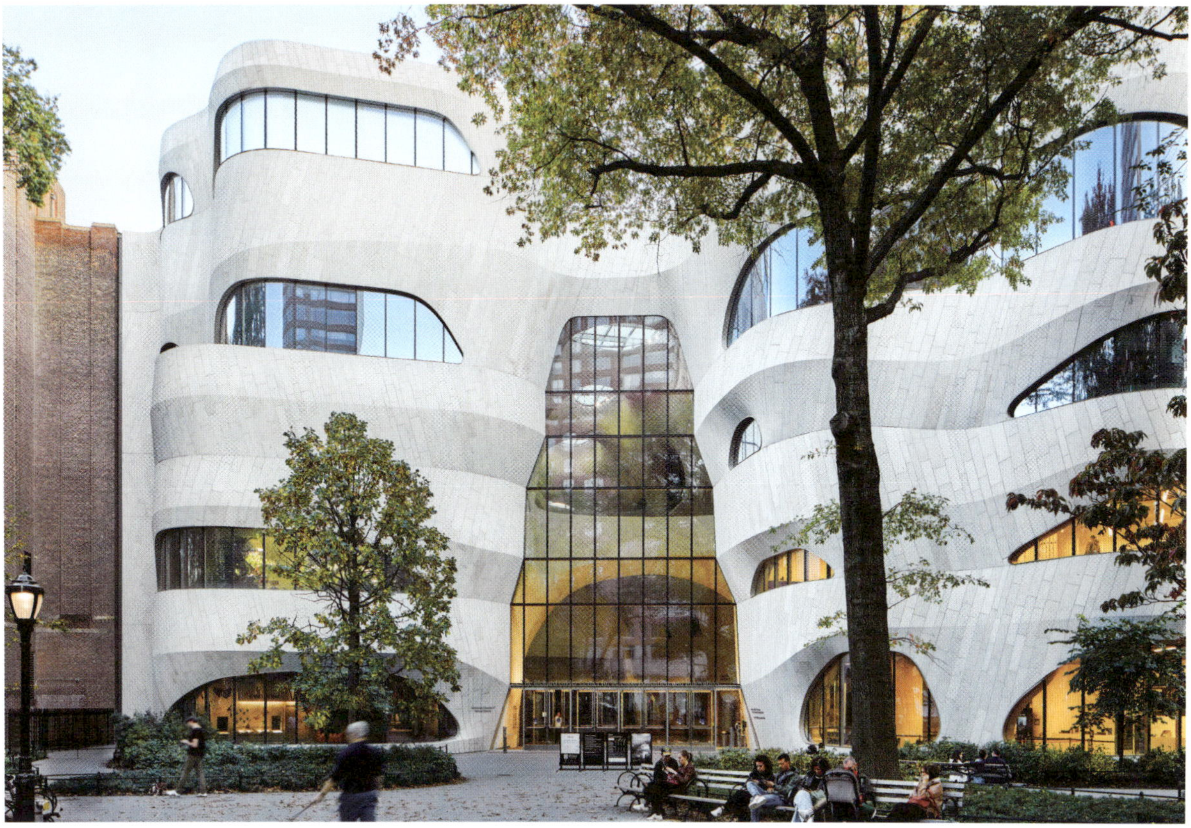

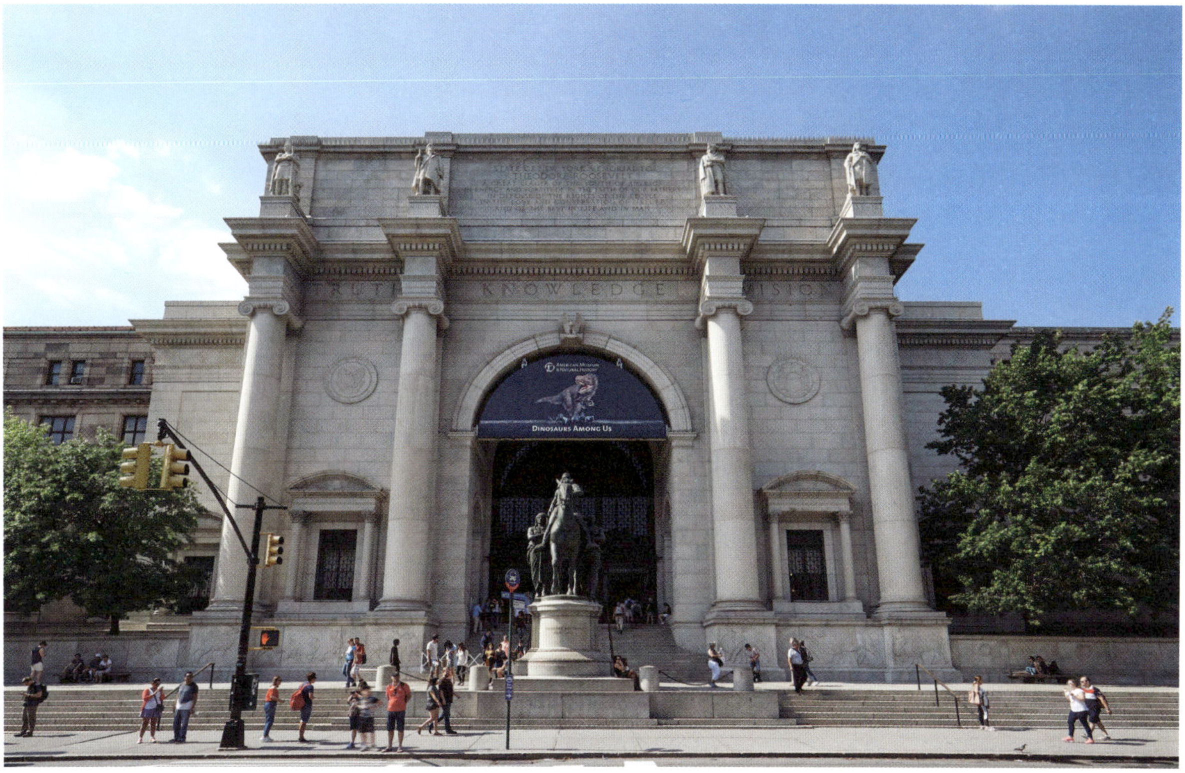

THE MUSEUM IS LANDSCAPE

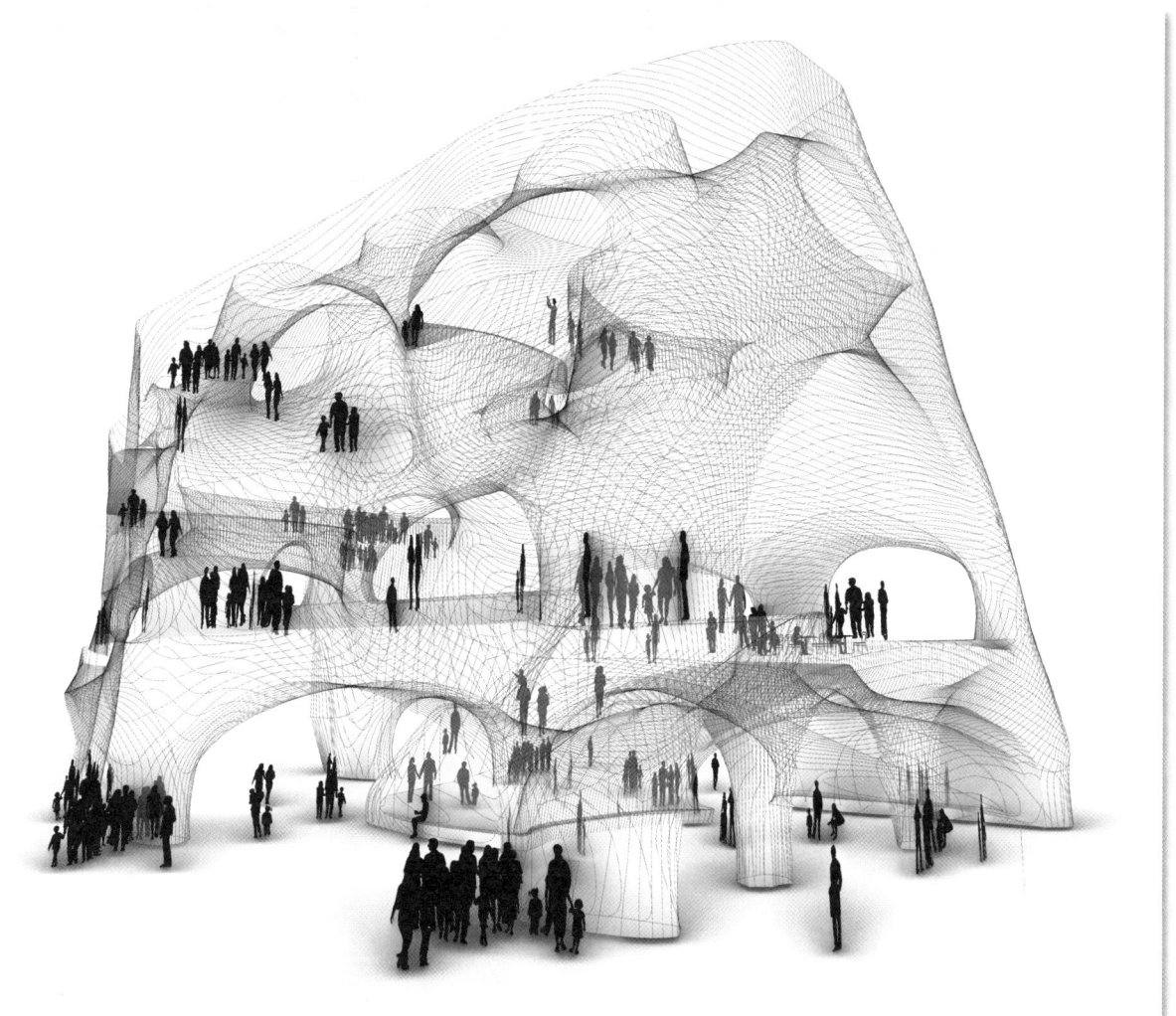

new opportunities for their future. Rather than repairing or restoring their subjects to a former state, Gang's grafts seek to augment a building's potential, setting in motion an interpenetration of culture and nature through architecture. By rethinking the AMNH as a graft-bearer, the Gilder Center improves circulation within the museum, while symbolically transforming its attitude toward the natural world. The graft serves a dual function: breathing new life into the institution and endowing it with a new civic image.

When you look at a map of Central Park, you will notice resemblances to the facade of Gang's building—everything is curvilinear and asymmetrical, unlike the imperial-Roman facade on Central Park West. Gang's elevation is something of an anti-facade, one that immediately suggests a certain modesty and seems to extend an organic form of hospitality. Inside, the organic forms are repeated in shotcrete, which requires hand finishing and gives the walls their fluid appearance. A large skylight fills the central atrium with daylight; lifting their heads, visitors discover cave-like forms leading to passageways, bridges, and classrooms, reminiscent of the rock formations found in Central Park.

The bridges that connect the galleries and link different parts of the museum are the perfect vantage points to experience Manhattanhenge—the moments throughout the year when the setting sun aligns with the cross streets of New York's grid. Two days each year, around May 28 and

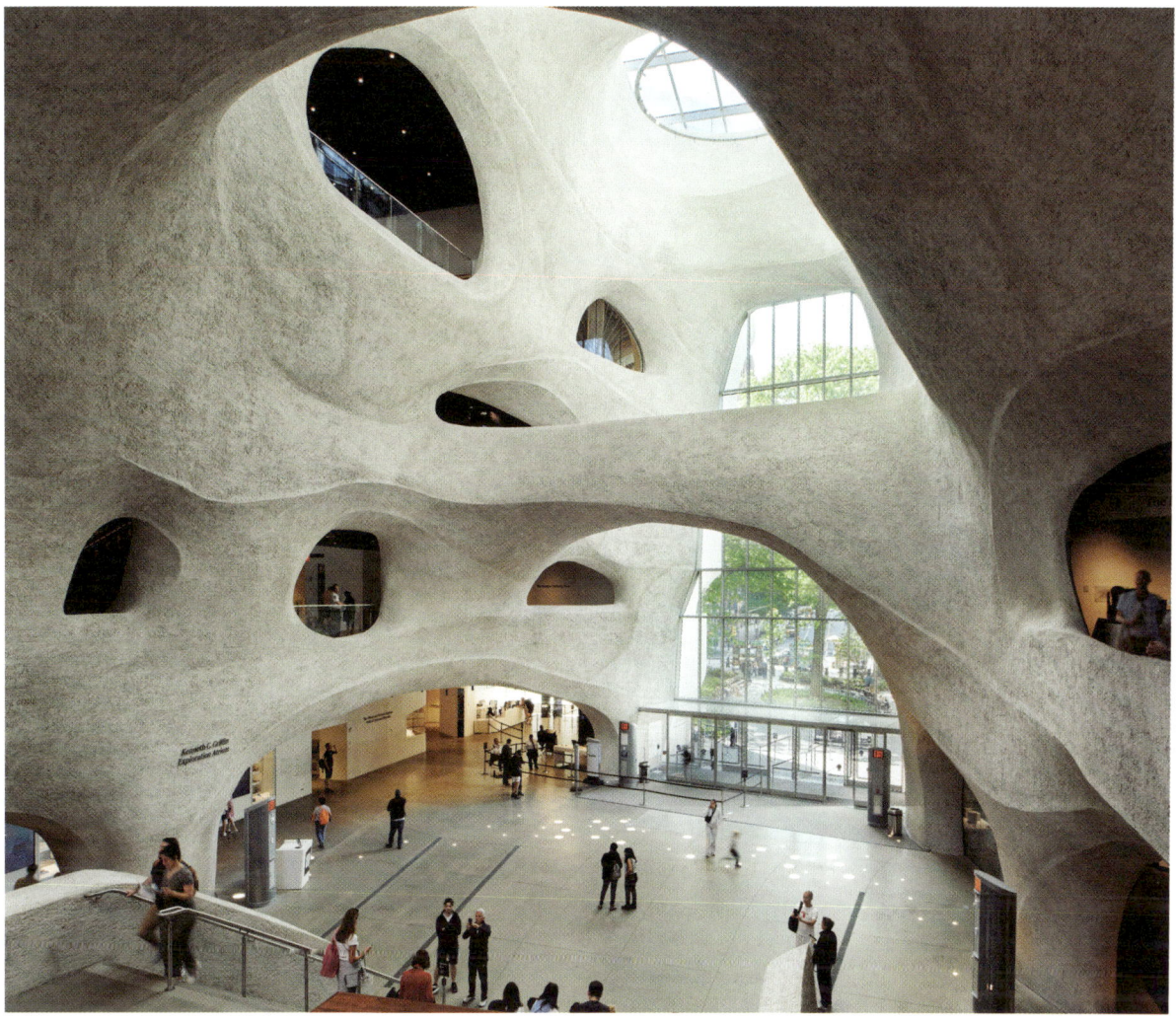

July 13, AMNH visitors can witness a spectacle when the city's skyscrapers, backlit by the sunset, suddenly resemble geological formations creating a landscape of canyons carved through rock. In a visceral, physical, and emotional sense, Gang's architecture expresses the inseparable relationship between the city and the museum. Indeed, the Gilder Center enables us to view, understand, and interact with the city in a way that is both intimate and panoramic. By forming an urban space that challenges the notion of nature versus "the museum" (as symbolized by Central Park), Gang's building highlights the fact that our environment is always both built and natural, rendering the opposition between city and wilderness invalid in the Anthropocene.

Previous page, right: The new Richard Gilder Center contrasts sharply with the neoclassical facade that remains a symbol of late nineteenth-century attitudes toward human knowledge of the natural world.

Opposite and above: Studio Gang's modeling of the new addition to the AMNH reveals the cave-like forms punctuated with skylights, providing a sensation akin to that experienced in natural environments.

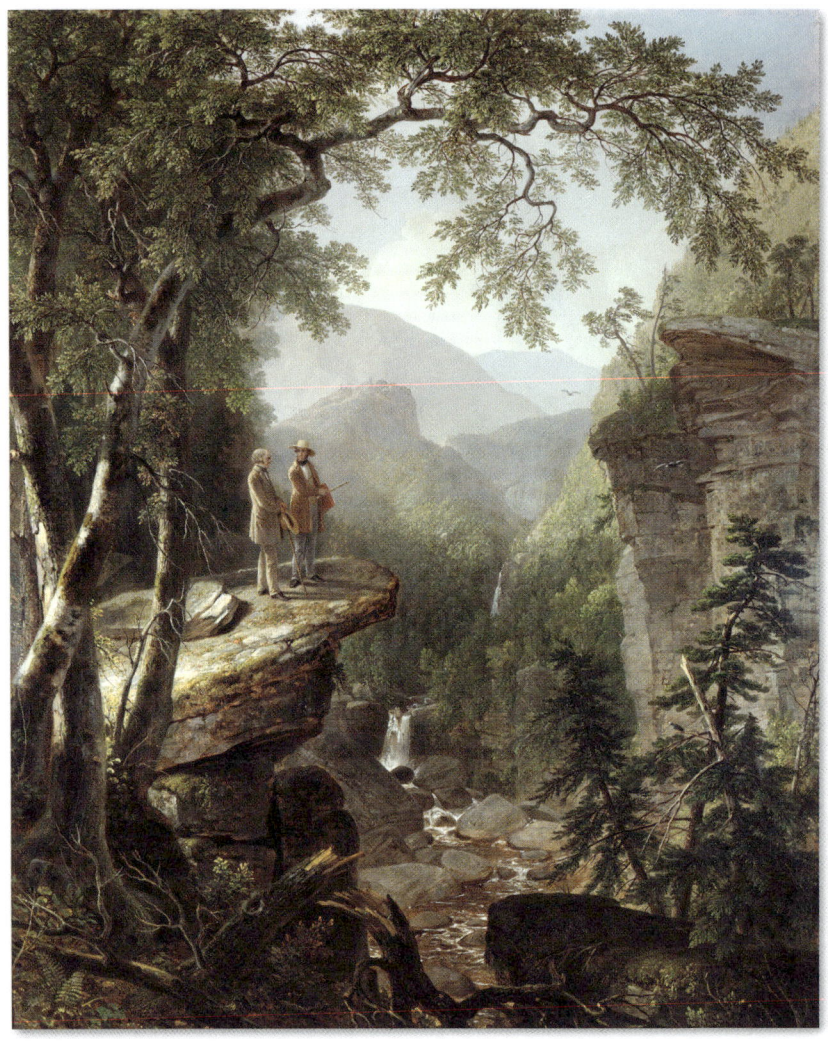

One of the museum's oldest paradoxes is that it contains representations of nature: indoors we find an illusory, augmented, controlled, and comprehensible vision of the wilderness, while outdoors, we can interact with the real thing. But what should one make of the threshold between the two? In his 1849 canvas *Kindred Spirits*, Hudson River school painter Asher Brown Durand would have us believe that humans and nature are completely independent. In the painting, two men, our supposed kindred spirits, stand above a valley, pointing authoritatively at the view below. Everything in the painting is precisely composed, with not a leaf out of place. However, one crucial element is missing: there is no semblance of a house, shed, or wall indicating a human-built structure.

Kindred Spirits was a founding work in the collection of the Crystal Bridges Museum of American Art. Sold by the New York Public Library in 2005, it is thought to have fetched $35 million, a record-breaking price for an American artist at the time. Upon acquiring the painting, Walmart heiress Alice Walton, who outbid both the Metropolitan Museum of Art and Washington's National Gallery, announced her plans to build Crystal Bridges on the outskirts of Bentonville, Arkansas, the city where her father opened his first store. In hindsight, it seems the picture may have been foundational

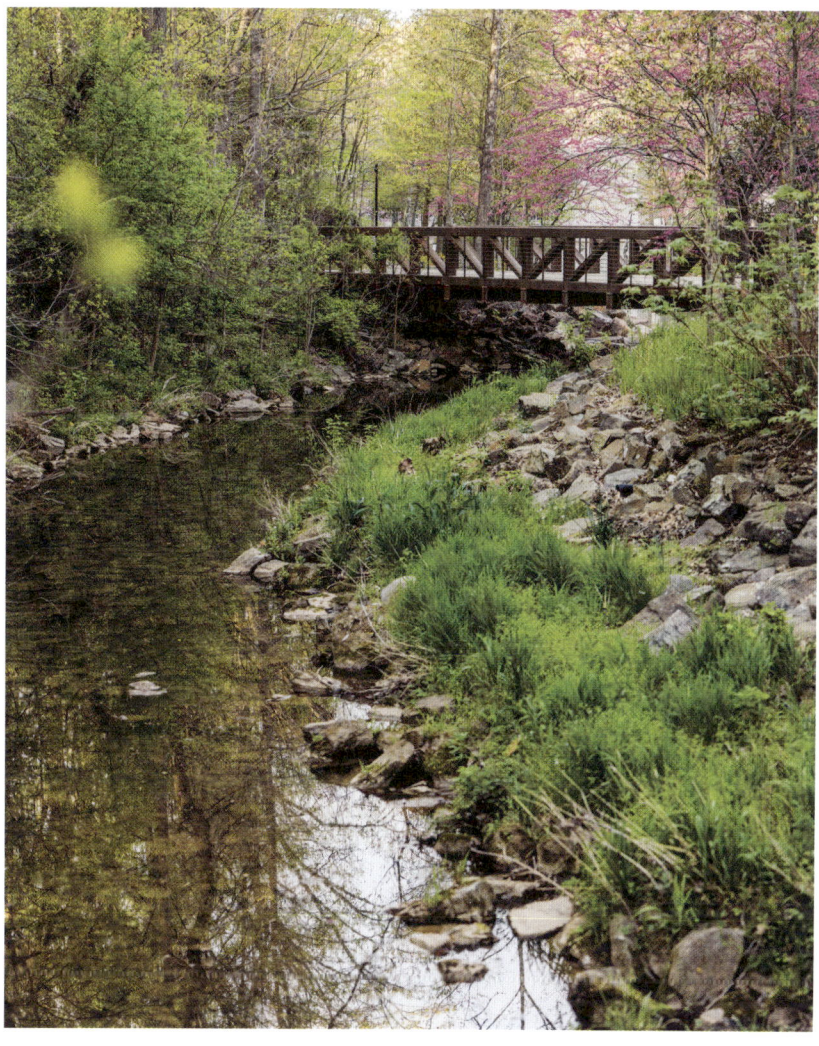

to the museum in more ways than one, as the vista depicted in *Kindred Spirits* foreshadows the location chosen by architect Moshe Safdie for its new building. At Crystal Bridges, Safdie created a blueprint for architecture as a threshold between art and nature. Inverting Durand's viewpoint on the American landscape, he chose to build the museum down in the valley at the level of the stream, imagining a series of pavilions that immerse visitors in the surroundings. A far cry from the imperial-Roman grandeur on Central Park West, the museum becomes the missing infrastructure in Durand's painting, allowing human culture to thrive in the face of nature.

 Engineered as a series of connected bridge structures on either side of the stream, the

Opposite: Asher Brown Durand, *Kindred Spirits* (1849), a founding work in the collection of the Crystal Bridges Museum of American Art.

Above: At Crystal Bridges, visitors can choose to explore the museum galleries or walk along pathways down by the river stream. The experience of culture is inseparable from the experience of nature.

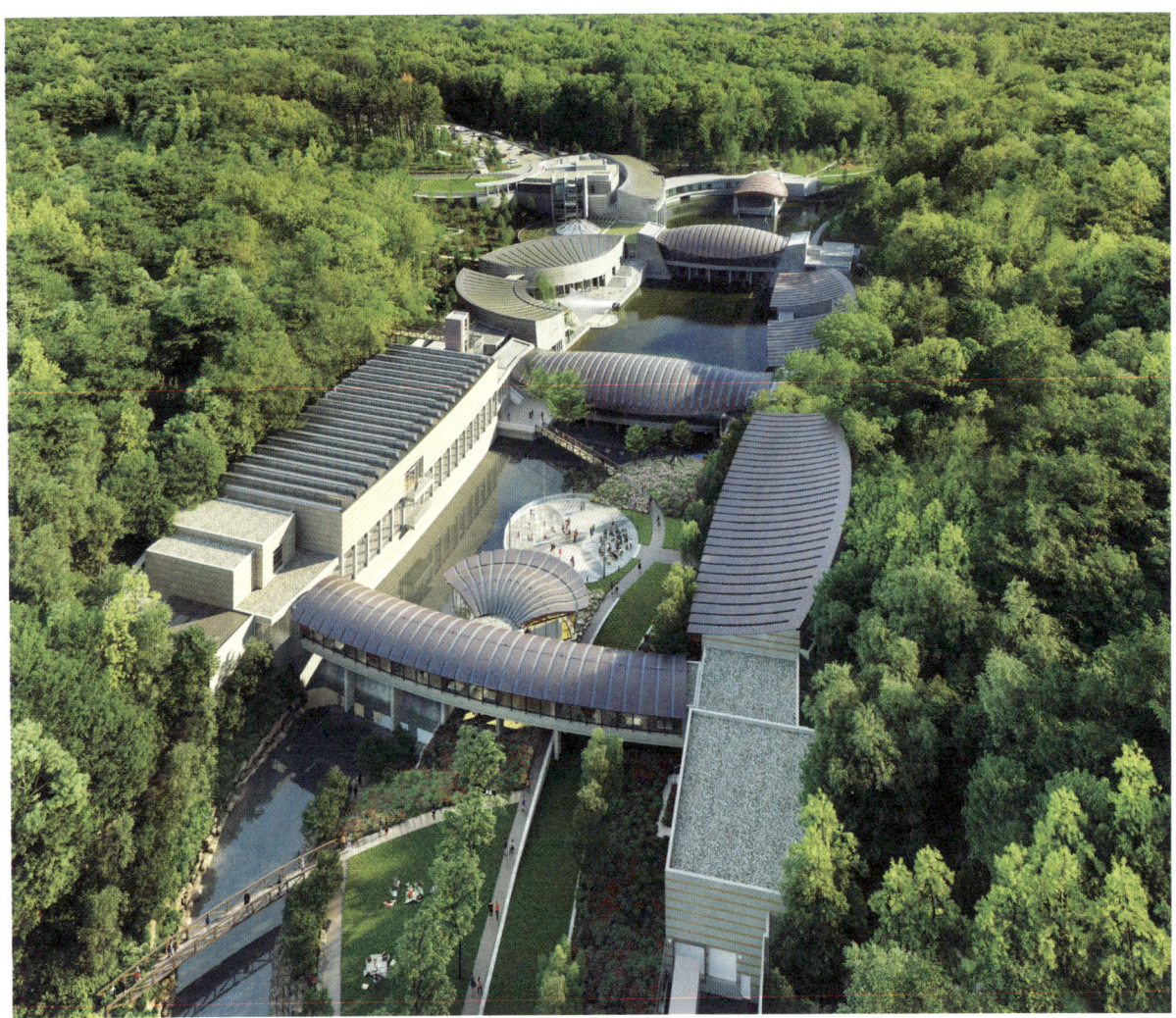

museum is entered at water level, after which visitors progress through a series of galleries that read like pavilions punctuating the landscape. Tilted outward, the galleries' glass facades resist the interpretation of a landscape being framed—you look within as much as without. Stretching away from the main building, trails allow visitors to explore the surrounding forest in a similar way to the museum, thereby extending the ambiguity regarding what is natural or artificial, wild or man-made.

Safdie's architecture updates the Hudson River school's viewpoint by imagining a museum that acknowledges nature's central role in the development of American culture. Among the works on display at Crystal Bridges is Frank Lloyd Wright's 1956 Bachman-Wilson House, transported to the museum's grounds from its original location in New Jersey. An exemplar of Usonian living,[2] the house further illustrates the ambiguity between landscape and architecture: rather than dominating the landscape, humankind lives symbiotically with it. Together, Wright and Safdie offer a microcosm of the reality of the American landscape, a three-dimensional illustration of how art, architecture, and nature are a constantly interpenetrating form of culture.

---

2. For more on Wright's vision of Usonian living, see John Sergeant, *Frank Lloyd Wright's Usonian Houses: The Case for Organic Architecture* (New York: Whitney Library of Design, 1976).

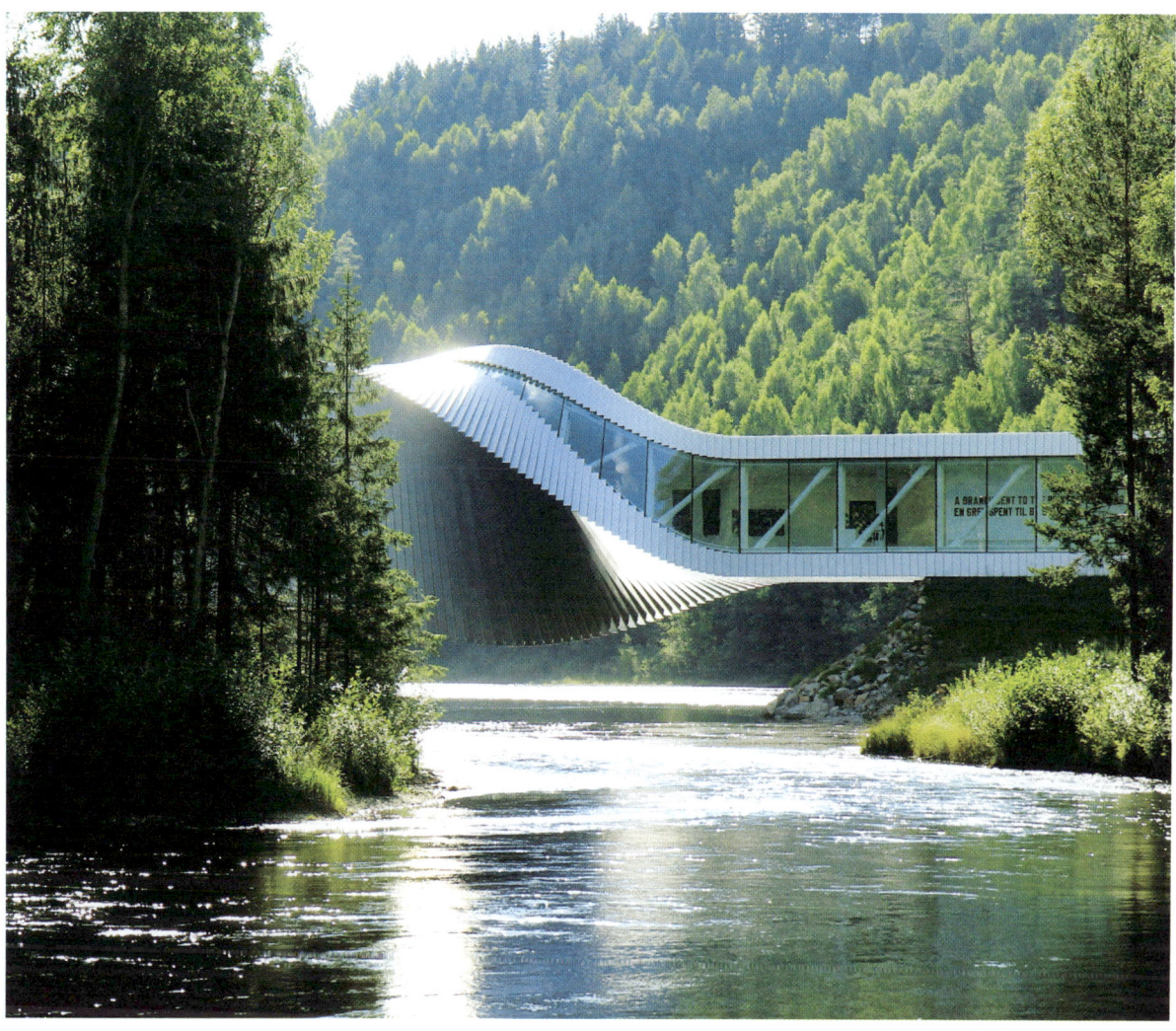

The architectural gallery conceived by Bjarke Ingels for Kistefos Museum's Park serves the function of a bridge across a river, connecting museum grounds, as much as it is an exhibition space. Entering the gallery, it is unclear which is exposed—is it the art within, or is it nature framed beyond the bay windows and perceptible through the skylights? The ambiguity is prolonged throughout the museum property, itself a sculpture park: Kistefos Museum refuses to assert itself as an enclosed space, suggesting instead that it is as much a collection of artifacts—be they architectural or industrial—as they are natural.

Opposite: Seen from above, the architecture of Crystal Bridges can be read as a series of pavilions that allow a total immersion in nature and a disappearance of the barrier between the landscape of the site and the boundary of the museum, as shown in this rendering.

Above: Kistefos Museum's Park is punctuated by sculptures and pavilions. Designed by BIG, the bridge connects the different parts of the landscape and sublimates itself to the experience of being one with the natural surroundings.

Following pages: Openness and flow imparted by the transparency between the city, the sky, the surrounding garden, and the building itself inspires a consciousness of nature in the visitors of the Fondation Cartier, Boulevard Raspail.

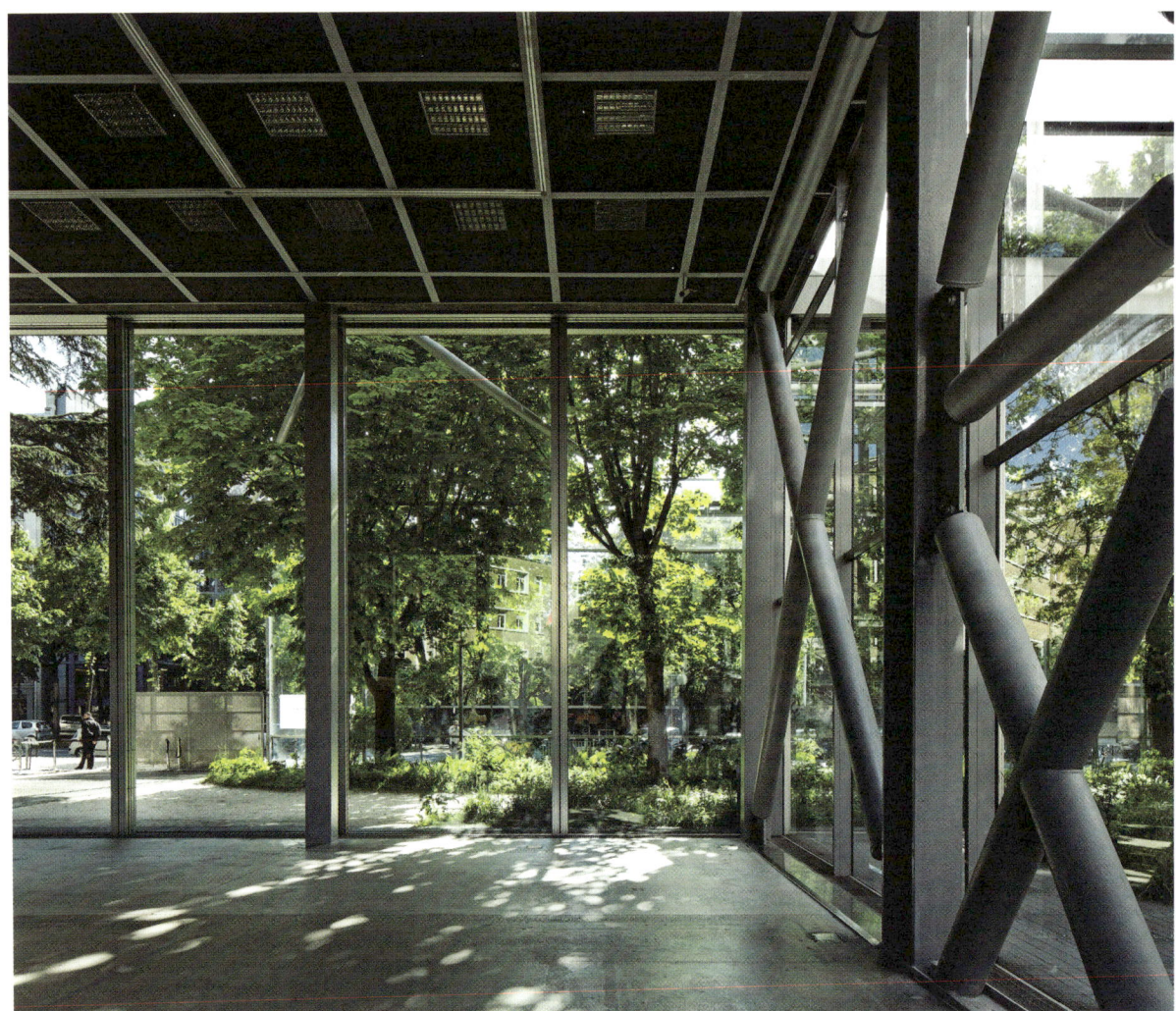

To enter Jean Nouvel's Fondation Cartier building on Paris's Boulevard Raspail, one must first confront the image of nature that is reflected onto a vast glass curtain wall. A second, three-dimensional garden appears between the curtain wall and the actual building, gradually revealing the entrance. After this enchanting initiation, one finally arrives indoors. Yet, perhaps this too is an illusion, as nature appears once again straight ahead—is it the memory of what one has just seen, its reflection, or reality? In the series of transparent screens that make up the Fondation Cartier, nature is constantly framed and reflected, elevating the architecture.

The starting point for the building's design was the preservation of a majestic old cedar, planted at the front of the plot by the author René-François de Chateaubriand in 1823. The rest was straightforward—a glass box eight stories high and twice as large, positioned parallel to the boulevard. This architecture, viewed from a distance, appears to be interrupted by a tree. Framed between the 50-foot-high glass screens rising from the street line, the cedar greets visitors as they cross the threshold between the sidewalk and the garden. The previous building on the site— the 1934 American Center—had been granted a construction permit on the condition that as few trees as possible be felled. Nouvel's design

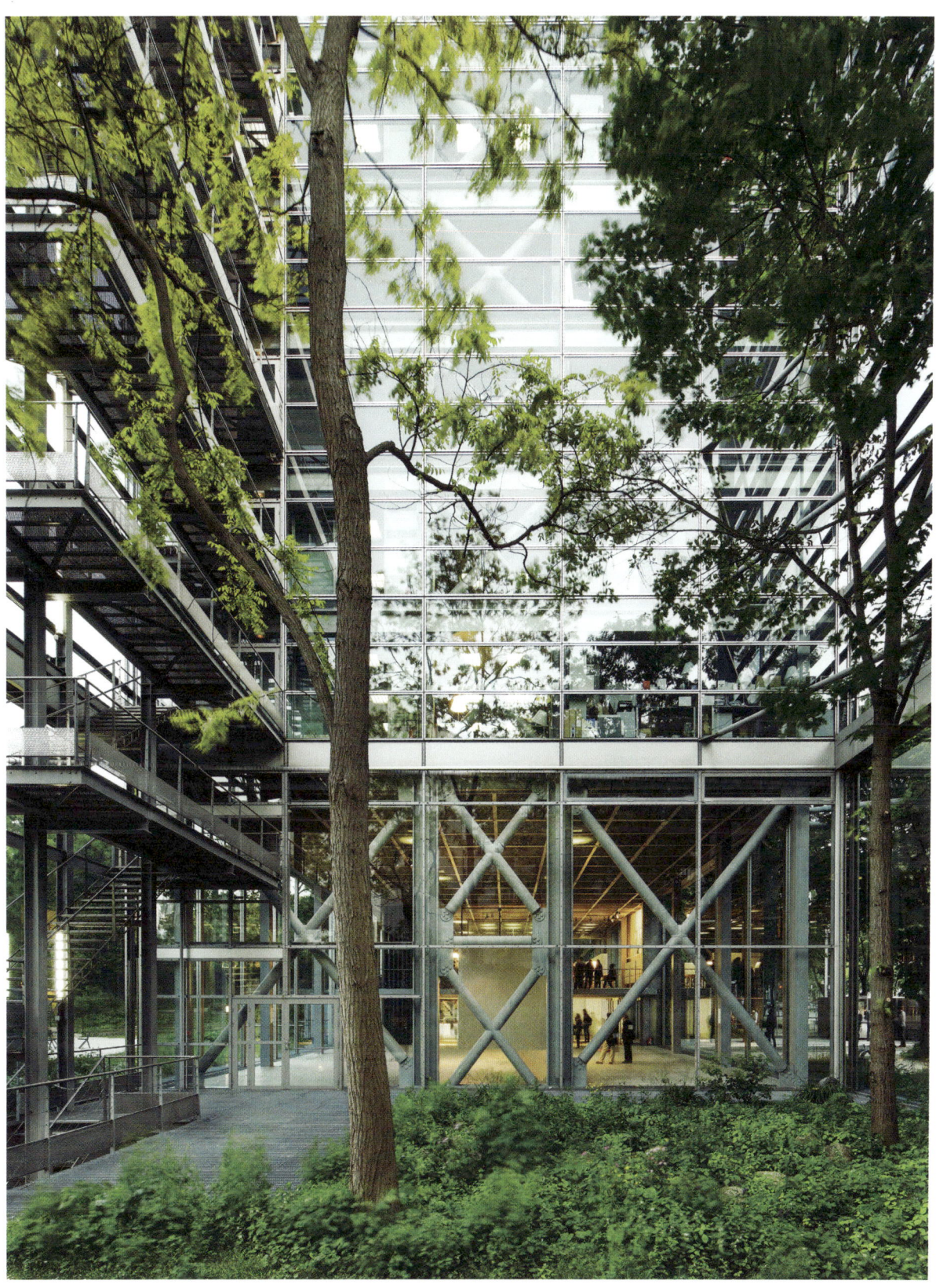

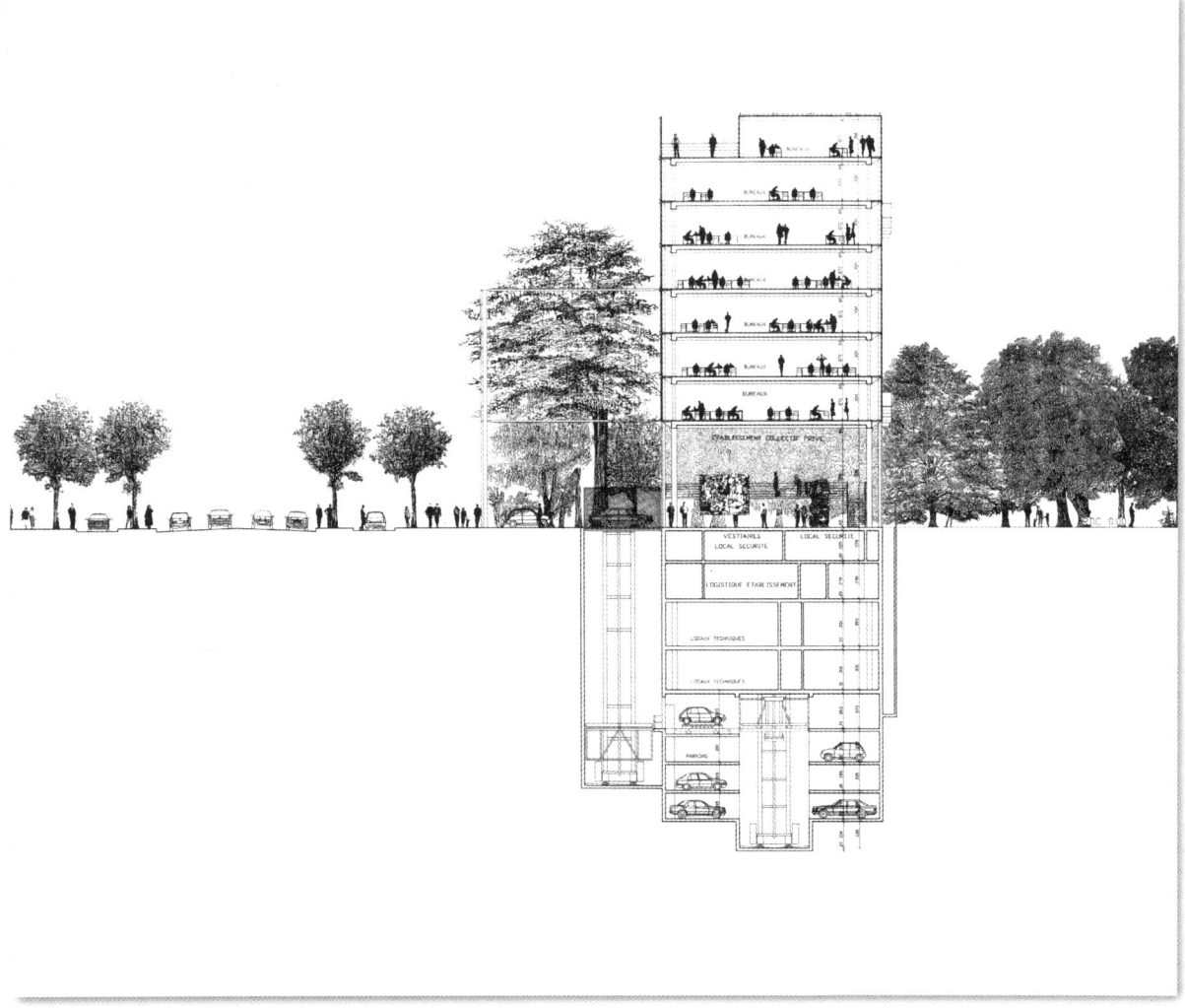

respected this same principle, aligning with his contextualist approach, which emphasizes historical preservation among its core tenets.

"Whatever the scale of the transformation of a site or a place, the question becomes how can we translate the uncertainty of the mutation of a living fragment? Can we tame the visible elements of composition—the clouds, plants, living beings of every dimension—with new signs, reflections, plantings?"[3] Nouvel asked in his 2005 *Louisiana Manifesto*. Written

3. Jean Nouvel, "Louisiana Manifesto," *Ce qui est là n'est pas ailleurs. Leçon inaugurale de l'École Chaillot* (Milan: Silvana Editoriale, 2008; first published by Copenhagen: Louisiana Museum of Art, 2005), 18.

for an exhibition at the Louisiana Museum of Modern Art, the text takes the celebrated Danish institution as its starting point, only to morph into a retroactive manifesto for the museum on Boulevard Raspail. Curiously, Nouvel's Fondation Cartier arouses such a heightened consciousness of nature that it seems purposefully built to reveal nature's importance and respond to a future urban imperative. With extraordinary vision, Nouvel materialized a new paradigm of architecture and cities, creating the conditions for the concept of urban beauty in nature to emerge.

Contrasting sharply with the stone-fronted apartment buildings that line the Boulevard Raspail, the glass curtain wall reveals, as

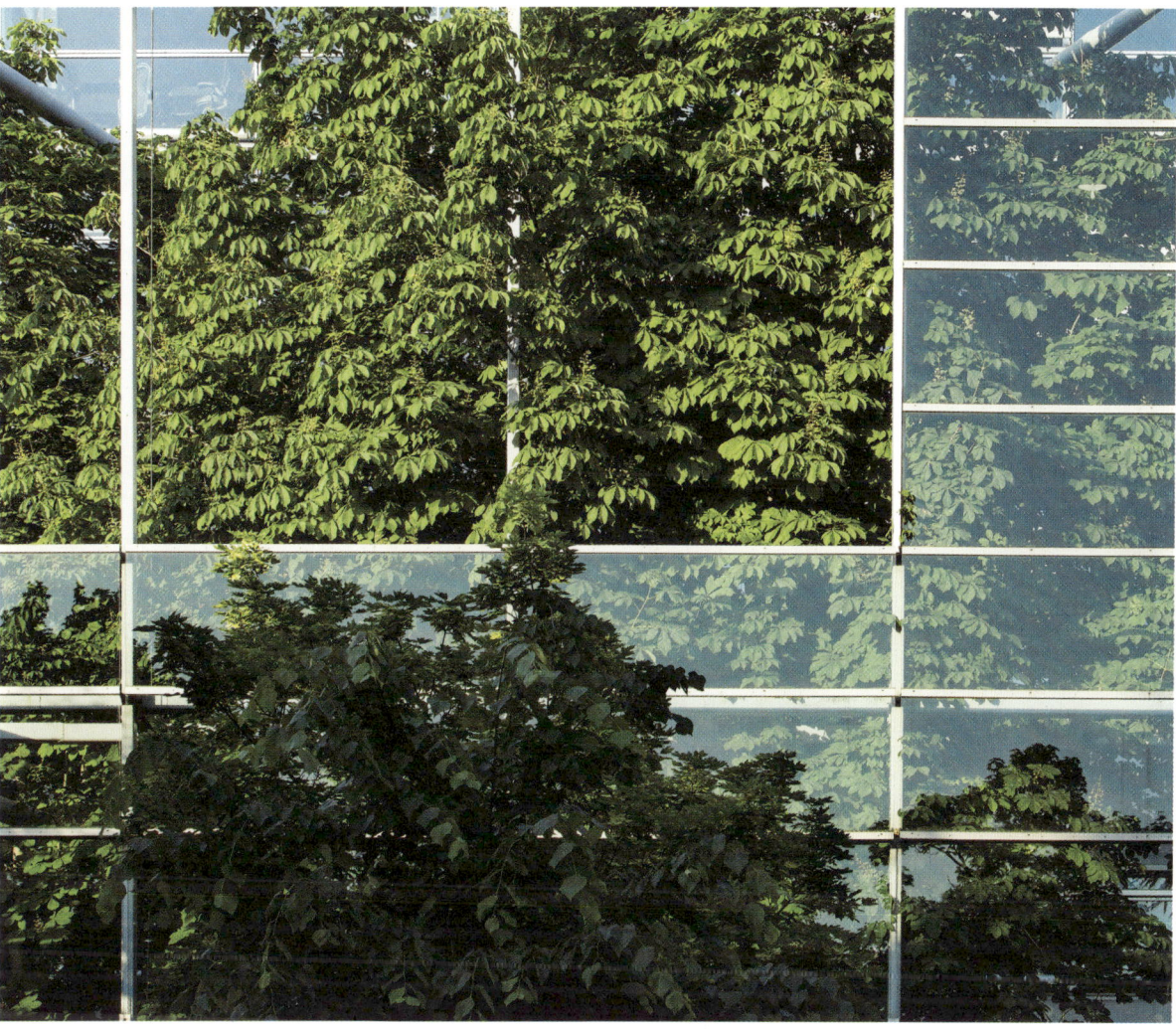

if it were an apparition, a dense volume of trees in a planned wilderness. Only after crossing this glass boundary—tangible yet evanescent—does the actual building enter our consciousness (a trick Nouvel would repeat at Paris's Musée du Quai Branly), appearing as something of a mirage itself. Fitted with immense sliding screens, the double-height ground-floor exhibition galleries can dematerialize entirely, further emphasizing the reciprocal porosity between the notions of garden and city, nature and urbanity.

Opposite and above: Originally designed as sliding walls, the gallery space could open onto the street and onto the garden, completely collapsing the notion that the gallery spaces should be isolated from the city or from the garden.

Following pages: The majestic Lebanese cedar was central to the original plan drawn by Jean Nouvel. It welcomed visitors to the American Center, and later to the Fondation Cartier.

Pages 124–127: At the Zaishui Museum of Art, designed by Junya Ishigami, there is no divide between nature and the museum. An architectural gesture that seeks to dissolve the distance between nature and culture.

THE MUSEUM IS LANDSCAPE

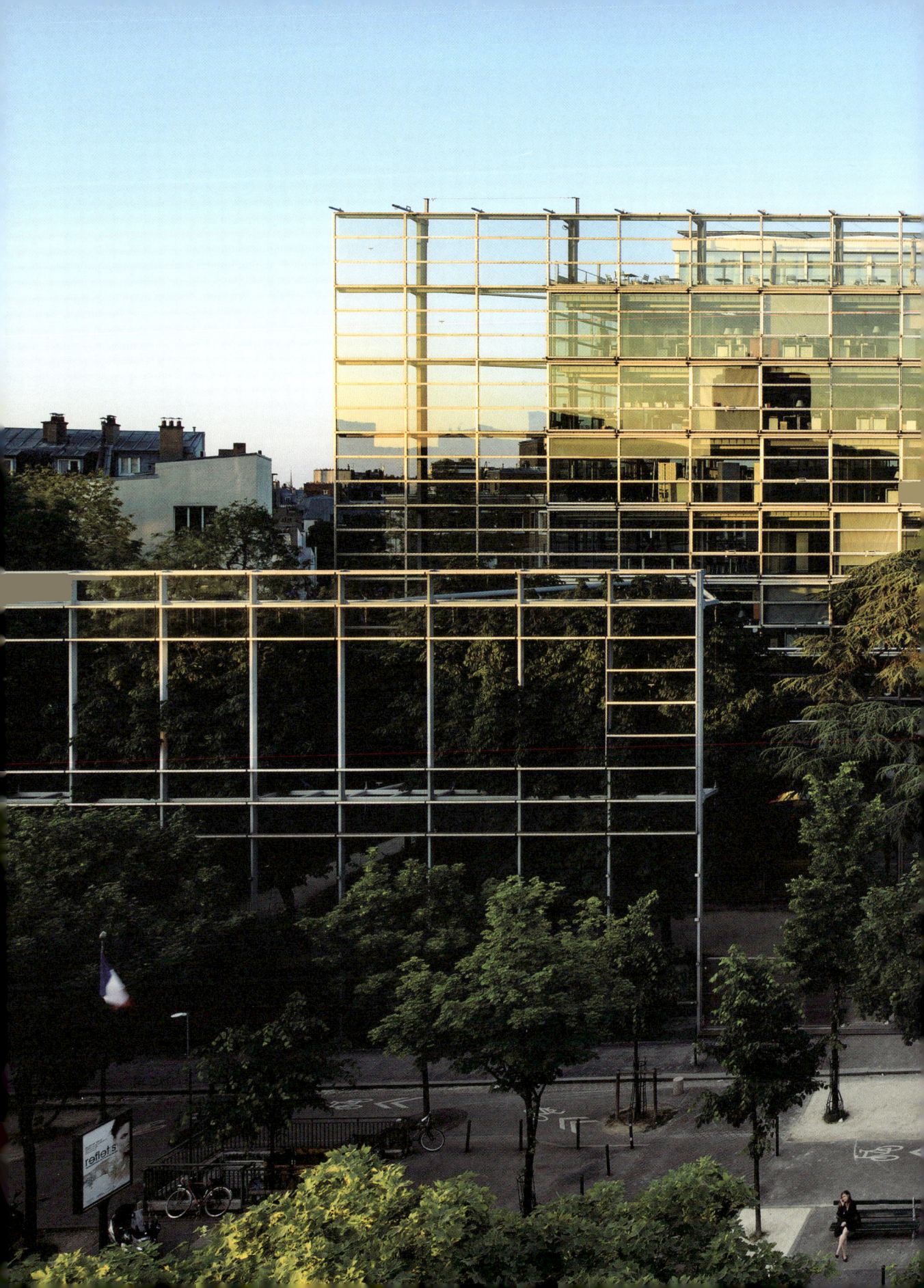

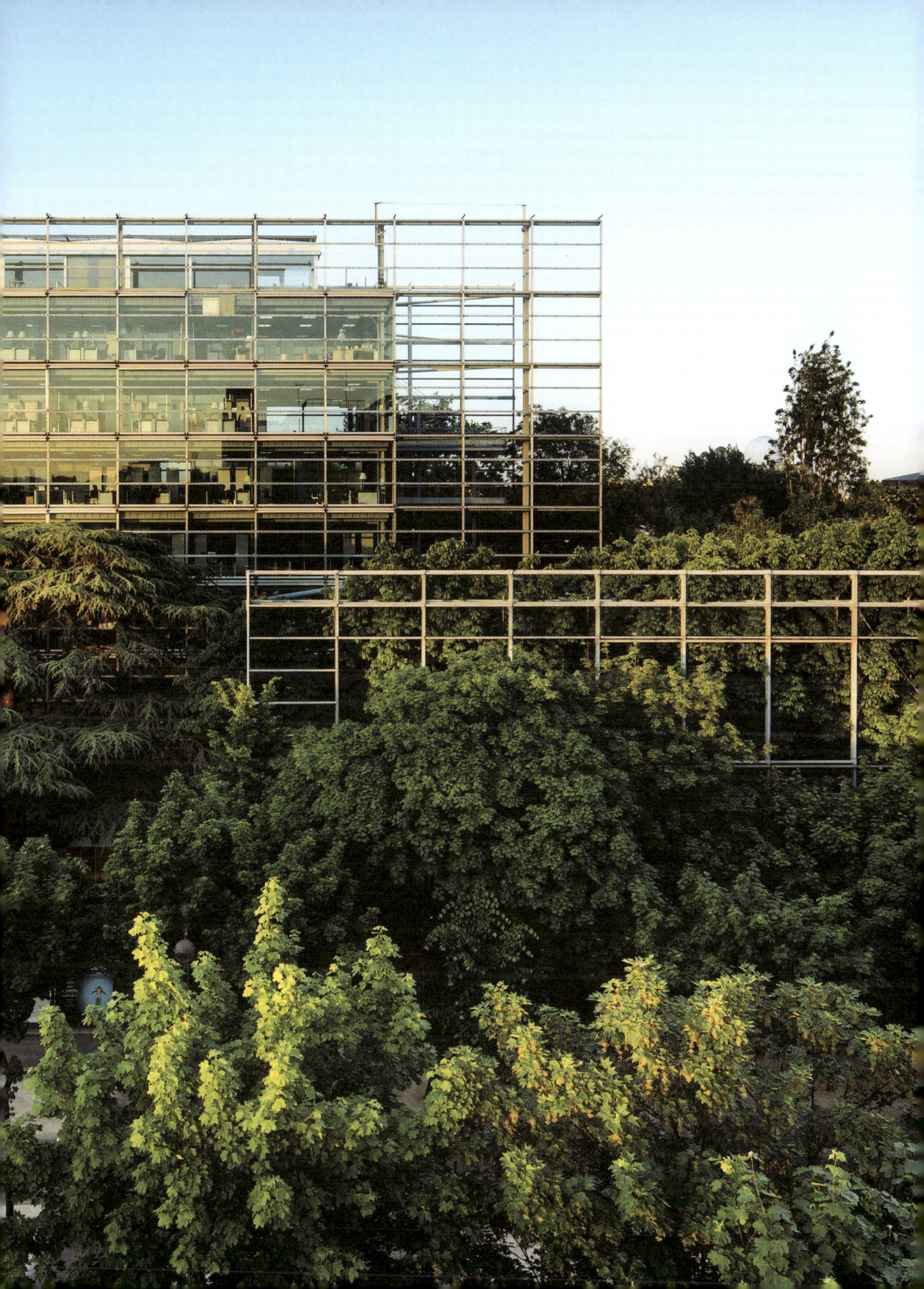

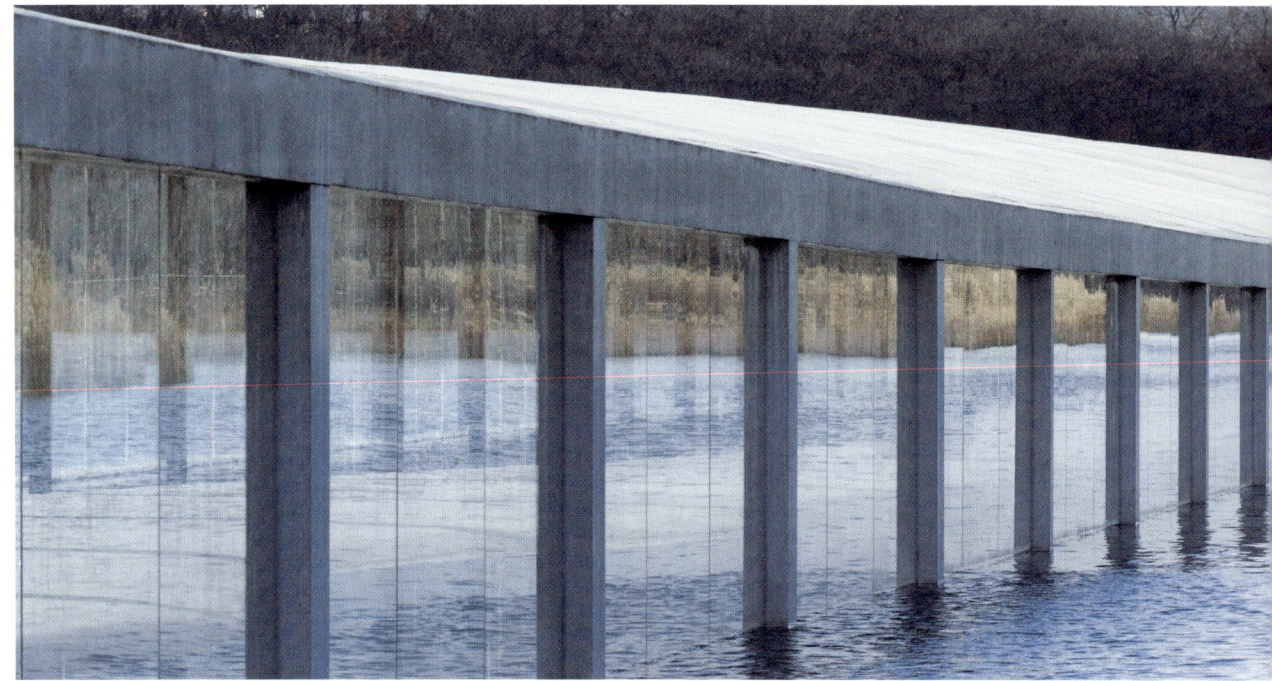

In Rizhao, China, there is no divide, as there is neither pure nature nor pure architecture—at Junya Ishigami's Zaishui Art Museum, the two categories dissolve into one. An interpretation of Chinese landscape painting in three-dimensional form, the museum foregrounds the pavilion, the ultimate architectural typology, while simultaneously merging it with the surrounding nature. Though it is just one element of the landscape, the man-made is central, as it allows visitors to walk on water—both to exist within the lake and to faze out upon it. Architecture disappears into nature in an interdependent, interwoven, and beautiful whole.

In Zaishui,—literally "at the water"—the scenery exists both indoors and out, since the two cohere in a continuous landscape. Stretching out over 1,000 yards, the museum's glass walls allow water to enter and possibly touch visitors' feet, collapsing the distance between the human and the natural. Reduced to a narrow line, the building itself entirely reinterprets the boundary between landscape and architecture. It is unclear whether the architecture anticipates a future ruin—one where entropy has triumphed, erasing historical forms of architecture and transforming the museum as we know it—or whether, conversely, it foretells a future where the museum has learned to restore the relationship that has always existed between humankind and nature. In place of art, this philosophical ambiguity becomes the museum's content.

In Rizhao, we are far from Central Park. Here, Ishigami has succeeded in materializing how we have moved beyond the opposition between building and nature; his museum embodies the threshold where culture recognizes its intertwined nature, at once human and non-human. By collapsing the distance between nature and architecture, his disappearing architecture seamlessly merges the two into a new form of landscape. In the narrow interstice that constitutes the building's "inside," Ishigami spatially reveals that nature and culture are one and the same. Every city needs such a place.

In Japan, the Teshima Art Museum, designed by Ryue Nishizawa, lives with the rhythm of natural light and of the four seasons of the year. Stepping inside this white shell, one is surprised by the absence of objects. "Art" in this museum, is replaced by the possibility of being overcome by the all-encompassing performance of nature: the traveling clouds above our heads, as well as the droplets of water that emerge from the ground embrace visitors' feet. The exhibition spaces are turned into a privileged viewing platform of meteorological phenomena.

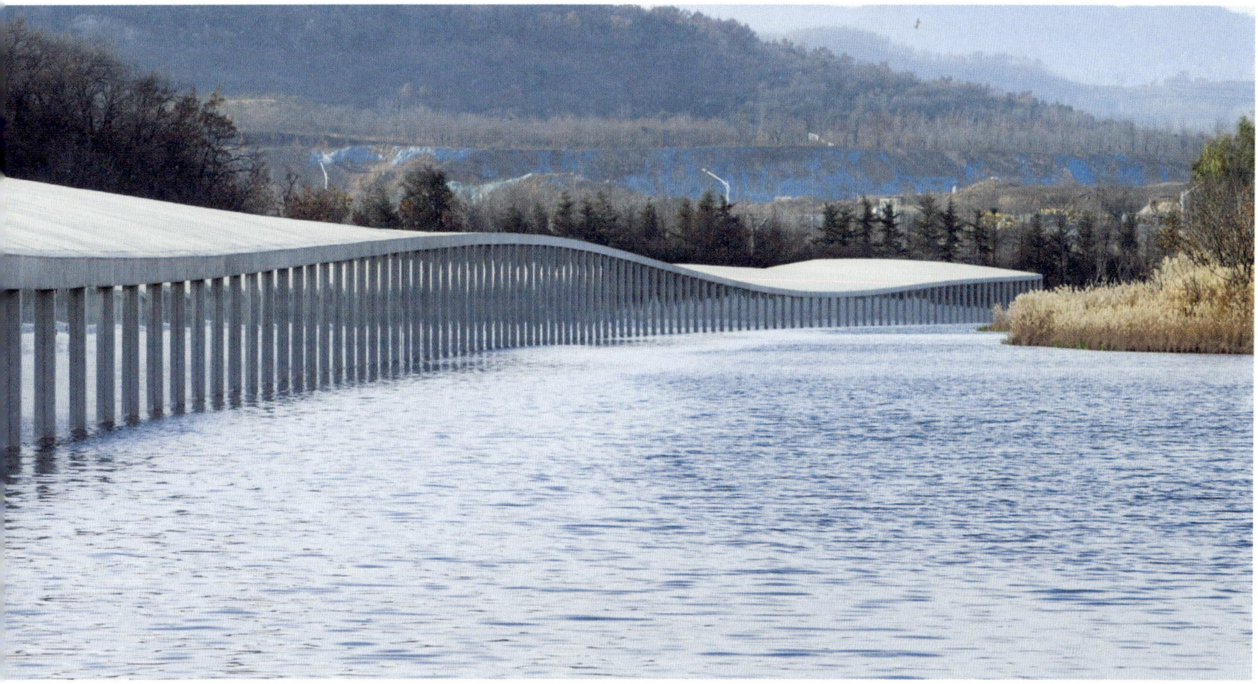

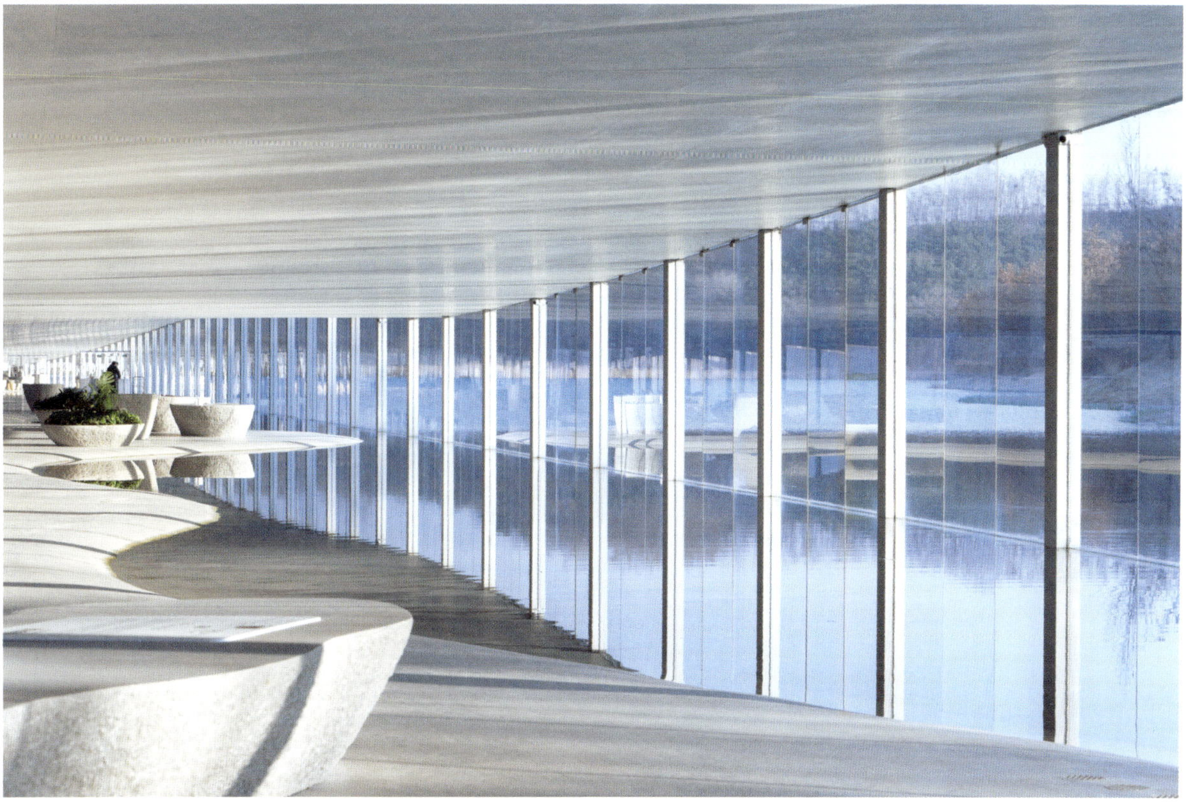

THE MUSEUM IS LANDSCAPE

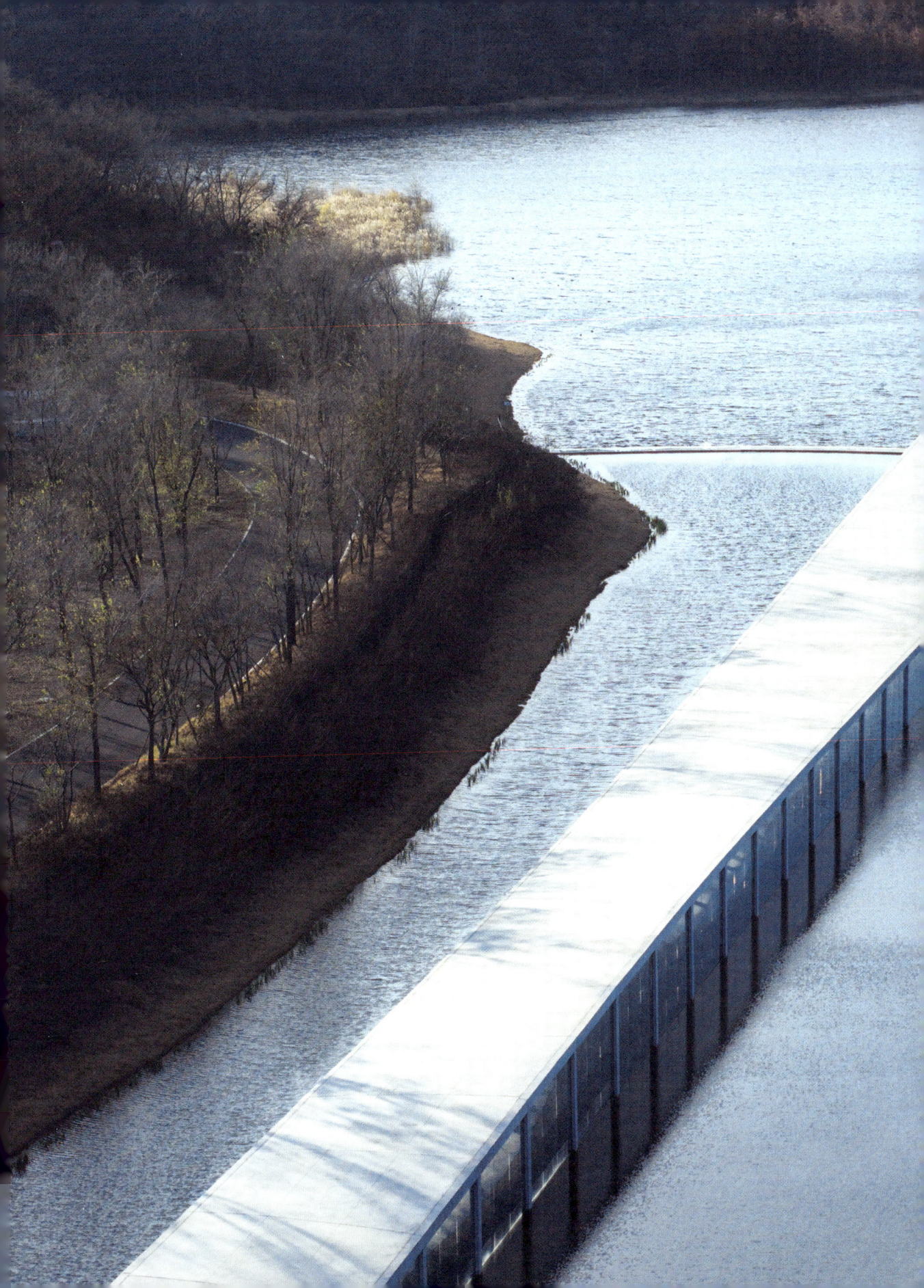

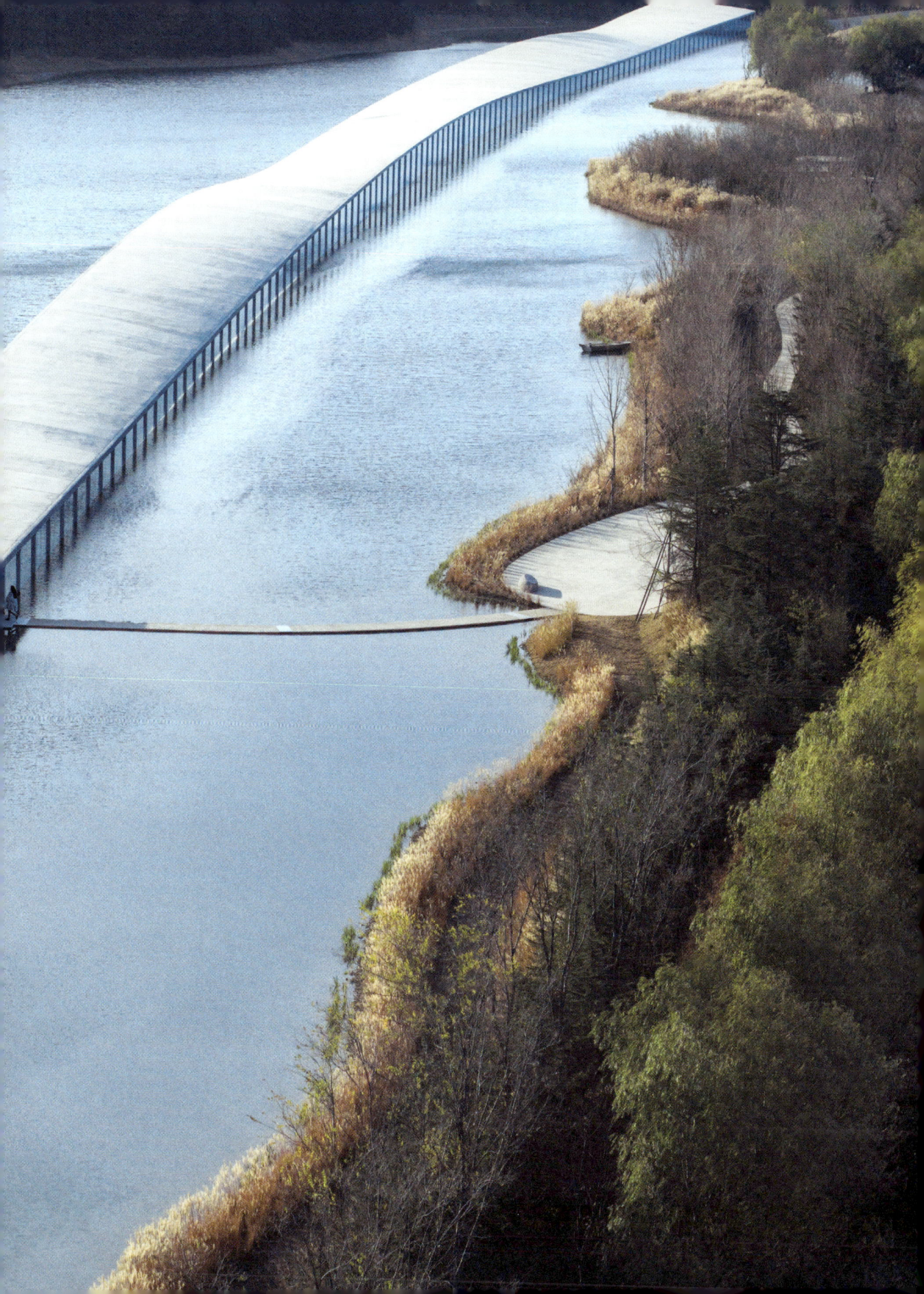

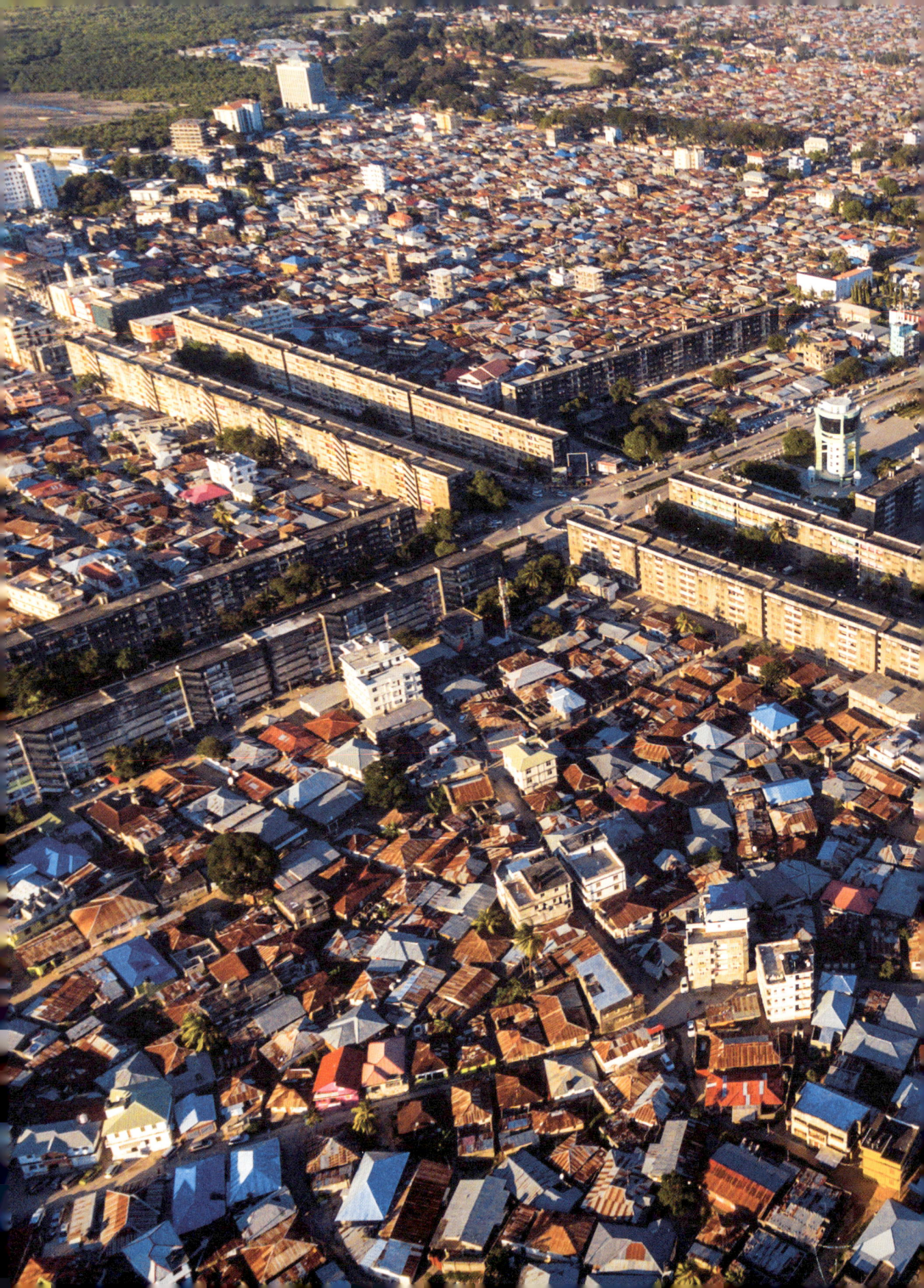

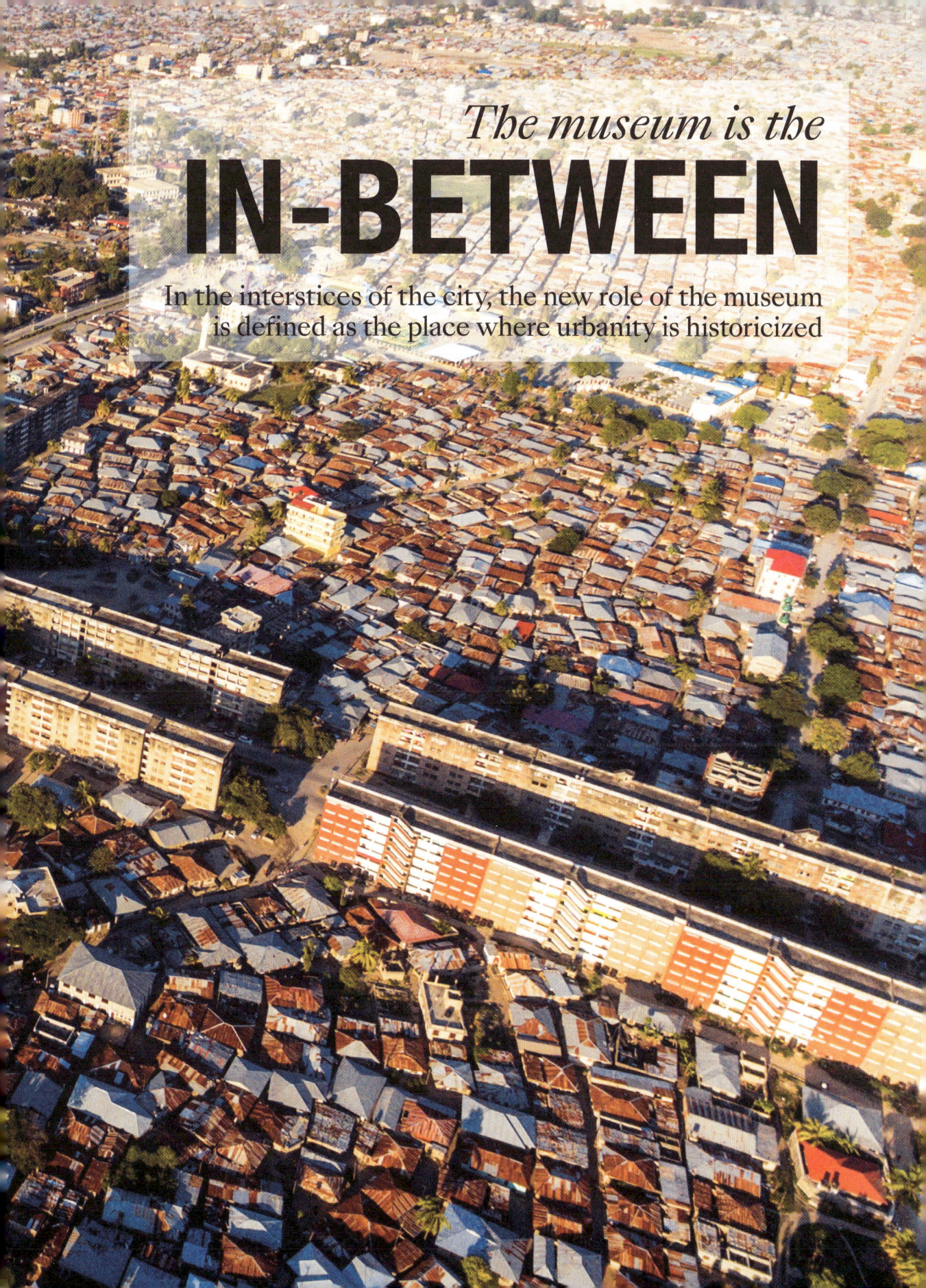

The museum is the
IN-BETWEEN

In the interstices of the city, the new role of the museum is defined as the place where urbanity is historicized

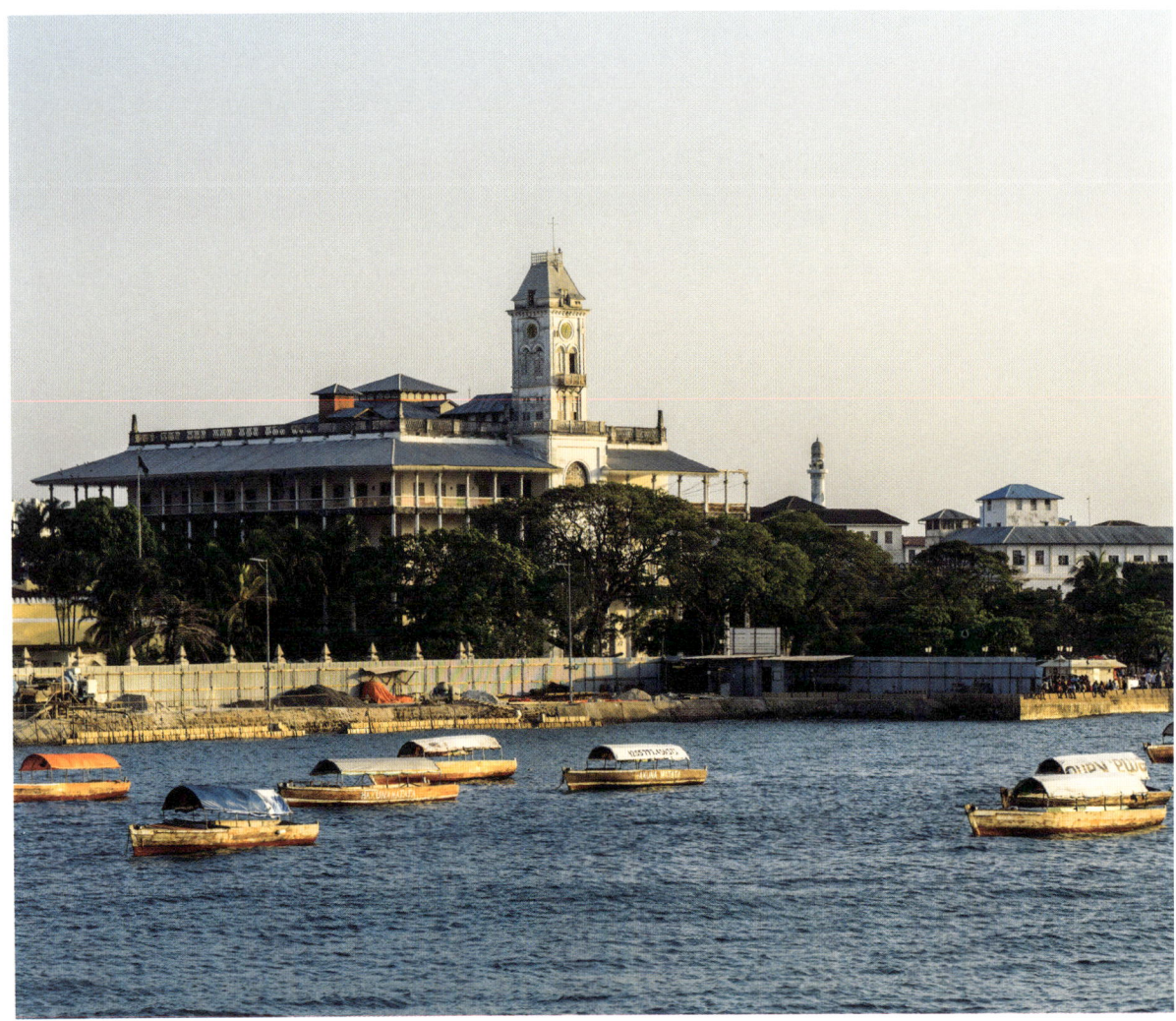

Architecture has continuously reinforced the distinction between buildings and nature by treating the man-made city as distinct from the "natural" landscape, framing the world in terms of binary opposites, such as Central Park versus the Metropolitan Museum of Art.[1] Yet, this city-nature divide is as impossible as it is ahistorical—a fantasy nourished by romantics who view nature as either abandoned by the city or never conquered by it in the first place. In reality, nature is integral to the city, which has always depended on it: the condition we call urbanity is merely the historical development of that relationship. Rivers gave rise to Paris, Rome, and Cairo; lakes birthed Tenochtitlan and Beijing; and mangroves nurtured to Zanzibar's Stone Town. No continent has been spared, and urbanity is now ubiquitous across the globe.

Zanzibar City, Tanzania. Under the scorching heat, Benjamin Mkapa Road—which was once a creek but now a river of asphalt—serves as a major divider, with its incessant flow of buses, cars, and motorbikes. On one side of the noise and dust lies Stone Town, with its shady canopy of almond trees and beautiful balconies suspended above the foliage. "Zanzibar might have been one of the most beautiful cities in the world,"

---

1. In response to this binary opposition, the park emerged as an attempt to assert the otherness of nature by staging it within the city as a theatrical simulacrum. See chapter "Landscape," p. 107.

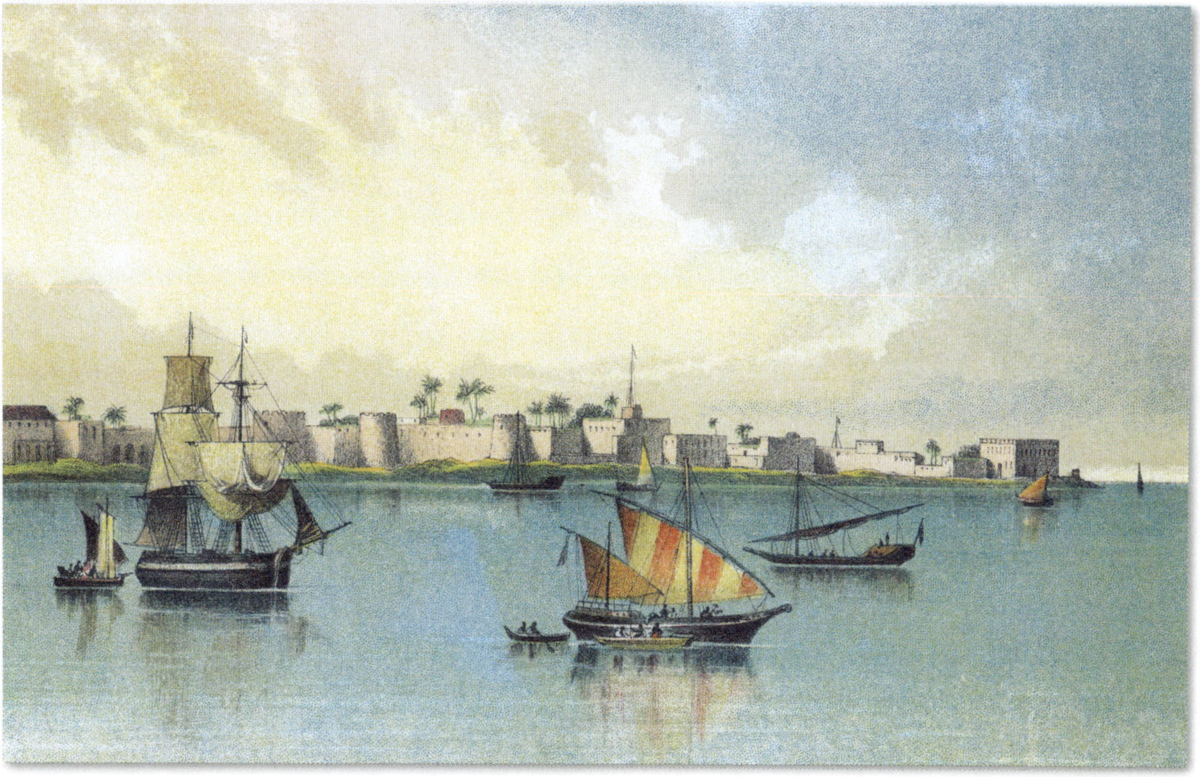

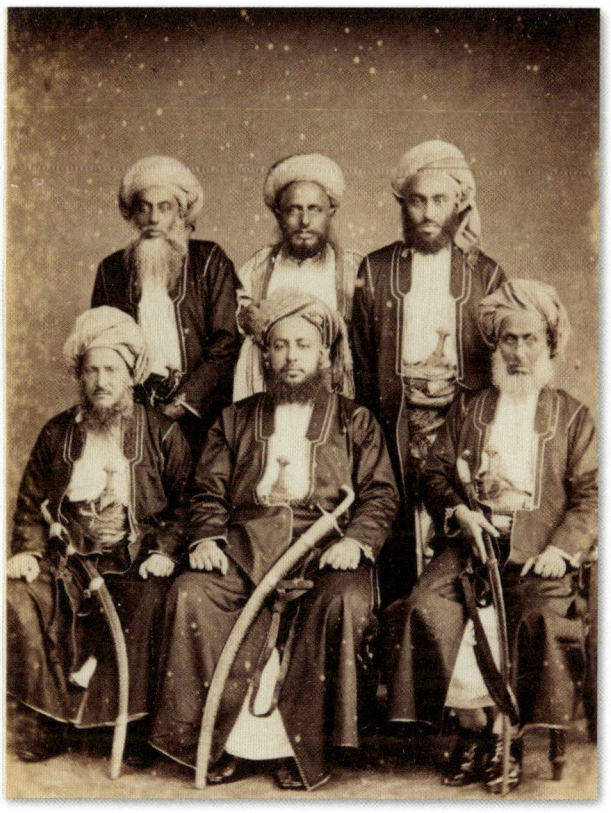

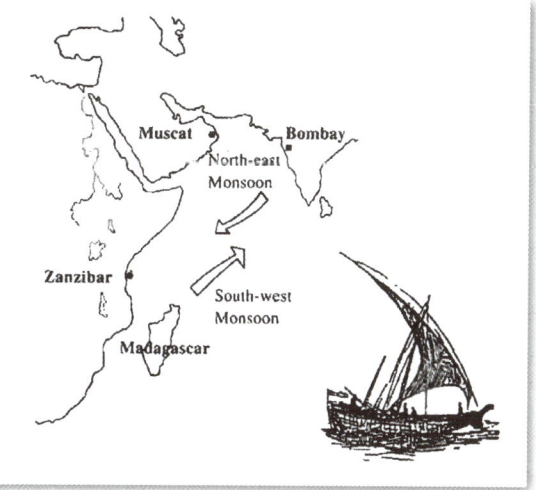

Previous pages: The lesser-known cityscape of Zanzibar is Ng'ambo, meaning "the other side." Four rows of socialist modernist housing break apart vernacular constructions, traditionally home to the Indigenous merchants of the island.

Opposite: The Beit al-Ajaib, the House of Wonders, was built in 1883 as the Sultan's ceremonial palace. The clock tower was added after the bombardment of 1896. Today, the building is being converted into a museum.

THE MUSEUM IS THE IN-BETWEEN

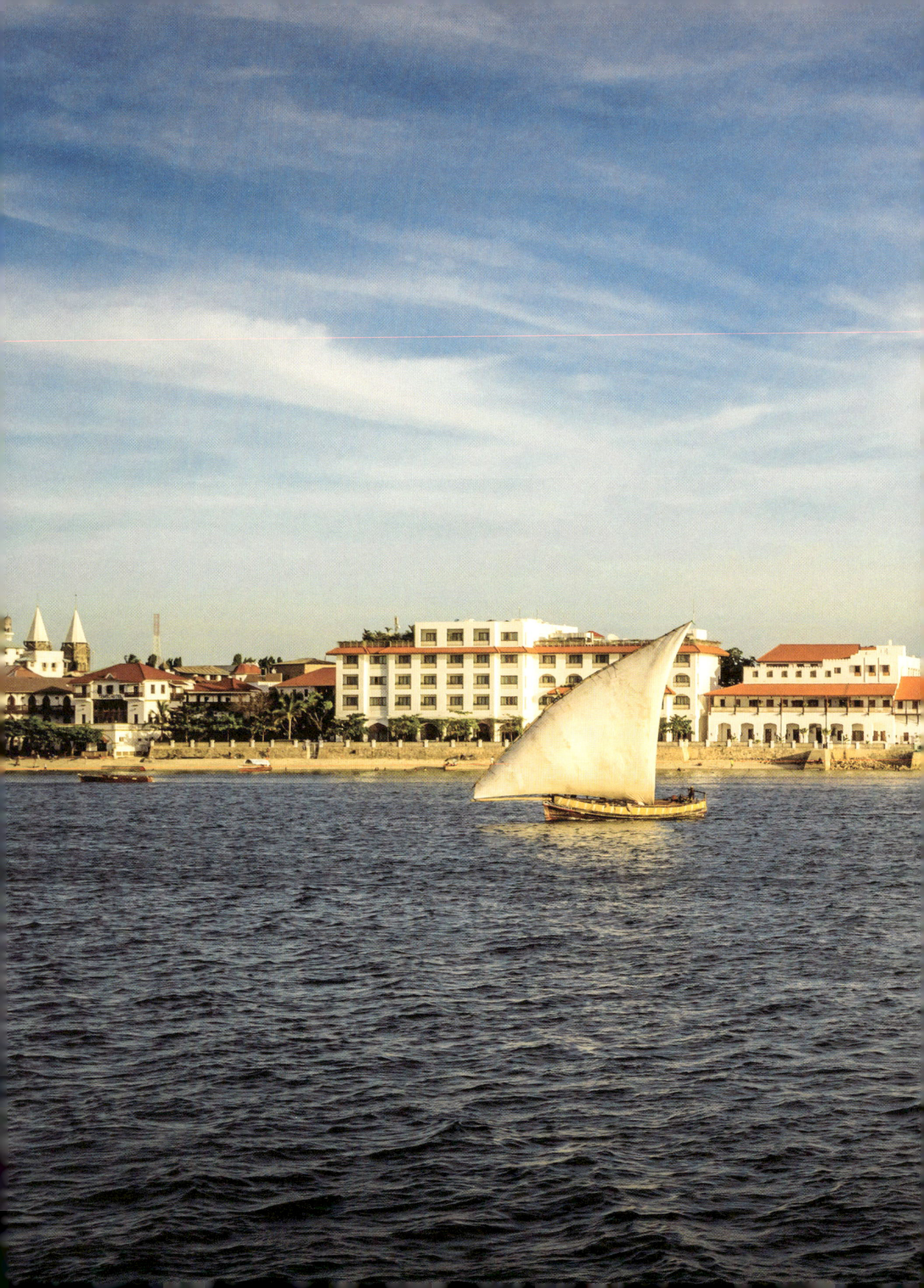

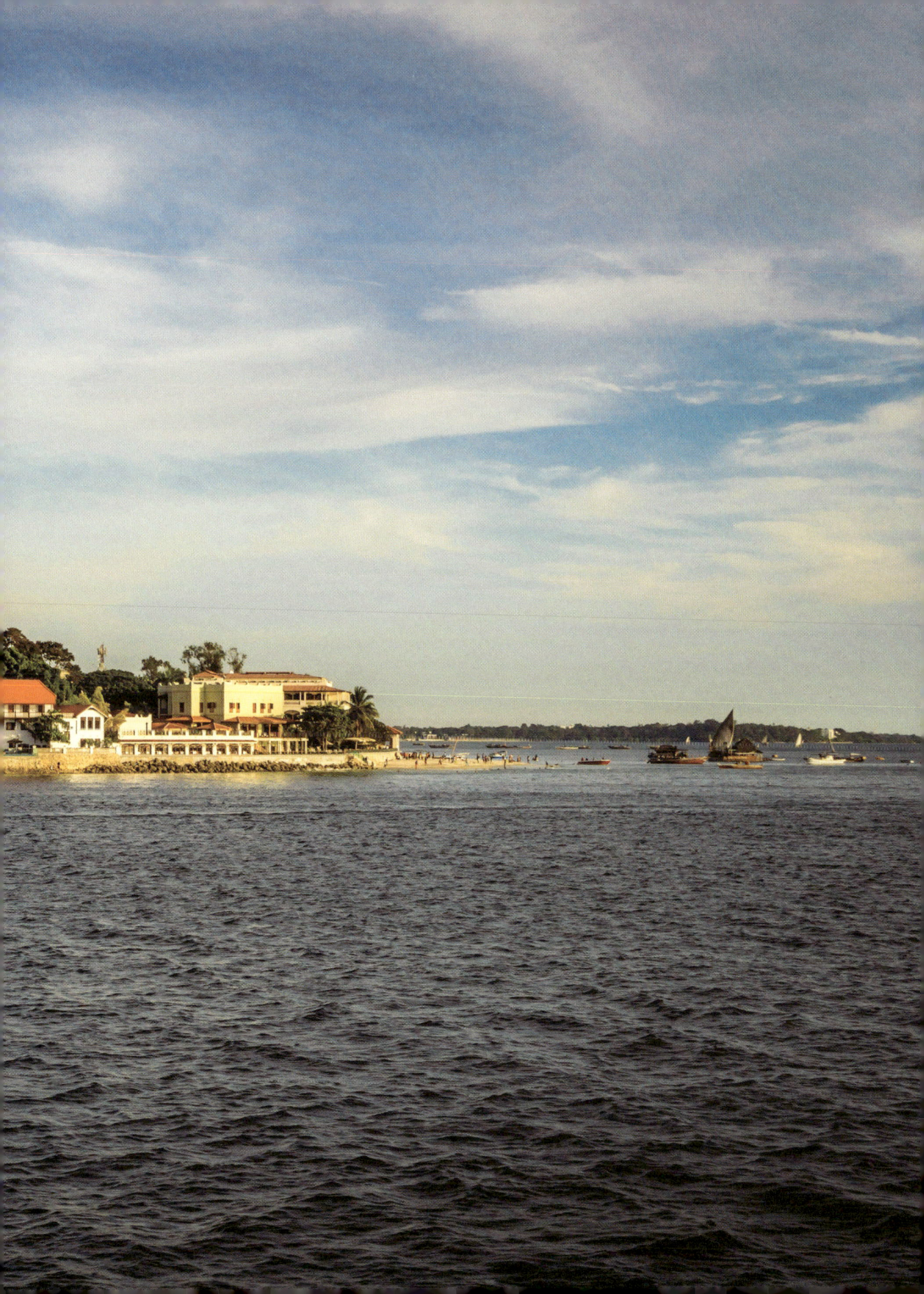

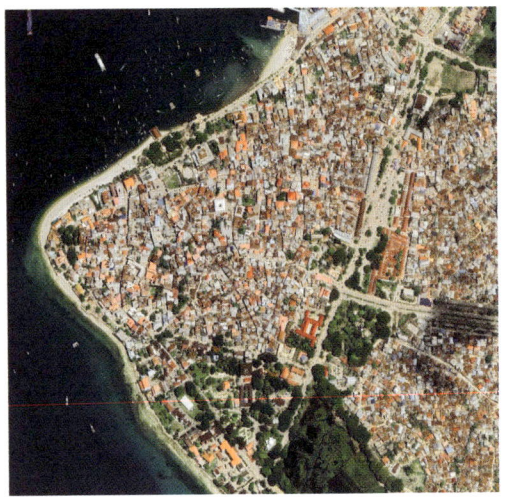
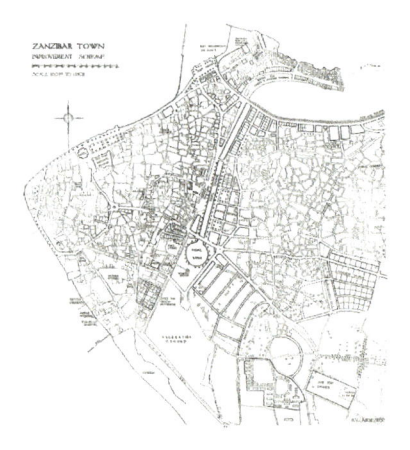
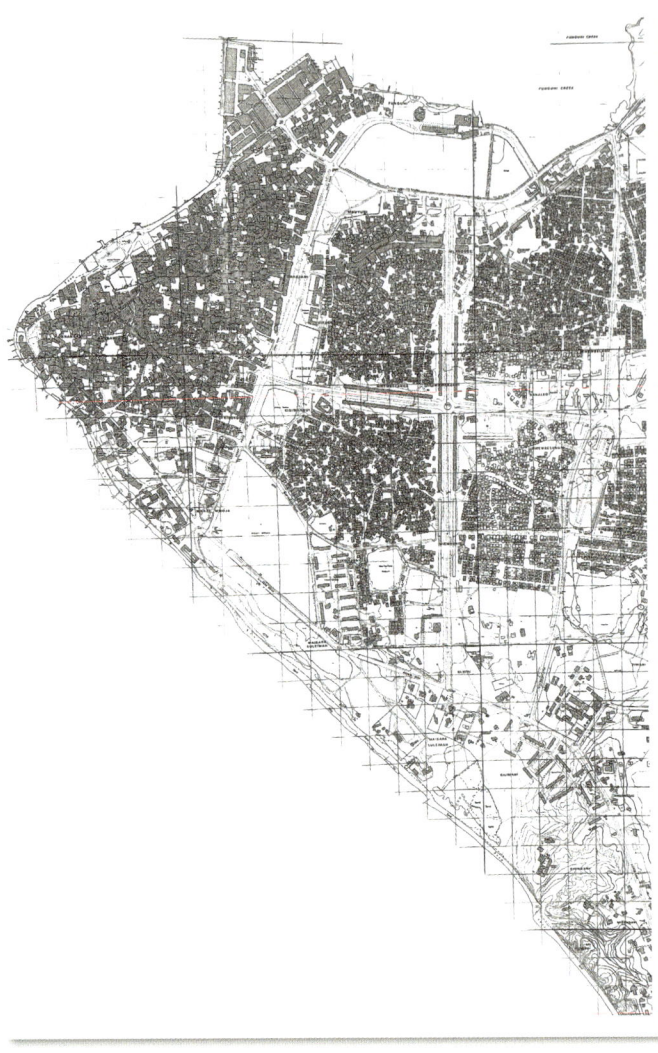

wrote the English town planner Henry Vaughan Lanchester in 1923. "Built as it is on spit of land jutting out into an azure sea, studded with green islets, and backed by verdant hills covered with waving palms, it should have no rival."[2] However, Zanzibar has another face: the neighborhood known as Ng'ambo, which emerged in the nineteenth and twentieth centuries on the other side of the creek. This creek originally constituted the natural geomorphological eastern boundary of the area, whereas to the North and South, its boundaries consist of the coast. What is now Benjamin Mkapa Road was at first a natural, eventually human-made separation of the historic city. Today, the city comprises two fragments of history, two distinct forms of urbanity, facing each other either side of Benjamin Mkapa Road: to the west, the World Heritage Site of Stone Town; to the east Ng'ambo—which literally means "the other side"—the historic home of the indigenous Swahili population, sometimes referred to as "the New City."

Zanzibar's history is one of constantly shifting sovereignty, and its identities are multiple. Long before it became part of Tanzania, the archipelago, located in the Indian Ocean off the East Coast of Africa, was home to several multi-ethnic merchant towns ruled over by a Muslim, Arabic-speaking elite connected

---

2. H. V. Lanchester, *Zanzibar: A Study in Tropical Town Planning* (Cheltenham: Burrow, 1923), 29.

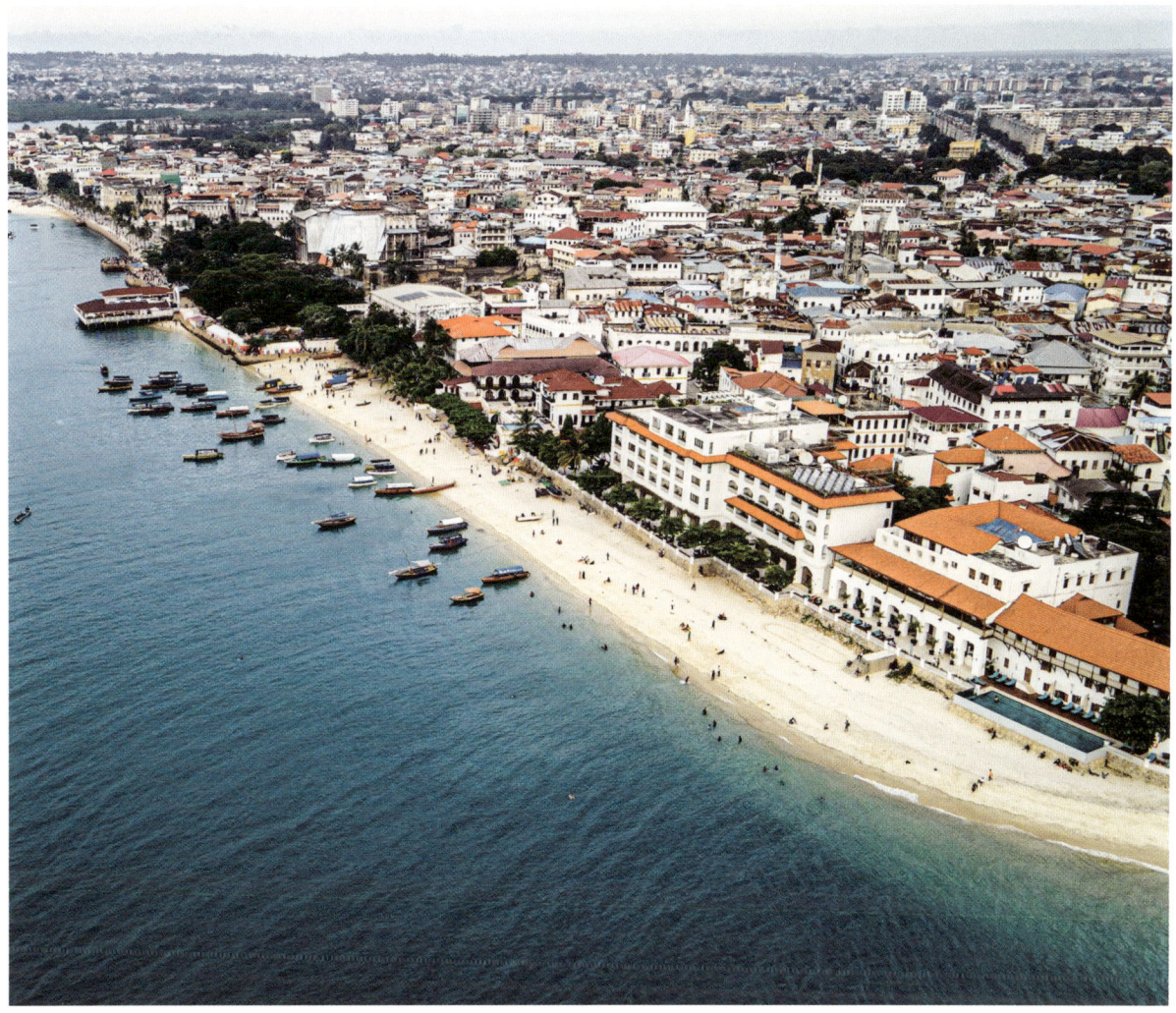

to international networks of trade. After first landing, in 1498, the Portuguese incorporated Zanzibar into their empire in the early sixteenth century, and remained there until the late seventeenth century, when local rulers called on Oman for help in driving them out. For the next century and a half, the archipelago was part of the Omani Empire until 1856, when the sultanate of Zanzibar separated from Muscat. In 1890, it came under British protectorate rule, gaining independence in late 1963. In January 1964, the majority Swahili and Shirazi population rose up against the ruling Arab minority; the sultan was overthrown, and in April of that same year, the archipelago merged with mainland Tanzania.

Page 131, above: As a strategic point along trading routes separating South Asia from the Middle East and Europe, Stone Town emerged as a dynamic commercial center, fought over by various colonial powers throughout the nineteenth century. **Bottom left:** Omani Sultan Sayyid Said, eager to promote trade on the island, is portrayed in the center of the first row in the photograph. Behind him is Tharia Topan, the man responsible for the Old Dispensary. **Bottom right:** A map of the western Indian Ocean with arrows indicating the direction of the trade winds that carried the large trading dhows back and forth between East Africa, Arabia, and India.

Previous pages: Today, Stone Town is the historic center of the city of Zanzibar, as well as the urban focus for the island and surrounding archipelago.

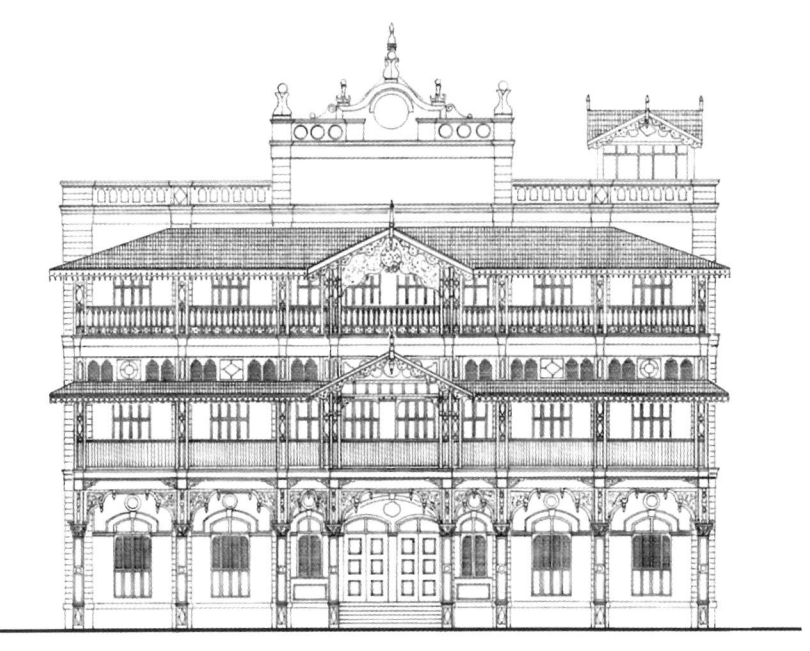

The unique cityscape of Stone Town represents an outstanding material manifestation of cultural fusion: a visible accumulation of overlapping traces from successive periods, each trace modifying and being modified by new additions. It is a palimpsest of multiple cultural layers brought in by diverse social groups over the centuries. This blending includes indigenous Swahili culture alongside influences from Arab, Persian, and Indian traders. While only a brick fort and a stone arch remain from the Portuguese presence, the architecture built during the Omani rule is still visible in the old part of Stone Town,[3] where courtyard houses supplanted earlier medieval Afro-Arab Swahili houses.[4] In parallel, Indian merchants developed the bazaar with its narrow streets of shophouses, while seafaring merchants built dwellings, docks, and warehouses on the waterfront. Additionally, several palaces built by the Omani remain, albeit in poor condition.[5]

During the British Protectorate, the administration established infrastructure and a strict system of building control, and large civic buildings, such as the Peace Memorial (J. H. Sinclair, 1925), began to appear.[6]

Ng'ambo, known as "the Other Side," grew to a size comparable to Stone Town itself, blending Arab, Swahili, Indian, Persian, Comorian, Goan, and Madagascan communities, including merchants, freed slaves, fishermen, and traders. A rich history of residential housing developed: communities made homes in a city that organically evolved into clusters of Swahili houses, common rectangular single-story residences with three to six rooms arranged around an axial corridor; Omani bayts, which are courtyard houses for the elite; and Indian dukas, shopfronts with living quarters above located in commercial alleyways. However, division along racial lines began to be imposed by colonial authorities

---

3. For a detailed study of the Omani period of architecture see Daniel Rhodes, Colin Breen, and Wes Forsythe, "Zanzibar: A Nineteenth-Century Landscape of the Omani Elite," *International Journal of Historical Archaeology*, vol. 19, no. 2 (June 2015), 334–55.
4. While contemporary Swahili houses are rare in Stone Town itself, they are the common residential type in the Ng'ambo area east of the town; in fact, all along the East African coast. For detail architectural study of the Omani houses in Stone Town in the nineteenth century, see Gerald Steyn, "An analysis of an Omani house in Stone Town, Zanzibar," *South African Journal of Art History* 16 (2001), 110–31.
5. Arthur Jasinski, "Colors of Stone Town in Zanzibar From White to black and back again," *Cities*, vol. 117 (October 2021).
6. For more details on civic buildings, such as the present day Zanzibar Museum, formerly the Peace Memorial, see Sarah Longair *Cracks in the Dome, Fractured Histories of Empire in the Zanzibar Museum, 1897–1964* (London: Routledge, 2020).

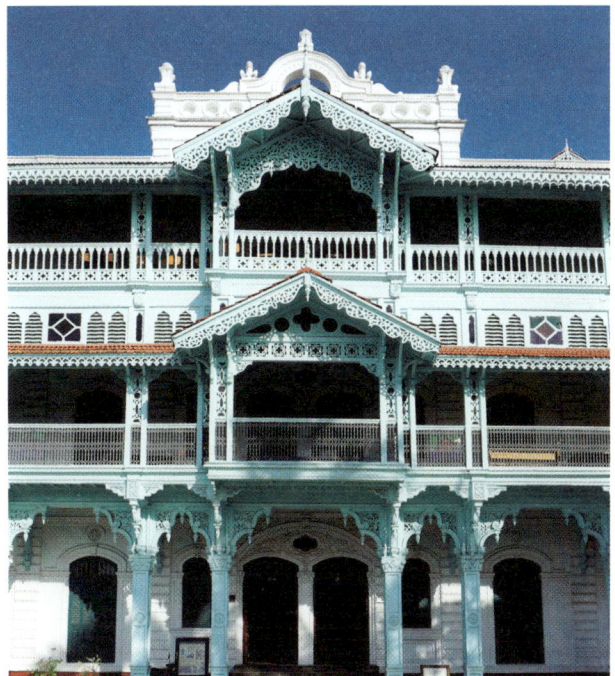 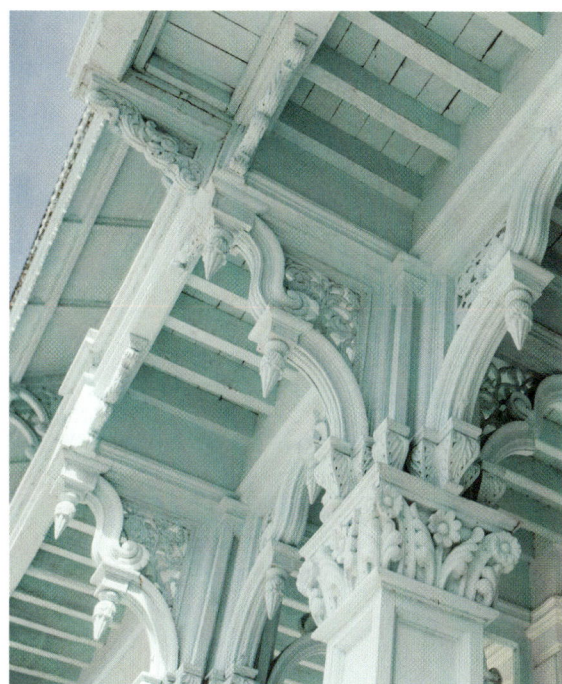

from the mid-eighteenth century onward, culminating in the 1930s with a system of racial segregation based on ethnic divisions among Africans, Arabs, Europeans, and Indians. This spatial divide can still be felt in today's city along the line of the creek.[7] After the revolution, which aimed to break with the colonial past, the new president, Abeid Amani Karume, decided to redevelop Ng'ambo as a modern socialist city with the help of East German building technology in the construction of roads, public buildings, workplaces, recreational parks, a centralized cemetery, and industrial areas. President Karume's vision, which sought to eliminate the racial divide, was only partially realized. The original master plan for Ng'ambo included the intention to construct more than 6,000 flats in approximately 200 buildings for around 30,000 people.[8] Between 1970 and 1973, more than a thousand flats, known as Michenzani flats, were built in the central part of Ng'ambo.[9]

---

7. Antoni Folkers, Iga Perzyna, Marie Morel, and Muhammad Juma Muhammad, *Ng'ambo Atlas,: Historic Urban Landscape of Zanzibar Town's "Other Side"* (Haarlem: LM Publishers, 2019).
8. Ludger Wimmelbücker, "Architecture and city," planning projects of the German Democratic Republic in Zanzibar, *The Journal of Architecture*, vol. 17, no. 3 (2012), 407–32.
9. Ibid.

Previous pages: The triangular shape of the former peninsula is clearly visible, separated from the main island by Creek Road which runs north from the Mnazi Mmoja playing fields to the swamp at Funguni.

Opposite and above: Isolated buildings in the UNESCO World Heritage city of Stone Town have benefited from preservation programs. In 1990, the Aga Khan Trust for Culture leased the Old Dispensary—formerly the Jubilee Hospital—from the government to restore this major landmark to its former splendor. Its design was based on Anglo-Indian motifs, and both the craftsmen responsible for the decoration and the timber were brought directly from India. The moldings and carved multistoried wooden balconies were highlighted in the modern restoration.

Following pages: Detail of the Old Dispensary, completed in 1894. The projecting double balcony with its carved posts and tracery bargeboards is the centerpiece of this elaborate building.

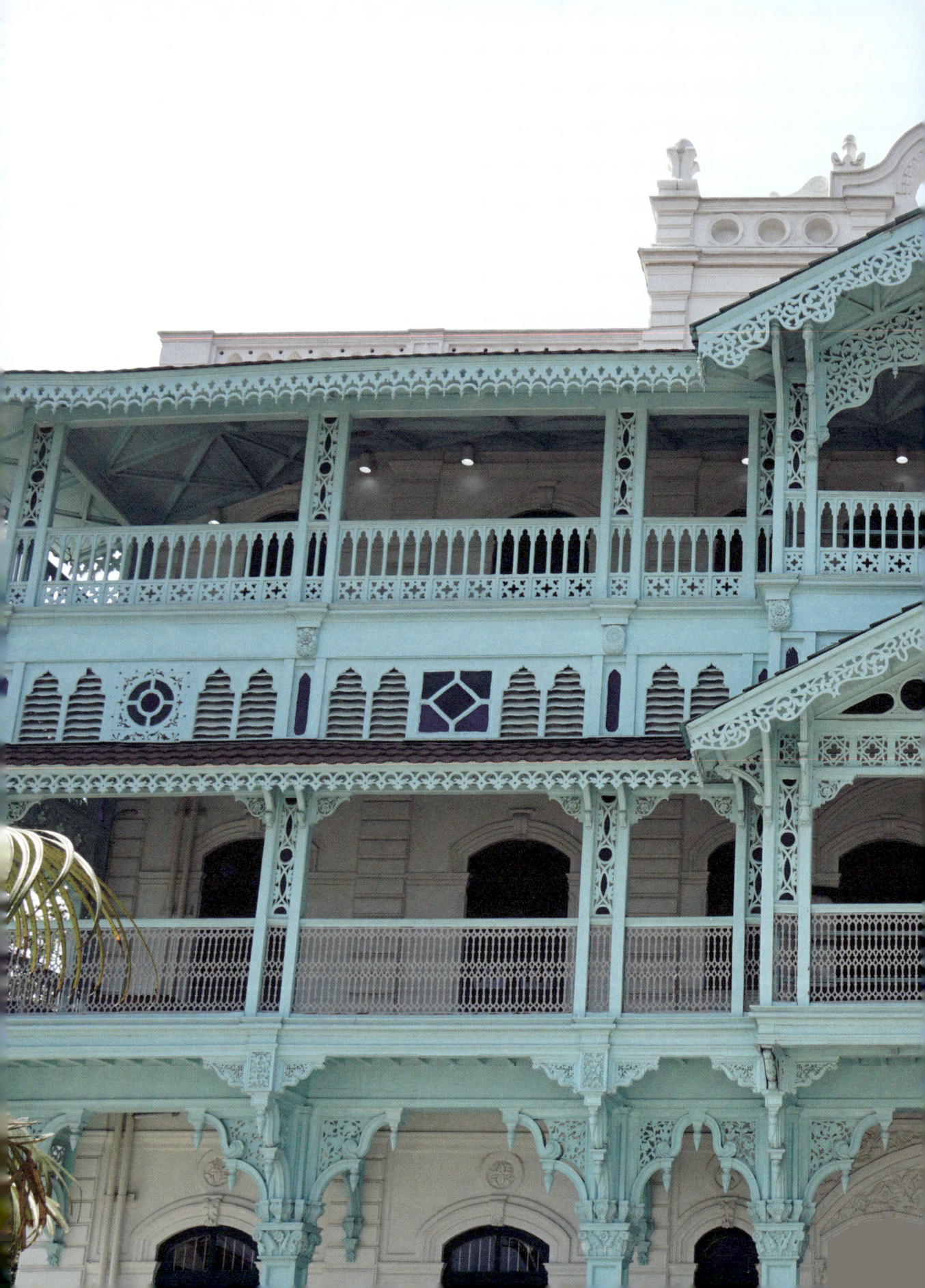

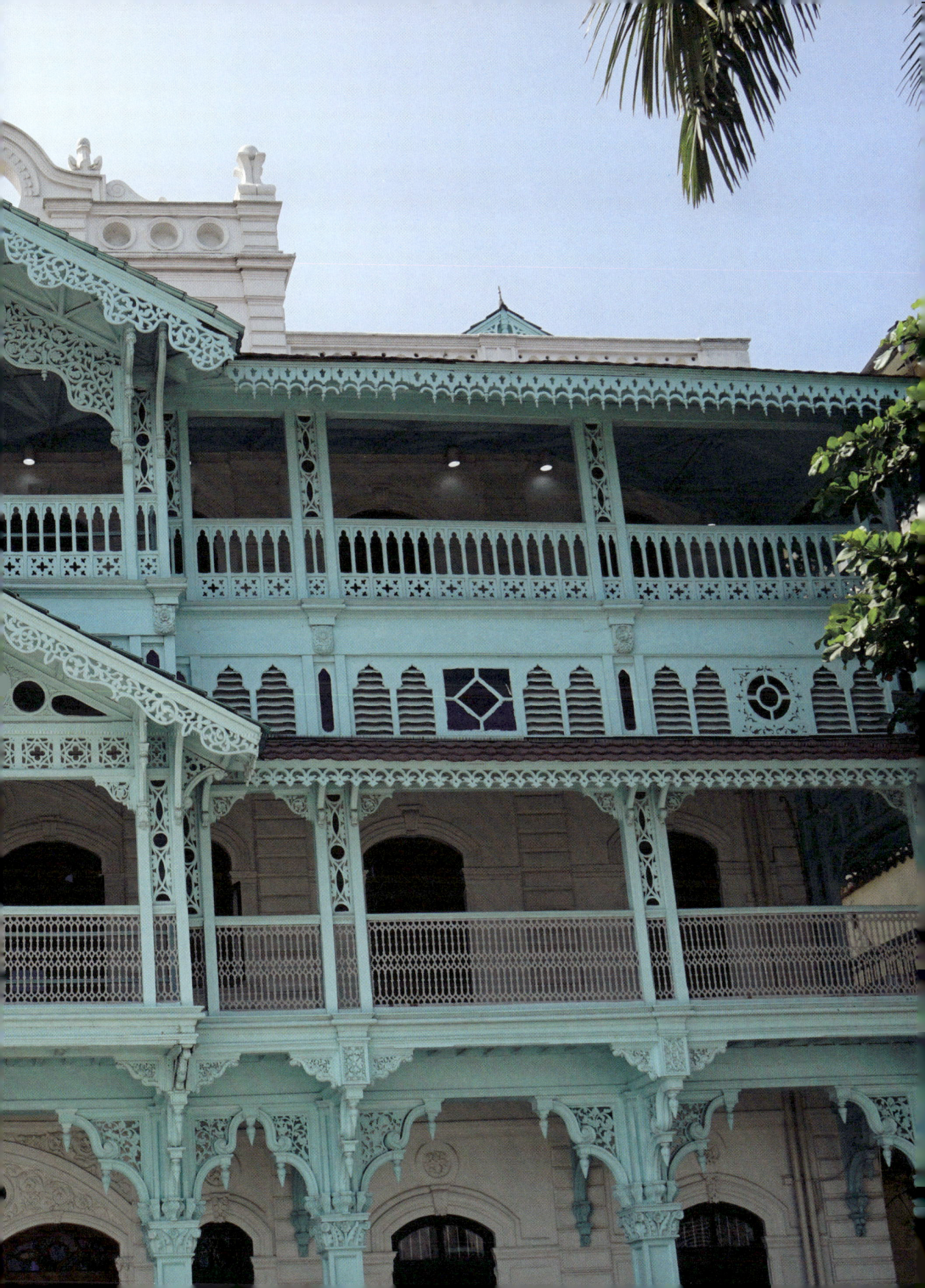

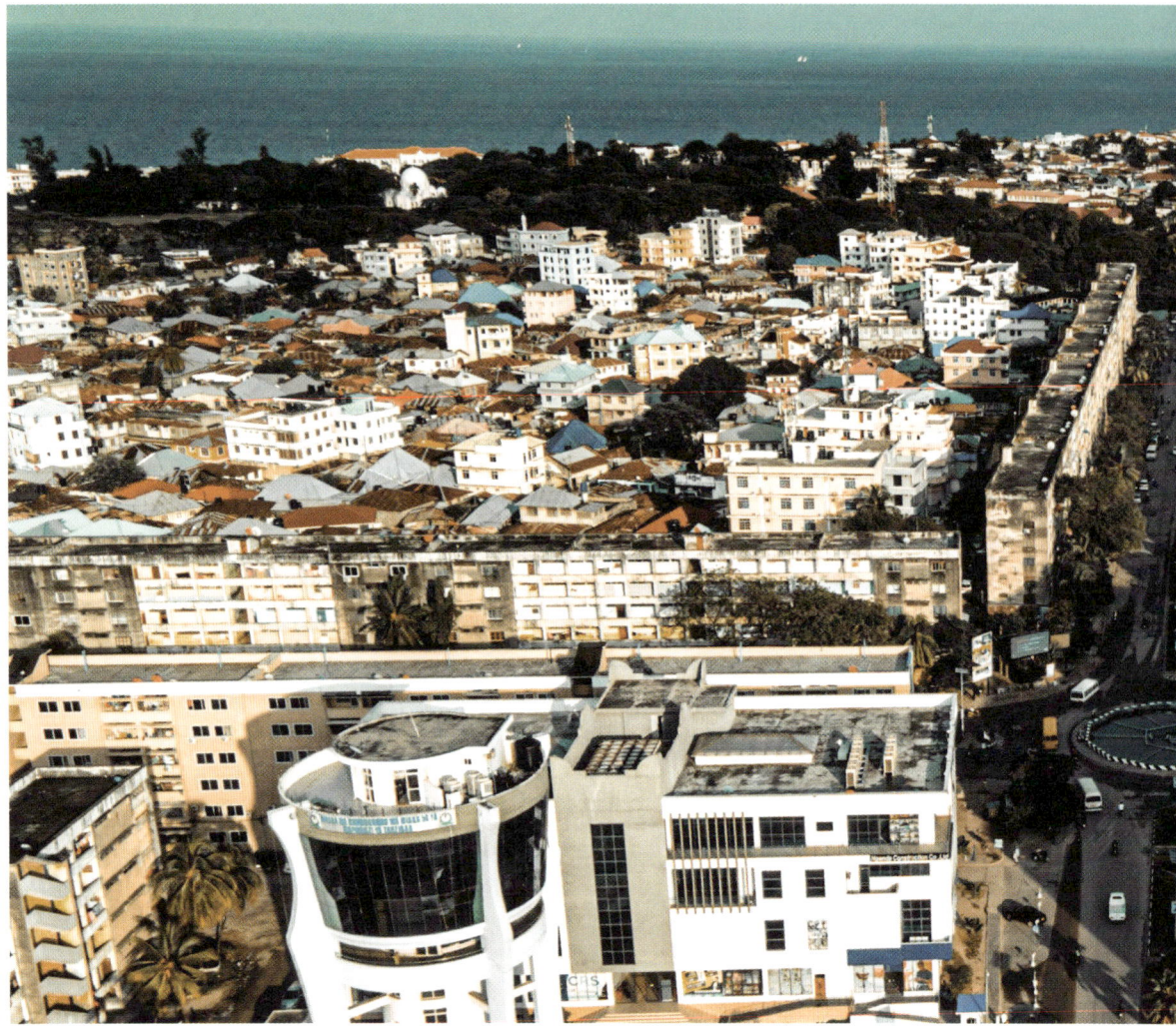

Highly standardized, with decent sized large apartments of about 1,076 square feet, the complex symbolizes the ambition of a revolutionary regime triumphing over the inequalities of the colonial past—an attempt to redefine modernity. Middle- and low-income families still reside in these complexes today, known as "the Trains." Constructed in an X shape, the complex stands in clear historical opposition to the preserved part of Stone Town across Creek Road.

In 2000, UNESCO recognized Stone Town as a World Heritage Site, a designation that transforms it into a form of an open-air museum.[10] This recognition symbolizes a moment in time, the departure of the British from Zanzibar, and marks the "building up" of Stone Town as having been "completed" by the first quarter of the twentieth century. With the UNESCO label, an invisible veil has been cast over the historic city: since nothing may now change, history has become fixed and flattened. Past modernities are denied any future. Paradoxically, its preservation, in the name of history and beauty, halts the very mechanisms

---

10. Stefano Bianca and Francesco Siravo, *Zanzibar: A Plan for the Historic Stone Town* (Geneva: Aga Khan Trust for Culture, 1996). This publication, which followed the Aga Khan Conservation Management Plan of the same year, has played a pivotal role in preserving the colonial legacy of the region.

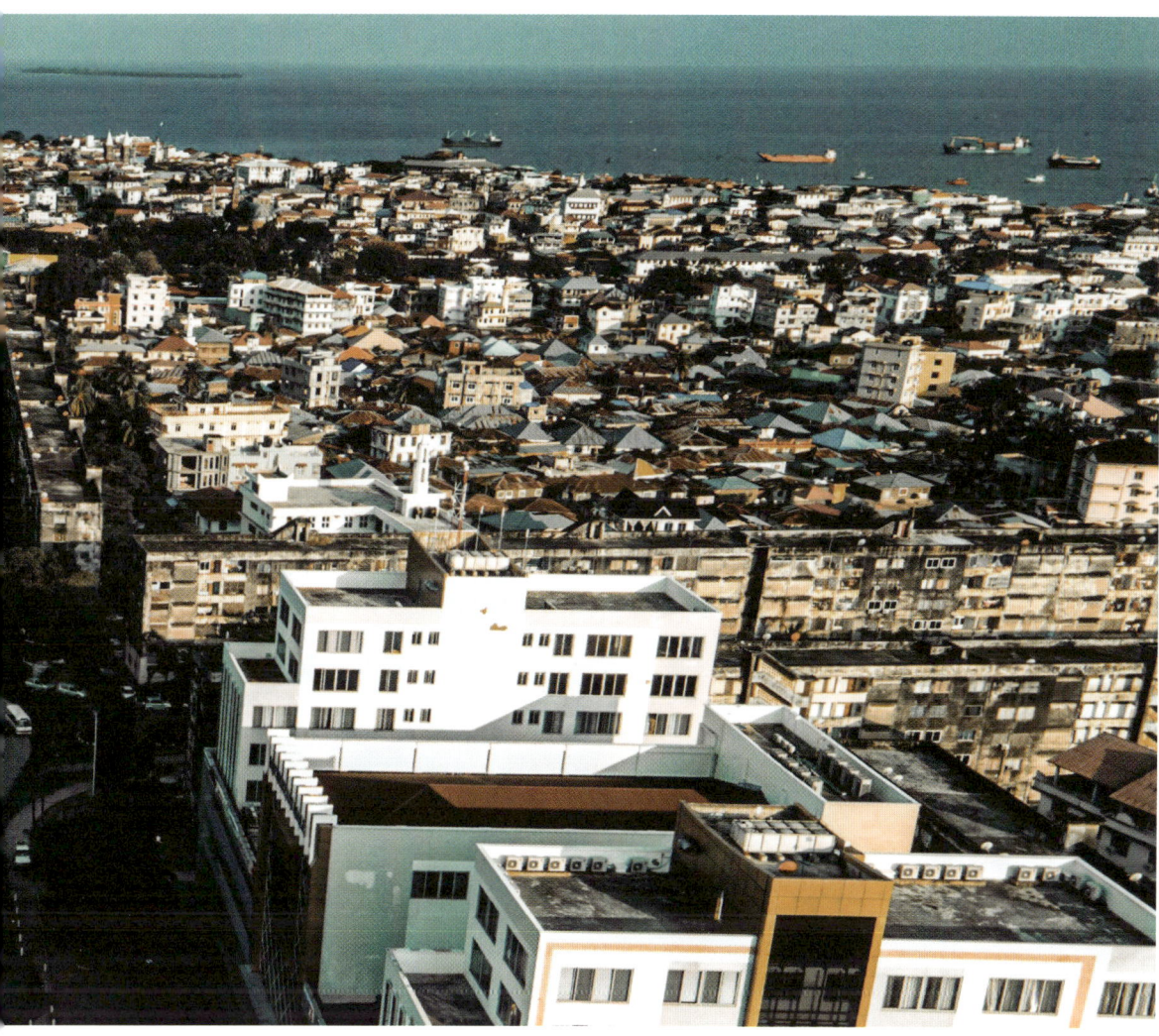

that made this outstanding example of human culture possible in the first place, which is to say its infinite adding of different material culture over time.

Moreover, the UNESCO designation focuses solely on the colonial history on one side of the creek. Two narratives of the past—one recognized by UNESCO, and the other excluded from preservation discourse—exist side by side, representing the colonial fabrication of a dual city, one that turned the creek, a natural barrier, into a social and racial divide. While UNESCO-inspired initiatives have contributed significantly to the preservation of Stone Town, the distinct experiences and residential heritage

Above and following pages: The social modernist housing projects known as the Michenzani, built after independence, are left out of any preservation program yet stand out as a symbol of the ambition of the Independence regime triumphing over inequalities of the colonial past. The massive arrangement of housing in a row owed to this part of town being nicknamed of "the Trains."

Pages 144–145: View of Ng'ambo from the Michenzani, showing the sloped metal roofs of the single-story Swahili houses below. The details of the doors of the houses in the colonial part of Stone Town reveal the Indian influences in the architecture.

Pages 146–147: The twin spires of St. Joseph's cathedral, built by the Roman Catholic mission from 1896 to 1899. The design of this French Neo-Romanesque church was influenced by the school of Leon Vaudoyer, an important architect active in France during the Second Empire.

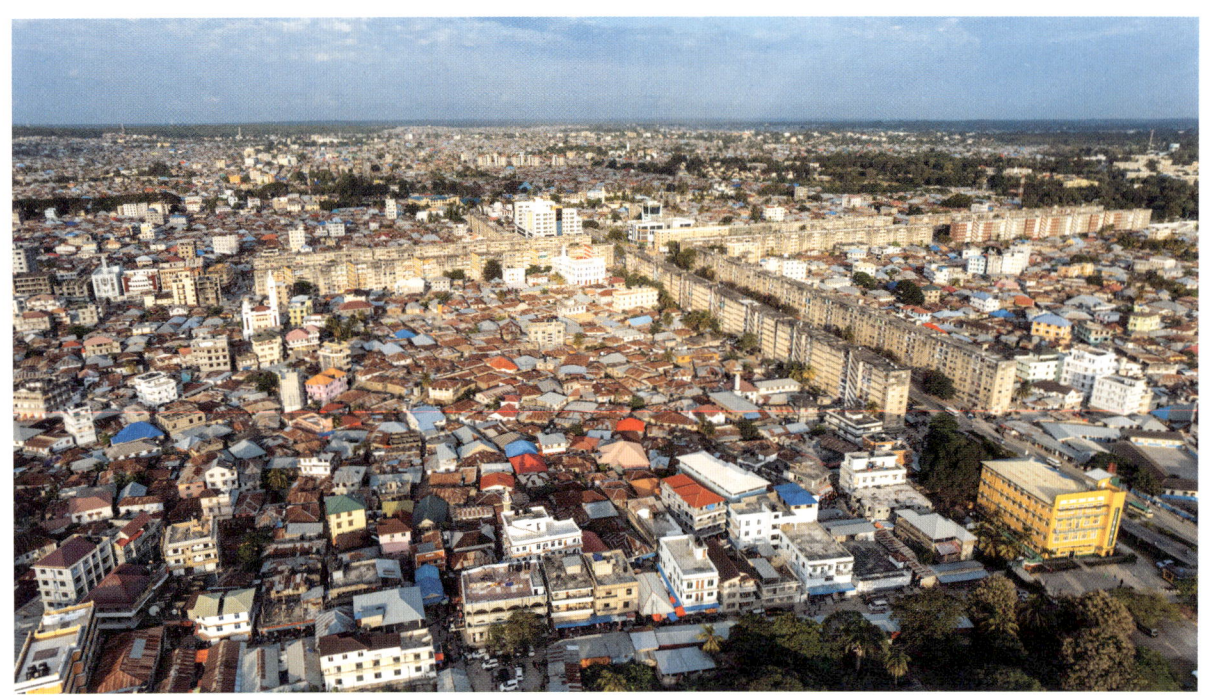

of both indigenous forms of life and subsequent modernist developments remain under-explored and are considered a separate history.[11] Benjamin Mkapa Road now serves as the threshold between three different forms of urbanism: a colonial seat of power, an organic vernacular town, and a modernist megaproject undertaken in the name of emancipation. The interstitial space of this creek-made road becomes the site of viewing within a museum-city that preserves the memory of past urban forms.

Zanzibar is a microcosm of the twentieth century: at once a history of architecture and, today, a history of architectural preservation. Standing on Creek Road and, crossing to either side represents a symbolic decision to explore a record of architecture emblematic of contrasting periods and ideologies—a colonial past, whose architectural fate has been the object of preservation initiatives, and its more recent socialist modernist post-independence opposition. It is at this former stream-made road, that one is exposed to the juxtaposition of these scenes, facing the reckoning of the existence of former concepts of cities that were adopted, rejected, and made absolute by the spaces that are not only in between the two but are the places of their viewing. In this museum-city, one experiences the realization of the city as the past object of architecture.

Entire fragments of landscapes, built up on past ideas of cities, are undoing the preservation process or are prevented from development due to strict conservation guidelines. In this sense, preservation, such as that represented by the UNESCO World Heritage designation, can be thought of as a planetary geopolitical curatorial project, where past urban forms expressed in architecture are prioritized over others through preservation. Symbolically, the artworks of this planet-scale museum collection of cities are the buildings themselves, laid out on a map of the globe. Preservation singles them out as exhibitions of past cities.

---

11. Antoni Folkers, Iga Perzyna, Marie Morel, and Muhammad Juma Muhammad, *Ng'ambo Atlas: Historic Urban Landscape of Zanzibar Town's "Other Side"* (Haarlem: LM Publishers, 2019). Despite being the most comprehensive recent study of Ng'ambo, the book paradoxically reinforces the binary between the "two sides" of Zanzibar City. A unified study of both is currently being led by a team under architect Aziza Chaouni at the University of Toronto's Daniels Faculty of Architecture, initiated by the Conservation Authority in 2023.

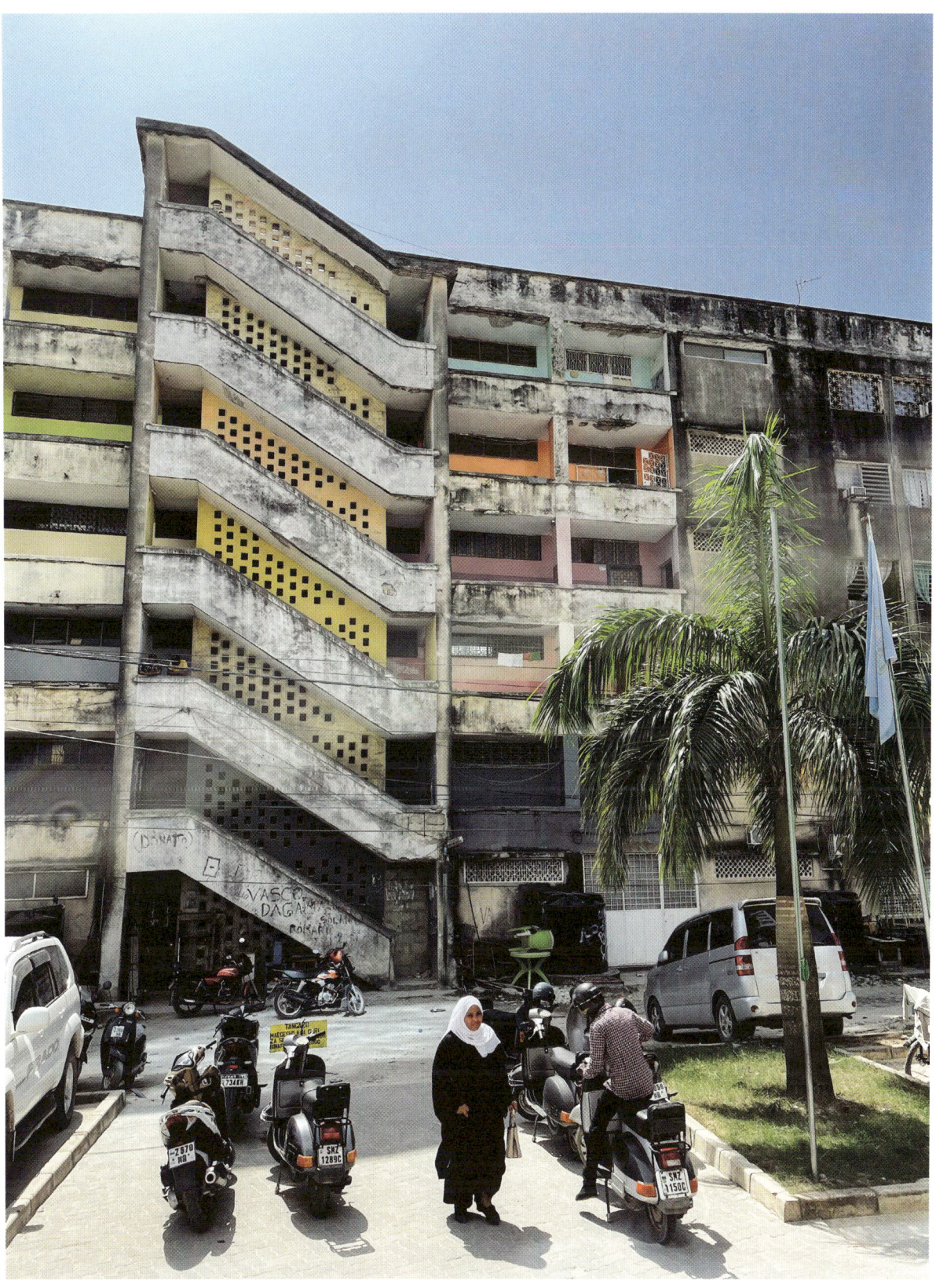

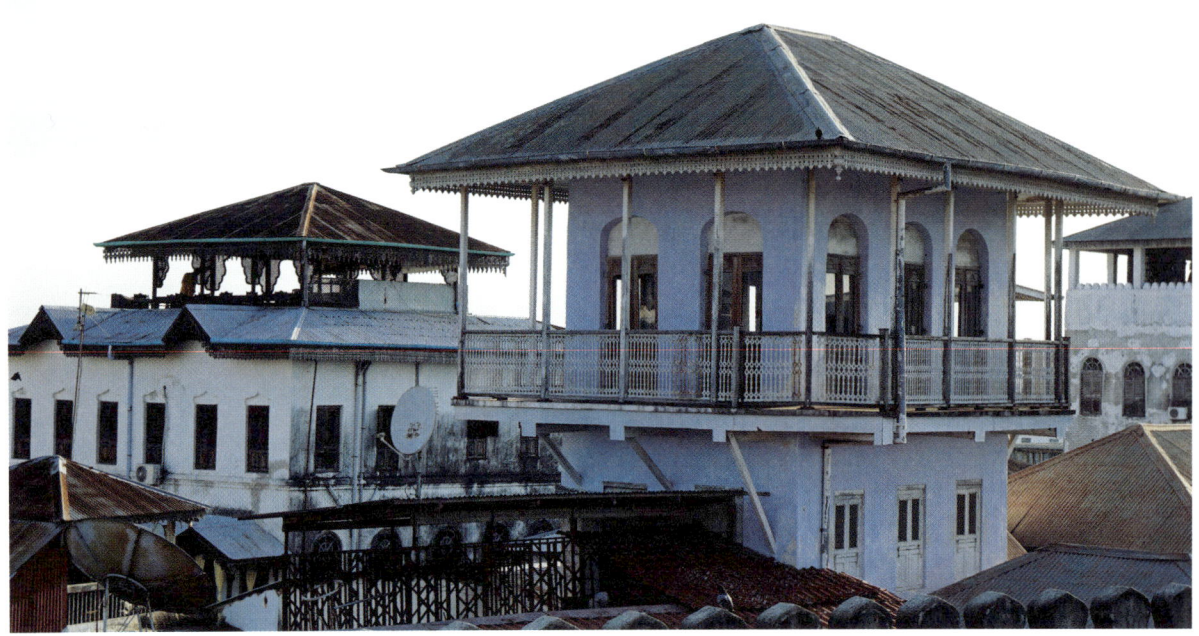

The history of Zanzibar and its preservation can be understood as a planetary sampling of a contemporary global phenomenon. Indeed, planet earth is a palimpsest of various layers of cities. If we consider that the city has extended to every corner of the globe, the example of Zanzibar is relevant as it represents issues of preservation that can be examined on a planetary scale. While we may like to think we live and work in cities, with "nature" lying beyond an imaginary wall at the end of the urban zone, in fact both land and cities are designed, making urbanity ubiquitous across the globe. Architecture has always been central to this process. In its most contemporary form, the museum's new task should be to identify spaces where it is possible to recognize our planetary urban condition and formulate avenues for a preservation methodology that balances different notions of what can be considered "heritage" across time.

The museum is arguably complicit in designating the city as the only worthy terrain for architecture's attention, preventing the recognition of the artificial divide that exists between the city and "nature" which reflects our globalized urban condition.[12] Indeed, this is particularly evident in the "Bilbao effect"—the naïve belief that a museum, enhanced by important or notable architecture, has the power to elevate a place's status or name a city. This collusion between the museum—symbolizing culture—and the instrumentalization of spectacular architecture has exacerbated our forgetfulness that what is not recognized as nature is not necessarily untouched by architecture or undesigned. Indeed, what is not acknowledged as the image of the city is not necessarily "nature" or "wilderness," is simply not the accepted "image" of a city.[13]

---

12. This divide has been repeatedly challenged by the discipline of landscape, most recently by James Corner and Charles Waldheim. Rem Koolhaas addressed this oversight architectural practice in the 2021 New York Guggenheim exhibition *Countryside: The Future*. By highlighting that architecture had historically focused on the city, Koolhaas sought to draw attention to the countryside. However, his emphasis on two distinct categories inadvertently reinforced the divide between the artificial and the wild.
13. It is useful to think of these spaces in the terms defined by Gilles Clement vis-à-vis landscape studies. The influential French landscape designer developed the notion of "friche," whereby landscape can be understood as a third space between the artificial and the wild, a space that, despite its potential, is marginalized by architecture on an urban scale. See Gilles Clement, *Manifeste du Tiers Paysage* (Paris: Éditions du Commun, 2020; first published in 2003).

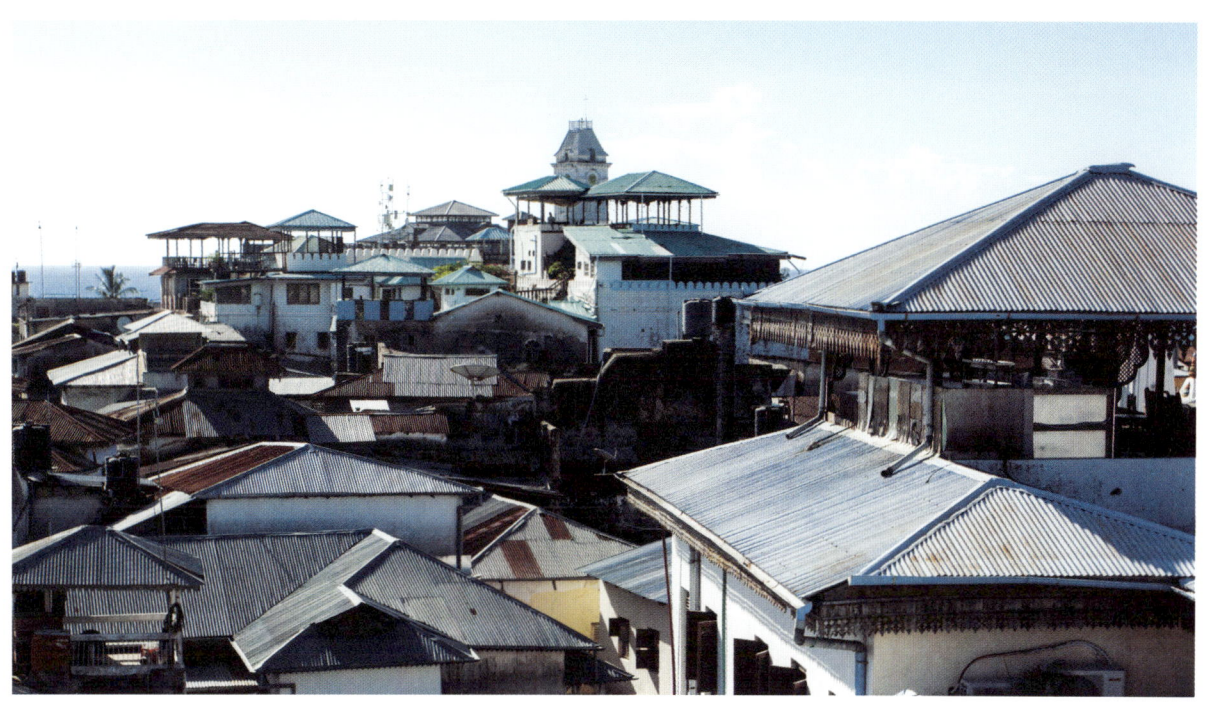

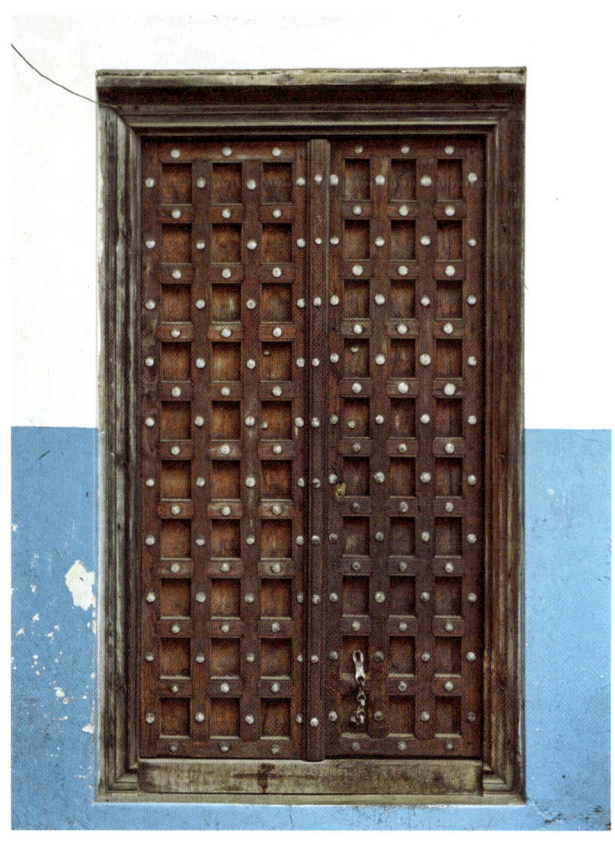

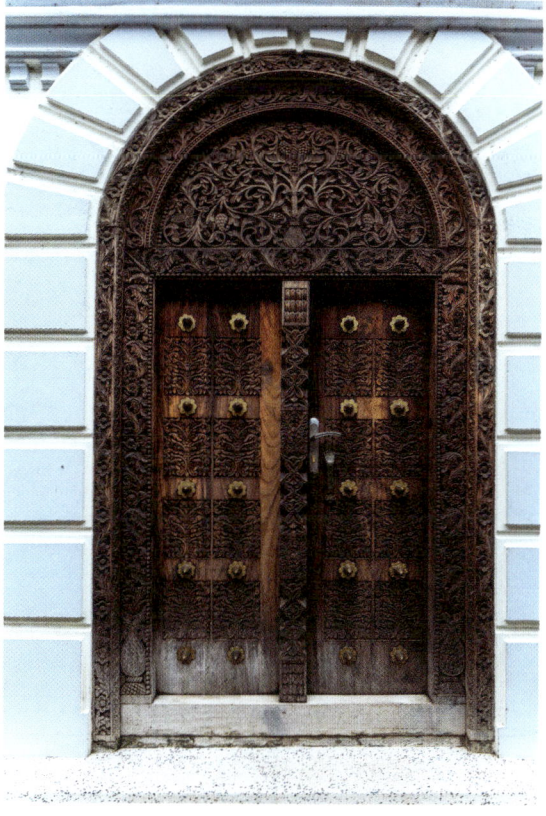

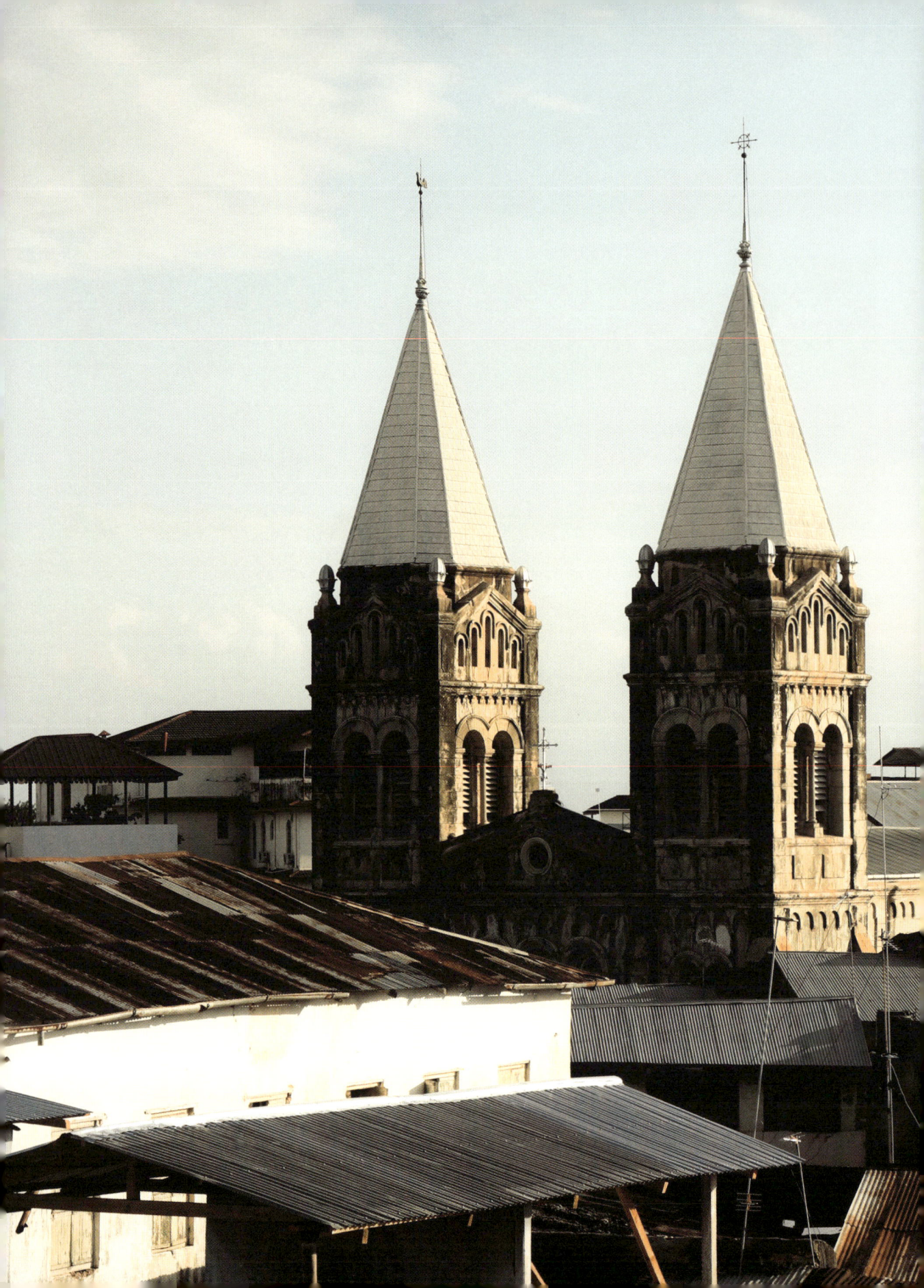

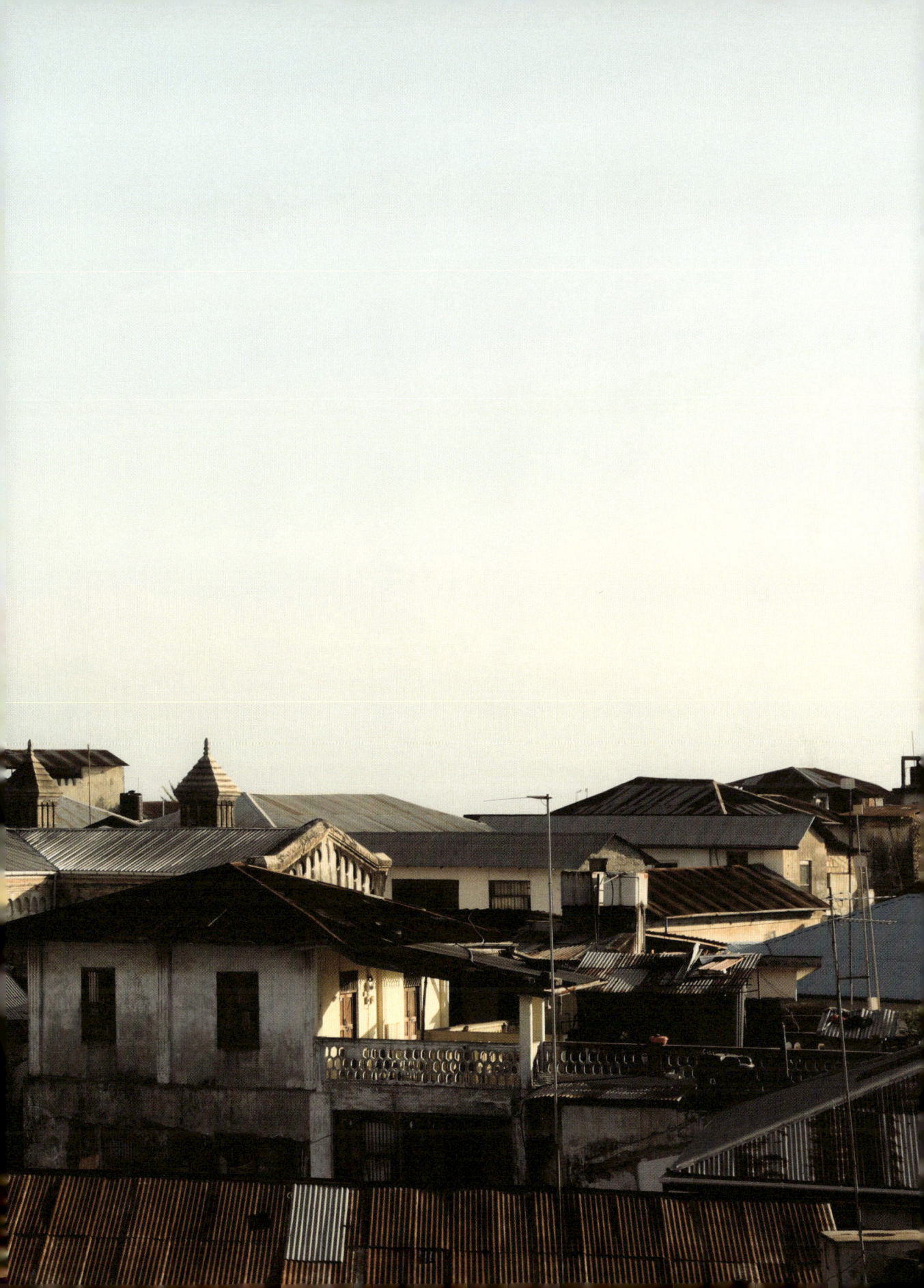

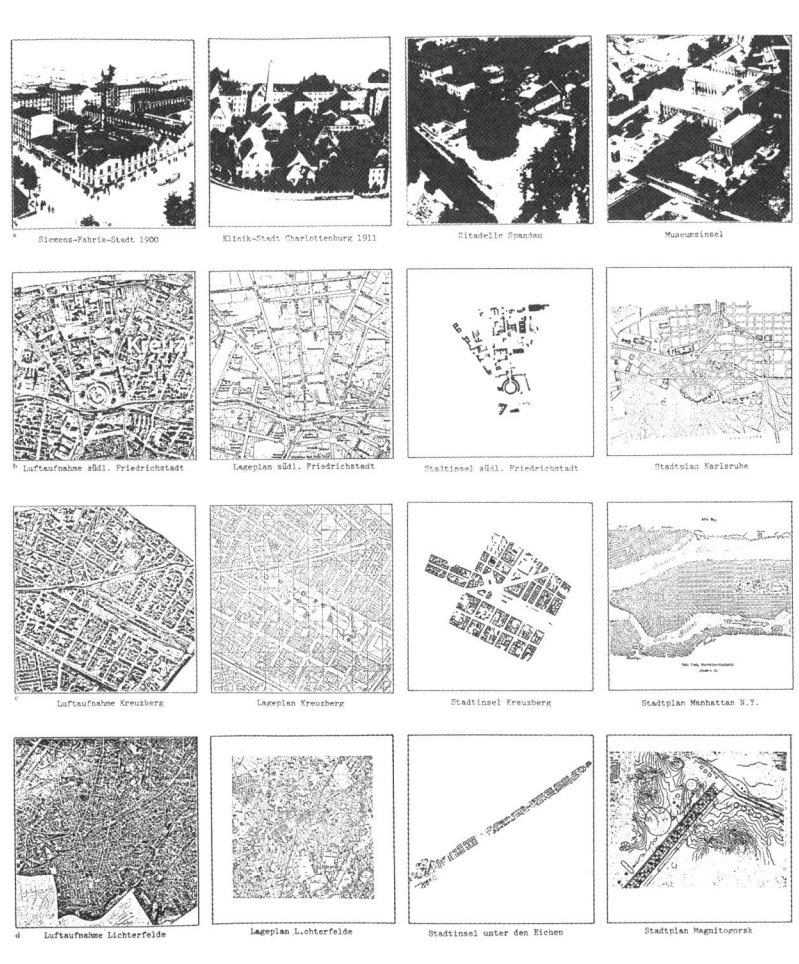

Rem Koolhaas understood this planetary urban reality early on, as outlined in his seminal study on Manhattan in 1972, a speculative project he called City of the Captive Globe, in which he imagined Manhattan as a museum, with each city block representing an avant-garde architectural movement supposedly incompatible with one another.[14] The UNESCO World Heritage designation can be seen as a collection that spans the globe, its landscape composed of city-museums, each symbolic of past and often contradictory urban ambitions: Ahmedabad, Athens, Bordeaux, Brasilia, Chandigarh, Paris, Zanzibar, etc. While these city-museums form a sort of archipelago around the globe, it remains crucial to acknowledge that the spaces in between—the

---

14. Koolhaas, Delirious New York. This idea is also present in the manifesto The City in the City—Berlin: A Green Archipelago which Koolhaas co-wrote with the Oswald Mathias Ungers, Peter Riemann, Hans Kollhoff, and Arthur Ovaska. They develop this idea in relation to postwar Berlin in their 1977. They suggested that a city comprising an archipelago of past cities and their interrelated zones could be a place of anticipatory action: instead of large-scale urban planning, such a conglomerate would operate at the level of the micro-city. As the founding partner of architecture firm OMA, Koolhaas further developed this idea of the surrounding voids as counter-forms in the office's 1987 Ville Nouvelle Melun-Sénart plan, which proposed an "archipelago of residue." Oswald Mathias Ungers, Rem Koolhaas, The City in the City—Berlin: A Green Archipelago (Zürich: Lars Müller Publishers, 1977).

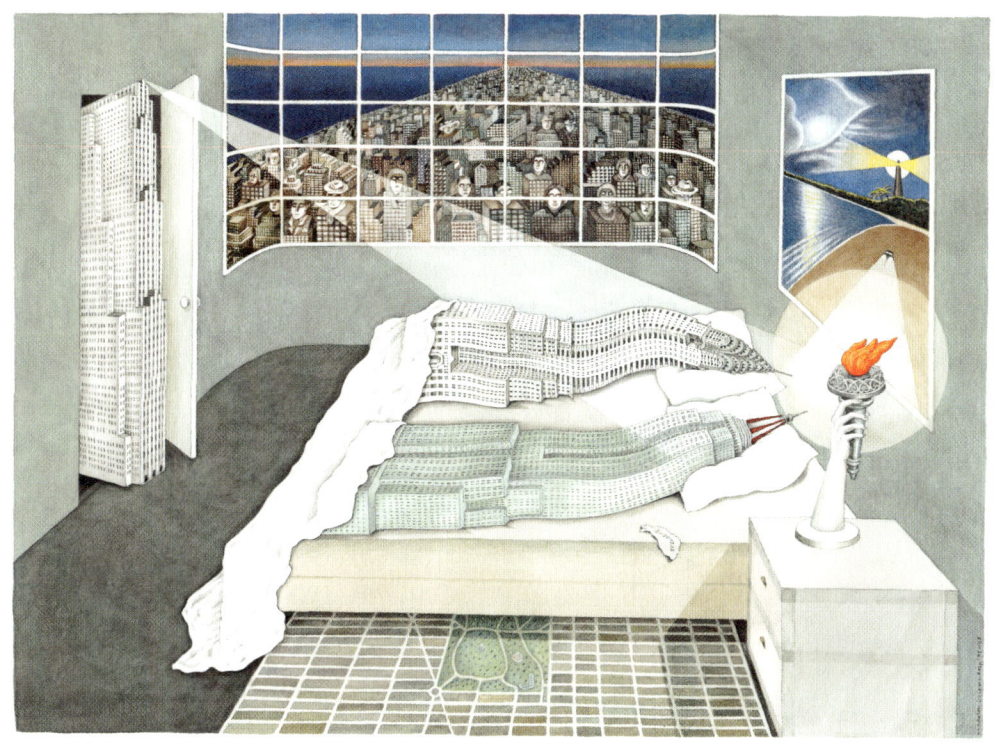

spaces of infinite urbanization—are where the actualization and self-consciousness of the modern city occur.

Already, in 1955, German architect Ludwig Mies van der Rohe wrote, "There are in fact no cities anymore. It goes on like a forest." This sentence was the opening of the groundbreaking book *Landscape As Urbanism* written by Charles Waldheim.[15] In this book, the landscape architect and Professor at the Harvard School of Graduate Studies, advocated for the absolute integration of landscape within the categories of twentieth-century

---

15. Charles Waldheim, *Landscape As Urbanism: A General Theory* (Princeton, NJ: on University Press, 2016).

Opposite: In *The City in the City*, Rem Koolhaas and Oswald Ungers suggest that a city can be an archipelago of different forms of urbanism interspersed with green areas.

Above and following page, left: The illustrations of Madelon Vriesendorp for Rem Koolhaas's *Delirious New York: A Retroactive Manifesto for Manhattan*, show how each block of the city is a microcosmic representation of a theory of urbanization.

Following page, right: The Seagram Building is recessed from Park Avenue, giving way to a large plaza, which make it stands out like a jewel in Manhattan's grid.

THE MUSEUM IS THE IN-BETWEEN

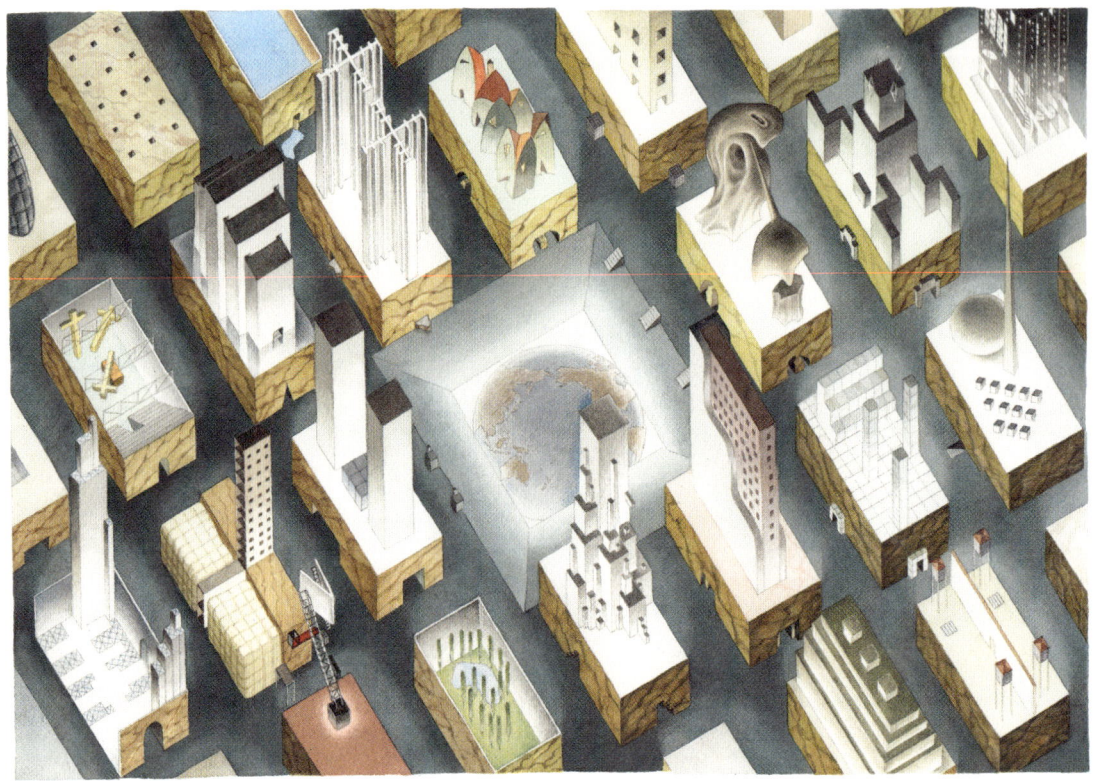

urbanism.¹⁶ Mies van der Rohe perhaps most eloquently illustrated this condition at New York's Seagram building, which, like a UNESCO World Heritage Site, stands apart from the surrounding urbanity on a metaphorical pedestal. The space that separates the Seagram building from the rest of the city is what makes this vision possible—this is the place of the museum, just as the interstices between points on UNESCO maps represent the generic never-ending city.

In its most contemporary form, the architecture of the museum allows for the acknowledgment of our planetary urban condition. We visit it to see and understand the past forms architecture has given to the city, actualizing the anticipation of its new understandings of its terrain. In Stone Town, Benjamin Mkapa Road is our contemporary museum-to-be. Standing at this intersection, the original natural enabler of the different iterations of Zanzibar City lies below our feet, its ecological antecedent and simultaneous condition. The revelation of this fact in the form of a museum illuminates essential ideas for the future of architectural culture.

---

16. In so doing, Mies van der Rohe prolonged the Italian radicals' insight into the never-ending city like Superstudio's Continuous Monument or Archizoom's No-Stop City.

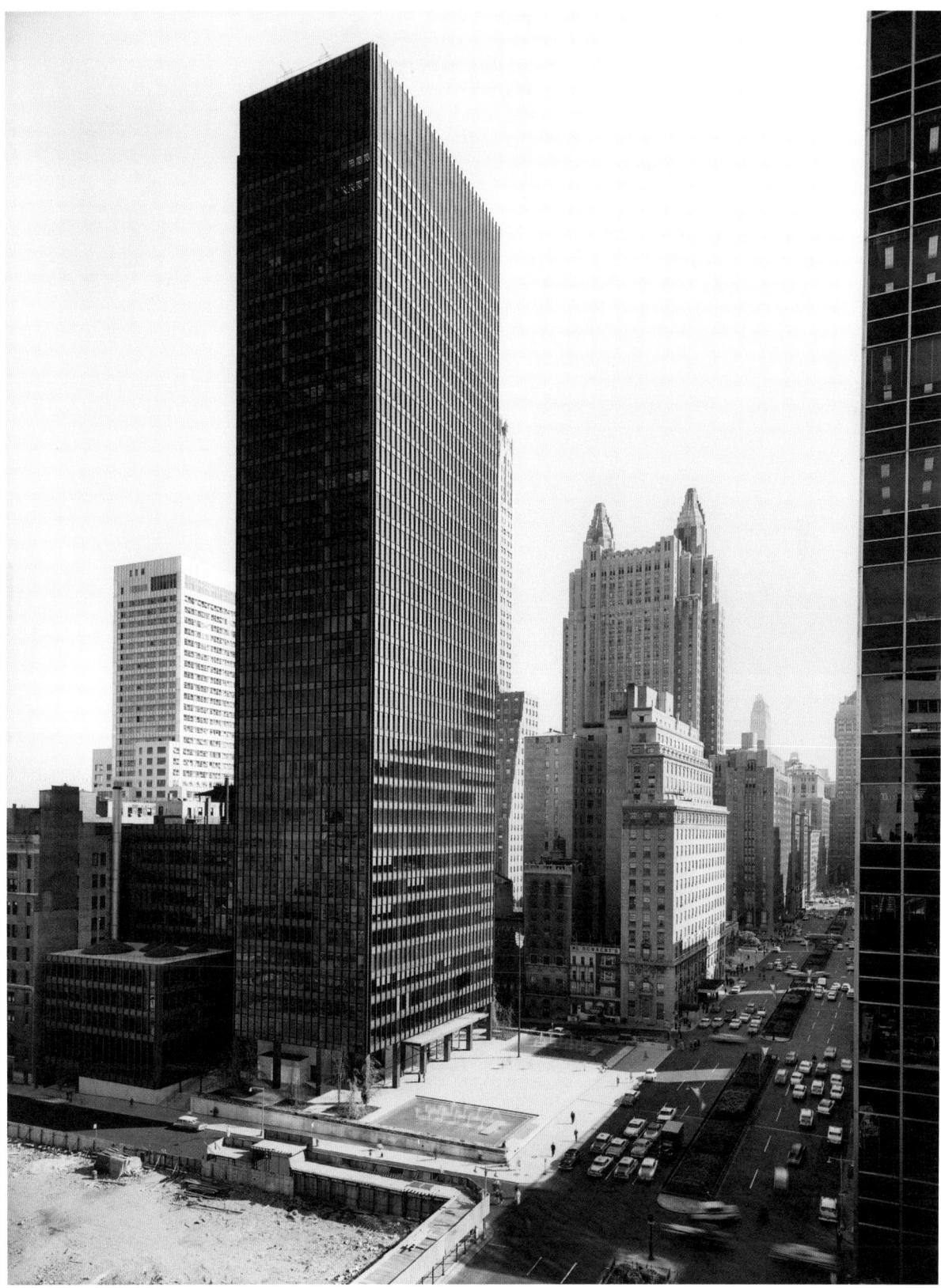

THE MUSEUM IS THE IN-BETWEEN

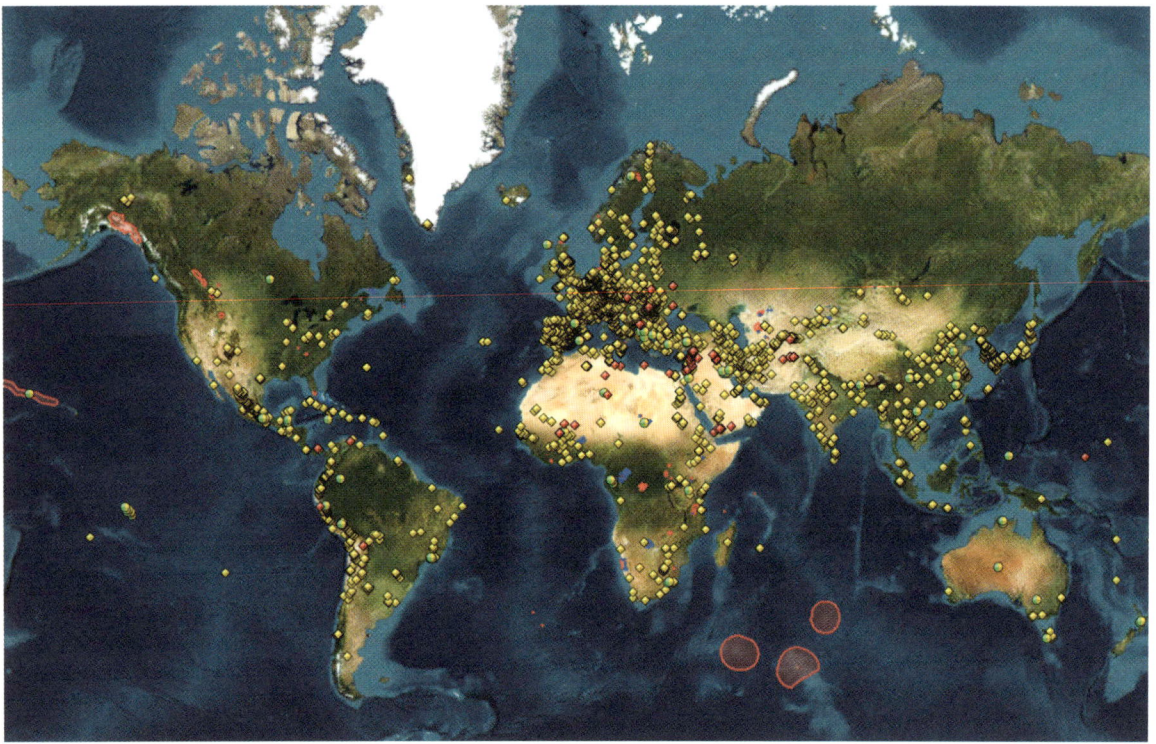

Category of property
- Cultural
- Natural
- Mixed

Property inscribed on the List of World Heritage in Danger
- Cultural
- Natural
- Mixed

On one hand, it frees a presupposed divide between the city and nature from a historical standpoint, enacting the acknowledgment of a planetary urban condition. On the other hand, it allows the coexistence of different architectural notions of cities as legitimate propositions, thereby surpassing the biases of preservation.

The significance of imagining Benjamin Mkapa Road as a museum resides in its potential to critique the limited notion of preservation while actively challenging the existing canon of global architecture in the twentieth century. If we make the space of transition—the road, the bridge, the river—the space of the museum, we can transform the institution into a place where the fleeting nature of things is revealed, the process of constant change becomes apparent, and our expectation of culture is transformed from being possibly finite.

Above: The places of human cultural significance revealed by the UNESCO World Heritage Sites Map can be seen, as a museum collection for the world.

Opposite: Zanzibar's historic facades reveal details that contrast sharply with Ng'ambo's modern Michenzani housing blocks.

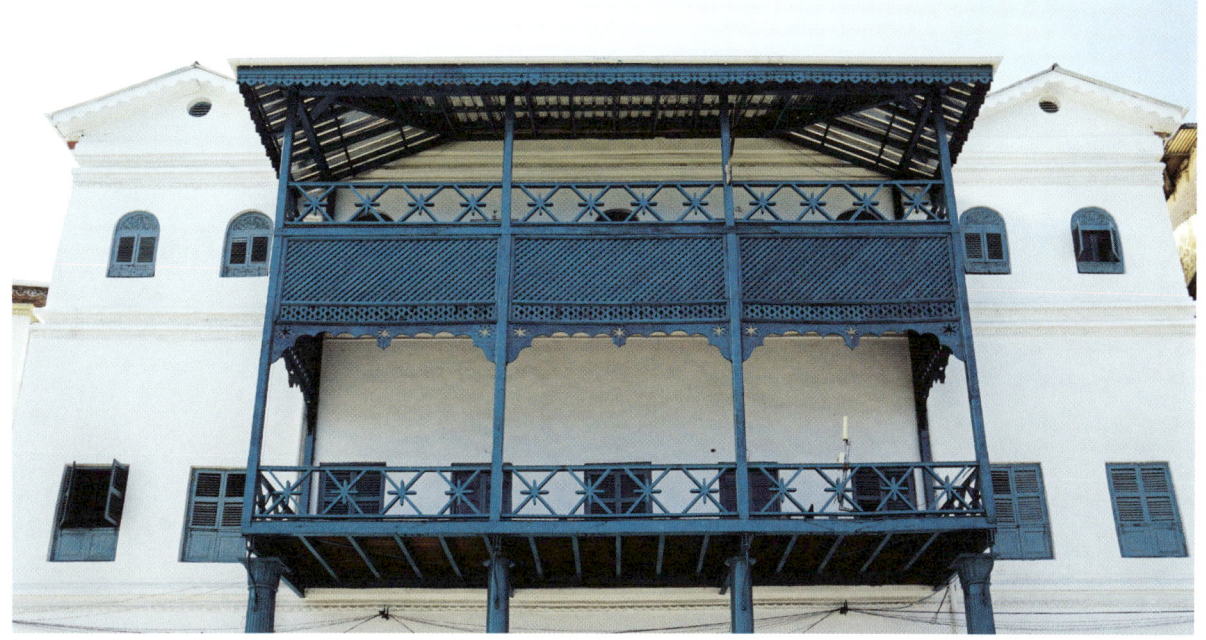

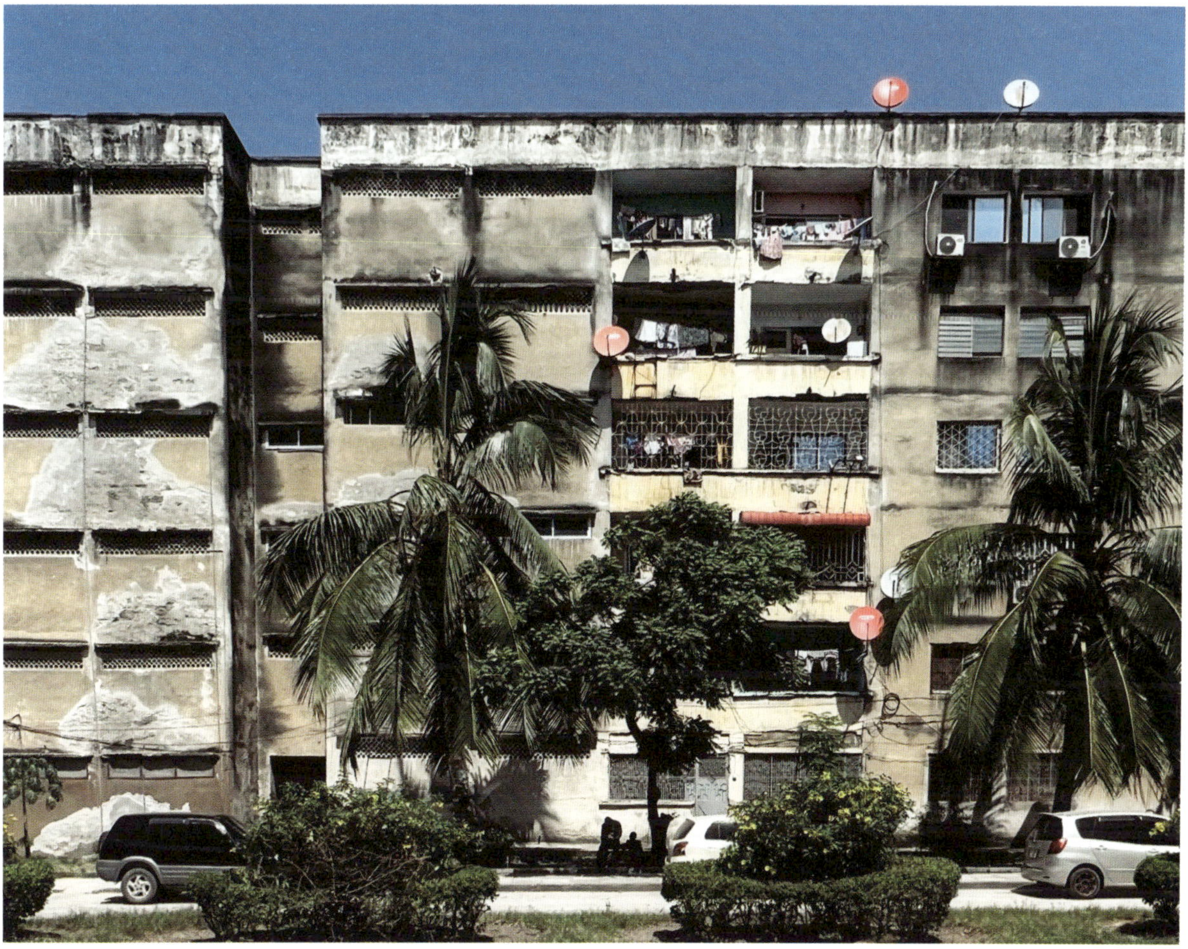

THE MUSEUM IS THE IN-BETWEEN

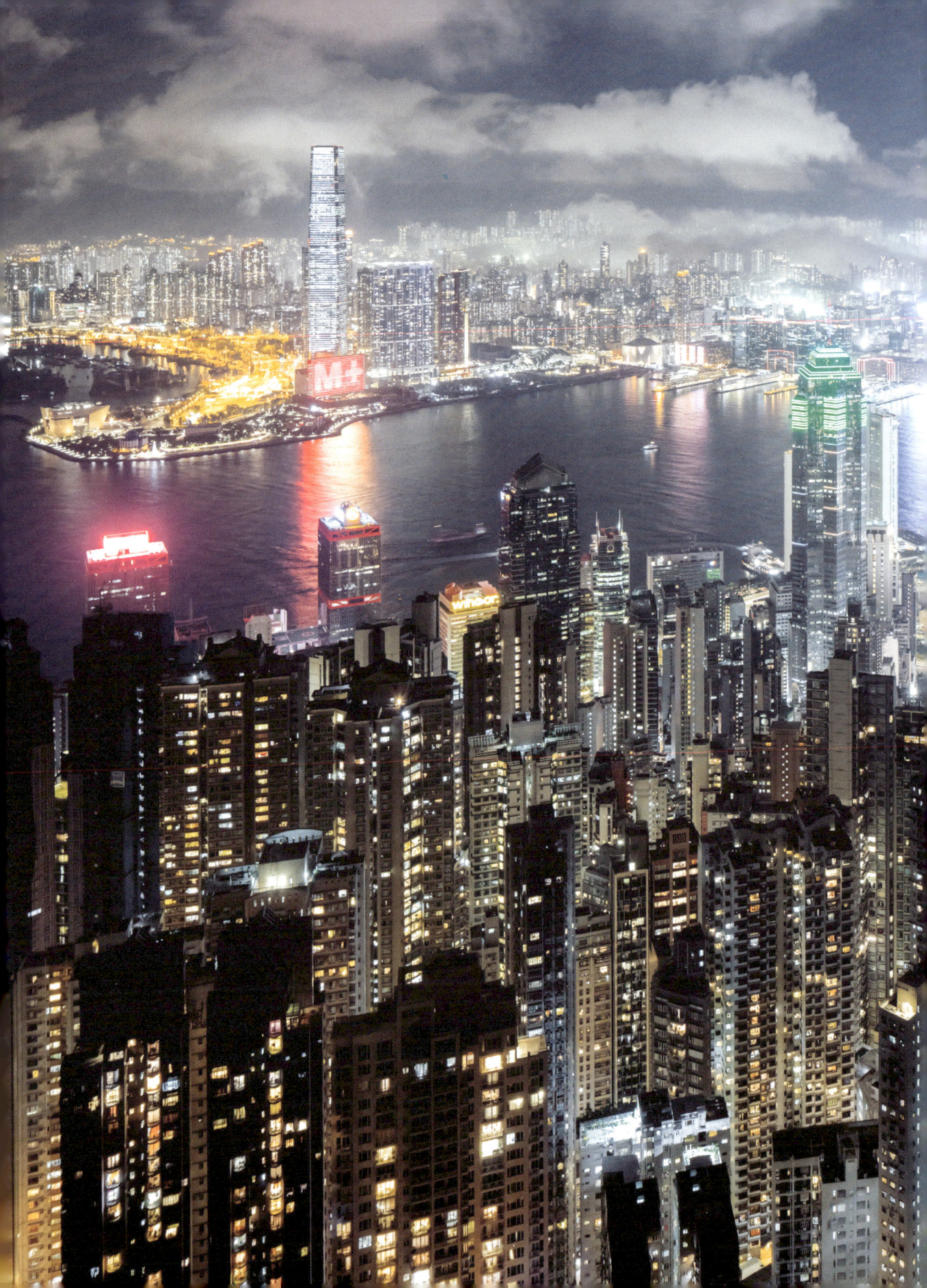

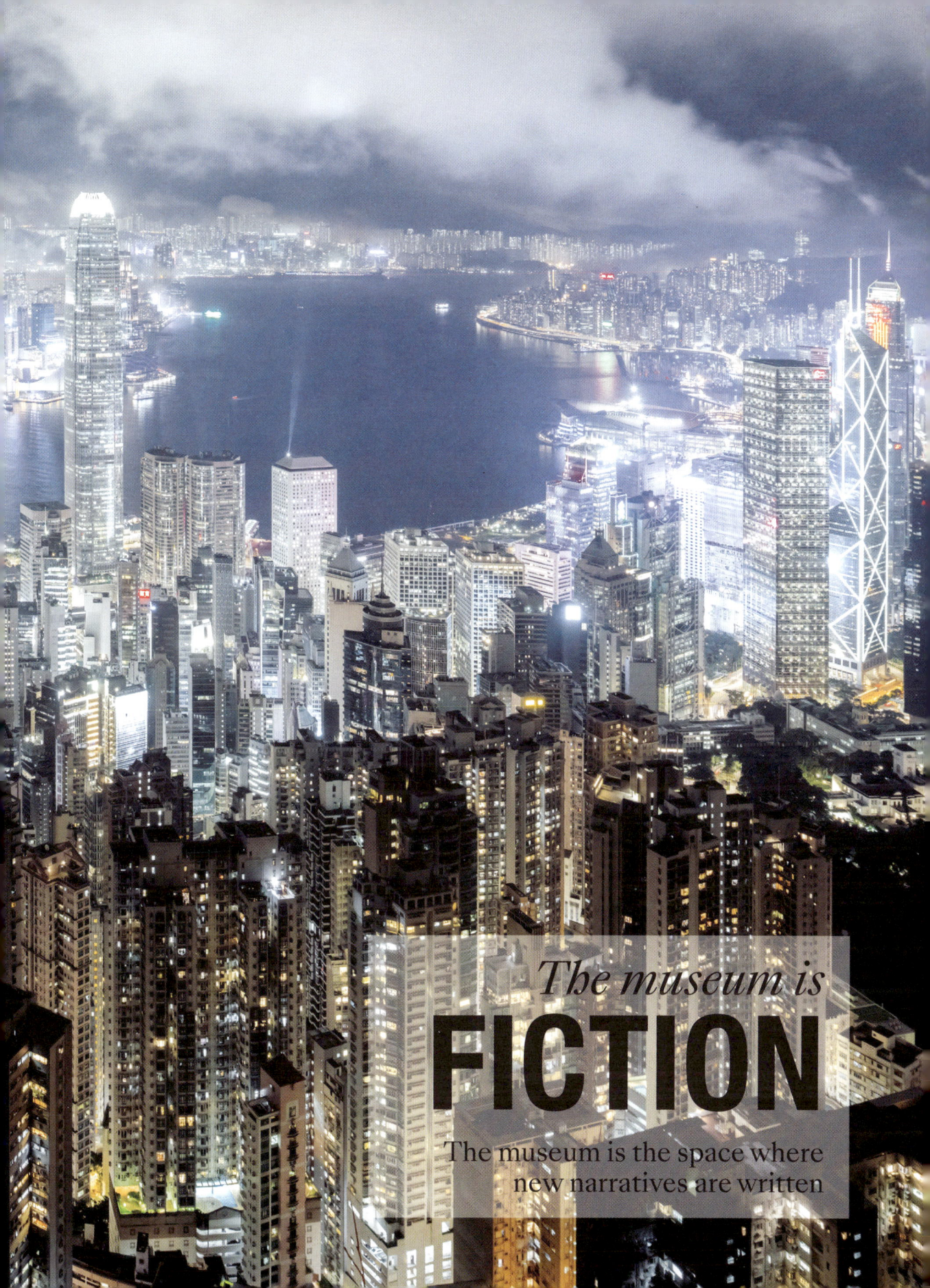

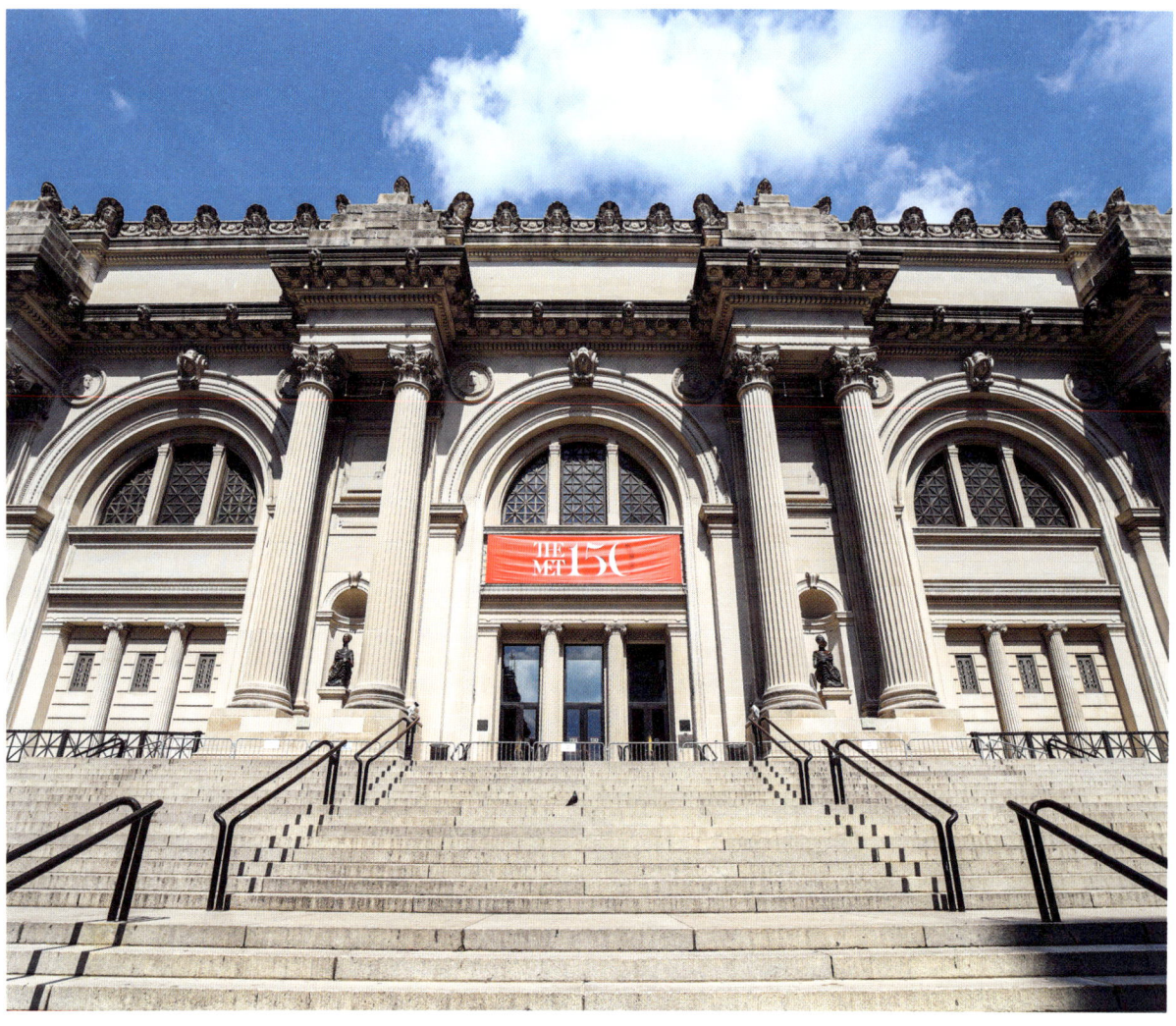

For limited periods of time, objects of disparate provenance are brought together to create a temporary new world—an alternative representation of the past or a novel formulation of the present. The exhibition, as we call these ephemeral worlds, is staged in a peculiar institution known as the "museum," a space that represents a possibility, a glitch, or an in-between zone. Here, memories and imaginations from different times, places, and cultures come together in dialogue.

On New York's Fifth Avenue, at the level of East 82nd Street, past the hot dog stand, a ceremonial staircase leads to the threshold of one such place, the Metropolitan Museum of Art (Met). Designed by Richard Morris Hunt, the Met's Beaux-Arts facade, completed in 1902, stands as a gateway to a suspended reality, hiding the institution's original building, whose High-Victorian Gothic style had come to seem outdated after the 1893 World's Columbian Exposition in Chicago. Hunt's frontispiece, whose elevation corresponds perfectly to the monumental entrance hall it defines, features three giant arches flanked by pairs of freestanding columns—an imperial-Roman combination of two distinct structural systems arranged in harmony. The architect's plans for the facade included a sculptural program that announced what visitors would find inside, with groups of figures representing "the four great periods of art"—ancient, classic, Renaissance, and

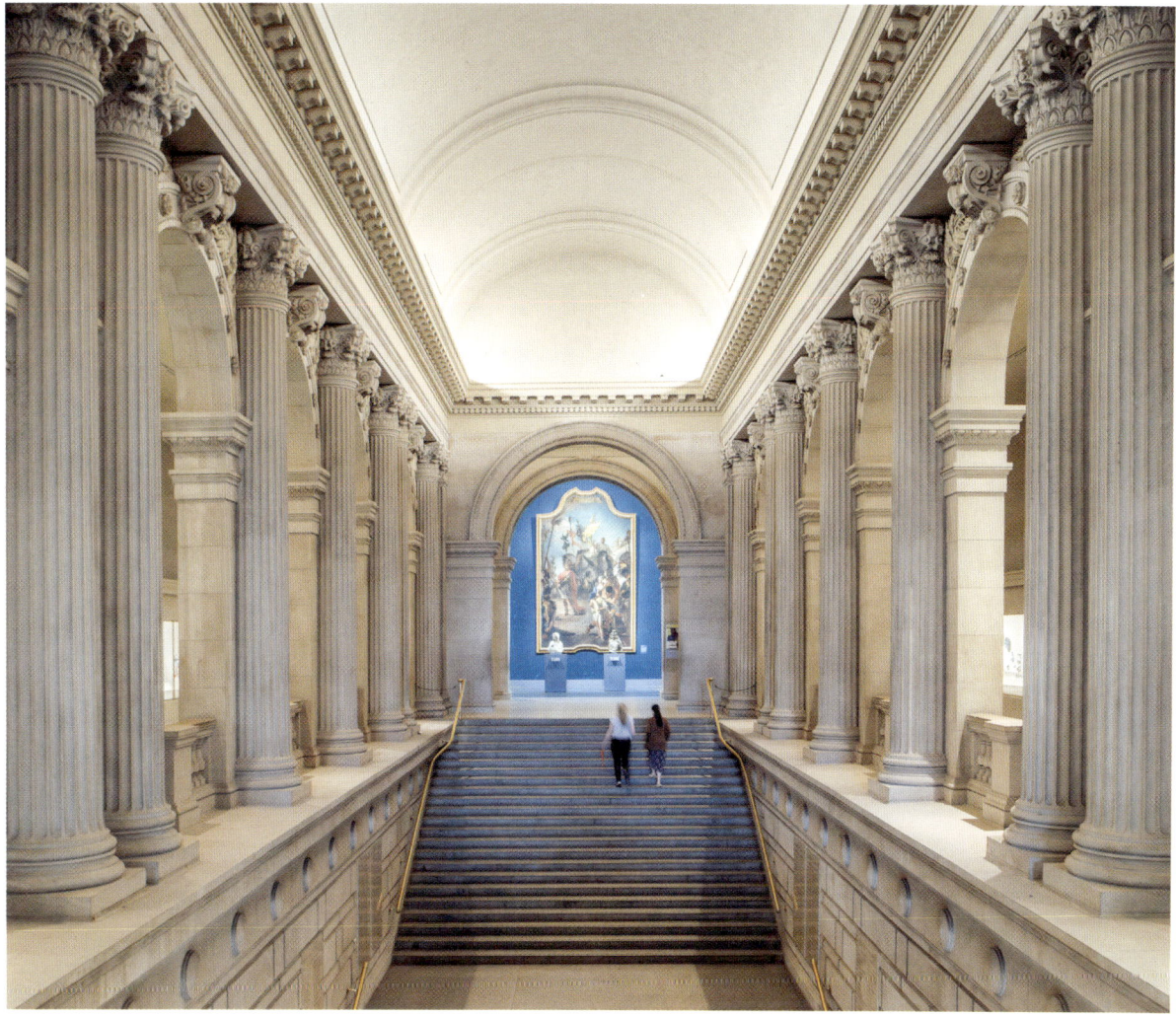

modern—under which he proposed placing reproductions of the best artwork from each period. Had his decorative program been executed, it would have made explicit the facade's role as the material manifestation of the point of communication between the city and this, its three-dimensional encyclopedia.

After crossing the facade, this crucial mediator of the museum's dramaturgical space with the rest of the city, visitors enter the museum and are propelled into a universe that incorporates the possibility of many different worlds and worldviews. Like in many museums, the Met's painting department is to be found on the upper floor, a location that is as much a matter of pragmatism as of classical

Previous pages: The giant screen is the facade of M+, which speaks to Hong Kong. The architecture of the museum adopts the language of the city, which is a landscape of high rises and billboards, and is densely populated.

Opposite and above: Crossing the Beaux-Arts facade of the Met, designed by Richard Morris Hunt, visitors climb the staircases to the European Painting galleries.

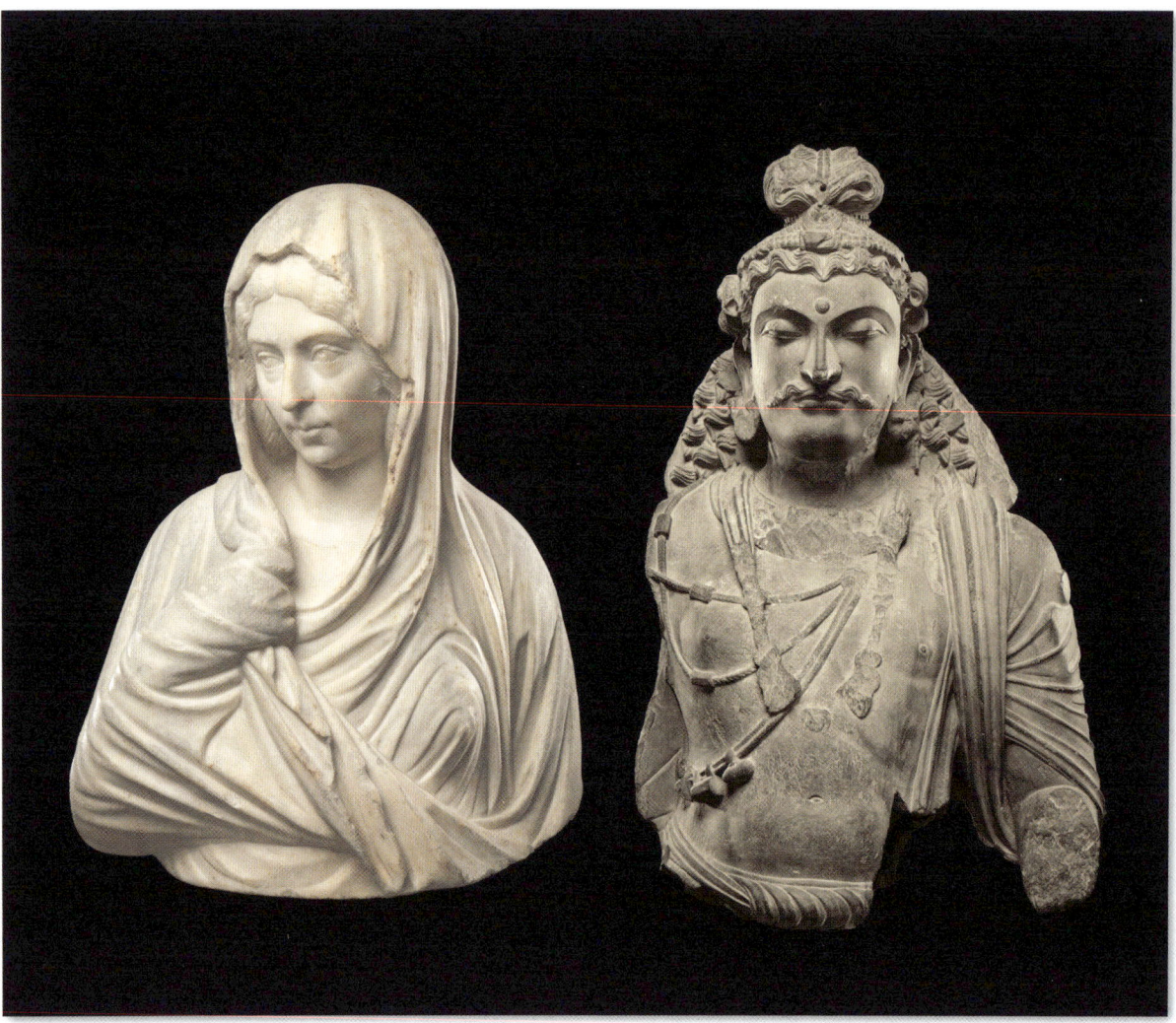

hierarchy, since paintings need daylight from above to be viewed properly.[1] To connect his entrance hall to the painting galleries, Hunt built a monumental stair, at the top of which visitors today encounter Giovanni Battista Tiepolo's *The Triumph of Marius* (1729). The painting, hung theatrically, depicts the victory parade of the eponymous Roman general in 104 BCE: riding high on a chariot, he displays the captive Numidian king Jugurtha before the people. In many ways the focus of the painting, the prisoner is represented with great dignity, while in the foreground captives and Roman soldiers carry precious objects looted from the conquered lands.

In the context of its current home, the painting appears as a self-contained event, but originally it would have been read as part of a mise-en-scène of political theater in the palazzo of a powerful Venetian family.[2] With their protagonists dressed in highly inventive costumes, the artist's vivid and dramatic

---

1. Jason Farago, "700 Paintings, 45 Galleries: A Guide to the Met's New European Wing," *New York Times*, November 23, 2023.
2. Tiepolo painted several such scenes, many of which were directly integrated into the walls and ceilings of Venetian churches and schools. Federico Zeri, *Italian Paintings: A Catalogue of the Collection of The Metropolitan Museum of Art, vol. 2, Venetian School* (New York: The Metropolitan Museum of Art, 1974).

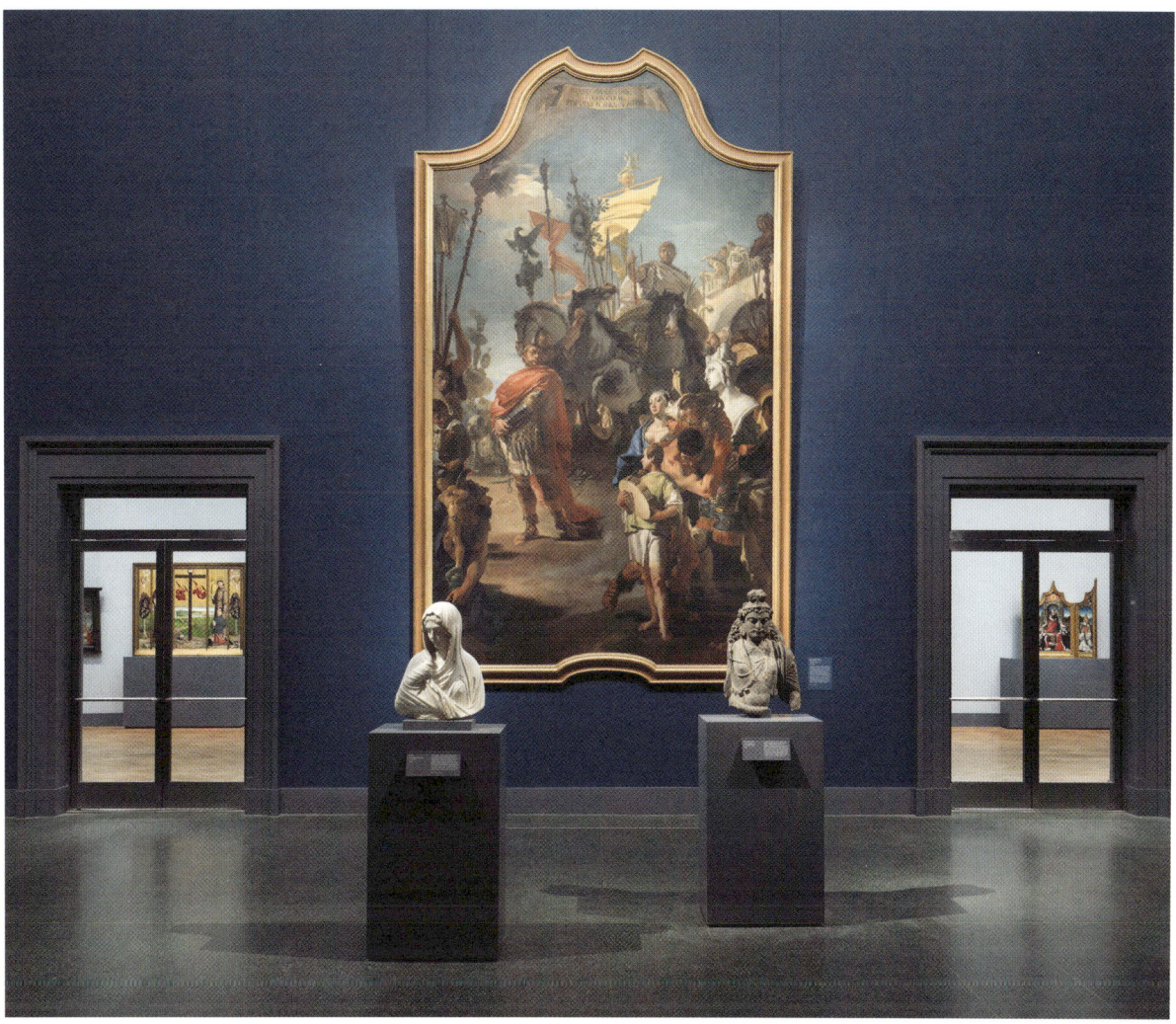

depictions of myth and history, many of which were directly integrated into the walls and ceilings of Venetian churches and schools, brought him fame across Europe. The combination of his paintings and their sumptuous architectural settings functioned as complete environments that engulfed viewers, transporting them into a history narrated as a three-dimensional world of staged fiction.

As an introduction to the Met's European painting collection, Tiepolo's canvas provides a tangible link between illusionistic painting and scenography: ancient Roman history is staged with dramatic movement and expression in a highly theatrical manner. Characteristic of eighteenth-century painting, this theatricality

Opposite: A second-century marble portait bust of a woman, and a fourth/fifth-century bust of a Bodhisattva, whose provenance is given as modern Pakistan, both in the Met Museum collection.

Above: Giovanni Battista Tiepolo's *The Triumph of Marius* (1729) is theatrically hung at the entrance of the European Painting galleries. It depicts the victory parade of the eponymous Roman general in 104 BCE.

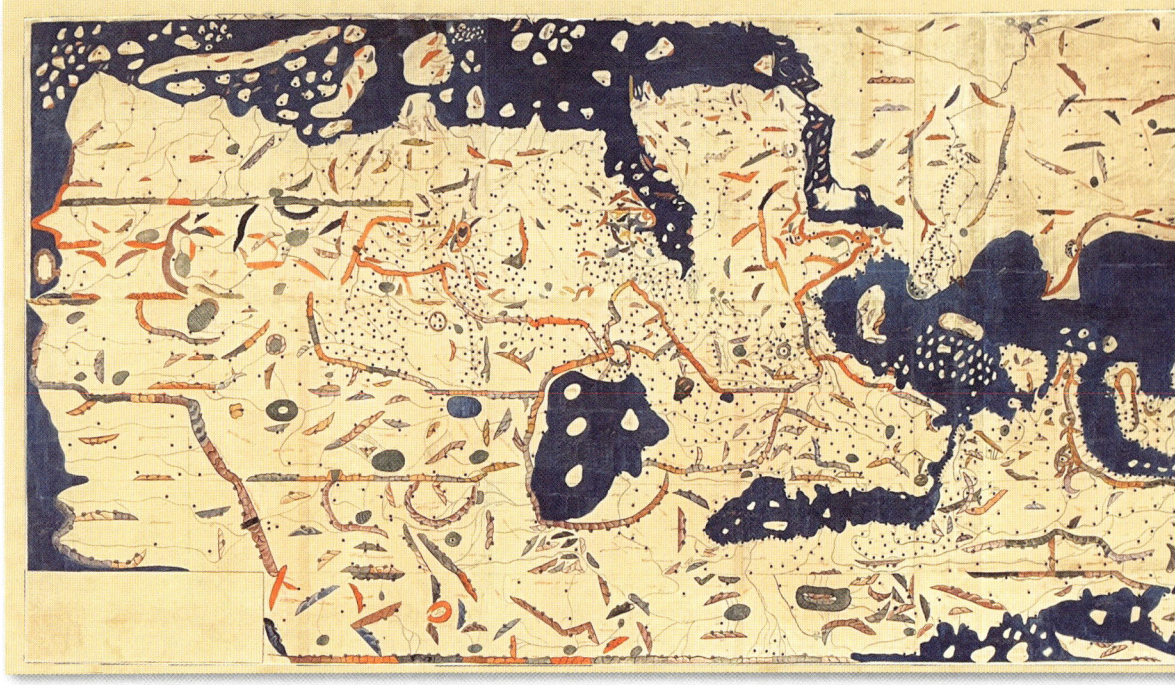

also functions as the key to reading the current hang in the Met's European Painting galleries, which was unveiled in November 2023 following a five-year project to renovate the skylights. Indeed, the staging of the forty-five rooms—enhanced by the newly improved skylights, a thematic organization, and the colorful palette of the gallery design—mirrors the historical ambiguity in Tiepolo's paintings, acknowledges the fictional quality of the exhibition as a space conducive to questioning history. Whereas Tiepolo used the codes of theater to signal this fiction, the Met's curators employ the codes of the exhibition to signal and question a finite definition of "European painting" as a canonical area of study.

A certain consciousness of the incompleteness of the Met's collection can be observed in this new installation, titled *Look Again*. Displayed in front of *The Triumph of Marius*, like props that have literally fallen out of the picture, are a fourth/fifth-century bust of a Bodhisattva, whose provenance is given as modern Pakistan, and a second-century marble portrait bust of a woman. Intended to point to the geographic boundaries of the museum's holdings while simultaneously inviting consideration of the dynamic nature of European borders and the diverse global afterlives of Mediterranean antiquity (of which Tiepolo's rendering of an ancient event is one example), they appear like part of the spoils taken from the conquered Numidians. Their presence enhances the understanding of Tiepolo as a painter-dramaturge and at the same time signals the intention to offer an expanded narrative of the legacies of the ancient Mediterranean world.

After *Marius*, the European galleries present juxtapositions of artworks across time, medium, and provenance over five centuries. For example, a gallery of anonymous paintings from the Spanish colonies stands adjacent to a room mostly showing works by Velázquez; further on, a self-portrait by Francis Bacon hangs beside a depiction of Veronica's veil, which one might interpret as a representation of Christ's self-portrait. Such juxtapositions seek to create dialogues beyond national contexts, questioning a historically Christian and unified image of Europe. In this manner, the Met proposes new ways of mapping the continent, free from fixed boundaries—whether national, temporal, or religious—creating a continental mass without nations, where identities are constantly evolving. By proposing an examination of the present through objects from the past, *Look Again* gives renewed relevance to the universalizing ambition of the Met's

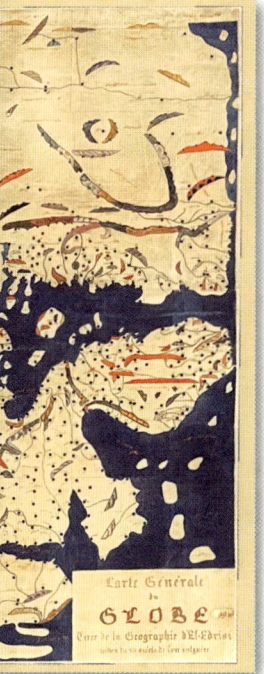 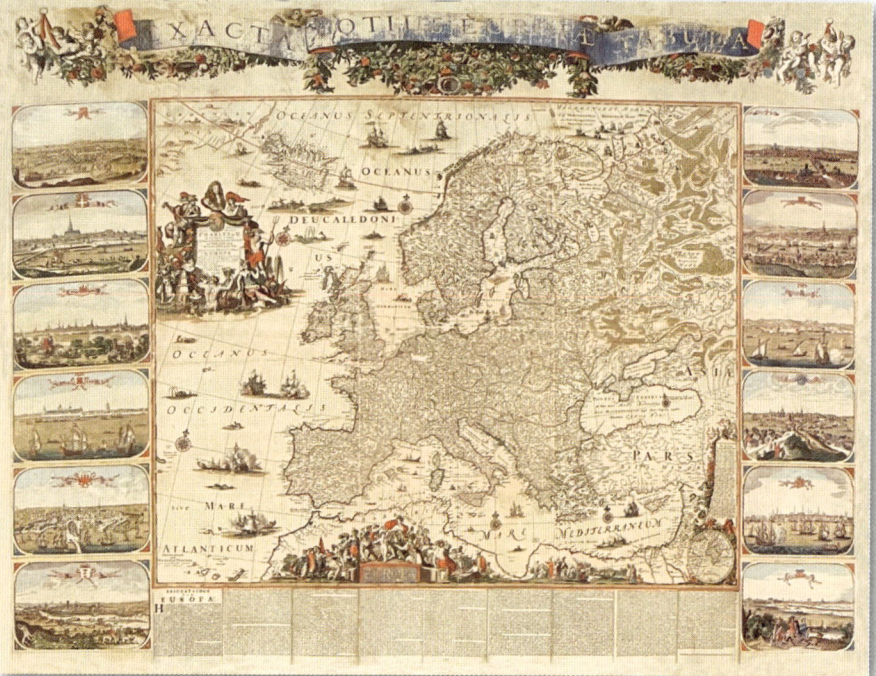

collections, "a universal museum of the world, in the world, and for the world."[3]

The exhibition *Look Again* demonstrates that the museum itself is not the space of "universality"; rather, this potential belongs to the artworks through the aggregate meanings they accrue over time and through displacement. The facade of any museum crystallizes the important task of architecture to delineate a space where narratives about the history of the world are performed in a particular city. In the case of the Metropolitan Museum of Art in New York, if these objects are found on the upper floor of this universal museum, it is because of their significance and potential, through juxtaposition with others, to narrate both past and present formulations of the world. Beyond the facade and the threshold it represents, the relationships between artworks become divorced from all proprietary notions or national paradigms. Through the subtle dramaturgic and theatrical potential of the exhibition format, *Look Again* tells us that "Europe" is a fiction that requires constant rewriting in the present tense.

Opposite: Different maps of Europe are displayed at the entrance of the exhibition, demonstrating the ever-evolving notion of the continent as a fluid geographic and political concept.

Following pages: M+ connects to the city as a whole through a giant screen that broadcasts in real time its participation in the culture of Hong Kong, the planetary city. This facade offers immediate connectivity.

---

3. As its CEO, Max Hollein, described it in 2023, https://www.metmuseum.org/perspectives/how-we-collect.

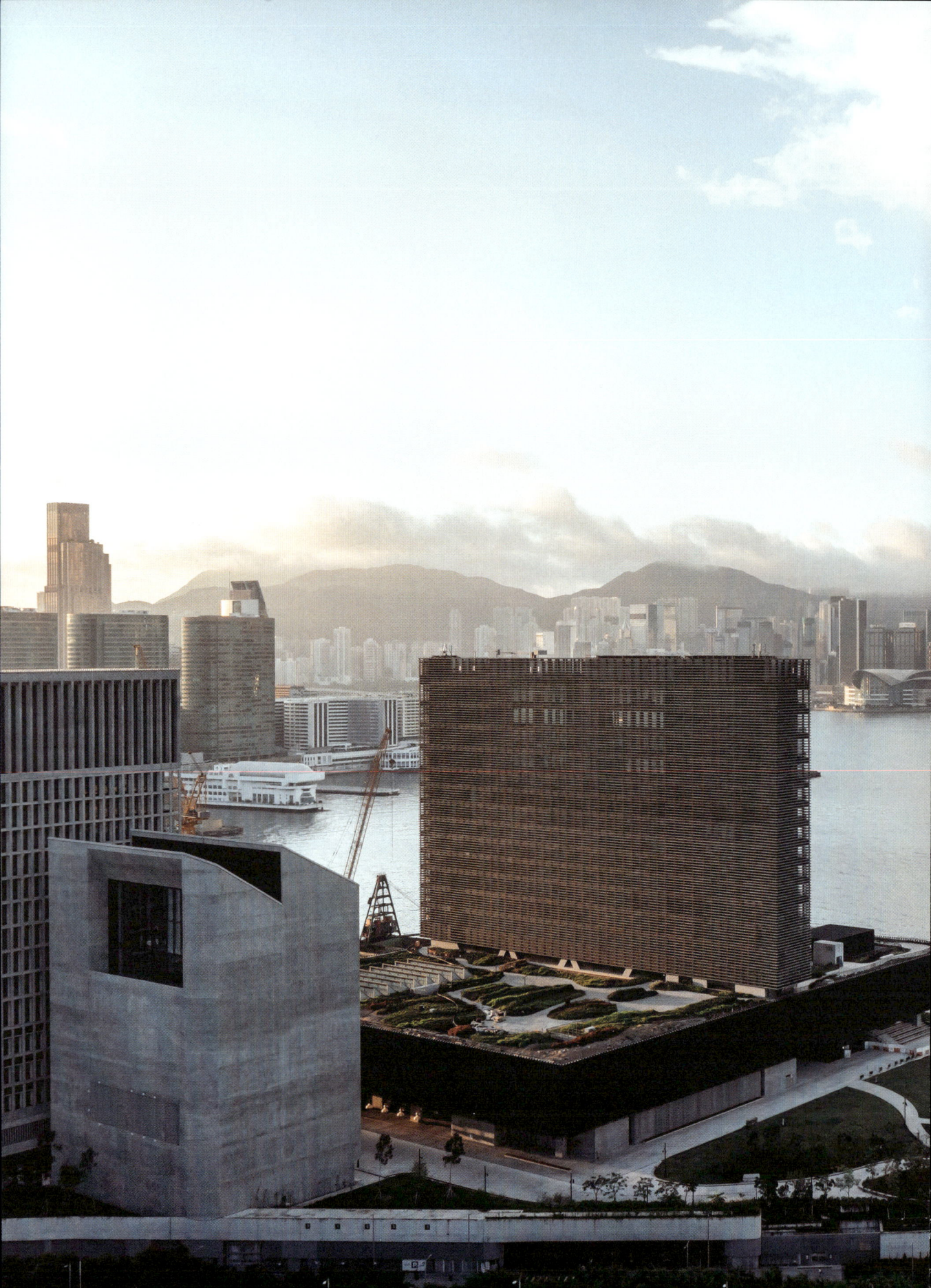

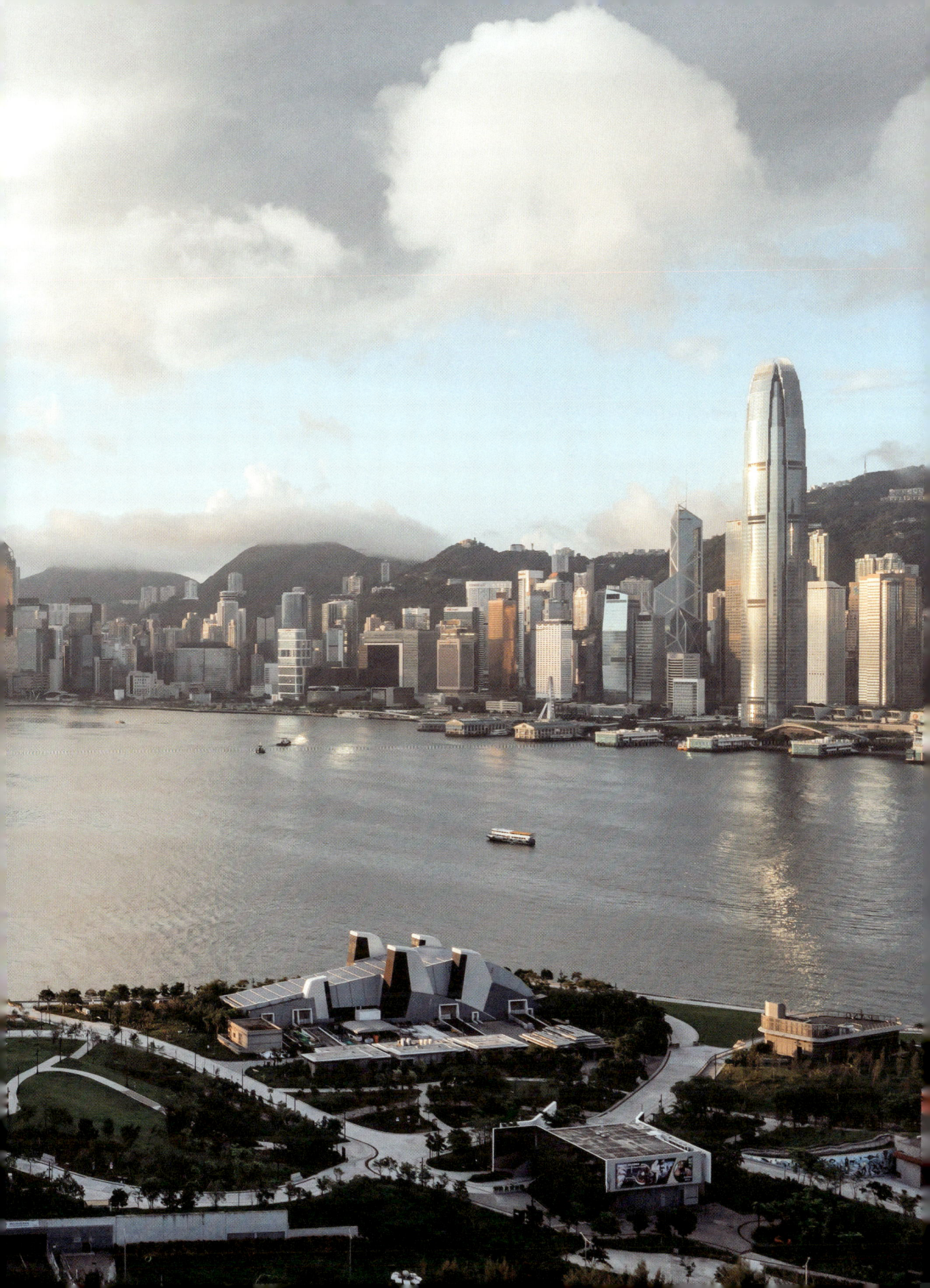

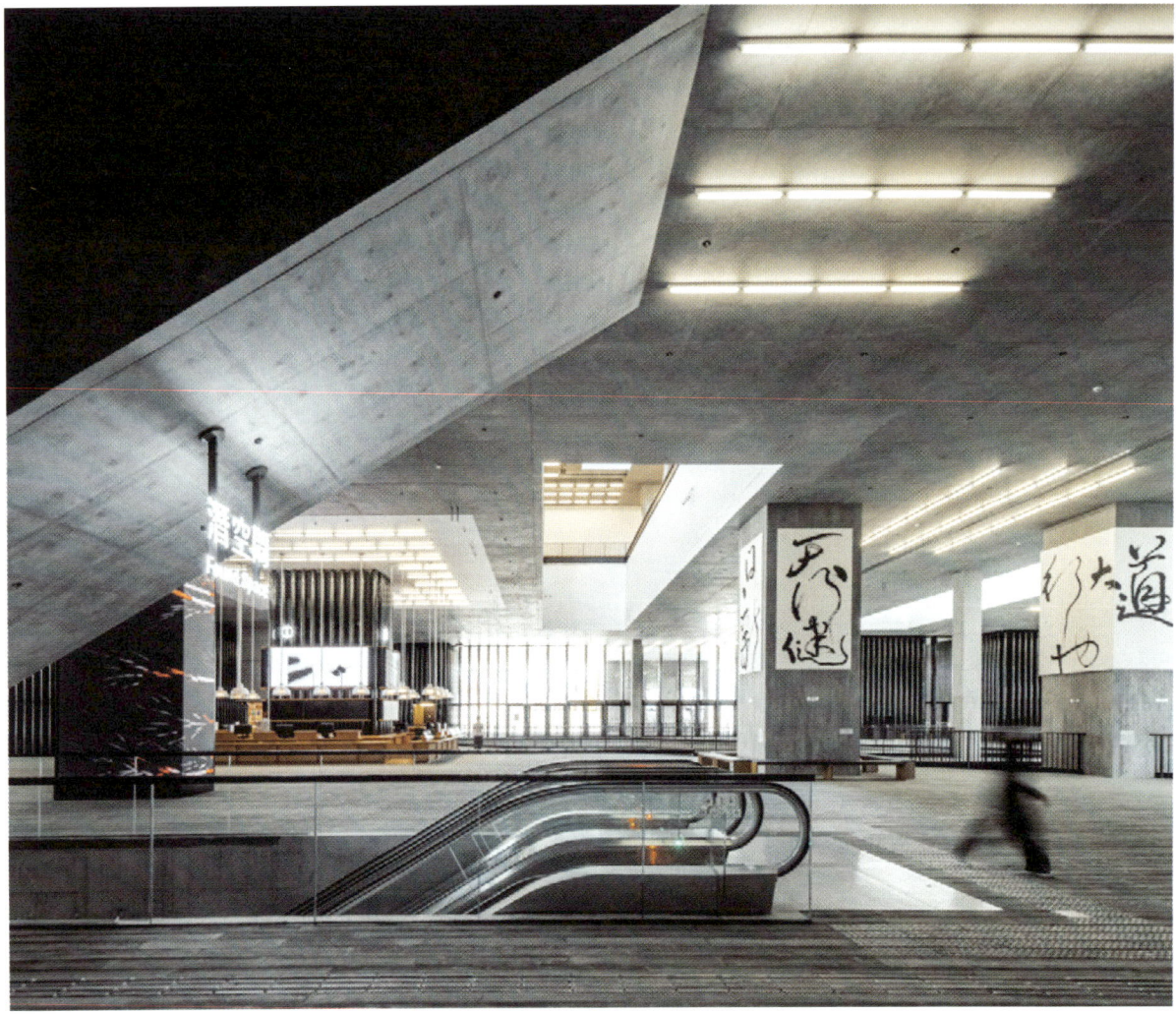

Not all museums are accessed via grandiose flights of steps that imitate Roman temples. In Hong Kong, visitors enter M+, the city's new temple of modern art, directly from the underground, the park, the streets or via escalators. The building's architects, the Swiss firm Herzog & de Meuron, who completed the project in 2021, may have had in mind one of Archigram's best-known projects, Plug-In City, a visionary urban megastructure incorporating residences, access routes, and essential services for its inhabitants.[4] A fitting idea for a metropolis that looks like something designed by the radical 1960s British architecture group, with its transport viaducts winding around and sometimes even through its countless tall buildings, and its numerous escalators connecting, the street to spaces both above and below, making the publicly accessible realm feel uniquely three-dimensional. Indeed, Hong Kong itself is a plausible plug-in project, with its perpetual stacking, infinite steps, elevations, and adaptations. Imagine the Centre Pompidou designers' dream of connectivity, synchronous belonging, and mirroring of

---

4. Plug-in City was intended to accommodate and encourage adaptation based on need the building were conceived as infinite add-ons: houses, offices, supermarkets, universities. Each unit was to have a different lifespan and would plug into a main "craneway."

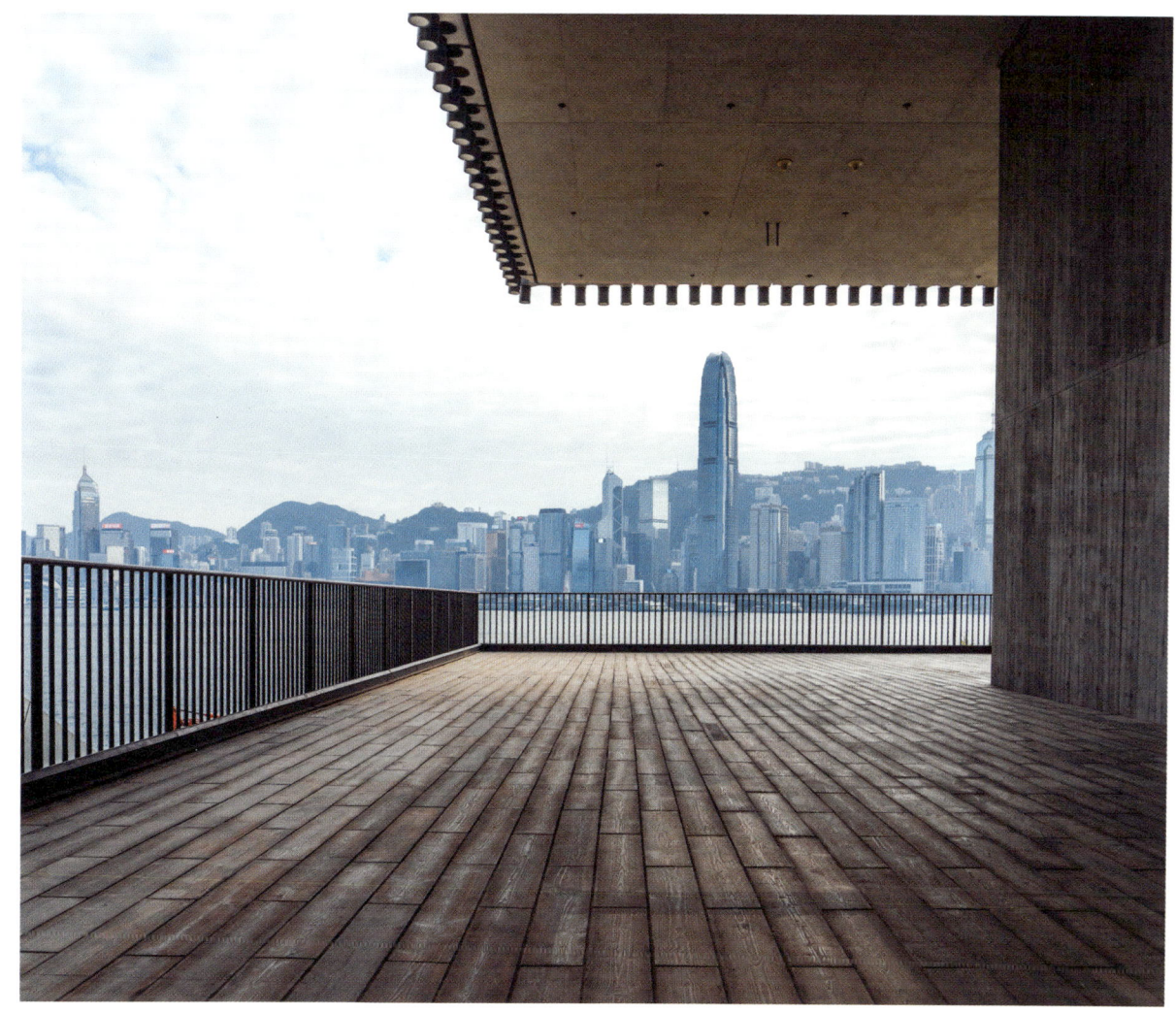

the city as an information hub translated into urban-scale infrastructure—Hong Kong is a close approximation, and one could plausibly envision a giant overarching crane as the city's mega-machine.

As a museum and collection, M+—branding itself as a "museum and more"—seeks to respond to its locality. A former British colony that returned to Chinese rule in 1997, it strives to respond to its immediate context while also being relevant to world culture, acknowledging the necessary globalized history of the

Opposite: The atrium entrance of M+ sits above the tunnel which connects trains to the airport. From an infrastructural standpoint, M+ directly plugs into the planet. The spaces connecting the different galleries function like public spaces within the museum.

Above: Suspended above street level is a large terrace that connects the museum lobby onto a generous view of Hong Kong Bay.

The overall flexible and impermanent form would thus reflect the needs and collective will of the inhabitants. For more on Archigram see Annette Fierro, *Archigram and the British High Tech* (London: Lund Humphries, 2023). See also Peter Cook, Warren Chalk, Dennis Compton, David Greene, Ron Herron, and Mike Webb, *Archigram* (New York: Princeton Architectural Press, 1972).

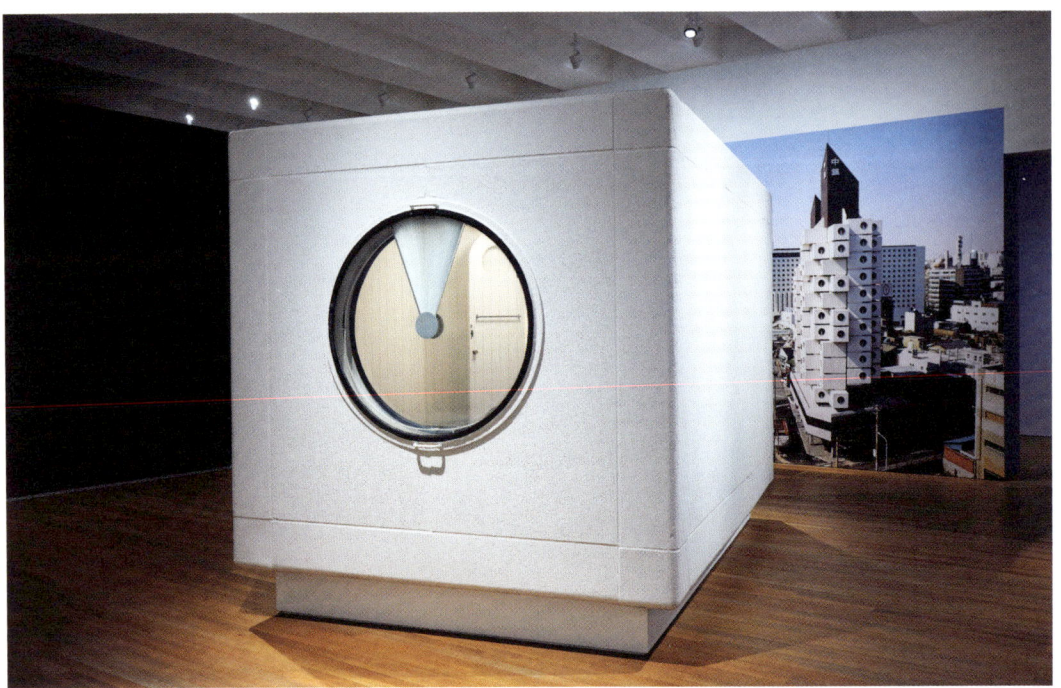

twentieth century. This was first and foremost the task of its collection, which comprises visual art, design, architecture, and moving images, organized in concentric circles beginning with Hong Kong, then extending to Mainland China and the rest of Asia, and finally to the rest of the world, limitless and total.[5] The various objects and archives collected prior to the museum's opening between 2012 and 2020 range from neon signs of Hong Kong storefronts to a recent sculpture by Korean artist Haegue Yang, and even reconstituted fragments of the now-demolished Nagakin Capsule Building in Tokyo.[6] The ambition of situating the museum's relevance to a planetary audience is also manifest in the historical acquisition of the Archigram archive, even before the museum opened to the public. Beyond the fact that the museum's architecture could aesthetically and conceptually be understood to borrow from the Archigram playbook, this administrative and curatorial feat disrupts a historical trend where archives are often displaced from the colony to the metropole; here, the archive has moved from the metropole to the former colony, taking its place in a museum that seeks to reflect and reinforce Hong Kong's critical importance in global visual culture and affirm the city as a historical center of modernism.[7]

As a museum, M+ attemps to define a cosmology of the modern and the "universal." At the Metropolitan Museum of Art, while the new installation at the European Painting galleries has opened up new narratives through exhibition-making, acknowledging the fiction of any finite encyclopedia, M+ seeks to redefine the history of Asia as a starting point for a possible encyclopedia. The contemporary philosopher Wang Hui has theorized this quest for a new cosmology

---

5. The museum's own definition: "an interdisciplinary and transnational compendium of twentieth- and twenty-first-century visual culture, encompassing the disciplines of design and architecture, moving image, and visual art, and the thematic area of Hong Kong visual culture." See Ikko Yokoyama, Lesley Ma, Doryun Chung, and Pauline j. Yao, eds., *M+ Collections Highlights* (New York: W. W. Norton, 2022). See also the M+ website, https://www.mplus.org.hk/en/about-the-collection/m-collection/.
6. The significance of this is immense, considering that the Nagakin Capsule Tower was one of the few extant built examples of the Metabolists movement. Designed by Kisho Kurokawa, it the tower anticipated modular replacement: each capsule was attached to a central concrete core. Mark Dytham, "A Successful Failure: Remembering the Nakagin Capsule Tower," *Architect's Newspaper*, June 22, 2022. Artist Haegue Yang draws on both the history of technology in the modern movement and early twentieth-century craft traditions. The dialogue she creates within history and across disciplines shows the universal potential reach of artistic language.

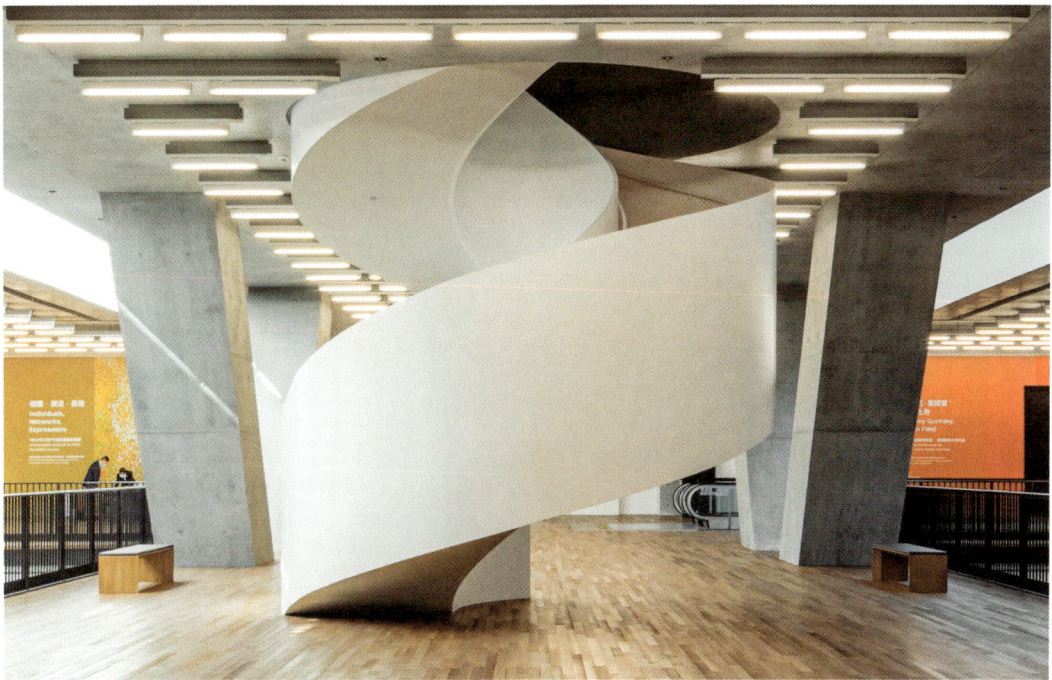

which goes beyond the modern nation-state paradigm, in *The Politics of Imagining Asia*. In this seminal work, Wang Hui demonstrates that historically, Asia was a European concept and not an "Asian" one. He argues that both Euope and Asısa were constituted as part of the process of forming new knowledge in eighteenth- and nineteenth-century Europe, underpinning the European Enlightenment and colonial expansion. His work reveals that criticism of Eurocentrism should involve a reimagining of "Asia" as well as a revision of nineteenth-century European vision of world history. For Wang, considering modernity in China and Asia is inseparable from rewriting of a history that weighs the complexity of networks and relationships between regions and societies: "A new idea of Asia—which is neither the beginning of a linear world history nor its end, neither self-sufficient subject nor subordinating object—provides an opportunity to reconstruct world history."[8]

Opposite: The collection display of M+'s permanent galleries places fragments of architecture, such as a salvaged part of the Nagakin Capsule Building in Tokyo, on the same level as paintings and contemporary art installations, illustrating the diversity within the category of "visual arts."

Above: A dramatic staircase at the center of the gallery floor of the museum connects with the upper level and adds to the architectural variety of the optical experience designed by Herzog & de Meuron.

---

7. Arguably, this gesture also echoes the ongoing debate about restitution, particularly intensified in Europe after the Benedicte Savoy report in 2020. Commissioned by the French govenerment, it launched a global reckoning with the presence of arfican artifacts in Europe and calls to restitue these objects to the former colonies of European powers.

8. As cited in Zhang Yongle, "New Forbidden Zone in Reading? Dushu and the Chinese Intelligensia," *New Left Review*,49 (January–February 2008). For the complete argument, the most important work by the philosopher Wan Hui is *The Rise of Modern Chinese Thought*, Harvard University Press, 2021).

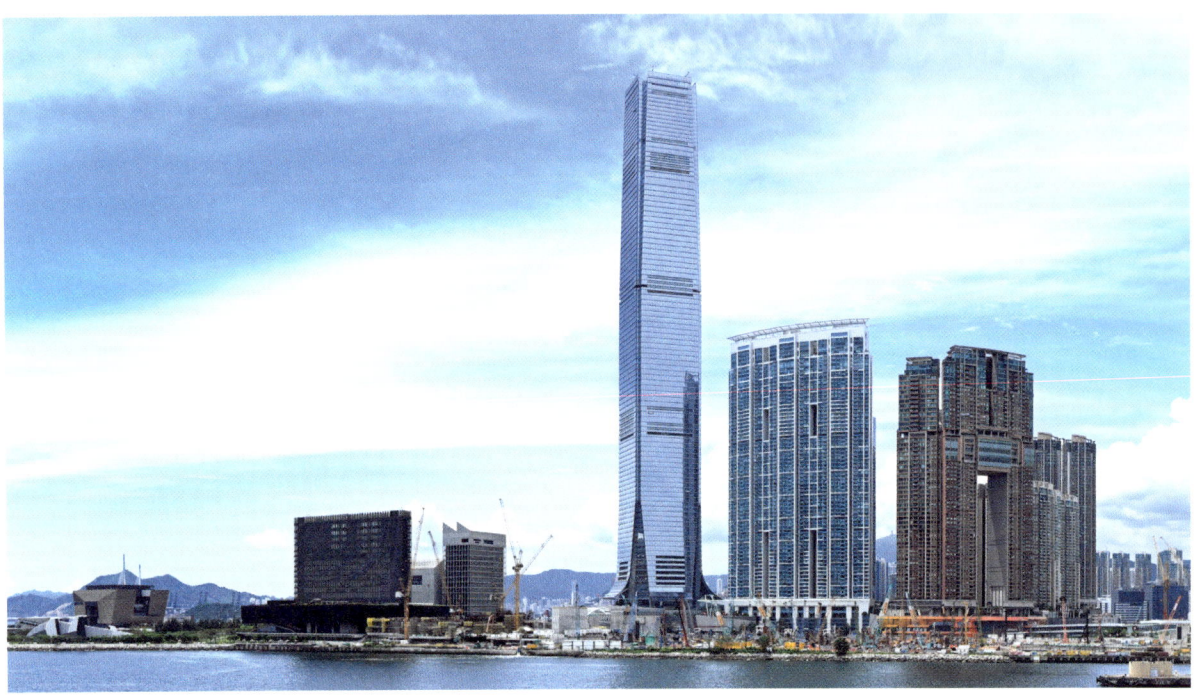

Reconstructing history from the viewpoint of Hong Kong is precisely what M+ sets out to do. The founding collection of the museum is the M+ Sigg Collection of contemporary Chinese art, the largest collection of artworks by Chinese artists active after the Cultural Revolution (1966–1976) in a public institution outside of Mainland China. The M+ Sigg Collection comprises works made during or after 1970, a date that seems unusual when compared to Western collections of twentieth-century modern art, such as that of MoMA, which are typically framed with pre and post-war narratives, with 1945 as a key date. It also diverges from conventional Chinese timelines; most art historians consider the 1921 foundation of the Chinese Communist Party as the starting point and Mao's death in 1976 as the endpoint. The 2017–2018 New York Guggenheim exhibition *Art and China after 1989: Theater of the World*, took yet another alternative approach to chronology when attempting to establish a canonical history of contemporary Chinese art.[9] The M+ Sigg Collection marks its beginning as early as the 1970s, when avant-garde groups like the No Name Group and the Stars Art Group began to reject the official style of Revolutionay Realism.[10] Bequeathing this collection to M+ holds immense significance as it aims to disrupt the typical twentieth-century timeline of modern and contemporary art by being housed within the walls of a global museum in Hong Kong.[11]

Xu Bing's 1988 *Book from the Sky* is an example of a seminal work in the collection which encapsulates the museum's philosophy as a place of both local history and global significance, independent of any national temporality or culture. Trained as a printmaker at Beijing's Central Academy of Fine Arts, Xu Bing came of age during the '85 New Wave, which emerged in the more relaxed atmosphere following China's 1978 reformist policies.[12] To create *Book from the Sky*, Xu developed a system of 4,000 fake Chinese characters based on the rules of the eighteenth-century *Kangxi Dictionary*

---

9. This exhibition was the largest of its kind at a major US institution in terms of defining a narrative of post-Mao China. The 1989 date refers of course to the collapse of the Berlin Wall, a date that has very different connotations in China, as the year of the Tiananmen massacre. See Alexandra Munroe with Philip Tinari, Hou Hanru. *Art and China after 1989: Theater of the World* (New Yoork: Guggenheim, 2017).
10. Pi Li, "Chinese Art: Object of Method?" in Pi Li (ed), *Chinese Art Since 1970: The M+ Sigg Collection* (London: Thames and Hudson, 2021), 13.
11. It inscribed in the recent history of contemporary art an alternative to the timeline the "postwar" framework of the Western world.

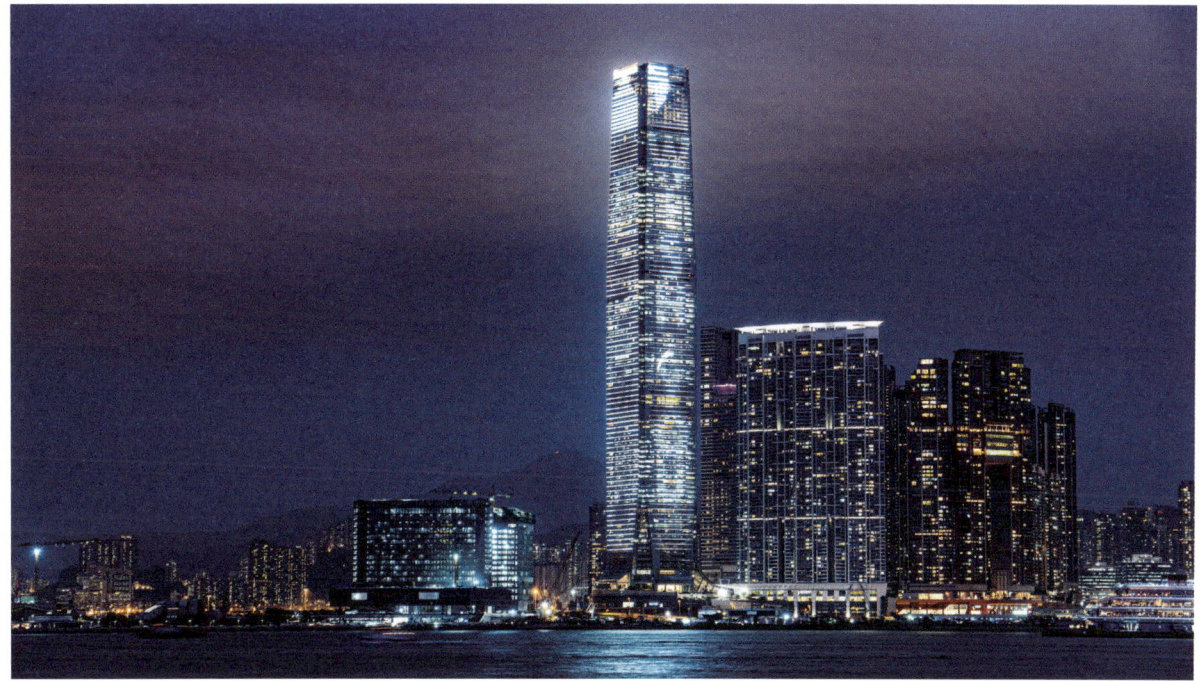

Opposite and above:
The construction site of M+, visible across Hong Kong Bay. The museum, whose collections span the modern period, is part of a series of other cultural infrastructure planned for the site, which is still under construction.

and the Song typeface, commonly used in official classical documents. The resulting installation consits of a hundred string-bound volumes that resemble an original classic, in the style of a Song dynasty block-printed edition. Intended to appear as a legible document, it subverts the expectation of a readability for a canonical script to crystallize and make visible the Chinese aesthetic experience. Viewers who approach the artwork often find themselves frustrated in their attempts to read it— the artwork's monumentality is futile, since it cannot be understood by any reader, Chinese or otherwise.

The questions that *Book from the Sky* confronts are those of locality; indeed, it calls into question the importance granted to script in Chinese culture and its status as a work of art.[13] Housed at M+ in Asia's new temple of modern art, the piece speaks to an international audience yet is dislodged

---

12. The '85 New Wave generation was fully open and receptive to new forms of culture—and crucially, to reading them. In forming an avant-garde, artists such as Xu Bing, one of—the most important intellectuals and artists of the post-Cultural Revolution era— fully embraced new sets of references while embodying the iconoclastic impulse that had characterized the 1970s.
13. See also discussion in chapter "Scroll Painting," pp. 14–19.

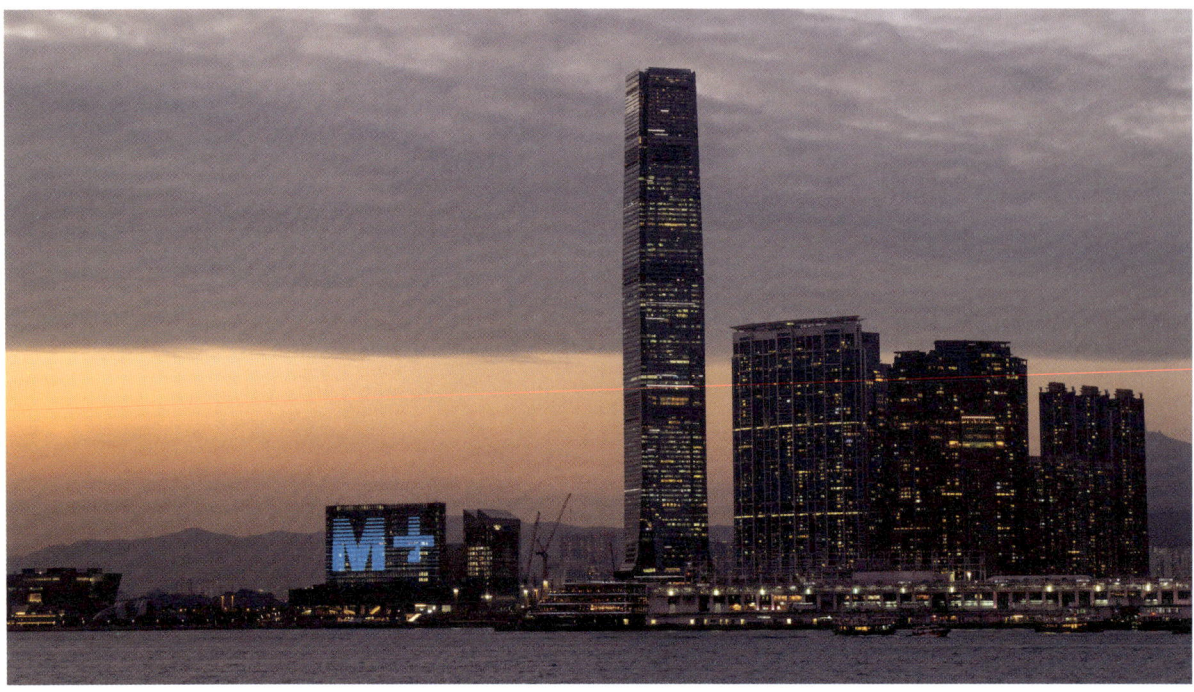

from the perceived specificity of the Chinese experience. It is located on a global playing field alongside other cultural backgrounds. Although it points to the specific relationship between the written word and the image in Chinese culture, *Book from the Sky* demonstrates how the language of art, in this case the history of calligraphy and the tradition of bookmaking, can address issues beyond its specific realm. Neither the Chinese reader nor the Western or non-chinese viewer can actually read what appears to be script; Xu Bing's *Book from the Sky* appeals to the potential for universality in artistic language.

If the museum anchors Hong Kong as a center in the global history of modernism through its collection, its architecture stands as this symbolic beacon in the cityscape. M+ is a gateway to a fictional world where the possibility of universality from a pan-Asian perspective can be represented. Its ambition to connect this worldview to the rest of the world is explicit in its infrastructural condition: one lands in Hong Kong, and via the express train from the airport, can reach West Kowloon station in just twenty-five minutes, the museum sitting above the station's tunnels. M+ is physically linked to the planet.

M+ is also connected to the city as a whole through a giant screen that broadcasts in real time its participation in the culture of Hong Kong, the planetary city. Across the breadth of Victoria Harbour, M+'s screen facade serves both as a programming space and an advertising symbol for the institution, its collections and activities. A thin rectangular beacon on an urban-scale pedestal, this media facade can be seen as a continuation of the 1960s avant-garde dreams of remaking cultural infrastructure in the image of the modern city. Archigram had imagined as one of the parallel studies of the Plug-in City, the Computer City Project involved an electric system running through the city that continuously feeds

---

14. At the time, Archigram and Cedric Price were applying emerging ideas in cybernetics to the field of architecture, which they viewed as technologically averse and conceptually stagnant.

15. Critics have questioned whether a screen can constitute legitimate architecture for a museum. See Oliver Wainwright, "A Throbbing Neon Powerhouse: Hong Kong's Gigantic New Billboard–With a Nice Museum Attached," *Guardian*, January 23, 2024. See also Giuliana Bruno's work on the question of "surface", which explores the intertwined histories of cinema, the architecture of the screen and the museum; Giuliana Bruno, *Surface: Matters of Aesthetics, Materiality, and Media* (Chicago: University of Chicago Press, 2014).

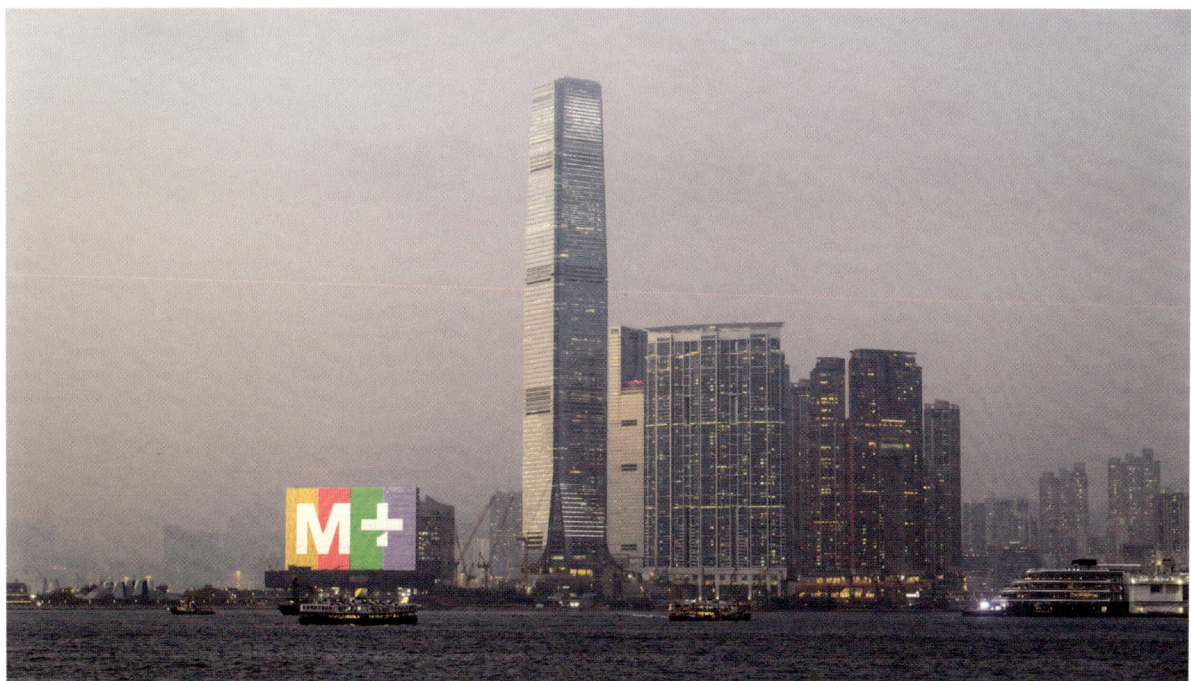

the central system with new requirements and adaptations to its architecture. Using the electronic summoning potential, the city's infrastructure would be responsive in real time.[14]

The screen of M+, plugged into the city, is the interface to a new worldview that directly engages with its skyline and interacts with the infrastructural and technological urban landscape.[15] Like Tiepolo's *The Triumph of Marius*, which sets the stage for a fictional space by using history as a dramatic backdrop at the entrance of the Metropolitan Museum of Art's European painting galleries, the M+ screen signals the gateway to a conception of an alternative worldview. The inherent quality of a screen to conceal the actual physical infrastructure to which it is attached allows for the potential infinite depth on its surface. This powerful statement made by the museum vis-à-vis the city announces its boundless nature—essentially offering a gateway to all the cross-temporal and cross-cultural implications that a pan-Asian cosmology may entail.

Opposite and above: M+'s screen facade is both a programming space, where the museum curatorial team can commission artists to create works as a site-specific medium, or an urban-scale cinema, as much as it is an advertising symbol for the institution, the collections, and activities housed within.

THE MUSEUM IS FICTION

171

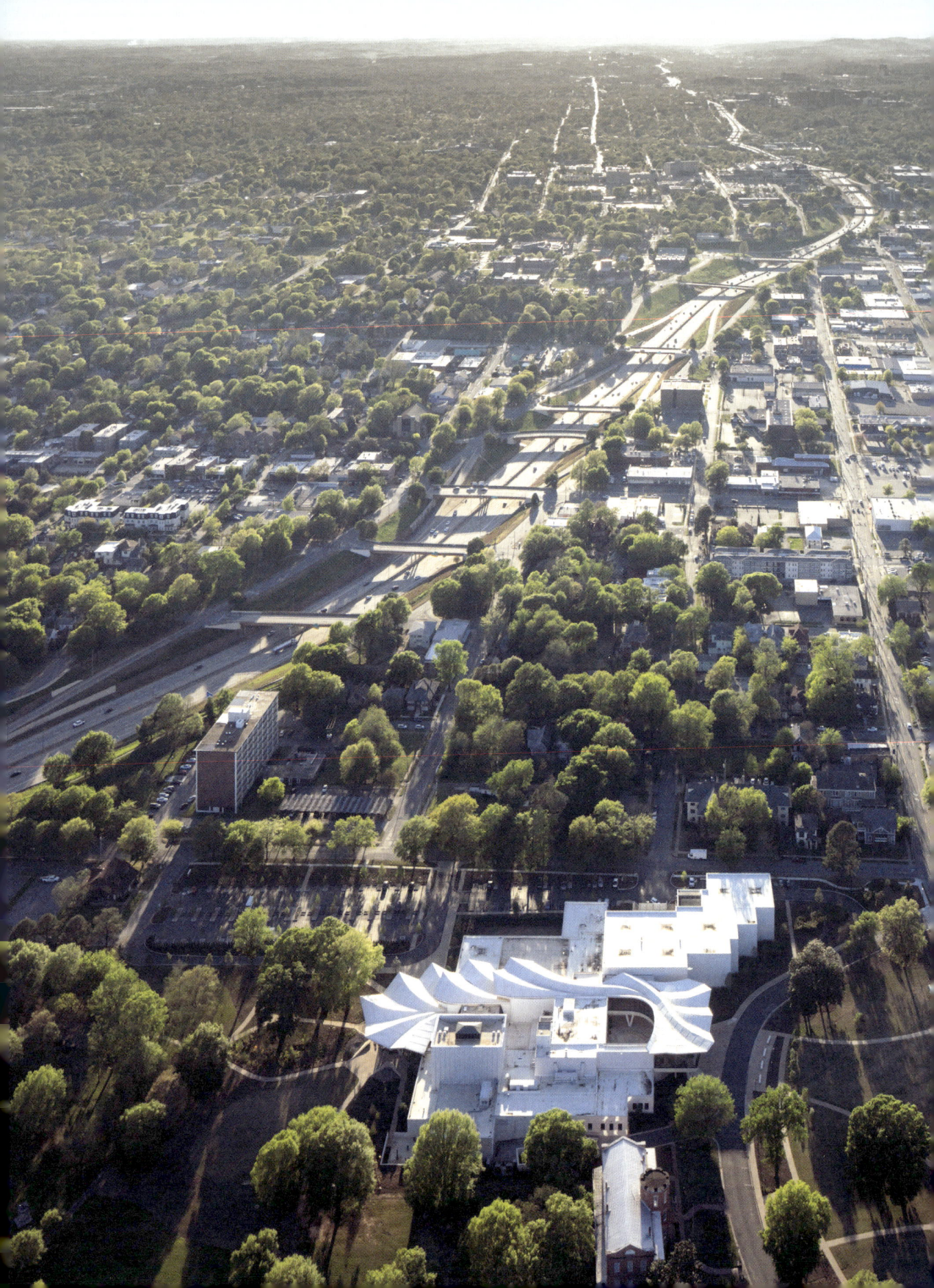

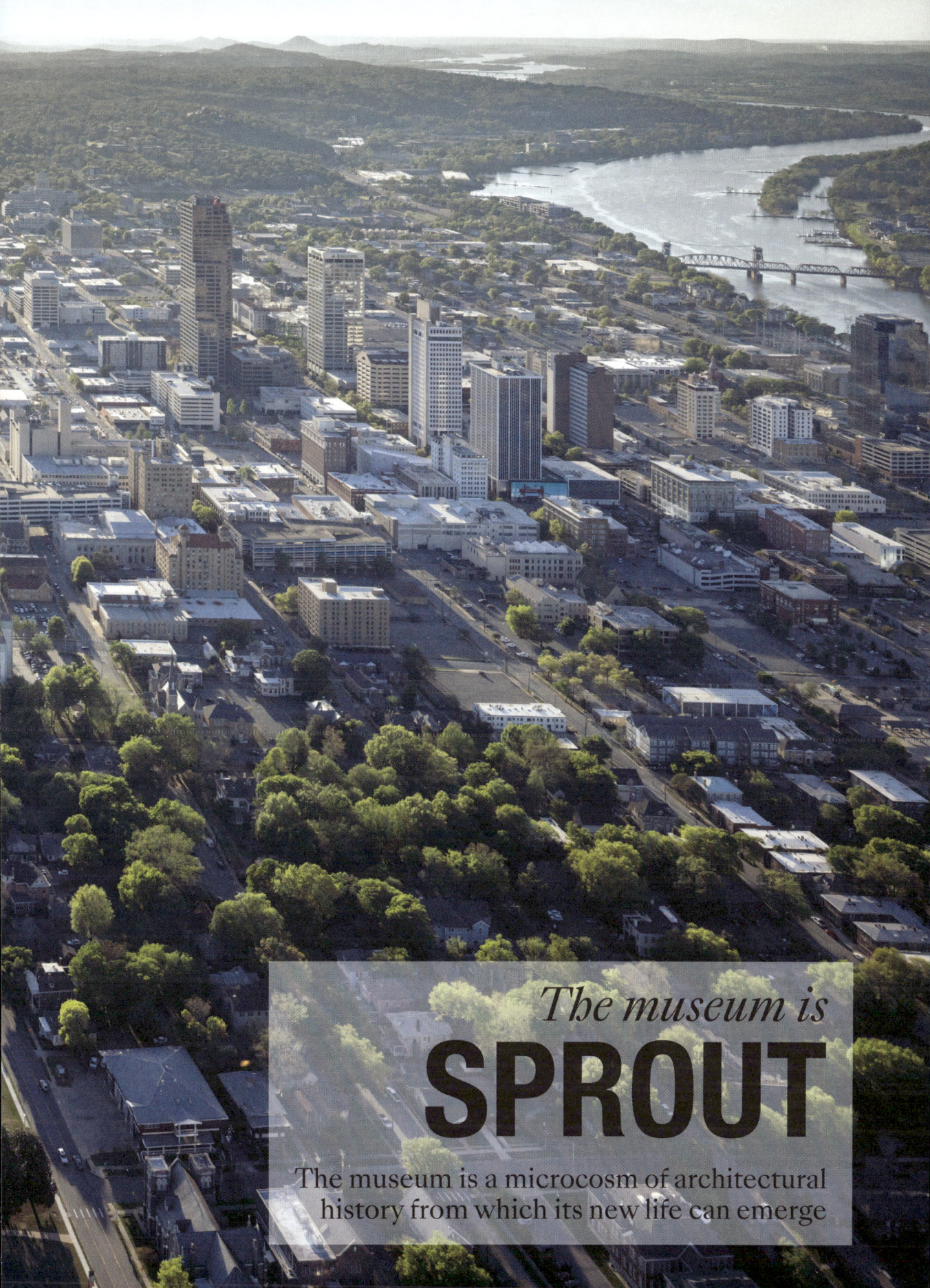

The museum is
SPROUT

The museum is a microcosm of architectural history from which its new life can emerge

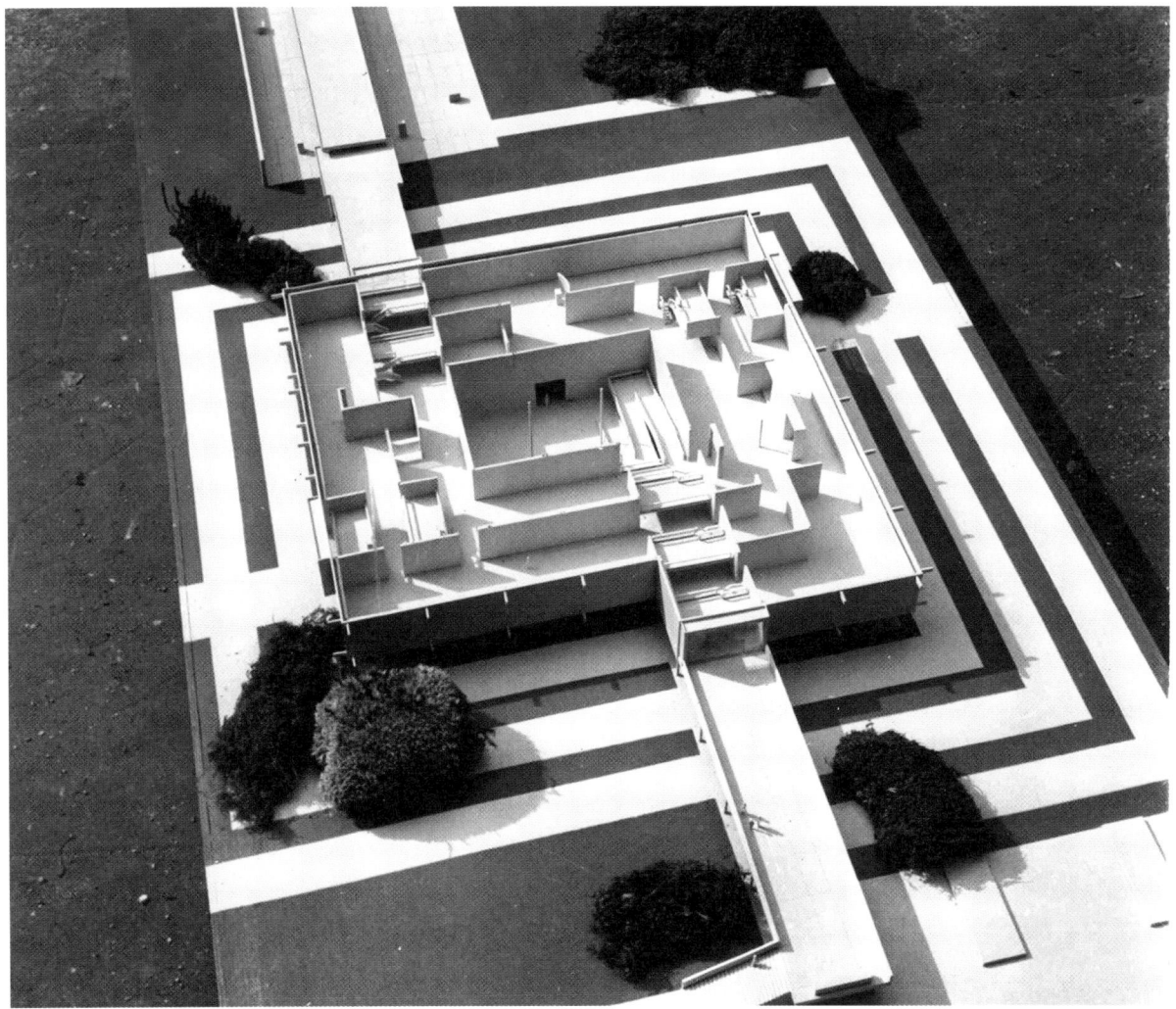

"The museum can be extended as desired: its plan takes the form of a spiral, a true form of regular, harmonious growth."[1] This is how Le Corbusier described his idea for a *Musée à croissance illimitée* or "Museum of Unlimited Growth" a project that first germinated in 1930 and to which he would return periodically over the years. In response to the endless accumulation that resulted from active acquisition policies, he imagined a single continuous wall folded into a square spiral to form a linear gallery that could grow along with the collections. The problem he attempted to solve was triggered in the mid-nineteenth century by the emergence of the world's fairs, the first of which was London's Great Exhibition of 1851, followed by Paris's Exposition Universelle of 1855.[2] With the

---

1. Le Corbusier, letter to Christian Zervos, December 8, 1930, *Le Corbusier et Pierre Jeanneret, Œuvre complète*, vol. 2, 1929–1934 (Zürich: Éditions d'Architecture, 1964; first published in *Cahiers d'Art*, no. 1, 1931), 73.
2. Beatriz Colomina, "The Endless Museum: Le Corbusier and Mies van der Rohe," *Log*, no. 15 (Winter 2009), 55–68. In this seminal article, architectural historian Beatriz Colomina highlights the contrast between Malraux's vision of the *Musée imaginaire*—enabled by photography's capacity for infinite juxtaposition of different objects across time and space—and Le Corbusier's advocacy for the physical museum wall, predicated on the assumption that the museum's dominant medium is the two-dimensional artwork.

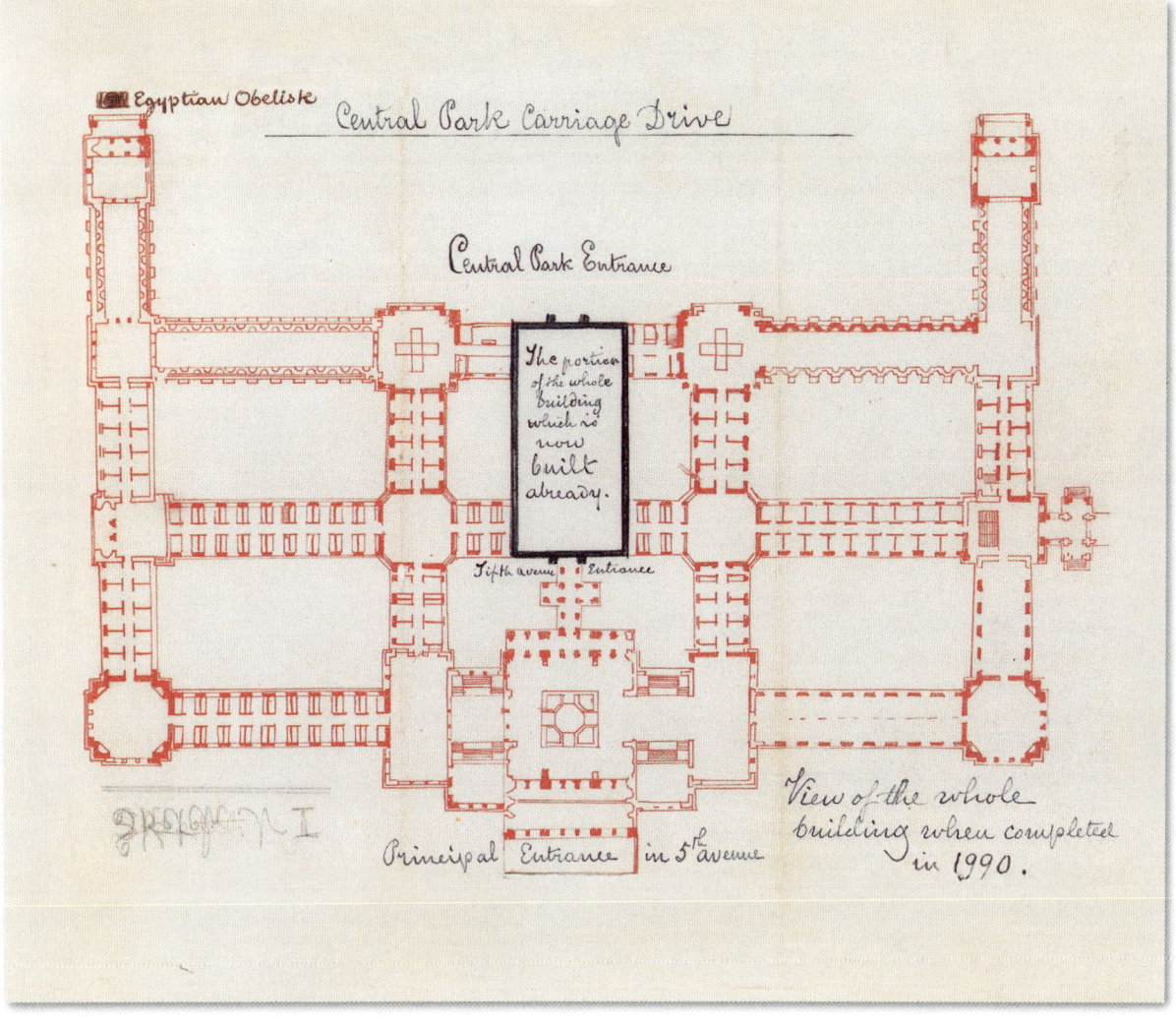

multitude of objects entering cities and their museums through these events, historic royal collections, as well as newer institutions, found themselves overwhelmed, and the question soon arose as to what kind of buildings should store and display these ever-growing holdings.[3] Over the course of the twentieth century, two main architectural tendencies emerged in this

---

3. In *Delirious New York*, Koolhaas wrote that "Manhattan's Crystal Palace contains, like all early exhibitions, an implausible juxtaposition of the demented production of useless Victorian items celebrating (now that machines can mimic the techniques of uniqueness) the democratization of the object; at the same time it is a Pandora's box of genuinely new and revolutionary techniques and inventions, all of which eventually will be turned loose on the island even though they are strictly incompatible."

Previous pages: Aerial view of Little Rock and the Arkansas Museum of Fine Arts.

Opposite: Le Corbusier's proposals for the "Museum of Unlimited Growth," whose walls were meant to be infinitely extended to accommodate ever-expansive collections.

Above: The drawing for the original master plan of the Metropolitan Museum is now lost, this crude copy probably drawn by Luigi Palma di Cesnola (1832–1904) in 1880 shows the projected construction of subsequent additions to the building over a century. The extensions actually built over the decades reflect a variety of styles and the evolution of museological concerns.

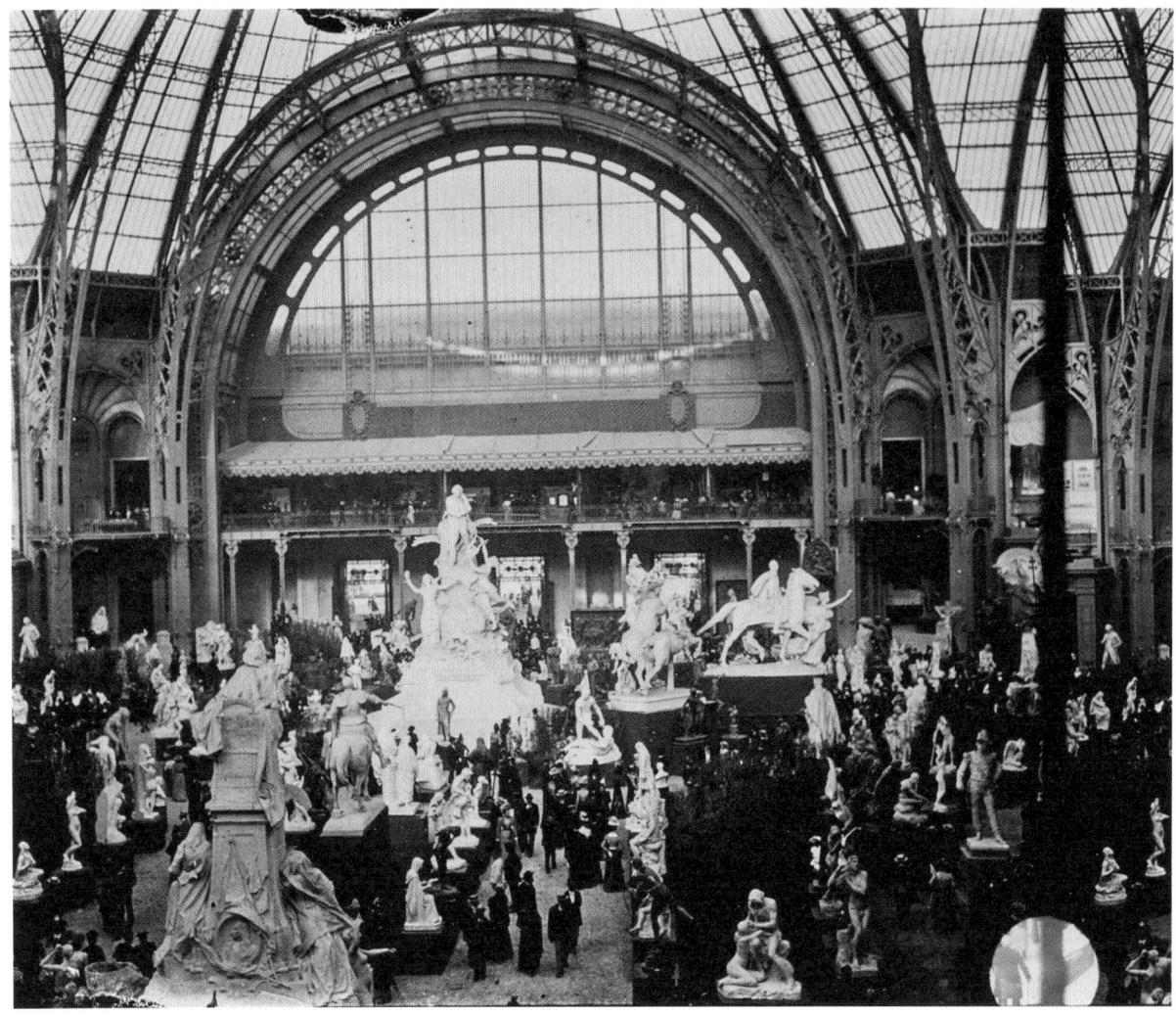

regard, alongside evolving notions of what should be conserved. The first was the *cadavre exquis*, the continuously growing museum, a core to which new parts are added over time. New York's Metropolitan Museum of Art followed precisely this logic, to the point where Calvert Vaux and Jacob Wrey Mould's original Victorian building has been completely engulfed (glimpses of its facade can still be caught at the museum's heart). With every addition and expansion, the Met adopted a new architectural style, but the process has now come to a halt with architect Frida Escobedo's renovation of the contemporary wing. Another famous example is New York's MoMA, extended four times in eighty years—Philip Johnson (1964), César Pelli (1984), YoshioTaniguchi (2004), and Diller Scofidio + Renfro (2019) all made major changes and additions to Philip L. Goodwin and Edward Durell Stone's original 1939 building.

This logic of unlimited growth also applies to New York's Guggenheim, which, rather than extending its Manhattan premises—whose spiral is the perfect ontological symbol of infinity—has opened satellites in cities across the globe in its drive toward universality. In this way, the spiral expanded its reach to locations as diverse as Venice (since 1979), Bilbao (since 1997), Berlin (1997–2013), and Las Vegas (2001–2008); though it failed to take root in Helsinki, and a new Frank Gehry-designed building in Abu Dhabi forms part of the Saadiyat Island cultural

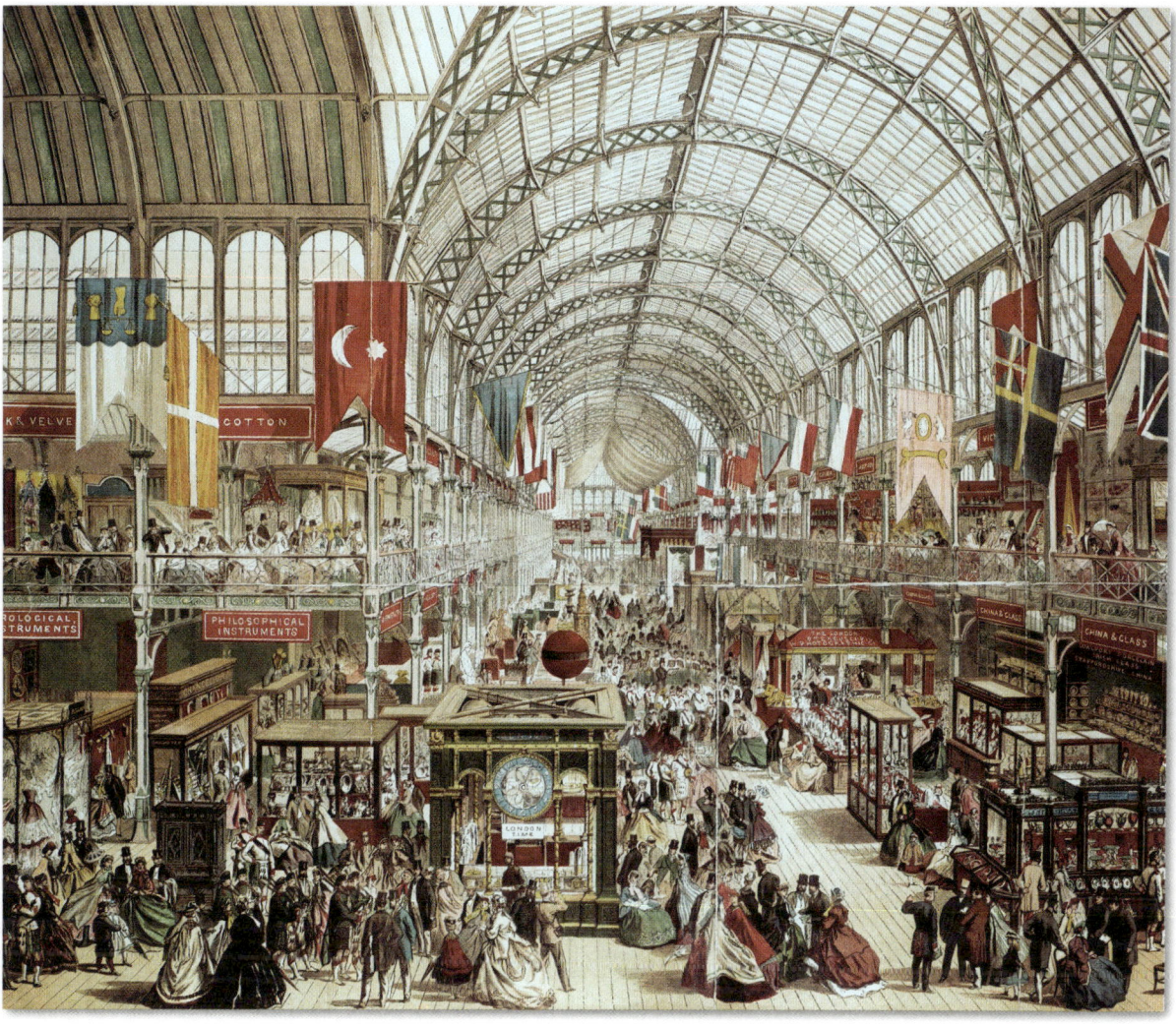

district, which includes no less than museums—Jean Nouvel's Louvre Abu Dhabi, Norman Foster's Zayed National Museum, teamLab Phenomena Abu Dhabi, and Mecanoo's Natural History Museum Abu Dhabi. This trend of unlimited growth is also evident in the vast quantity of new museums that have opened around the globe over the past thirty years. Saadiyat Island is a particularly extravagant example of this phenomenon. From a global standpoint, Saadiyat Island can be thought of as the final resting place of Le Corbusier's "Museum of Unlimited Growth."

The second architectural response to the proliferation of museum collections in the twentieth century was to create a temple of

Opposite: The 1900 edition of the Exposition Universelle was held at the Grand Palais for the first time, and was received to great fanfare by the French public. The monument was dedicated to French art and exhibits.

Above: The display of The Great Exhibition of the Works of Industry of All Nations at the Crystal Palace of London.

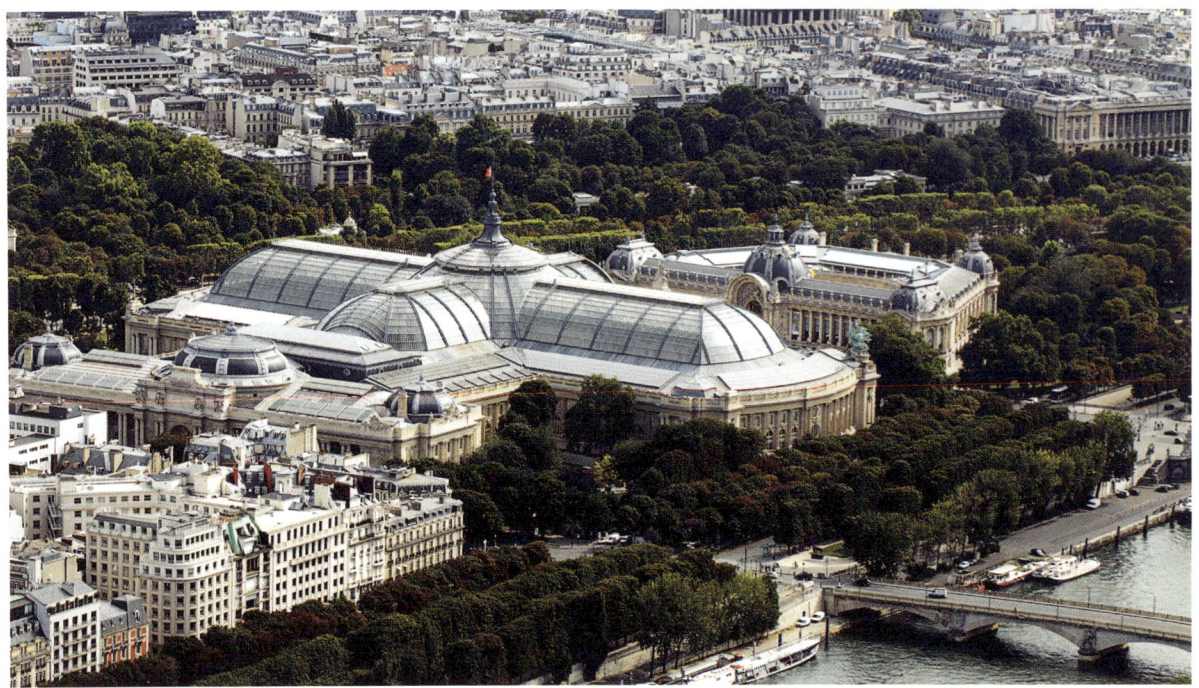

the ephemeral, making the museum the host of the new. The giant temporary exhibition hall built for world fairs were architectures for the display, advertisement and celebration of all the industry, innovation, and technology on which cities evolve and thrive. This was the role of Paris's Grand Palais, one of three permanent structures built for the 1900 Exposition Universelle, replaced the leaky old Palais de l'Industrie from the 1855 exhibition, itself a response to London's Crystal Palace of 1851. With its immense glass vaults floating above a Beaux-Arts stone facade, the Grand Palais has hosted events such as the Salon de l'aéronautique (air show), the Salon de l'automobile (auto show), and the Salon des arts ménagers (ideal home show), forming an ongoing mini world's fair—a sort of museum of the twentieth century. Like the world's fair themselves, these events, along with initiatives such as London's South Kensington Museum (now the Victoria & Albert Museum), provided a forum for radical proposals for the future of industry, technology, and the metropolis. In recent years, in what might be called a gesture of curatorial urbanism, the Grand Palais's original function has been brought back to the fore, and the importance of its role has been acknowledged through a multimillion-euro restoration program led by Chatillon Architectes (2010–2025).

Furthermore, the establishment of exhibition halls like the Grand Palais and almost half a century earlier the South Kensington Museum, later to become the V&A in London, solidified the need for temporary exhibitions that speculate on the future of the metropolis, much like the first World Expositions did. Before these two buildings, the pavilions of the world expositions served as radical places of architectural experimentation. Together with the building of permanent architecture for temporary programming, the museum inherited the responsibility of being the genesis and birthplace of the city from an architectural and urban perspective.[4]

---

4. Despite the interplay between the city and the exhibition, the latter's inclusion within architectural walls did not lead to a new museum form in Paris. In contrast, in the United Kingdom and the United States, museums swiftly integrated industry following the expositions. The hesitation to open the museum—the palace—to anything other than fine arts was an impressive paradox for a city that had hosted the first expositions. French institutions were the exception in the latter part of the nineteenth century, maintaining a narrow understanding of fine arts. As a result, technology, history, and ethnography were relegated to other architectural spaces and exhibition sites in the city,

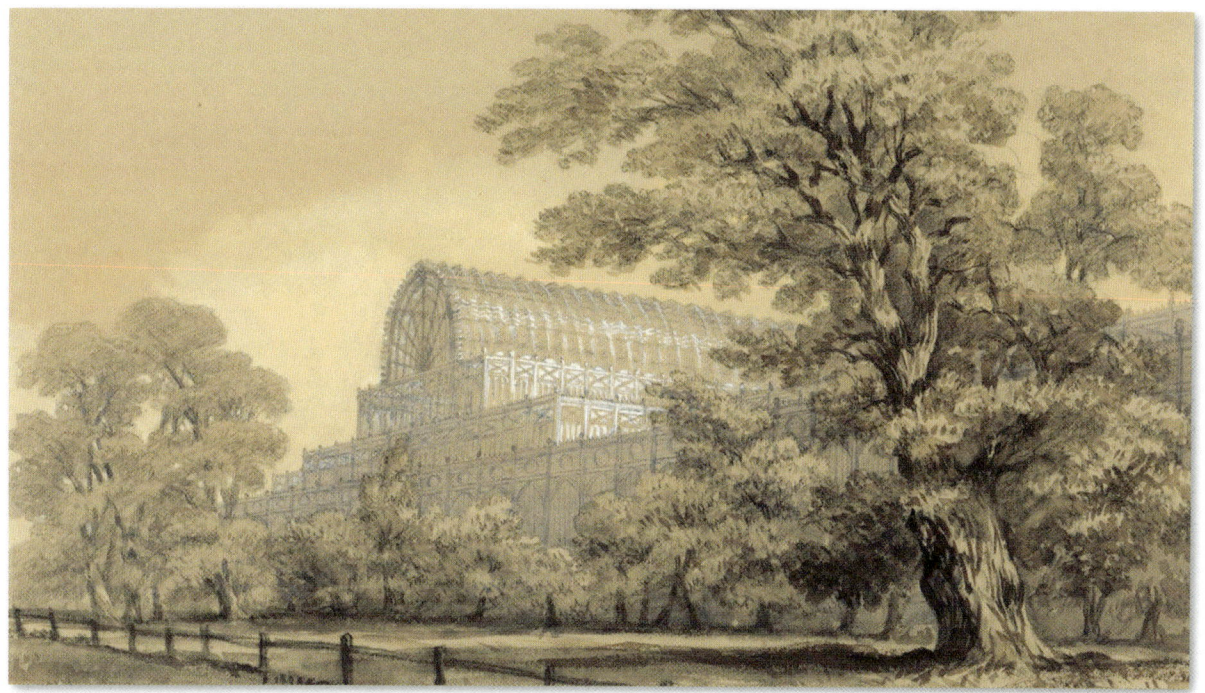

Reviving the original impetus of the Grand Palais through contemporary restoration in recent years has reaffirmed, as an urban curatorial gesture, the necessity of this architecture and its role as a sanctuary of ephemeral exhibitions. By highlighting this architecture on a city map and restoring the building to its original purpose of grand artistic, scientific, and technological display, we celebrate its original vision and raison d'être: to house within its walls the arrival and manifestation of new objects and phenomena that have the potential of disrupting the ever-expanding encyclopedia. As an institution without a collection, restoring the monument that serves as the headquarters and symbol of the Réunion des Musées Nationaux means reaffirming the museum as a non-collecting site of urban experimentation, against the legacy of Le Corbusier's proposal for a museum of the twentieth century.

Opposite and pages 180–181: An aerial view of the Grand Palais at the intersection of Pont Alexandre III in Paris. Initially built in 1900 as a palace of temporary exhibitions, it was meant to replace the leaky Palais de l'Industrie on Champ de Mars. The restoration of the Grand Palais is a celebration of a palace for temporary exhibitions in Paris. Careful choices were made during its restoration bringing to the fore details and hues and reinstating its beauty and glory as a site of discovery, learning, and life for the city: a century and a half later, it continues to host exhibitions and popular cultural events.

Above: The Crystal Palace of London, designed by Joseph Paxton, was built in Hyde Park, a half-century before the Grand Palais for the first Universal Exposition.

---

setting the stage for the continued distinction between design and art. In contrast, other cities experienced a less painful integration of technology and art, recognizing their shared ontology within the museum context. See Krzysztof Pomian, *Le musée: Une histoire mondiale*, vol. III, "À la conquête du monde: Art et industrie" (Paris: Gallimard, 2020), 35–53.

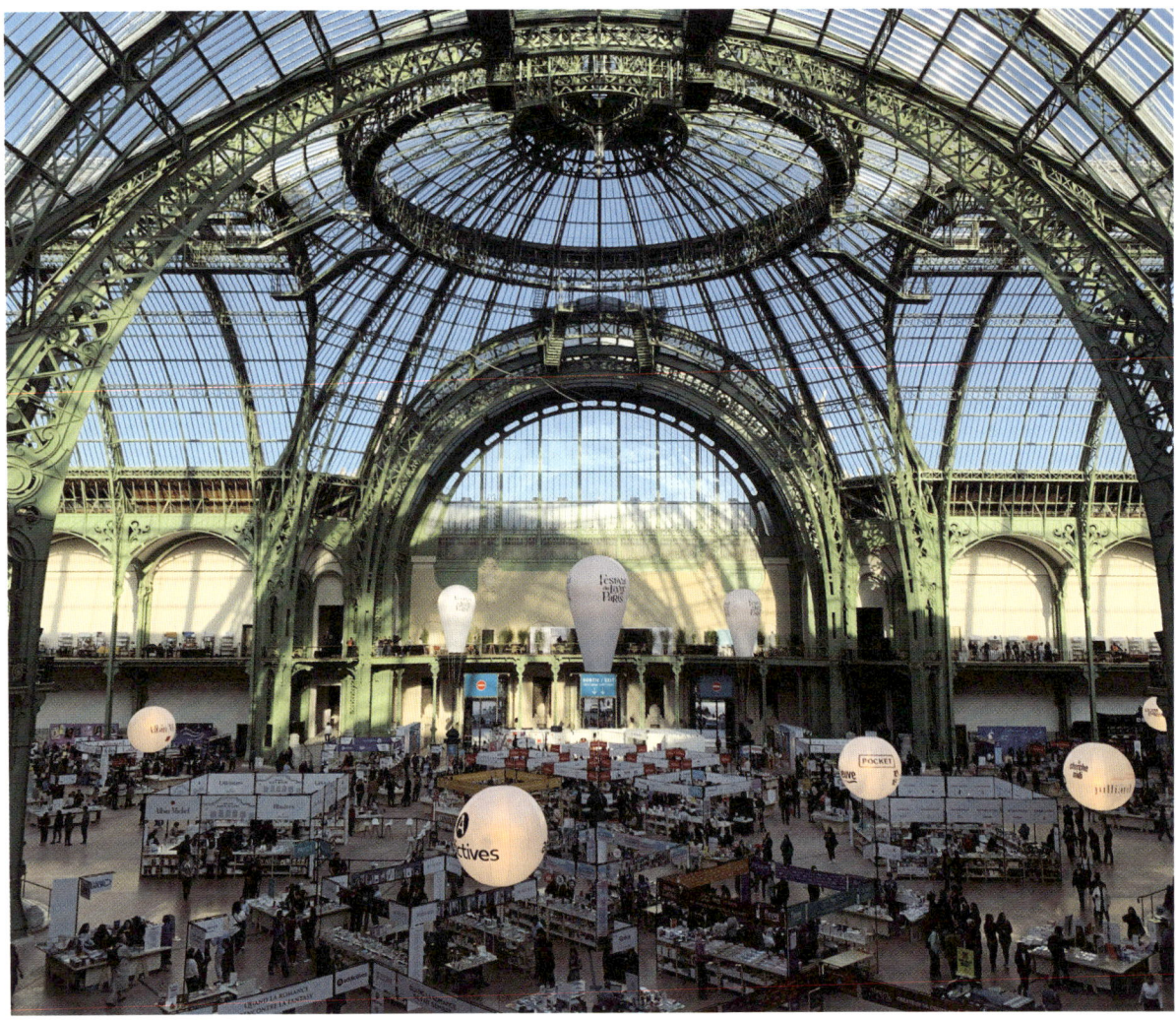

Indeed, what the Grand Palais renovation symbolizes is the museum as a space for hypothetical speculation, rather than an infinitely growing encyclopedia represented by an ever-expanding permanent collection—something which, in our digital age, might arguably be superseded by immaterial databases. The digital revolution has produced a situation reminiscent of nineteenth-century cities during the advent of the world's fairs. Today, just as cities are packed with information and knowledge, so are our handheld devices, and consequently, our homes or wherever we may be. At any moment, anywhere, anyone can access a wealth of knowledge that would have been unthinkable not so long ago. Perhaps we have achieved an even better version of Malraux's "Museum Without Walls" through a virtual realm that stores artifacts alongside books and knowledge in a ubiquitous, ever-available, go-to museum-encyclopedia. If this is the case, why would we still need ever-expanding museums or giant temporary exhibition halls?

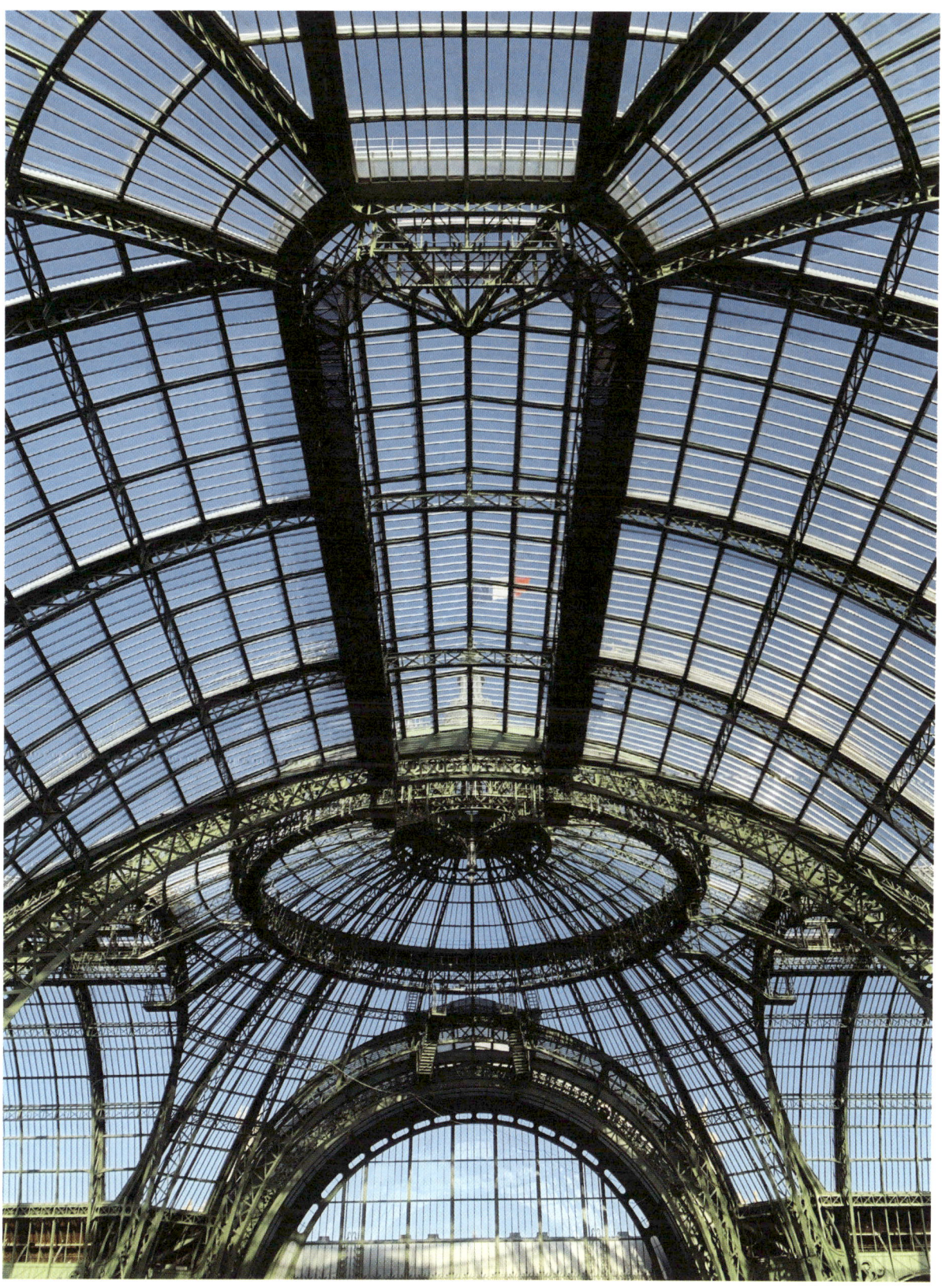

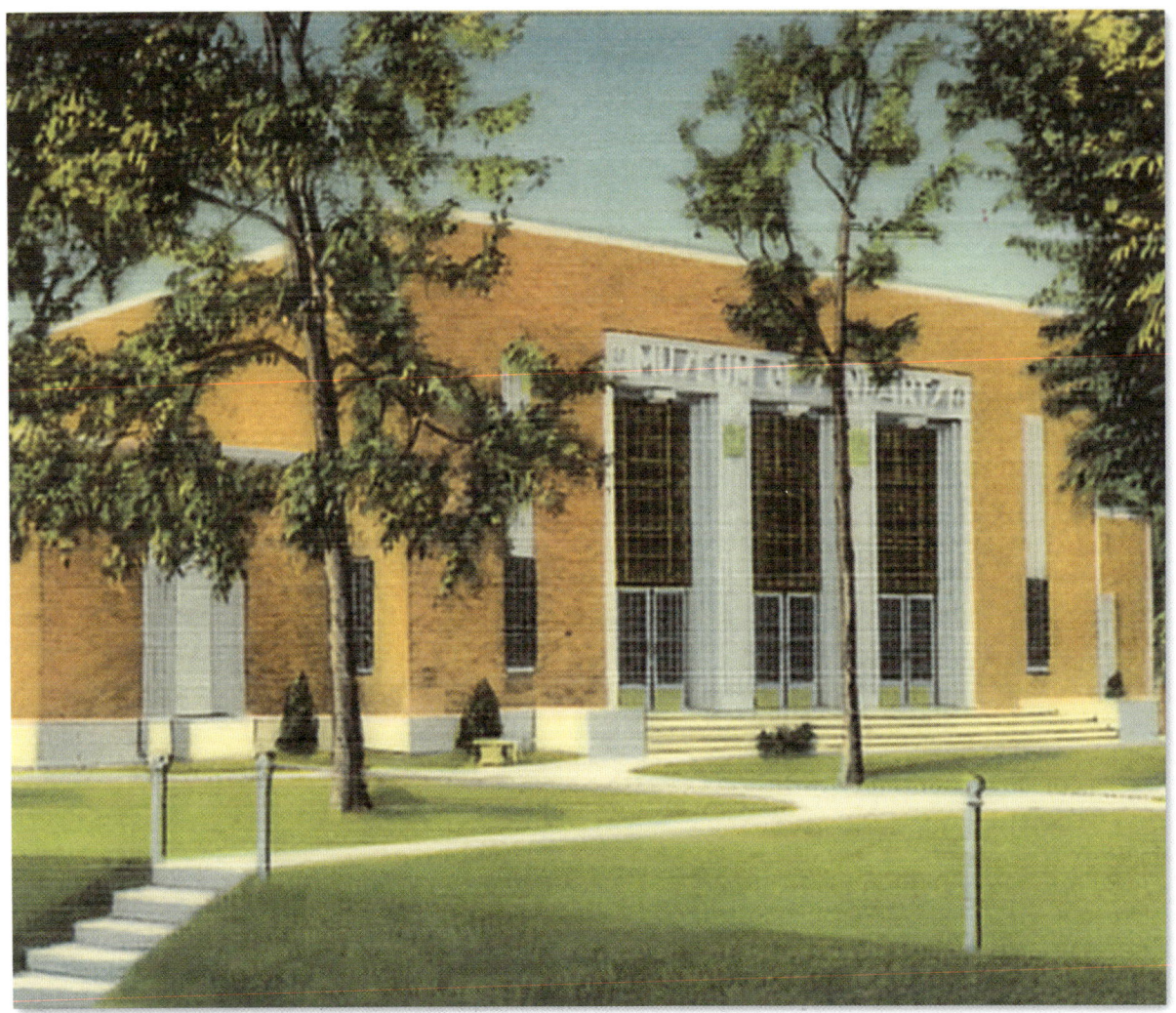

Paradoxically, it is this ubiquity of the archive in digital space that has conferred renewed strength on museums as physical spaces and cultural emblems. In response to the immateriality of the encyclopedia and its digital form, the twenty-first-century museum is redefining its spaces and its role. No longer is it to be infinitely extensible, either at a local or on a planetary scale, nor merely a container for ephemeral industrial exhibitions. Rather, this new museum becomes a place where life happens—a meeting ground where knowledge circulates through social means. For example, Studio Gang's 2023 expansion of the Arkansas Museum of Fine Arts in Little Rock, Arkansas, proposes a symbol of growth from within the museum that connects the city at both ends. Toward the northern end of the axis, Studio Gang undertook some surgical demolition in order to reveal the museum's original 1937 art deco facade, which had been hidden behind late-twentieth-century additions.[5] Designed by architect H. Ray Burks and built by the Works Progress Administration, it features carved allegories of *Painting* and *Sculpture* by the Little Rock artist Benjamin D. Brantley. Today, it serves once more as the main entrance, though not as the museum's street facade—that role

---

5. Its fate was similar to that of the original Met building by Calvert Vaux and Jacob Wrey Mould, as discussed on p. 176.

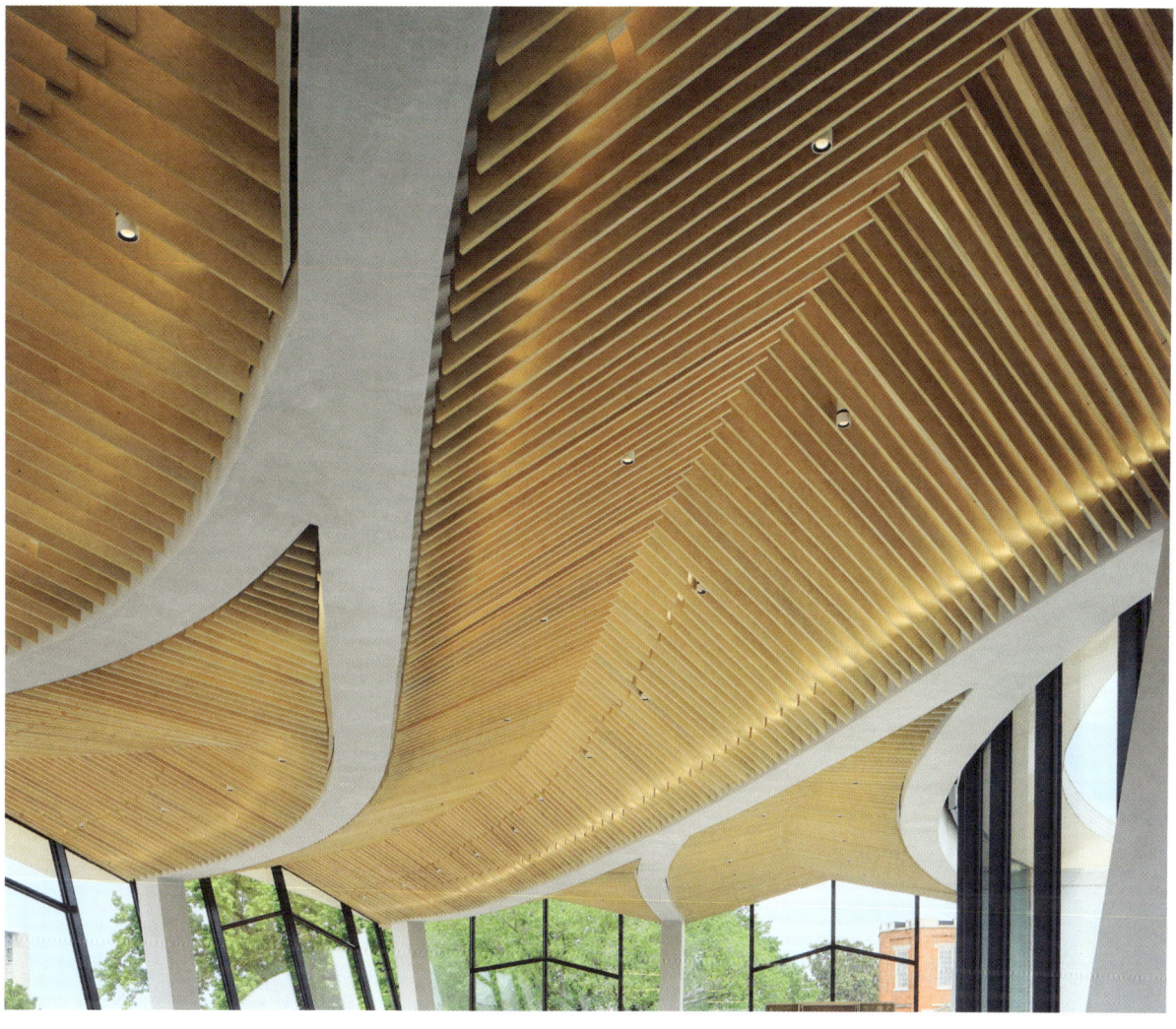

is played by a striking new addition mounted on pilotis, which enters into dialogue with the other structures. In this way, the mise en abyme of the original architecture of the building is itself exhibited thanks to the expansion (itself a restoration), and the original facade becomes its symbol. In this manner, the principle of expansion of the building is itself exhibited, and Studio Gang's signature is the evolving function of the architecture. It is made visible as responsible as it transforms the paradigm and function of space within the museum. The most visible addition to the museum, supported above the original entrance on pillars, in a very sophisticated manner signals a willingness for architectural coauthorship.

Opposite: The original art deco facade of the building designed by architect H. Ray Burks had been concealed by additions to the museum over the course of the twentieth century. Gang's project not only restores it as the main entrance from the north, but the extension provides a place from which to properly view it and understand the museum's own architectural history.

Above: The curve in the roof orients the visitor across the different programming spaces of the museum.

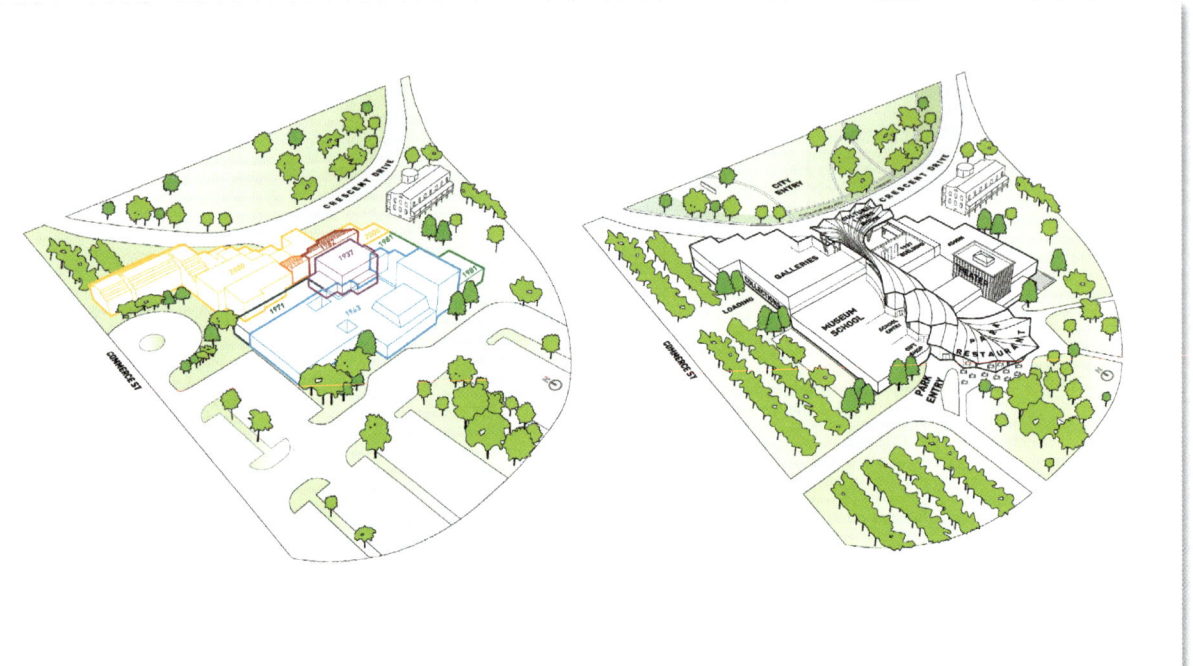

On one hand, the new architecture reveals the old, on the other, it speaks of itself as the object that makes visible the past and future of the city's icon—the museum.

This redevelopment completely reconsiders the logic of ever-growing architecture for ever-growing collections. Prior to the renovation, the museum comprised eight different buildings constructed over a period of seventy years. Rather than just adding yet another wing in yet another style, Studio Gang united the museum's existing buildings to enhance connections between all its different spaces. A drawing by Jeanne Gang shows a sinuous vegetal form, a "sprout" that links the architectural history of the museum along a north-south axis and opens the complex to the city. At either extremity, the new structures that define the axis fan out into space—Gang describes this as a "blossoming"—while new visitor amenities "anchor" the graft into the whole. Moving along the axis, visitors can see into exhibition, education, and performance spaces, inviting further exploration. Clerestory windows bring natural light into the heart of the building, while flowing ceiling lines allow for intuitive wayfinding. The project allows for action to occur in the museum, rather than it remaining a static site of display—visitors not only view objects in an exhibition but learn, interact, create new situations, and bring life into the institution.

In Arkansas, the museum's transformation has expanded the notion of architecture itself as the enabler of a different kind of space for the encyclopedia, one that is a place for sociability and shared human cognitive experiences. Unlike the spiral metaphor at the Guggenheim, extending endlessly over the globe, or Le Corbusier's "Museum of Unlimited Growth," which must constantly add linear meters of wall space, the sprout, while also potentially infinite, is a bud that generates new life from existing conditions. Gang describes her approach as "grafting," wherein additions to existing buildings, parks, and urban contexts transfigure the originals to create new opportunities for their future, augmenting a site's potential and setting in motion an interpenetration of culture and nature through architecture.[6] As an emblematic public building that, like the city itself, is formed from various historical strata, the reconfigured Arkansas Museum of Fine Arts stands as an example of how this approach might be applied to the urban fabric at large.

---

6. See Jeanne Gang, *The Art of Architectural Grafting* (Zurich: Park Books, 2024).

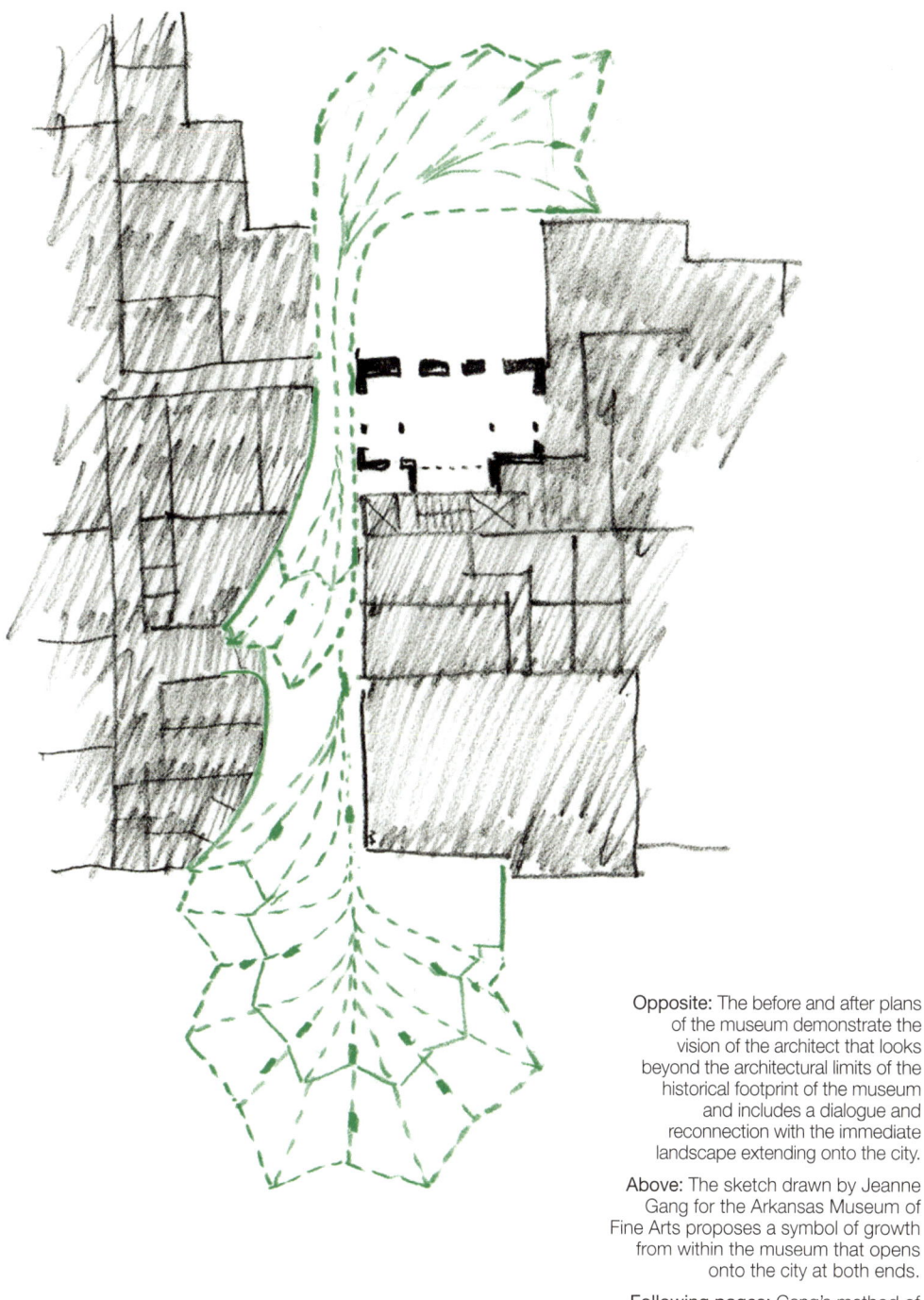

Opposite: The before and after plans of the museum demonstrate the vision of the architect that looks beyond the architectural limits of the historical footprint of the museum and includes a dialogue and reconnection with the immediate landscape extending onto the city.

Above: The sketch drawn by Jeanne Gang for the Arkansas Museum of Fine Arts proposes a symbol of growth from within the museum that opens onto the city at both ends.

Following pages: Gang's method of grafting shows how new and old can coexist and produce a new emblematic public building that, like the city itself, is formed from various historical strata.

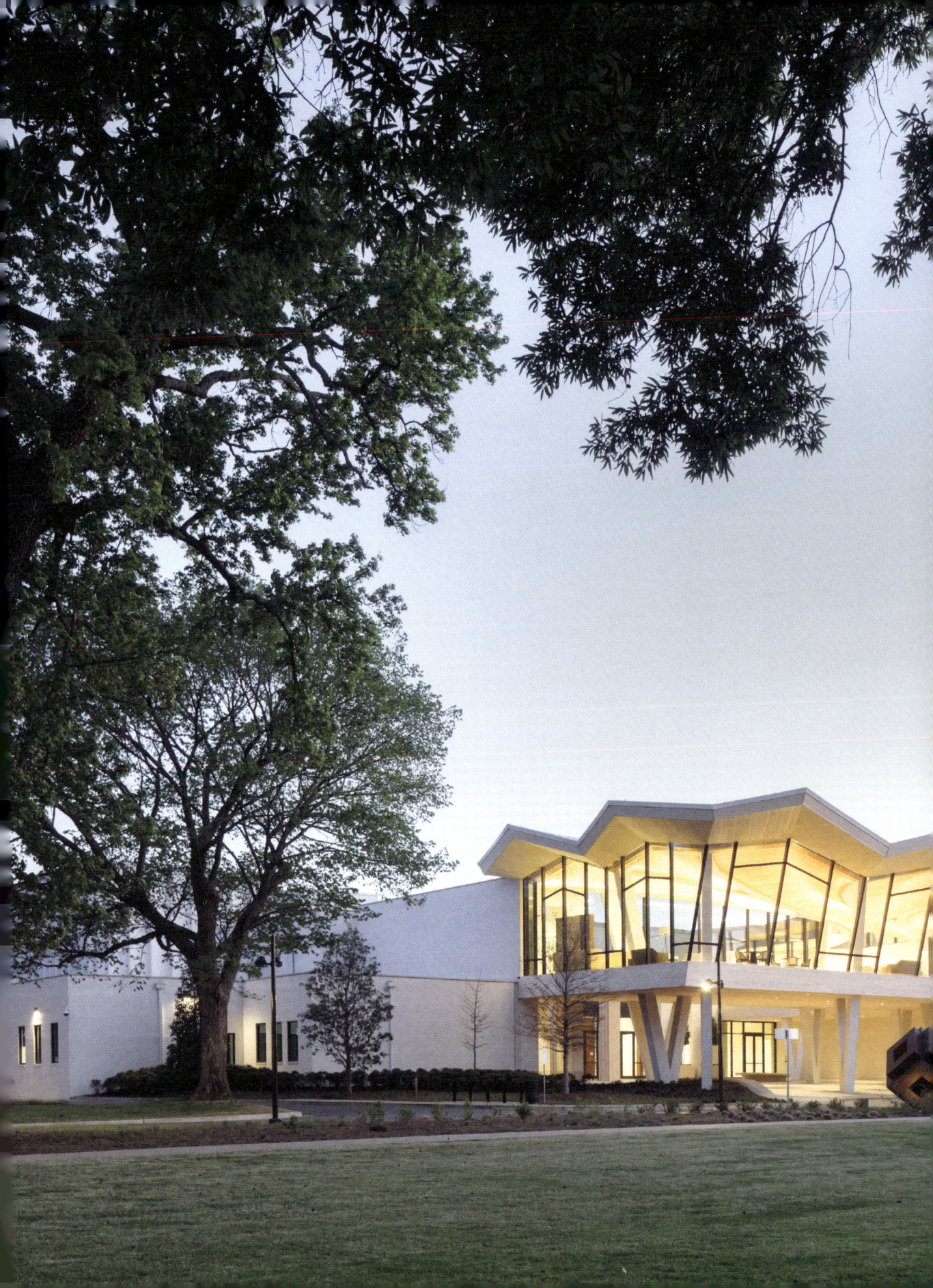

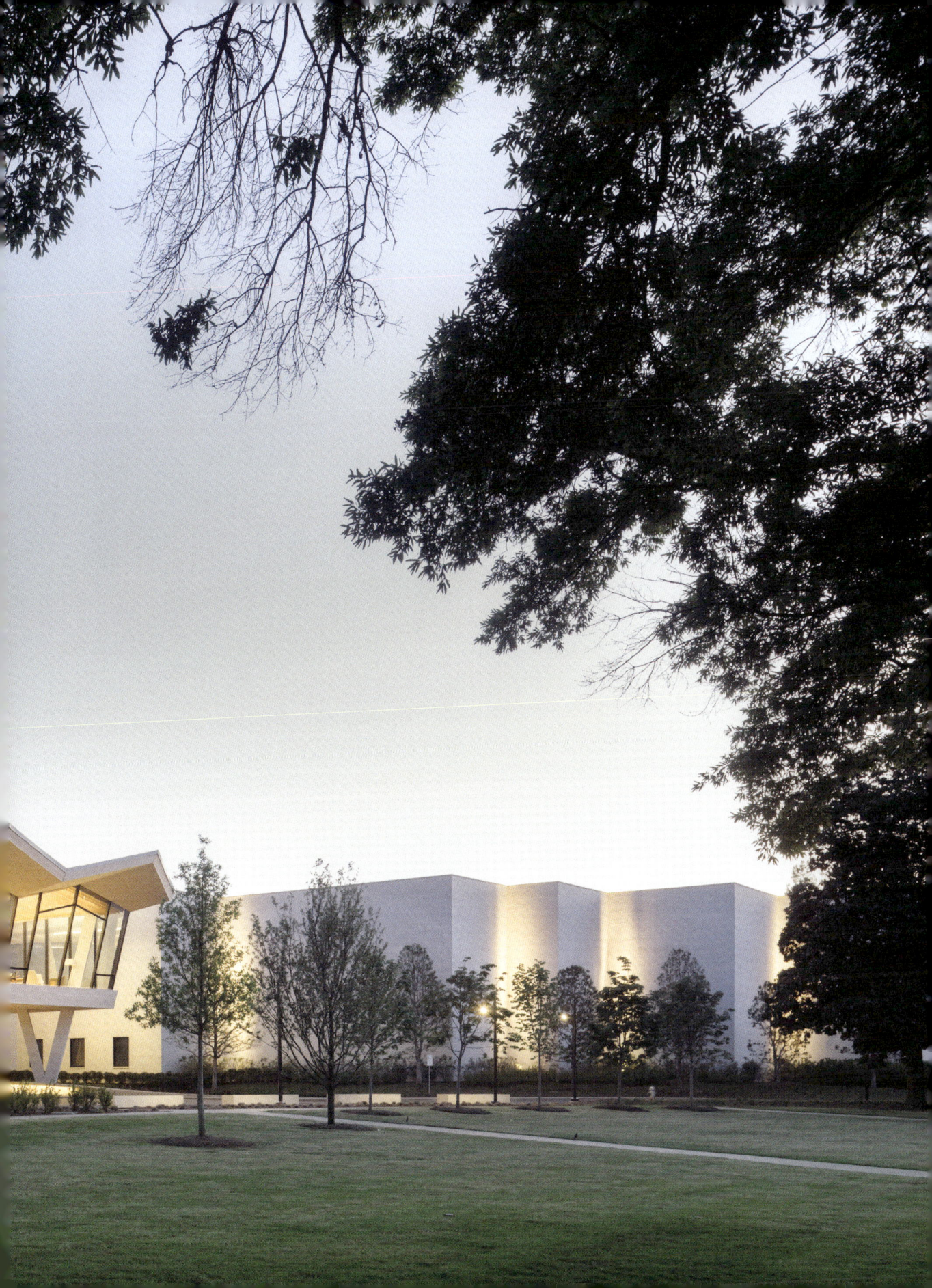

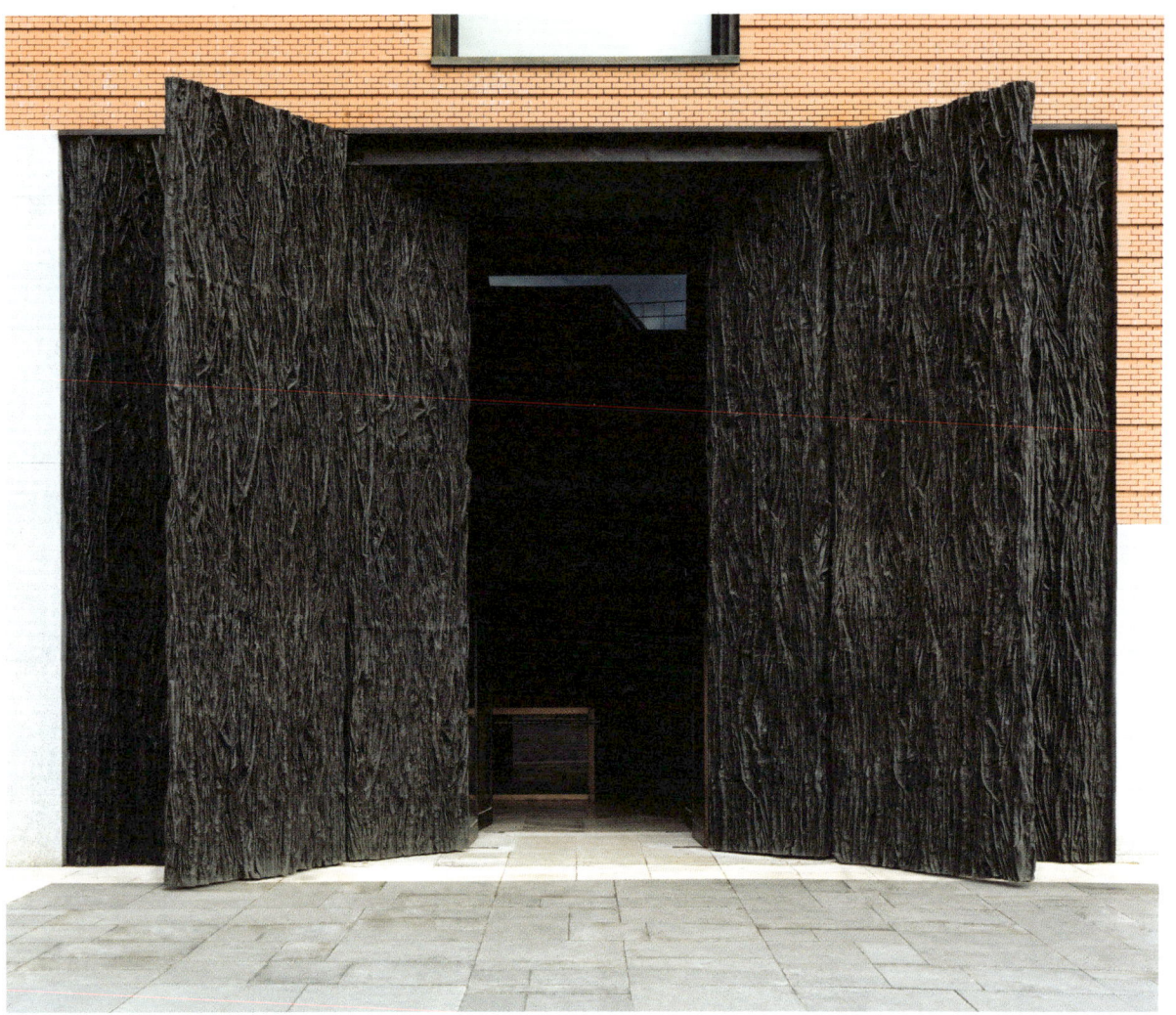

Similar to the intervention made by Studio Gang in Little Rock, an artwork by Cristina Iglesias realized for the extension of the Museo Nacional del Prado (led by Spanish Pritzker Prize-winning architect Rafael Moneo in 2008), is a vegetal allegory that suggests a new way for architecture to speak of itself in the museum and urban setting, consciously participating in the critique of the encyclopedia it holds inside its walls. Like Gang's concept drawing, Iglesias also used a form of vegetal grafting to transform the symbolic joint between the historical museum building and the modern extension. She designed the artwork *Portón–Pasaje*, a twenty-two-ton monumental bronze portal that marks the street entrance to the new addition, which is located opposite the historic building. Sculpted to resemble a dense thicket of roots or vines, the hydraulically operated ceremonial doors move six times a day, on each occasion creating a different form of threshold, a succession of spaces that form part of what Iglesias considers an autonomous artwork. This "vegetal fiction," as she describes it, also refers to the Prado's history (which is linked to the nearby botanical garden), since the historic building (begun by Juan de Villanueva in the 1780s) was initially conceived to house the Royal Cabinet of Natural History. The thresholds created by Iglesias's artwork are liminal spaces, where one stands

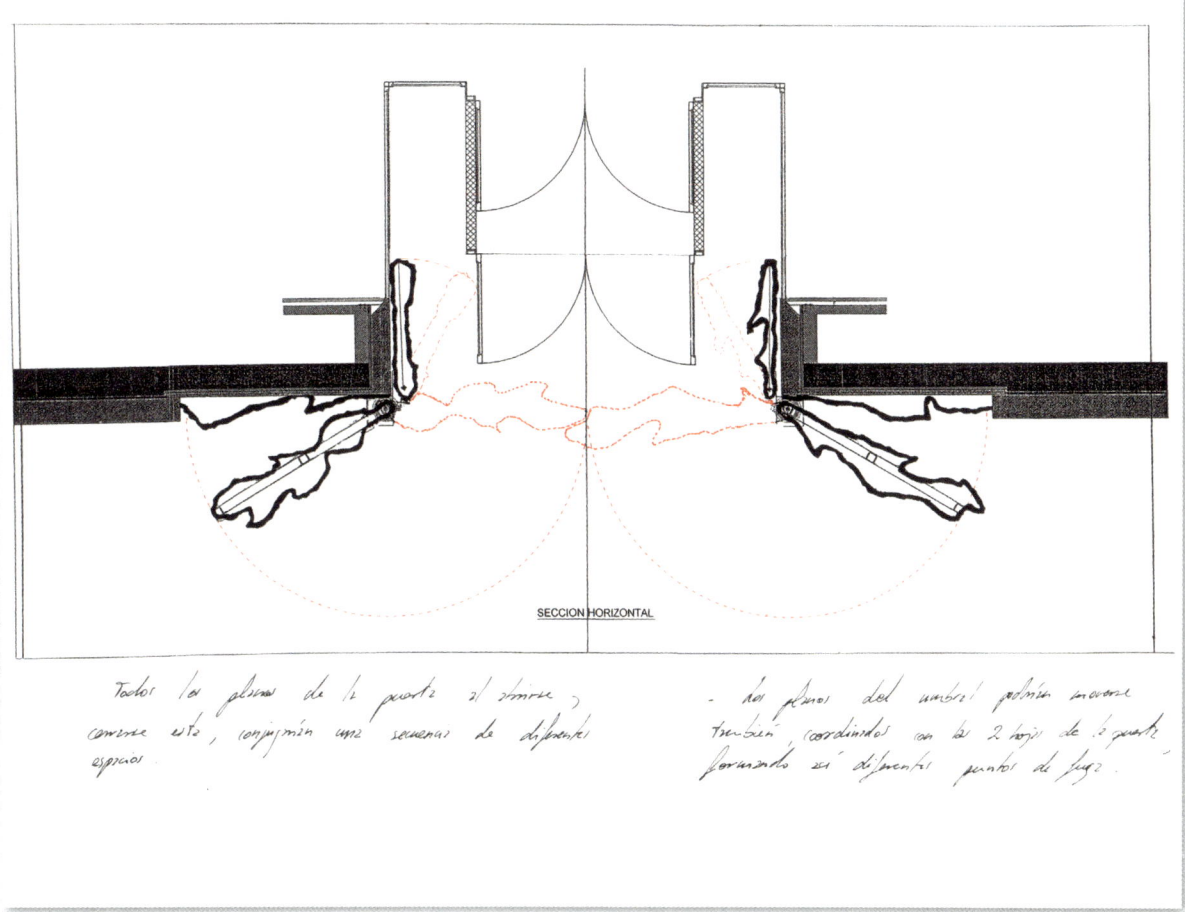

in transit between the city and the space of the imagination, between what is, what might be, and what might have been. The allegory of the vegetal actualizes architecture's role transforming spaces into opportunities for historical self-reflexivity.

Opposite: *Portón–Pasaje*, a twenty-two-ton monumental bronze portal by the artist Cristina Iglesias, marks the street entrance to the new addition of the Museo Nacional del Prado, opened in 2008.

Above: A sketch of the doors shows the movement of the sculpture at different times of the day.

Following pages: The artwork *Portón-Pasaje* serves as the threshold between the historical past of the Museo Nacional del Prado and the new extension designed by Rafael Moneo in 2008.

Pages 192–193: The plans and rendering for the extension of the New Museum reflect the changing nature of museums in the United States, beyond galleries and exhibition spaces. Architects are increasingly encouraged to reimagine their functions among performance, socialization, and events.

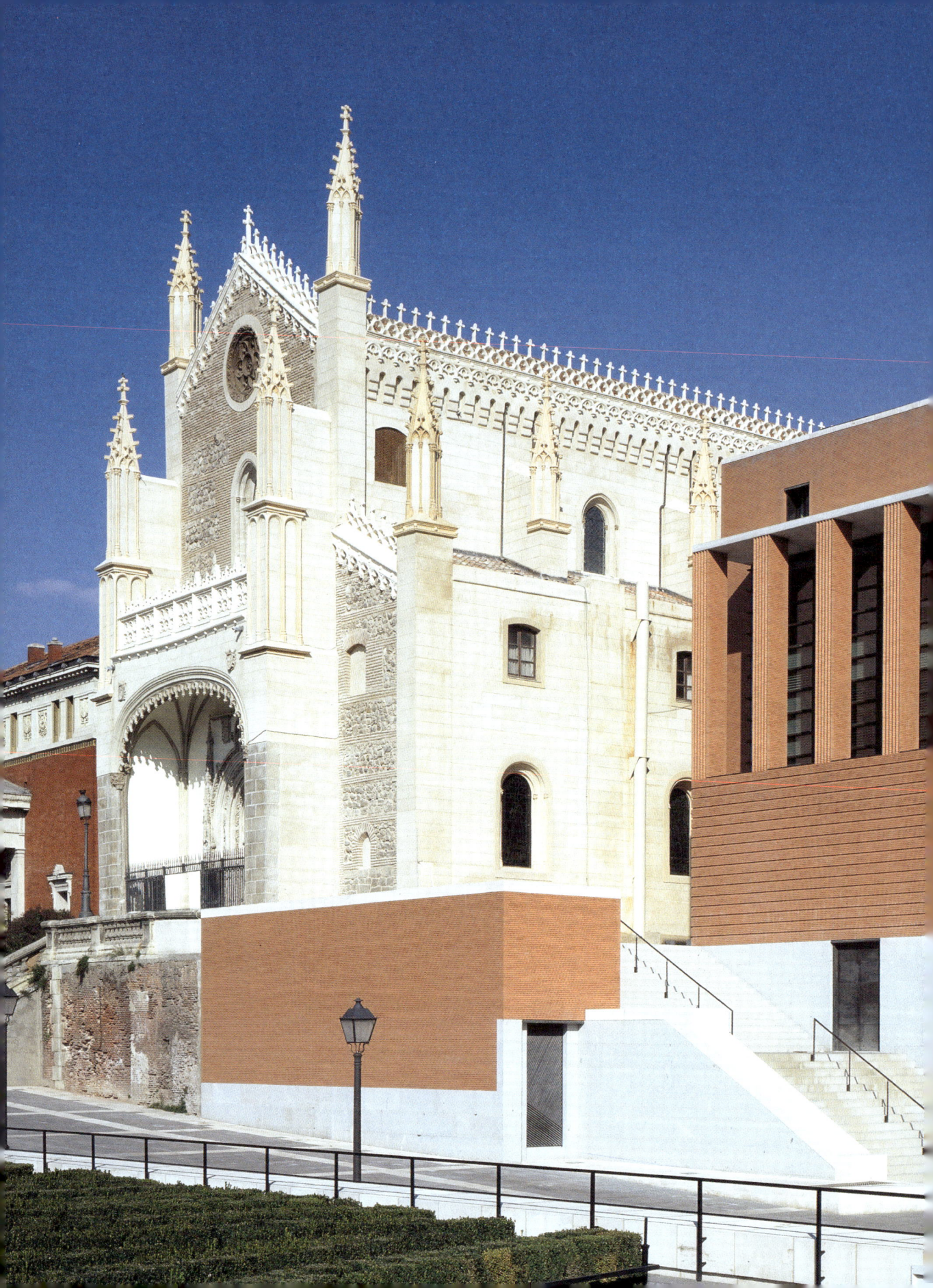

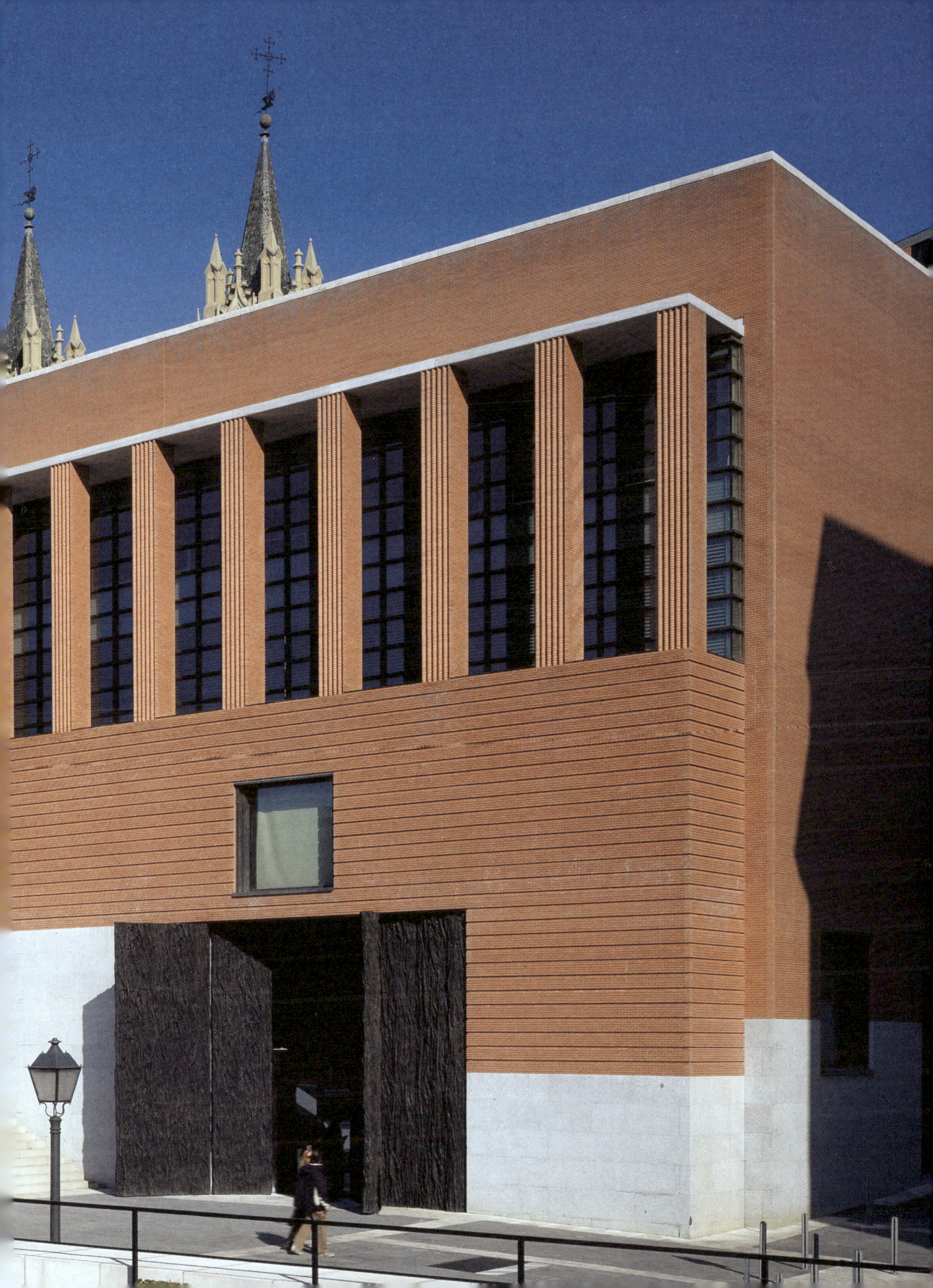

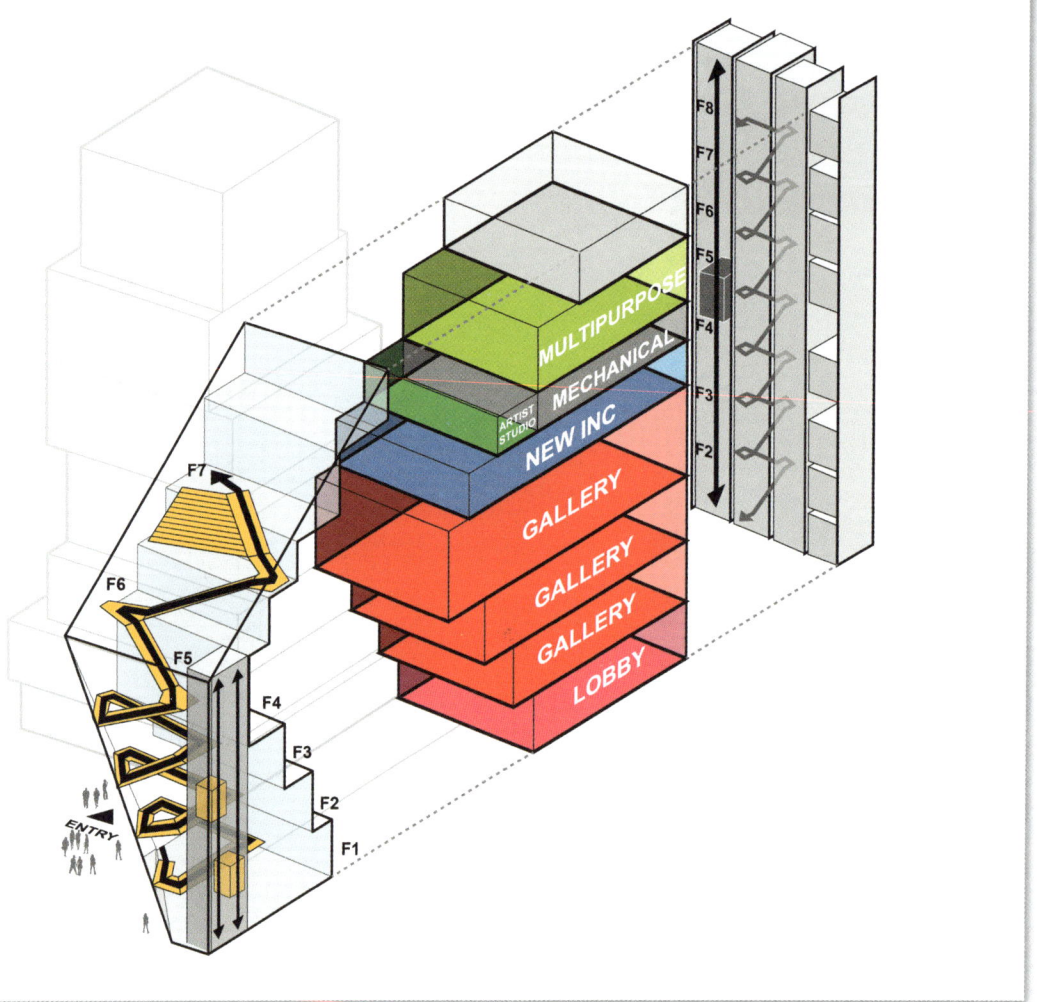

In 2025, New York's New Museum inaugurated an extension of its 2007 building by Pritzker Prize-winning firm SANAA. This expansion of contemporary architecture raises questions about the rapidly evolving function of museums in today's society. Critically positioned at the intersection of Prince Street and the Bowery Downtown, OMA's Shohei Shigematsu underscores the necessity for museums to include undefined spaces in programmatic terms, creating a project that goes beyond merely augmenting existing gallery space. The expanded New Museum not only enhances connectivity with existing gallery spaces but also integrates offices and artist residencies dedicated to Rhizome and New Inc, the institution's design and technology incubators. With this third museum design, the architect is expanding the definition and function of this space in North America as something in between a campus, an art gallery, and a commercial zone. As a non-collecting institution, the New Museum serves as a critical proof of concept for leaving behind the twentieth-century notion of a museum as an expanding body of art and architecture in favor of a community-centered place that space allows for spontaneous, self-organized programming, the exchange of ideas, and human interaction.

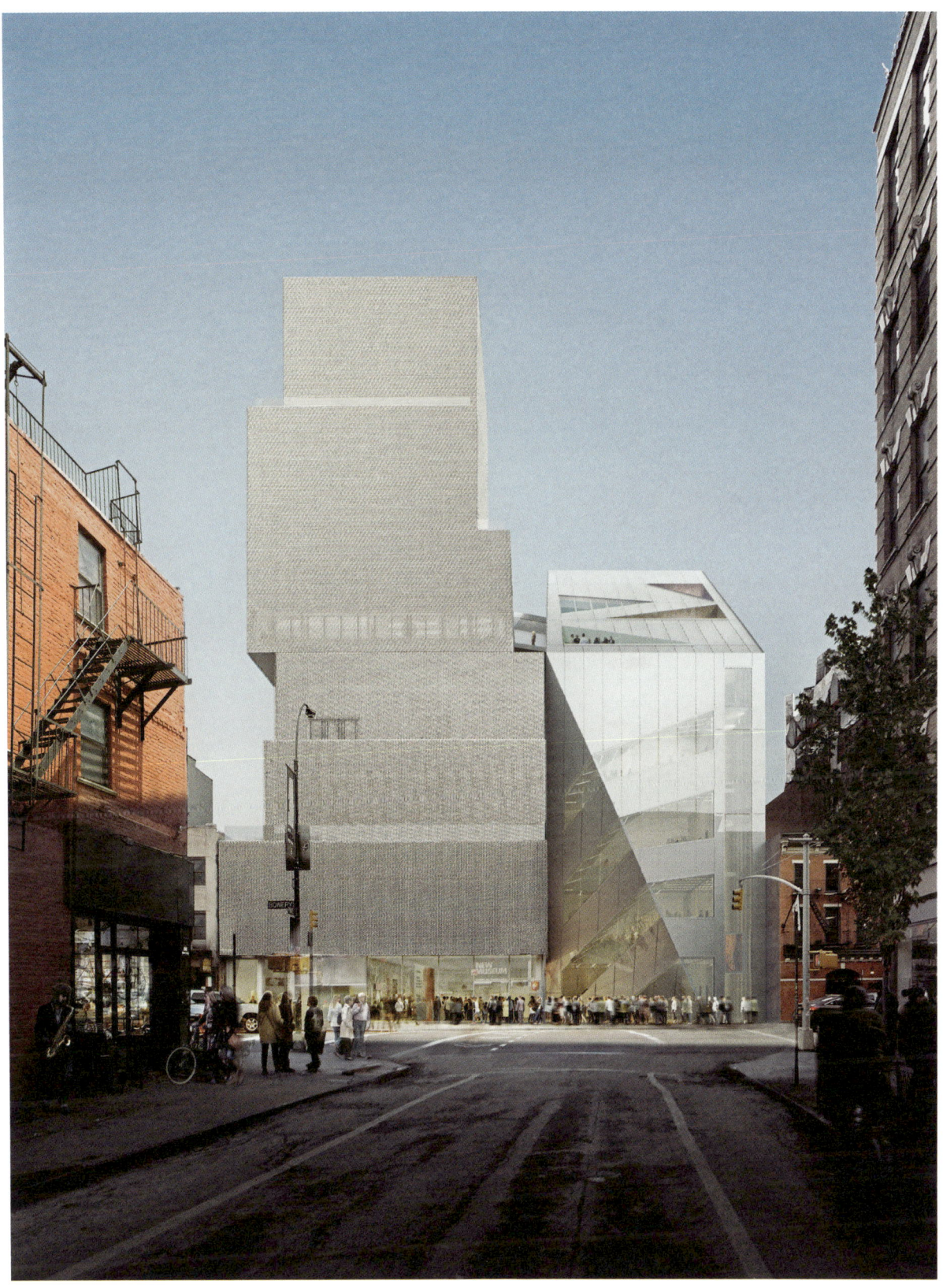

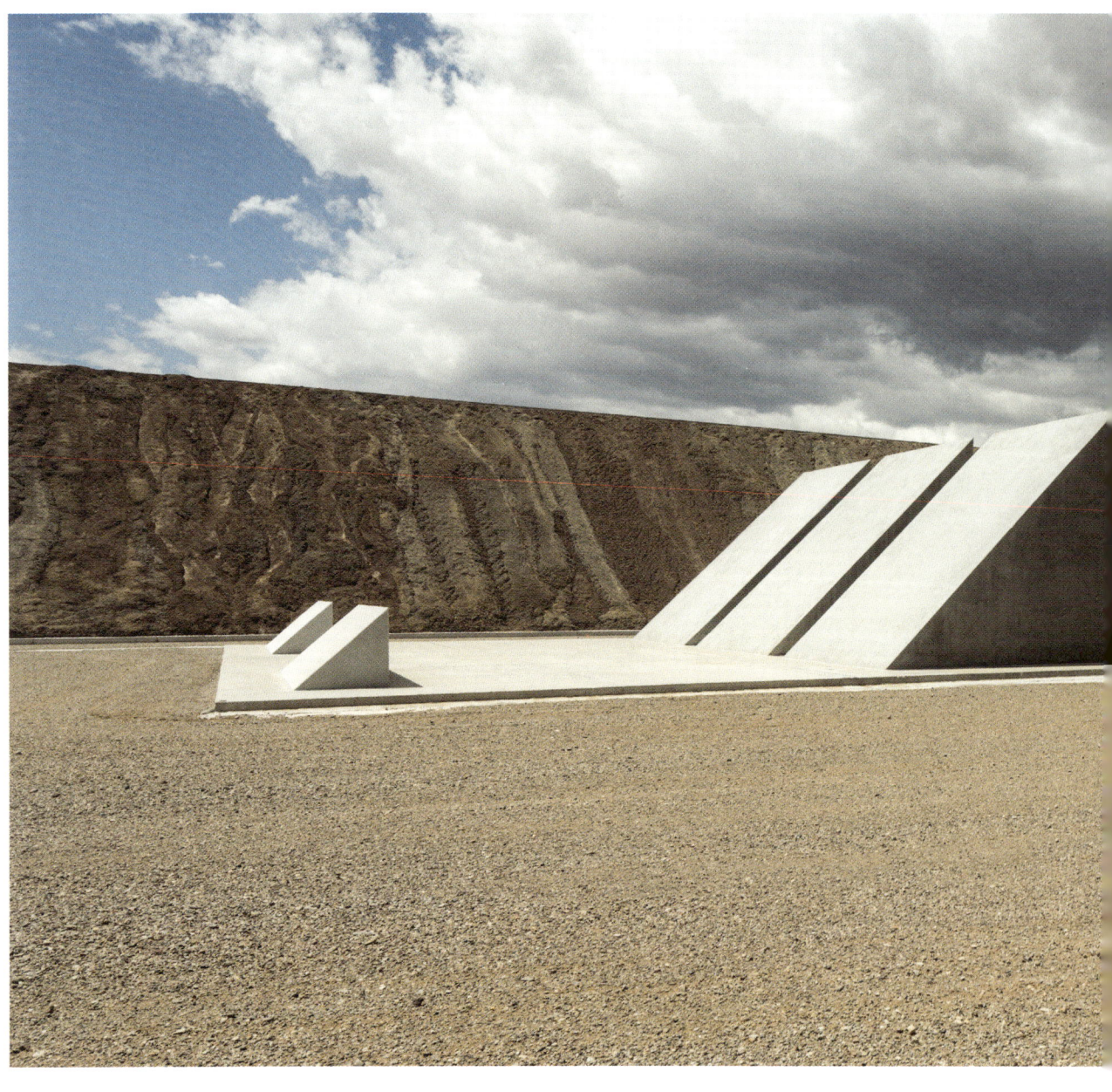

The museum is PLANET

The museum is an archive of the earth

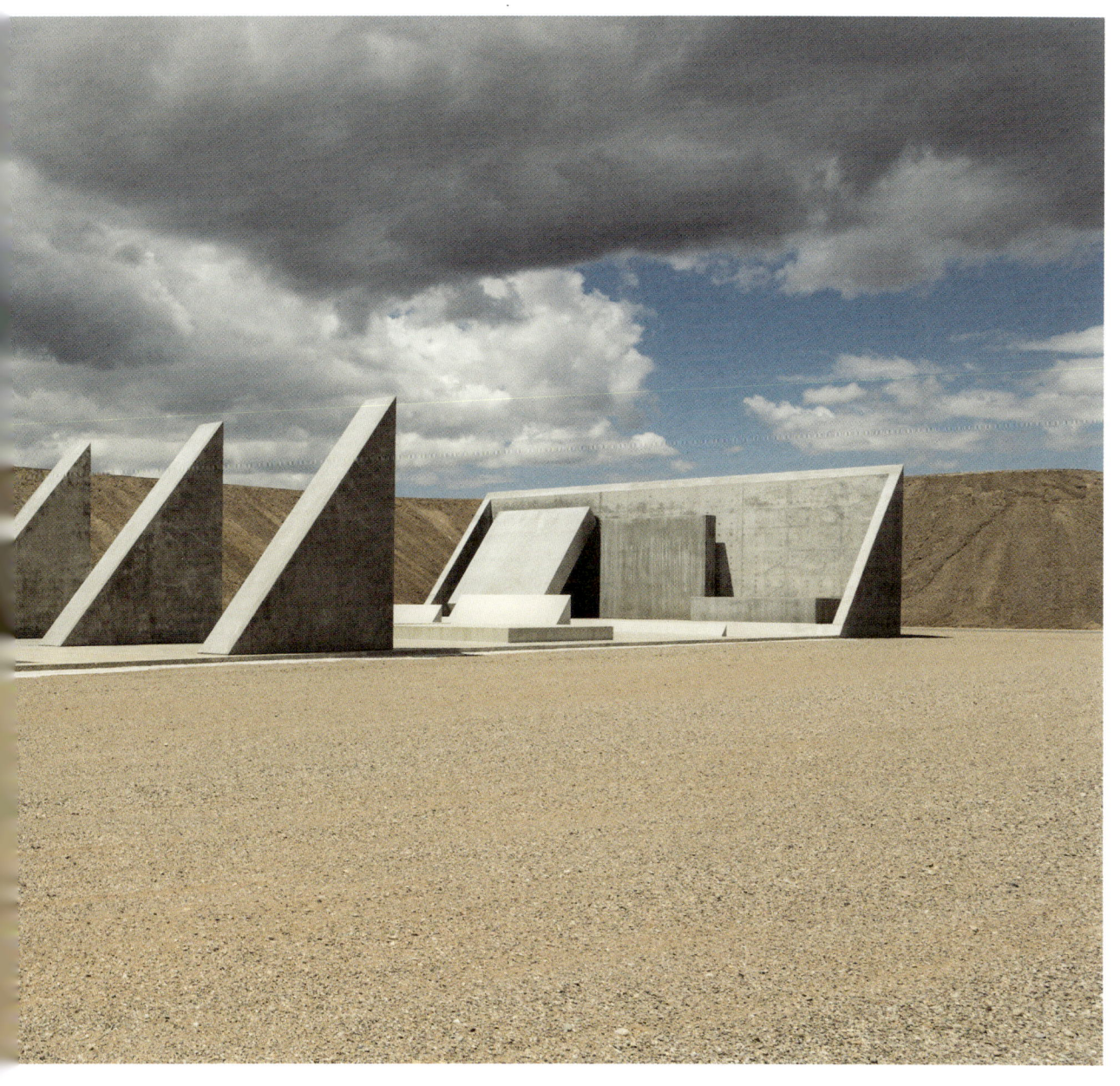

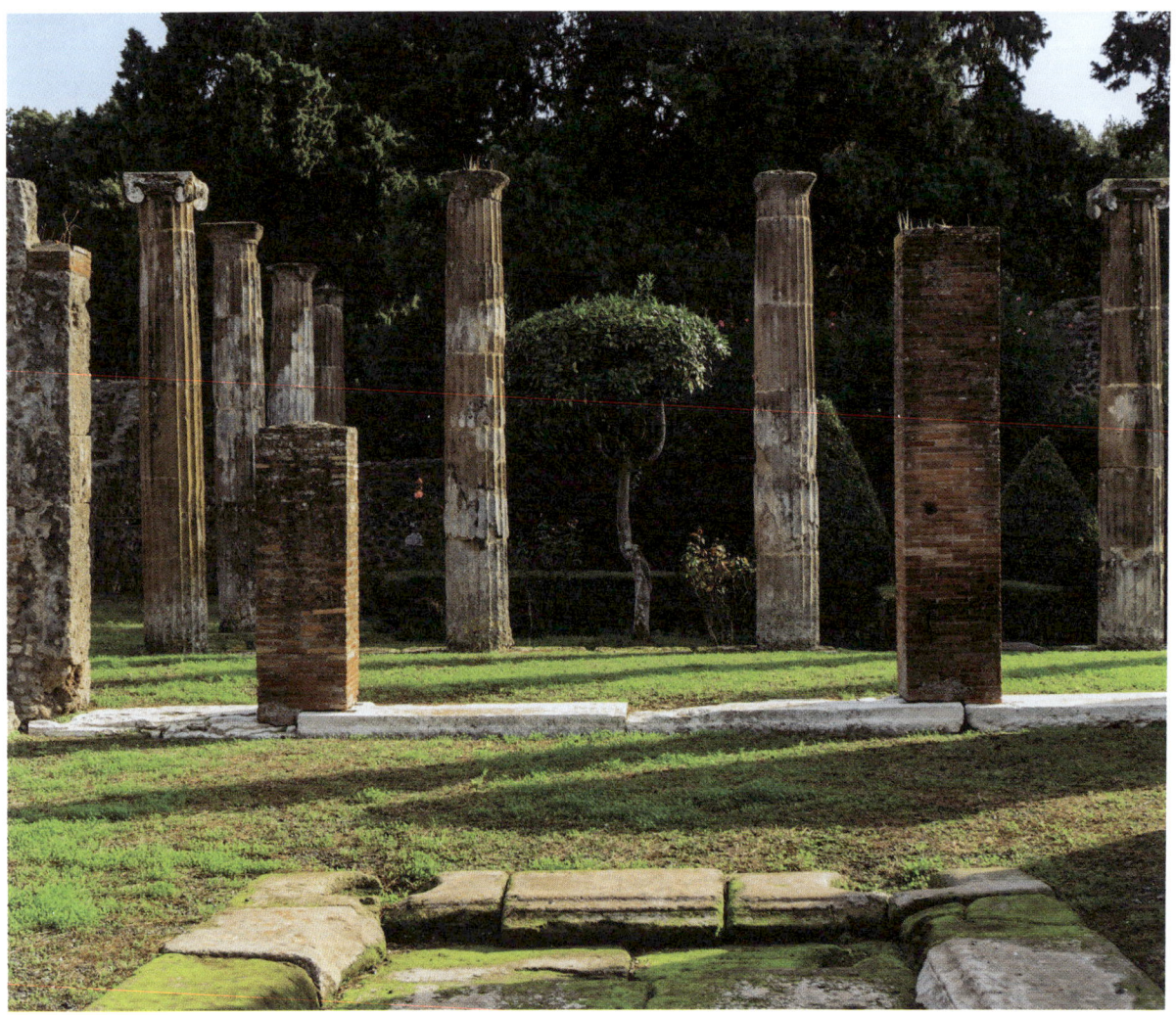

Ruined structures in various stages of returning to the earth attract tourism everywhere, perhaps for the sensations they convey: Easter Island, Chile; Stonehenge, England; Pompeii, Italy; and Jarlshof, Scotland. Indeed, evanescence is a sight to behold. In Rome, the city's ethos is reflected in the "exhibitions" of its past that can be stumbled upon at nearly every street corner, inviting visitors, tourists, and contemporary Romans to peer down and catch glimpses of what might have been a past version of the city, speculate on an absent future that never was. The suggestion of an additional part of a building is completed with the eye and the imagination as shapes are outlined everywhere in space. Accumulated literary associations add depth to the experience of melancholy at archaeological sites in global history. Today, tourists walk in the footsteps of Matsuo Bashō[1] in Hokkaido, Japan, or dream of Byron and Shelley in Italy and the Aegean. Places become pages for commentary, and landscapes transform into iconic cultural sites through the generation of a canon.

---

1. Matsuo Bashō (1644–1694), a Japanese poet active during the Edo period, wrote about the Japanese landscape. His texts can be interpreted as maps of an open-air museum that references canonical locations in Japanese culture.

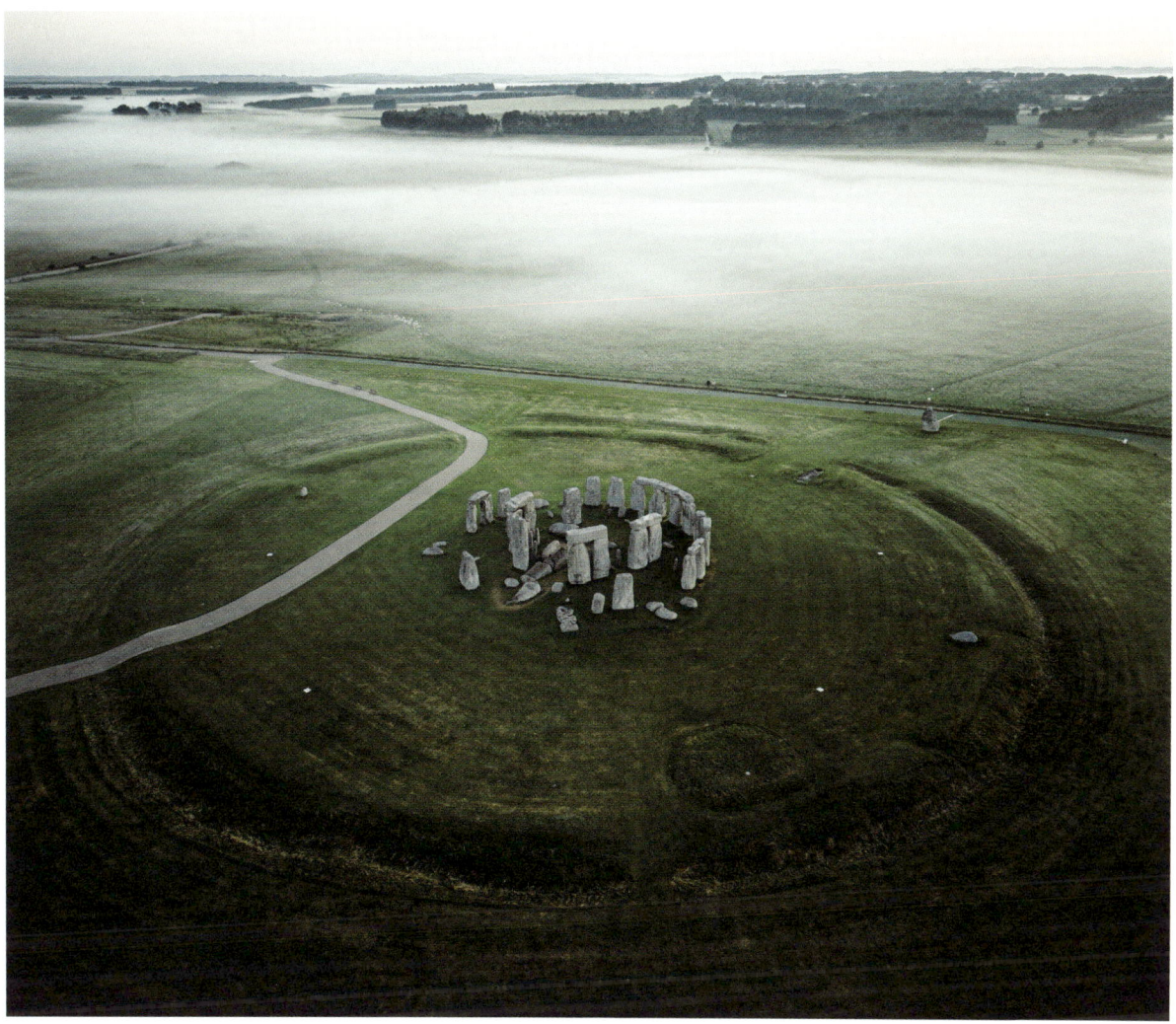

The museum encapsulates all the past expressions of a city—either as its own ruin, or as a collection of ruins representing historical artifacts and technologies. The architectural expression of the museum is a search for a timeless and universal form that embodies a site of memory while making space for new interpretations in the present. The contemporary and future museum faces the new challenge of acknowledging that the totalizing nature of urbanization has eliminated any meaningful distinction between built and natural environments, making the city itself a past form of architectural expression. The geopolitical curatorial project represented by the UNESCO World Heritage

Previous pages: A view of *45°, 90°, 180°*, a part of Michael Heizer's *City*, an artwork that took the artist over fifty years to build in a remote part of the Nevada desert, near the settlement of Hiko.

Opposite: The ruins of Pompeii, preserved by a sudden torrent of lava that overcame the ancient city, are a testament to the ambitions of the vanished civilization. Heizer's architecturally sized sculpture provokes the same sensation of awe toward our living civilization.

Above: In a symposium held at Cornell University in 1966, famed Land Artist Robert Smithson recounted that the ruins of Stonehenge were perhaps the least of spectacular monuments, considering that the entire country of England's land was itself a ruin of time, its coast eroded by the elements of nature.

THE MUSEUM IS PLANET

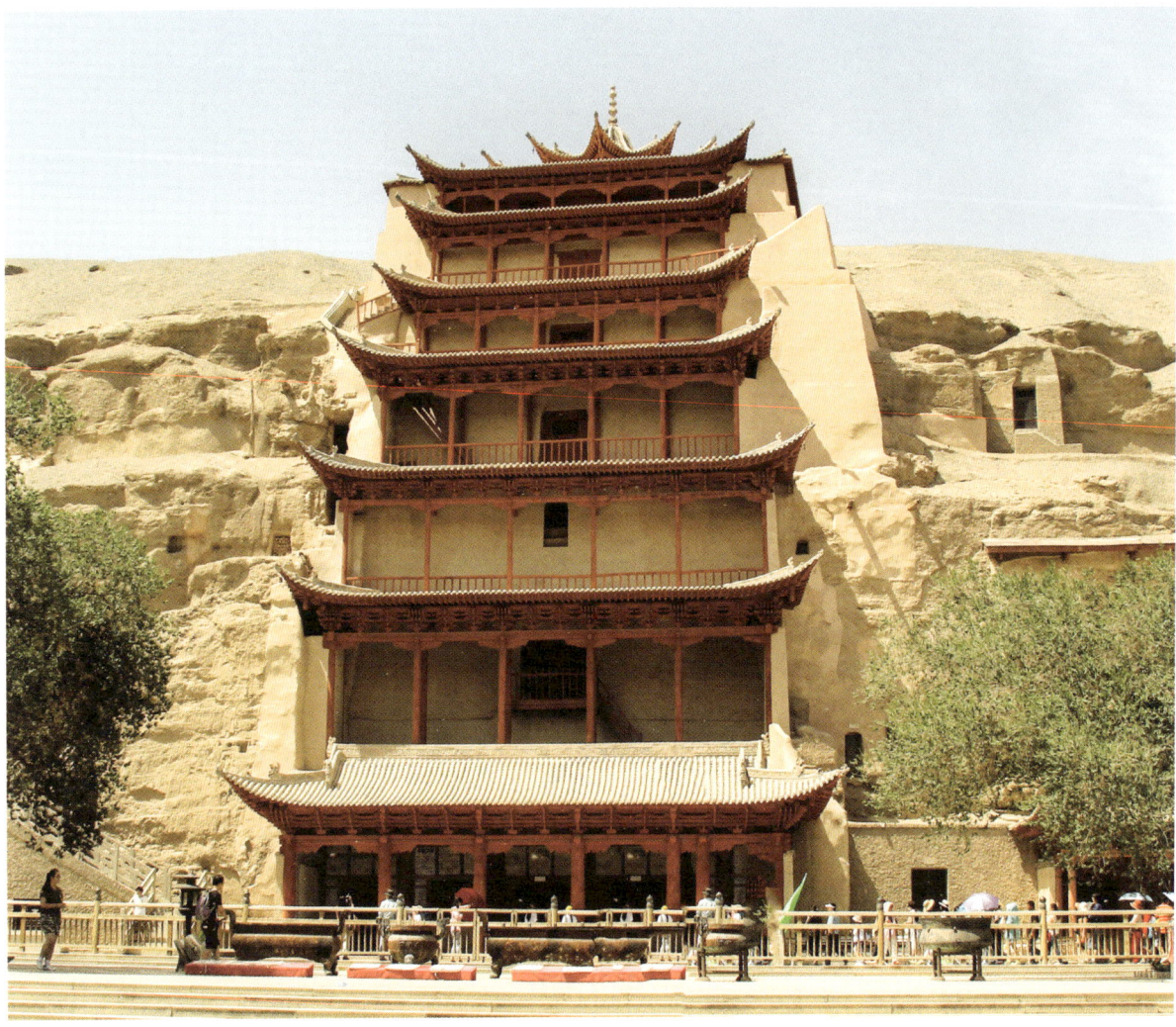

Site highlights our continued museumification of a past architectural definition of the city, a condition already established: the distinction between what is and isn't the city has been accelerated and enshrined by the widespread use of the car.[2] Indeed, Frank Lloyd Wright's proposal for Broadacre City, first put forward in the 1930s, imagined the entire American landscape becoming a giant, loosely structured urban continuum thanks to the mobility offered by the automobile. What the architect's speculative project demonstrated was the transformation of the planet's surface into the primary material of the twentieth-century art—the city.[3]

As such, it is no longer sufficient for the contemporary museum to exist merely as a jewel in the grid; its architecture must recognize a new philosophical form with the potential to manifest in the landscape as much as in exhibition spaces or urban infrastructure. The transformation of the earth's crust into the fabric of the city, and therefore the museum itself, has already been achieved thousands of years ago

---

2. See chapter "The In-Between," p. 129, for discussion on the notion of UNESCO World Heritages Sites as a geopolitical curatorial project.
3. See Frank Lloyd Wright, *The Disappearing City* (New York: W. F. Payson, 1932).

ARCHITECTURE FOR CULTURE

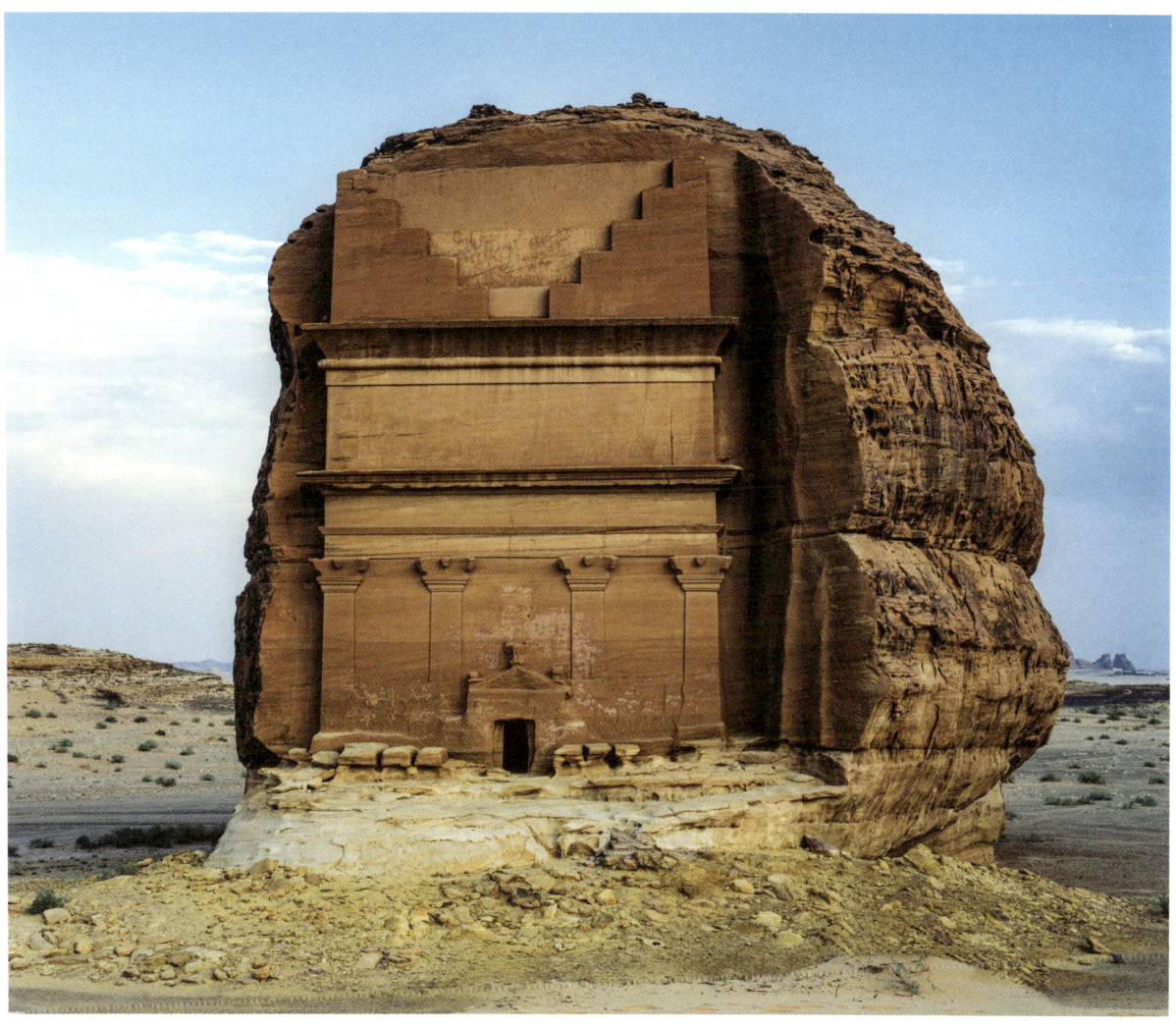

and several times over with the foundation of ancient cities. For example, consider the cave temples around Dunhuang, on the edge of the Gobi Desert in China's Gansu Province, dating back to the fourth century CE. The very geomorphic material of the city, carved into rock, constitutes its art and architecture. Within, the Dunhuang caves contain a thousand years of Chinese painting nestled in spaces within a hollowed-out cliff. For more than a millennium, walls of these rock formations, shaped by the earth itself, were a repository of Buddhist art.[4]

Opposite: The Dunhuang site is located at a historically strategic point along the Silk Road, at the crossroads of trade as well as religious, cultural, and intellectual influences. The 492 cells and cave sanctuaries in Mogao are famous for their statues and wall paintings, spanning 1,000 years of Buddhist art.

Above: Hegra is the largest preserved site of the civilization of the Nabataeans south of Petra in Jordan. It features well-preserved monumental tombs with decorated facades dating from the first century BC to the first century AD. The site also features some fifty inscriptions of the pre-Nabataean period and some cave drawings.

---

4. See Wu Hung, *Spatial Dunhuang: Experiencing the Mogao Caves* (Seattle: University of Washington Press, 2023).

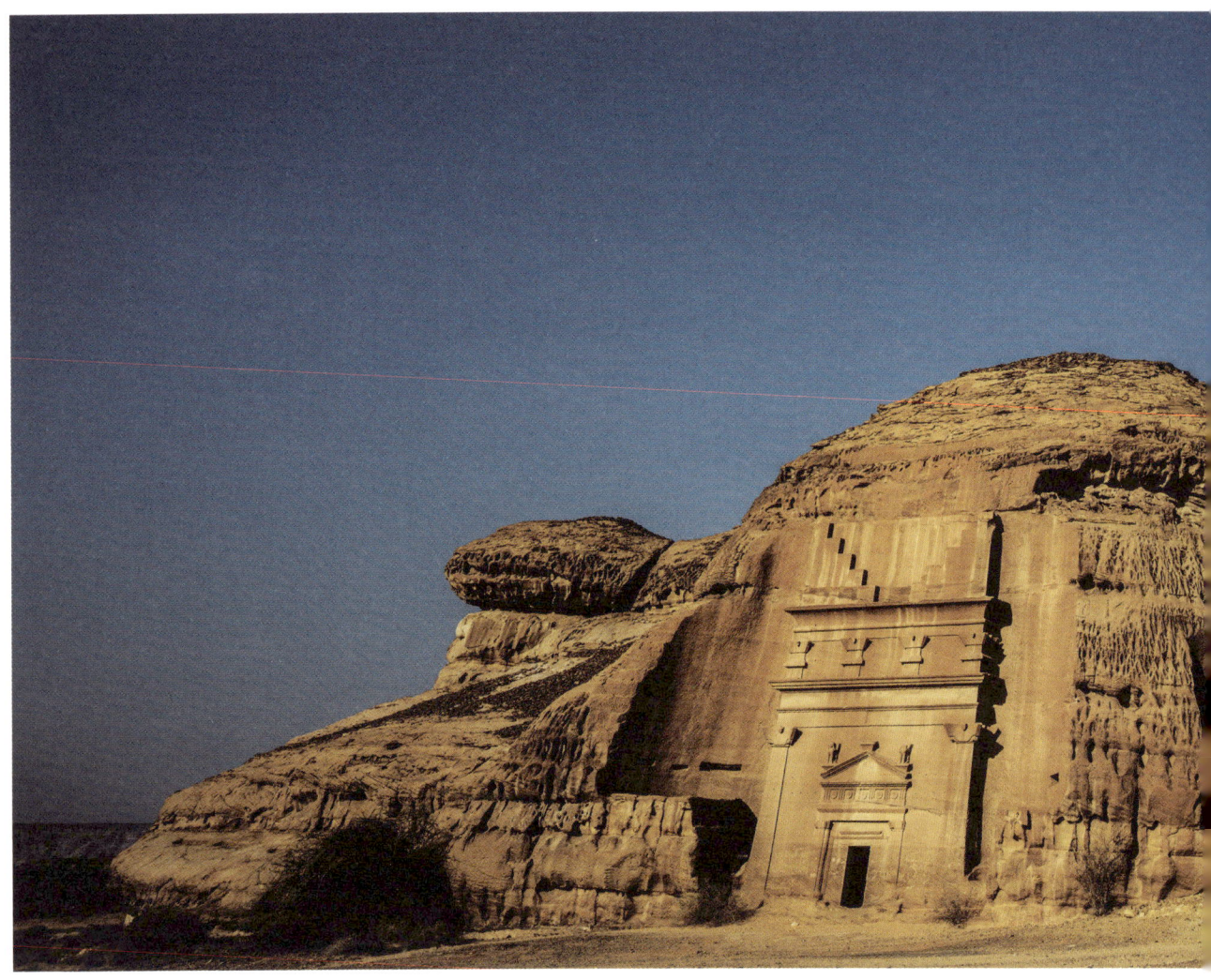

Contemporary museum architecture is an experiment that attempts to arrive at what might be the form of a contemporary city that encapsulates its past while allowing for spaces that future interpretations of the heritage it collects. As a typology designed to conserve collections, museum architecture is ontologically one that must project its existence into the future. As such, it rejects the nostalgia of ruins: its constant reinvention through new additions and transformations prevents petrification, while entropy must never be allowed to gain the upper hand.

In Saudi Arabia, an experiment is underway at two sites of archaeological and historical significance to formulate a new type of museum that acknowledges past expressions and cities while rejecting cultural petrification. Hegra, the country's first UNESCO World Heritage Site, designated in 2008, is located 186 miles north of Medina. It features well-preserved funerary architecture—monumental rock-cut tombs with decorated facades—built by the Nabataeans (whose kingdom also included Petra) between 9 BCE and 40 CE. The opening of Hegra to foreign tourism reminds us that Saudi Arabia has been an important stop on international trade routes for millennia. Spearheaded by the Royal Commission, the opening of Villa Hegra, a cultural center at this precise location with an ambitious program of artist residencies, commissions,

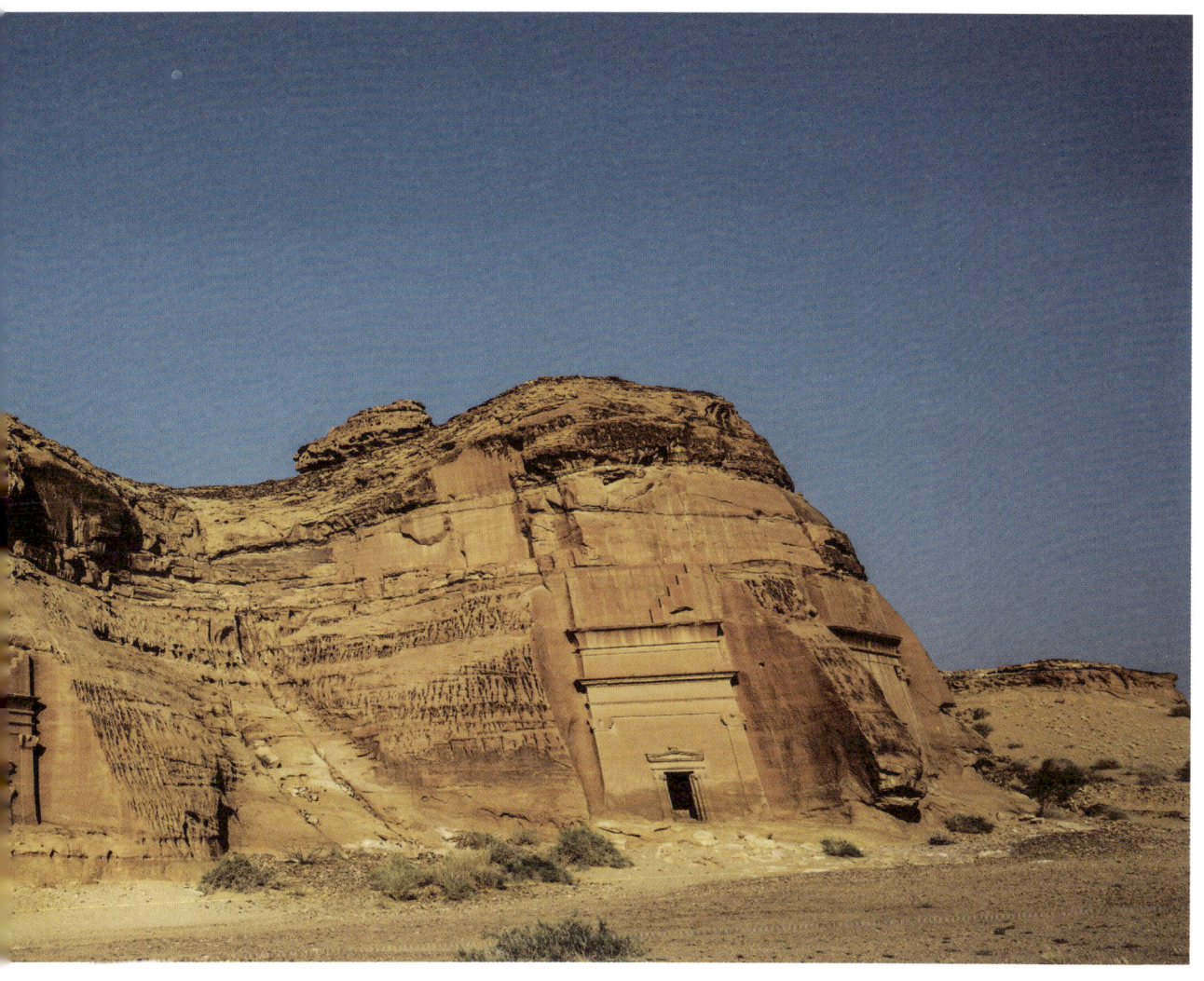

Hegra includes a major ensemble of tombs and monuments, whose architecture and decorations are directly cut into the sandstone. It bears witness to the encounter between a variety of decorative and architectural influences (Assyrian, Egyptian, Phoenician, Hellenistic).

open-air performances, and scientific workshops aim to prolong the history of this site as a witness to human culture. Meanwhile, 16 miles away at Wadi AlFann, the Saudi authorities are turning a natural landscape of rock formations into a "valley of the arts"—artists such as Manal AlDowayan, Agnes Denes, Michael Heizer, and James Turrell are working on original in situ commissions. Wadi AlFann's natural beauty alone would allow it to rival established destinations such as the Grand Canyon or Iguazú, and the addition of Land Art by internationally renowned artists suggest that landscape is, much like the case of Dunhuang in the fourth century, the walls of our planet's museum.

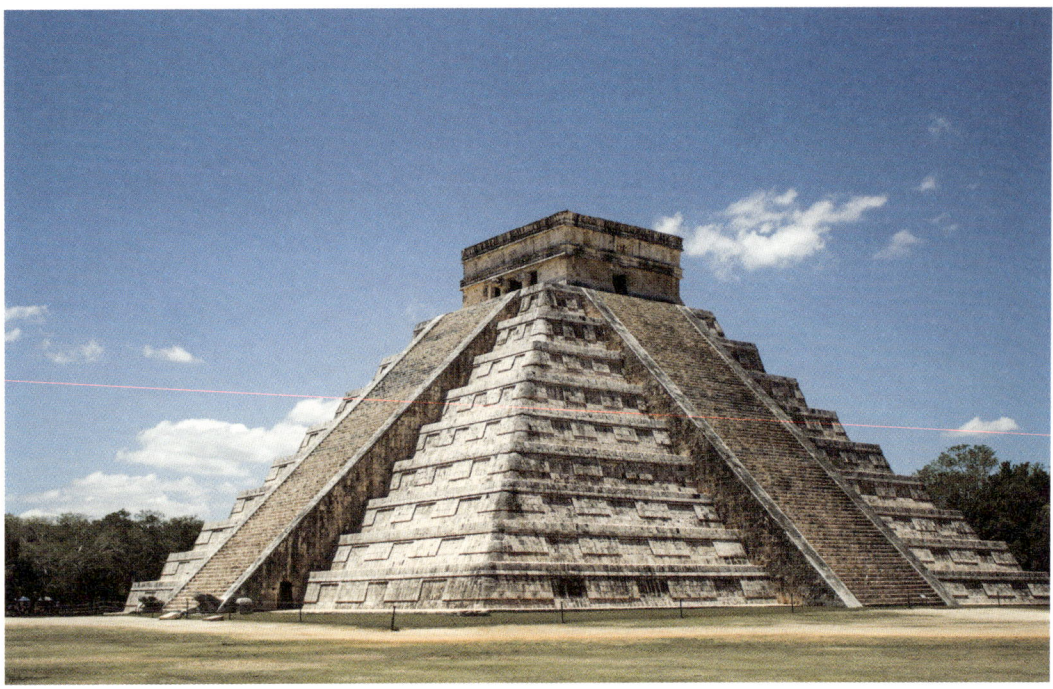

Over the past fifty years, perhaps the most contemporary idea of what form the new museum might look like has emerged in Nevada, in the tiny settlement of Hiko, about two hours north of Las Vegas. It is located in the Basin and Range National Monument, this vast rugged landscape includes the Garden and Coal Valleys, the Worthington and Seaman Mountains, the Golden Gate and Mount Irish ranges, White River narrows, and, just outside Hiko, *City*, a monumental piece of Land Art created by Michael Heizer between 1970 and 2022. Approaching the work, it is impossible to distinguish it from the wider landscape, which seems to go on indefinitely; only within its boundaries can the visitor differentiate its 0.8 square miles from the vast plain surrounding it. *City's* textures are those of leveling and landscaping—concrete, sand, gravel, and packed earth. This giant sculpture-architecture, made from the terrain itself, comprises carefully shaped mounds and lines etched in to the ground, forming traces of a possible urban occupation.

As such, *City* is intimately connected to the landscape: everything we see was already there but has been reformulated to leave a mark on the surface of the earth, whose strata become the museum itself. Walking among the various groupings of forms, some of which Heizer calls "complex," one could be deciphering a hypothetical map of an archaeological site or navigating a contemporary formal language. Time is in complete suspension: are these the burial mounds of a pre-Columbian civilization or an archaeology of the future yet to be unearthed? Is *Complex One* intended to evoke a generic modern billboard or the temples at Abu Simbel?[5] Either way, there is no nostalgia or decay, only the mineral material of the Earth transformed over time. *City* shares with ancient cities the use and manipulation of the earth's materials as the foundation of its architecture.

The Valley of the Kings, west of the Nile in upper Egypt, is one of the world's most famous burial sites, recognized by UNESCO in 1979. The architecture of these tombs was cut into the Theban Hills, using the rock formations and geological specificity to mold the landscape and create maze-like pathways leading to some sixty royal tombs. Heizer's citations are far-reaching, synthesizing humanity's ancient desire to make the surface of the earth a material record of human history. At *City*, one is not

---

5. Art historian Germano Celant questioned the relationship between Heizer's work and ancient cities like Abu Simbel. See Germano Celant, *Michael Heizer* (Milan: Fondazione Prada, 1997).

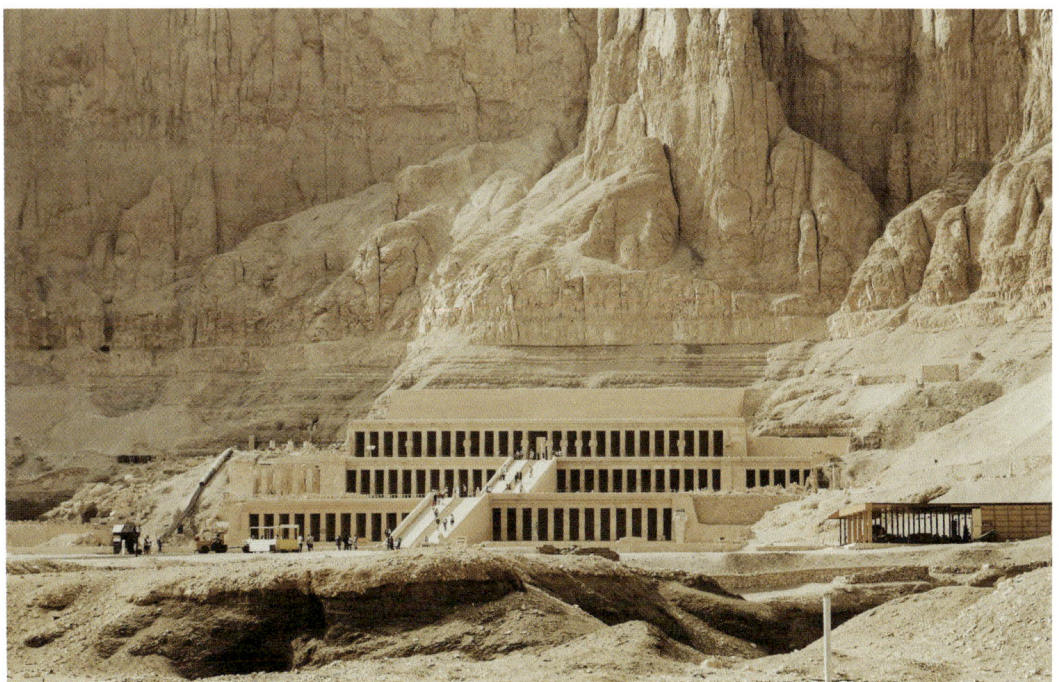

only confronted with the legacy of Egyptology but also reminded of other ancient civilizations that sought to unite earth with sky, such as the pre-Columbian Mayan civilization that built Chichen Itza (AD 600–900) on the Mexican Peninsula of Yucatan. The ancient plans of the city reveal an attempt to orchestrate its architecture according to astronomical knowledge, and much like Heizer's work *City*, could only be fully perceptible from above, to a fictional, non-human gaze.

In the endless expanse of the American West, Heizer has built the past, present, and future of planetary art. Half a century of digging, removing, excavating, and displacing fragments of a landscape has produced an entirely transformed one. The precision made possible by machinery inspires our awe; we are overcome by a desire to know, build, and experience at a totalizing scale, that of a city. But, unlike the Paris of the 1889 Exposition Universelle, whose giant steel Galerie des Machines displayed to the world the mighty engines that built modernity, nothing is shown of the means that made *City* possible, only the beauty they are capable of producing. An encyclopedia of earthwork forms, the piece offers us, at a human scale, the potential for a dialectical encounter between today's ever-expanding

Opposite: Chichen Itza is one of the most important extant examples of the Mayan-Toltec civilization in Yucatán, Mexico, and was built between the sixth and the tenth centuries AD in the characteristic Maya style. Heizer's megalith designs are similar to the sacred, spiritual buildings, such as the Mayan castillos.

Above: The entrance to the Valley of the Kings burial site where the bodies of the pharaohs were laid to rest in ancient Egypt. Several hundreds of tombs are cut deep into the rock and display intricate hieroglyphic carving and vivid painted decoration.

Following pages: Hills, valleys, and bumps separate *Complex One* and *45°, 90°, 180°*, the major monuments of *City*—a meeting point between an ancient ruin and a highway.

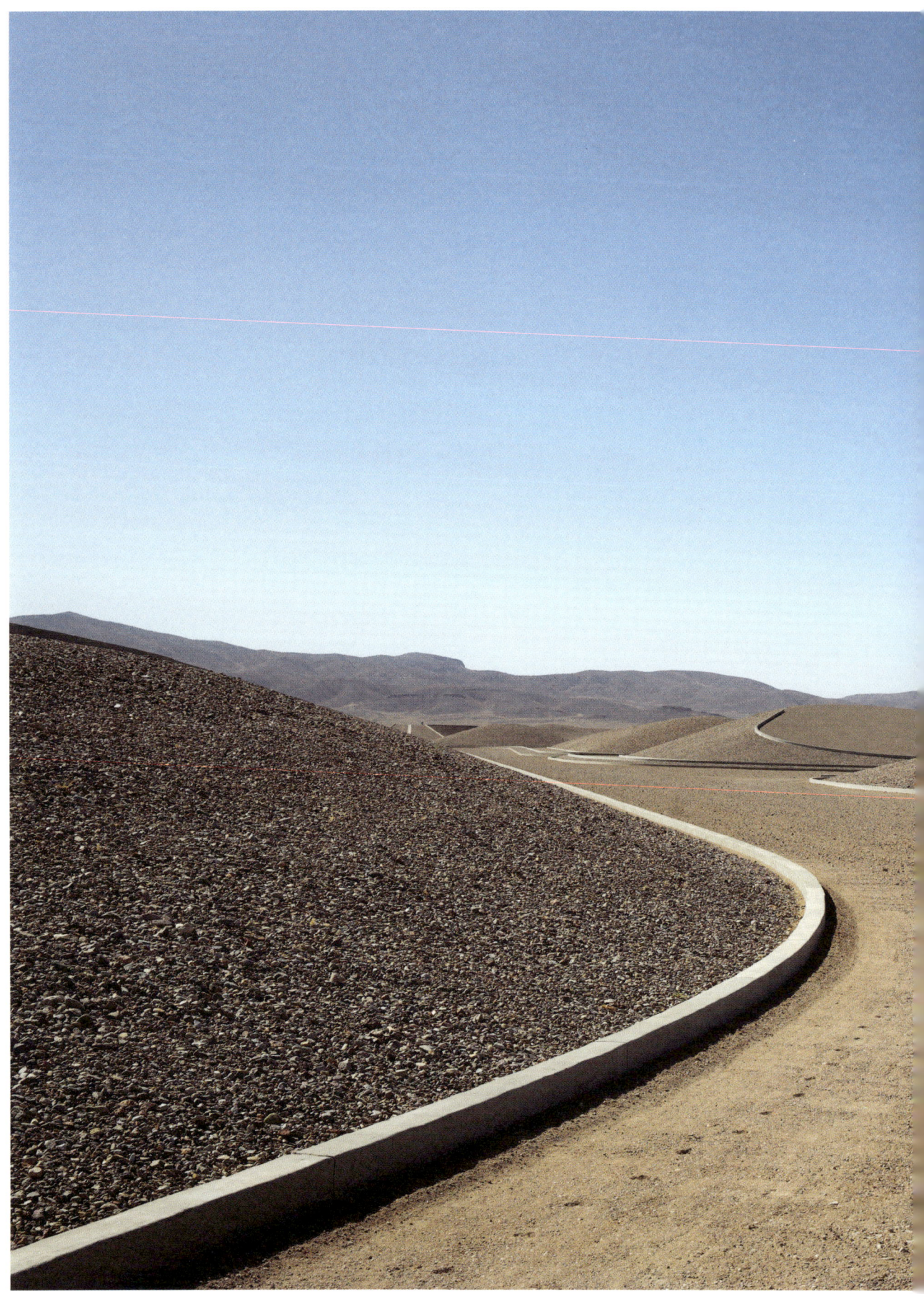

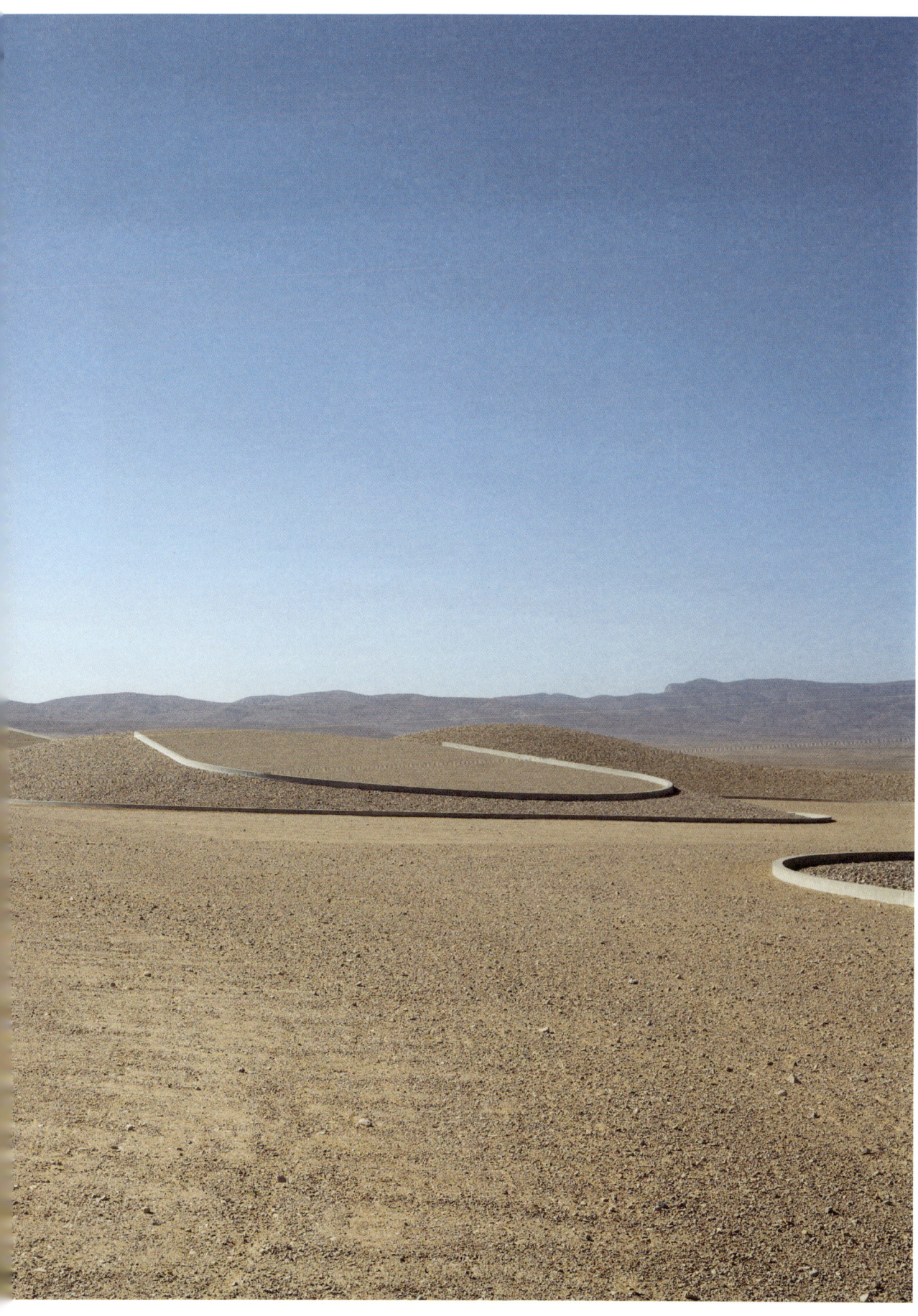

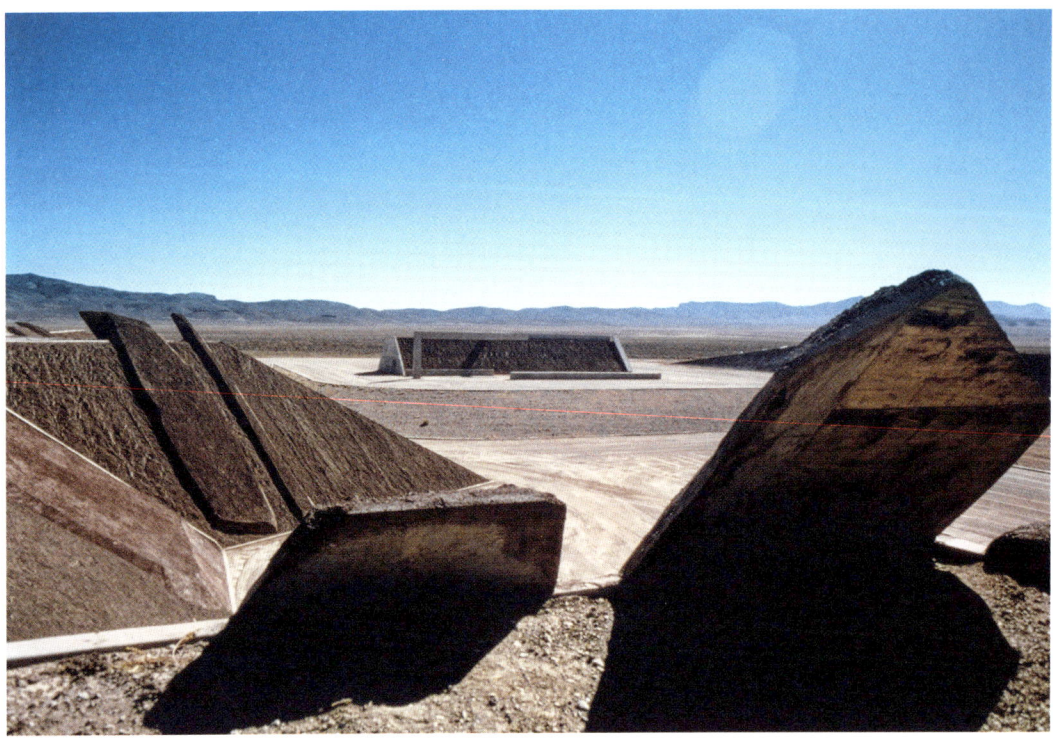

urbanity and the ancient, archaic forms that permeate the earth.

City makes it evident that if everything is now tending toward the urban, the earth's crust and the city become one. In a further illustration of this principle, one of its complexes, *45°, 90°, 180°/Geometric Extraction*, refers to the negative-positive of displacing material from one place to pile it in another. Earth constitutes pedestal mounds on which to exhibit the forms that are the result of transformed processes allowed by the physics of nature.[6] A new museum made from the earth, synthesizing past and future cities all at once, *City* is not a ruin because nothing is broken—time has not yet had the chance to erode its enigmatic forms.

The idea that the earth itself is a great work of architecture shaped over centuries was already present in Heizer's 1969 work *Displaced/Replaced Mass No. 1*, a constructive encounter between material from different environments. This piece takes the form of an excavation in the desert containing a giant rock whose weight is the same as that of the excavated material. At the advent of Land Art, in the late 1960s and early 1970s, its true consequences were not yet acknowledged in terms of its potential to redefine the inseparability of art and architecture. When Heizer began *City*, advances in space exploration and the emergence of the ecological movement enabled humans to understand their relationship with the planet differently. Between the first Moon landing in 1969 and the Oil Crisis of 1973, an entire counterculture came to see the globe as a fragile, interconnected whole—a worldview epitomized by the magazine, *Whole Earth Catalog*, whose Stanford-educated founder, Stewart Brand, believed that American industrial society needed major reform to become more socially and ecologically responsible.[7]

Within this "Whole Earth" framework, Heizer's generation of artists was the first to

---

6. *City* poses fundamental challenges to traditional media categories in art history. In her 1979 essay "Sculpture in the Expanded Field", Rosalind Krauss attempted to trace the evolution of what the term "sculpture" had come to mean. Under modernism, she posited, it had "ceased to be a positivity and was now the category that resulted from the addition of the *not-landscape* to the *not-architecture*"; with the emergence of Land Art, those two negative definitions became positives—"not-landscape" being a form of architecture and "not-architecture" a form of landscape. See Rosalind Krauss, "Sculpture in the Expanded Field," *October*, vol. 8, (Spring 1979), 30–44.
7. Stewart Brand, *Whole Earth Catalog* (Fall 1969).

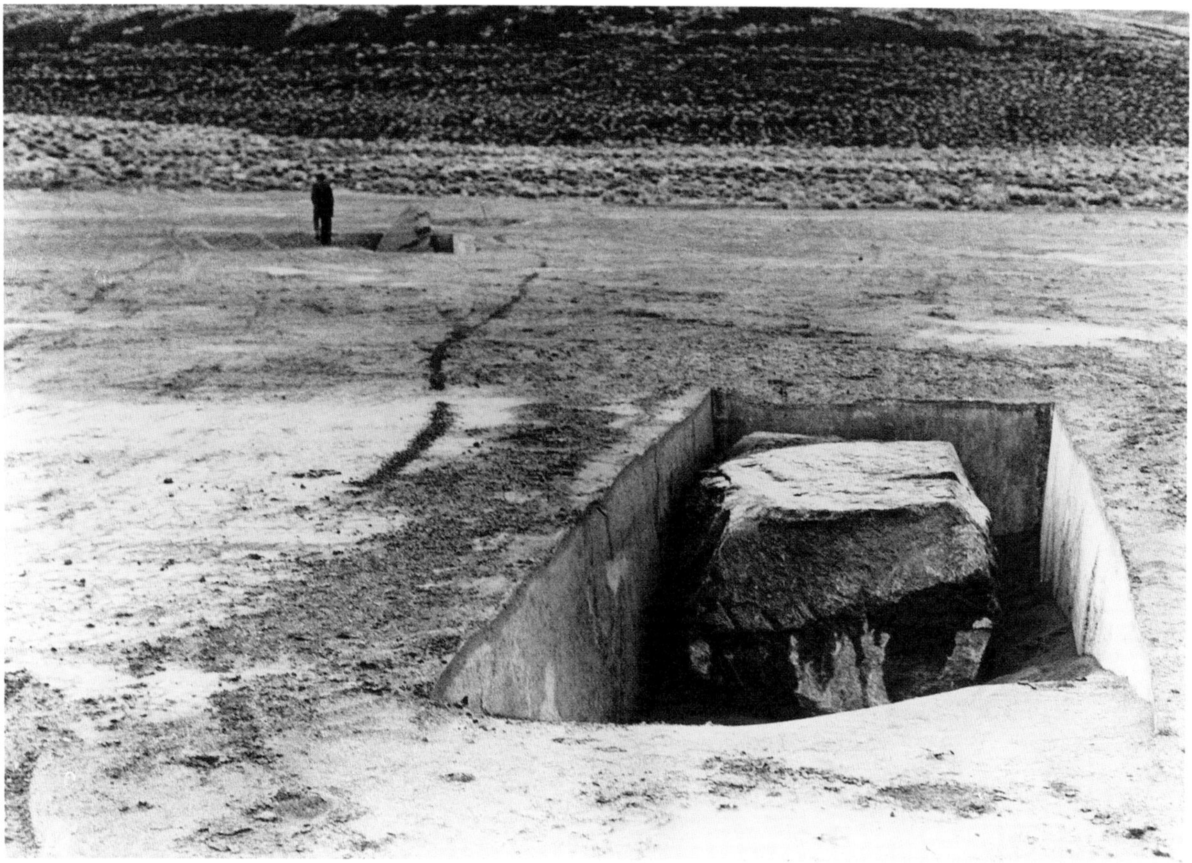

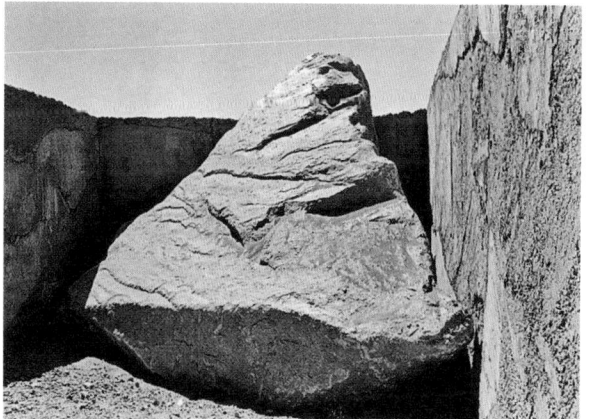

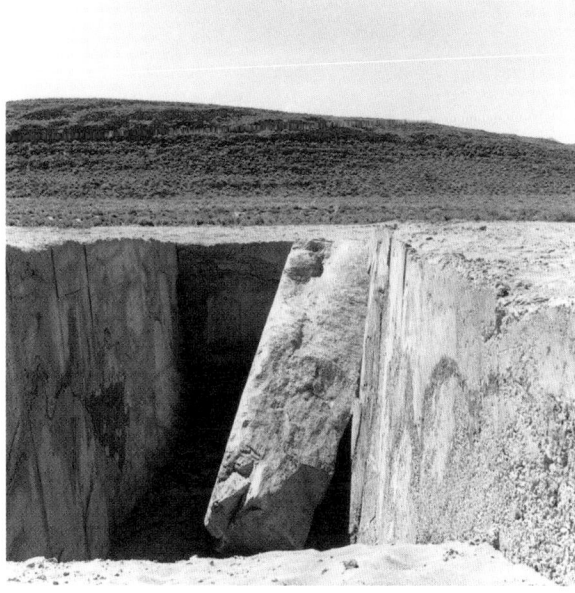

Opposite: *Complex One* is the first segment of *City* that Heizer built.

Above: *Displaced Replaced Mass* were the first sculptural objects that Heizer conceived. The orientation of the rocks inside the hollows dug into the desert correspond to a precise rhythm: they are respectively placed diagonally, vertically, and horizontally (at angles of 45, 90, and 180 degrees).

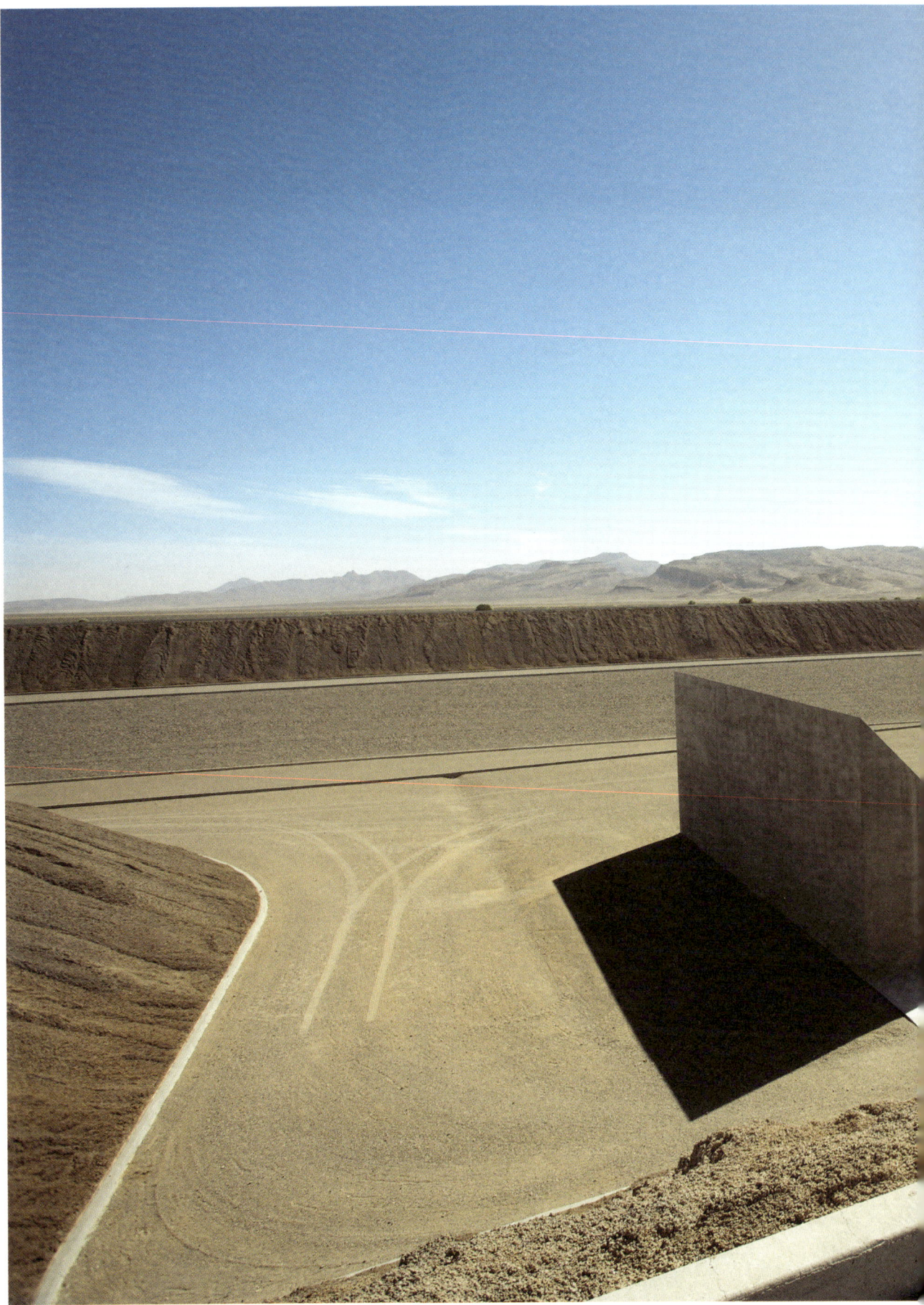

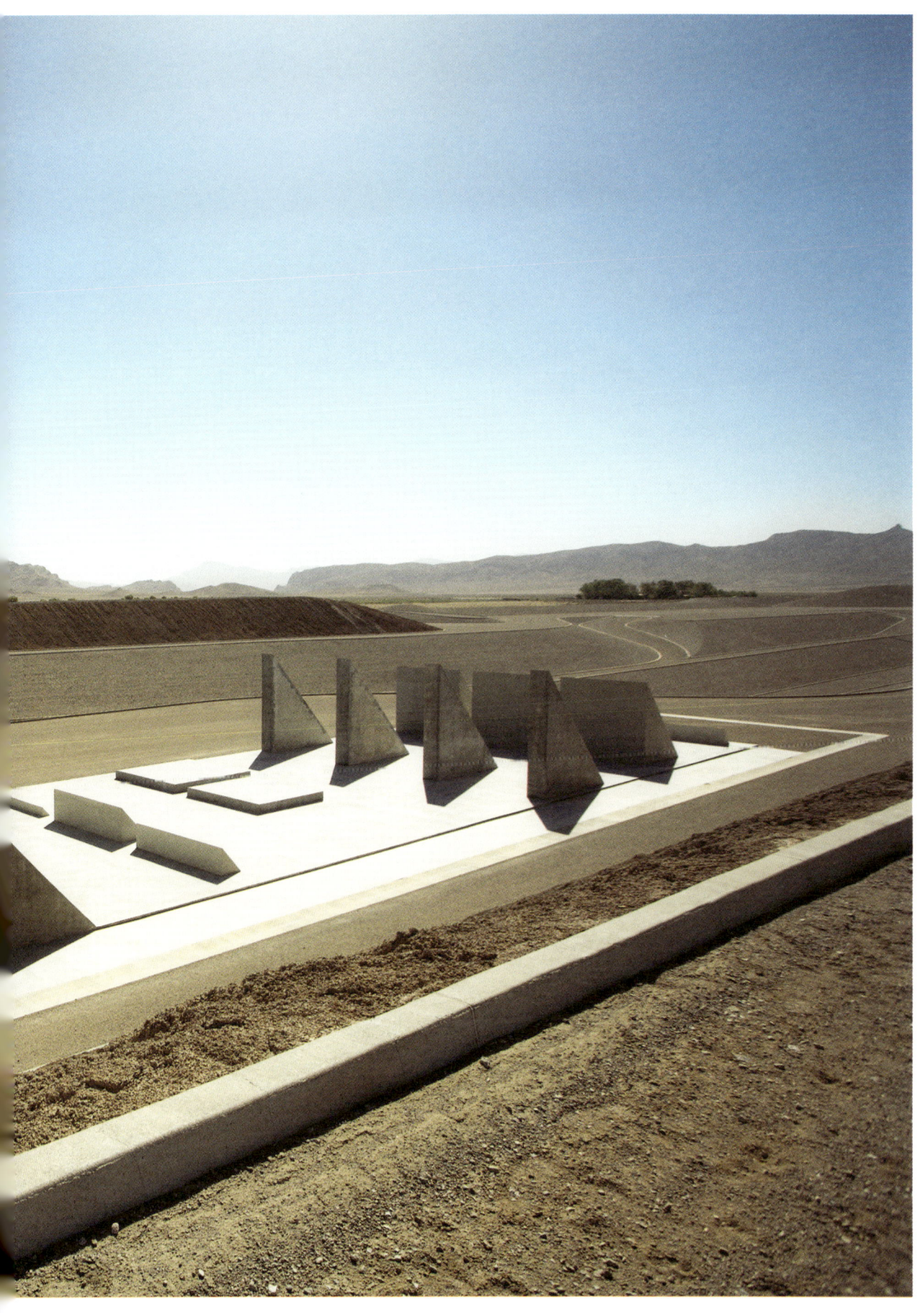

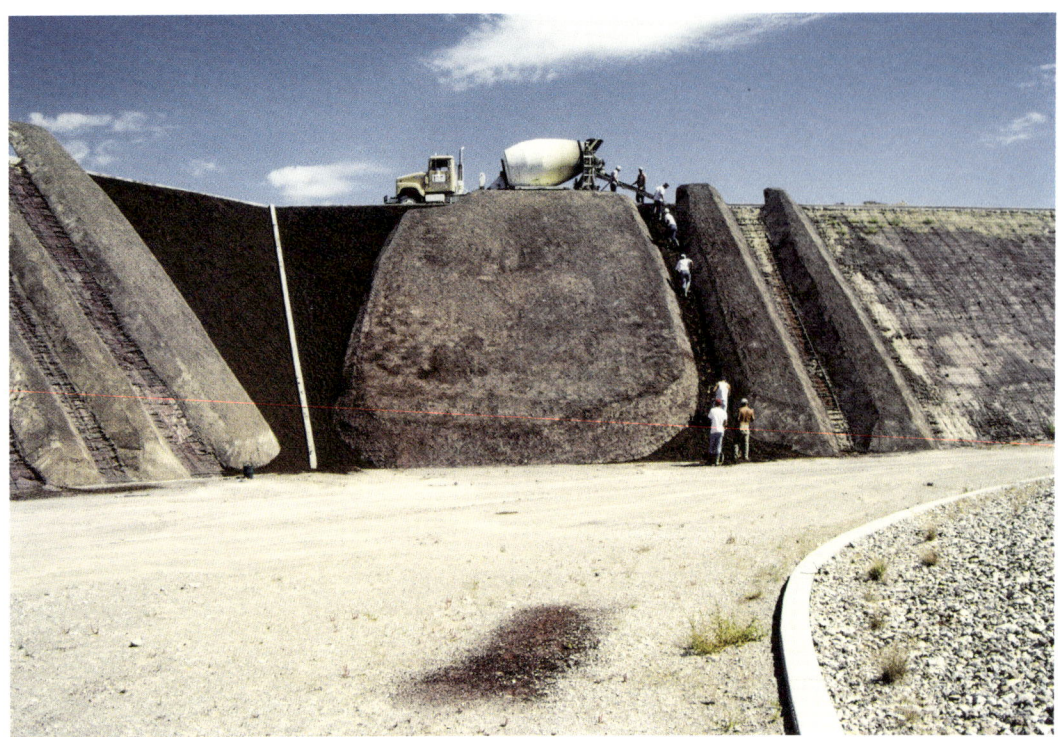

understand that art could occur at something approaching a planetary scale, creating a very material link between earth's surface and the sky, showing that humans are completely interdependent within this interplanetary scheme. Works such as Robert Smithson's *Spiral Jetty* in Utah (1970) and Walter De Maria's *Lightning Field* in New Mexico (1977) testify to a shift in the perception of our planet and art's role in relation to it. The cover of *Life Magazine*, which pictured the earth from above for the first time and was published globally, transformed humanity's recognition of its belonging to the planet. This image allowed humanity to picture the earth as something historical: as we could see the earth and move away from it in time and space, its very materiality became the repository of human memory.

It was only in 2015, over fifty years after the building of *City*, that the land and its surroundings were designated as Basin and Range National Monument, encompassing nearly 1,160 square miles. The significance of this designation holds immense symbolic potential in demonstrating the shifting nature of the museum according to the evolving definition of culture over time. The fact that the land which makes out *City*—a vast area transformed with the same machines and techniques used to build cities and freeways—is deemed an object of preservation acknowledges the evanescence of the materials that make up our planet. Art and nature merge within Land Art in the same manner that nature and urbanity become one in the twenty-first century. If museums are places where art is displayed and defined, then *City* itself is the most contemporary form of expression, and in many ways proposes a new definition of the concept where landscape, the techniques of its transformation, and its new expressions are unified.

With *City*, the relationship between art and architecture leaves the exhibition hall and becomes autonomous within the landscape, acknowledging that the site of contemporary art and culture is constantly shifting, and too should the place and architectural

---

8. Art historians have insisted on characterizing and in effect reducing the Land Art movement within an evolutionary historical framework of modernism. Indeed, the movement served as a seminal example of a modernist definition of sculpture after minimalism, where the medium is space-time experience—an idea visualized by Krauss's diagram in "Sculpture in the Expanded Field," where sculpture lies at the intersection of landscape and architecture.

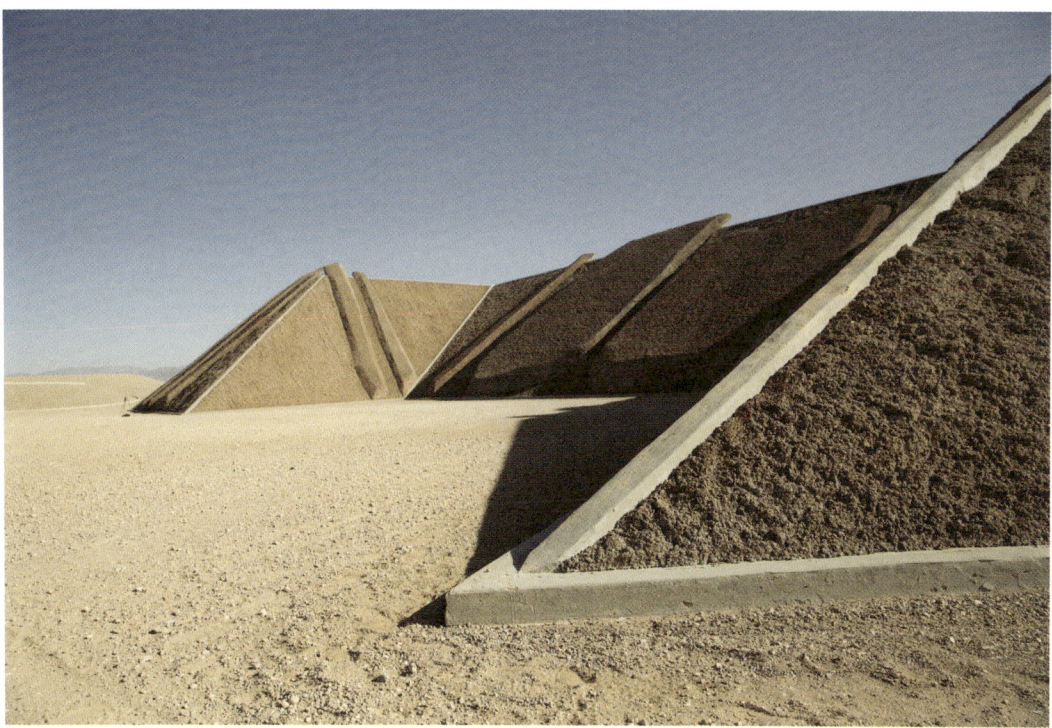

expression of the museum. Rather than sculpture's expanded field or redefining modern sculptures, *City* is the acknowledgment that architecture's manifold identities include its inseparability from art.[8] Viewed from above, *City* is a monument for the planet but also an amalgam of different abstracted shapes, expressed in a language that is illegible from within. It affirms that all cities are past cities, that future ones are reformulations of others, and that museum architecture is the means through which the anticipation of culture's future can exist.

Previous pages: A view of *45°, 90°, 180°*, another monument within *City*, which consists of a concrete plaza supporting several rows of increasingly enormous triangles and rectangles. They are a possible abstraction of a single wedge of concrete: if assembled they compose a single form.

Opposite and above: The building process of *Complex II*. The tools required to build *City* are the same scale as those required to build a modern city. On the right, a view of the work completed.

Following pages: Only from the air does the layout of *City* finally resolve into an elegant symbol or abstracted system. But *City* is not meant to be seen from above or all at once, or in photographs. The visitor never entirely sees *City*.

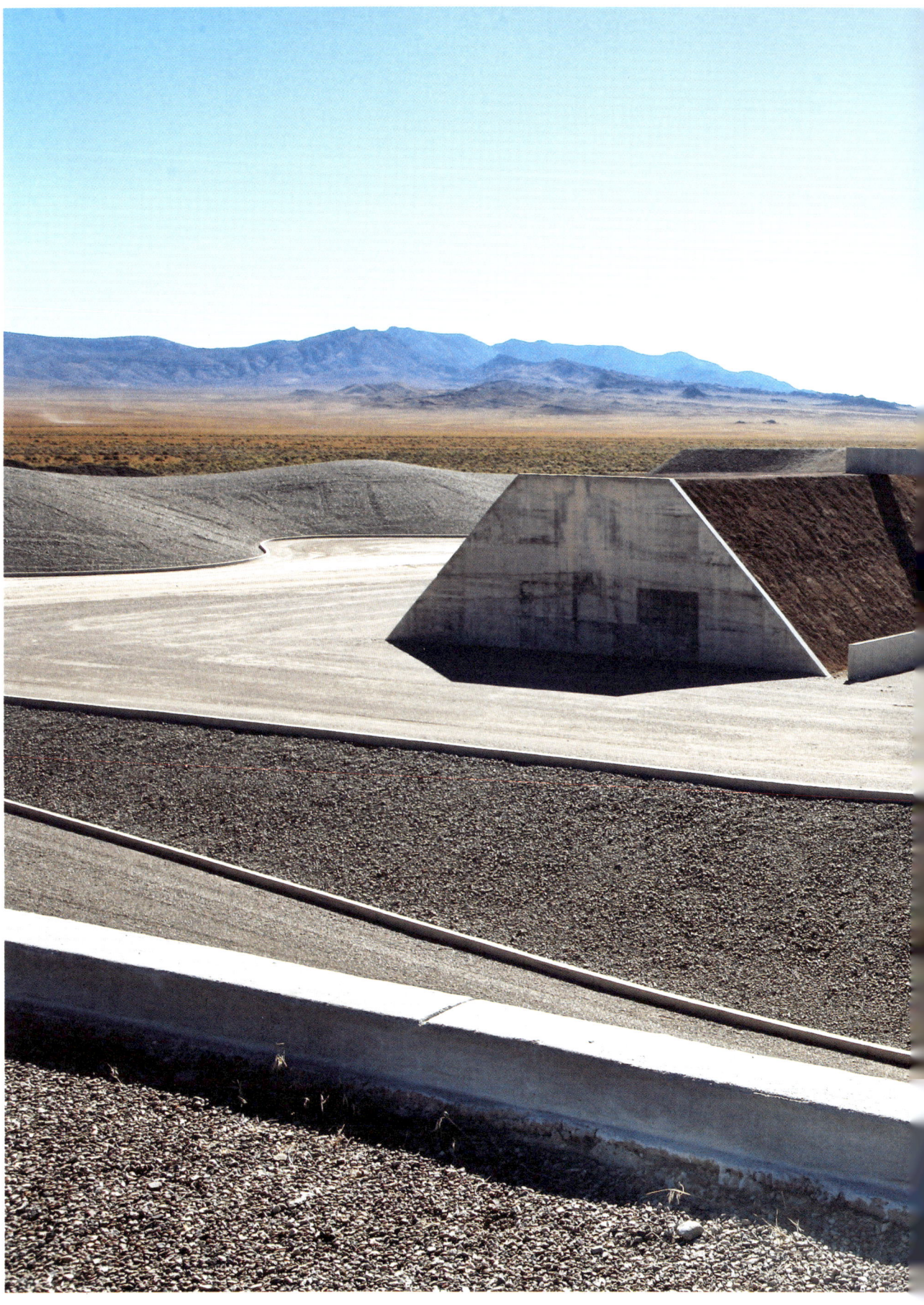

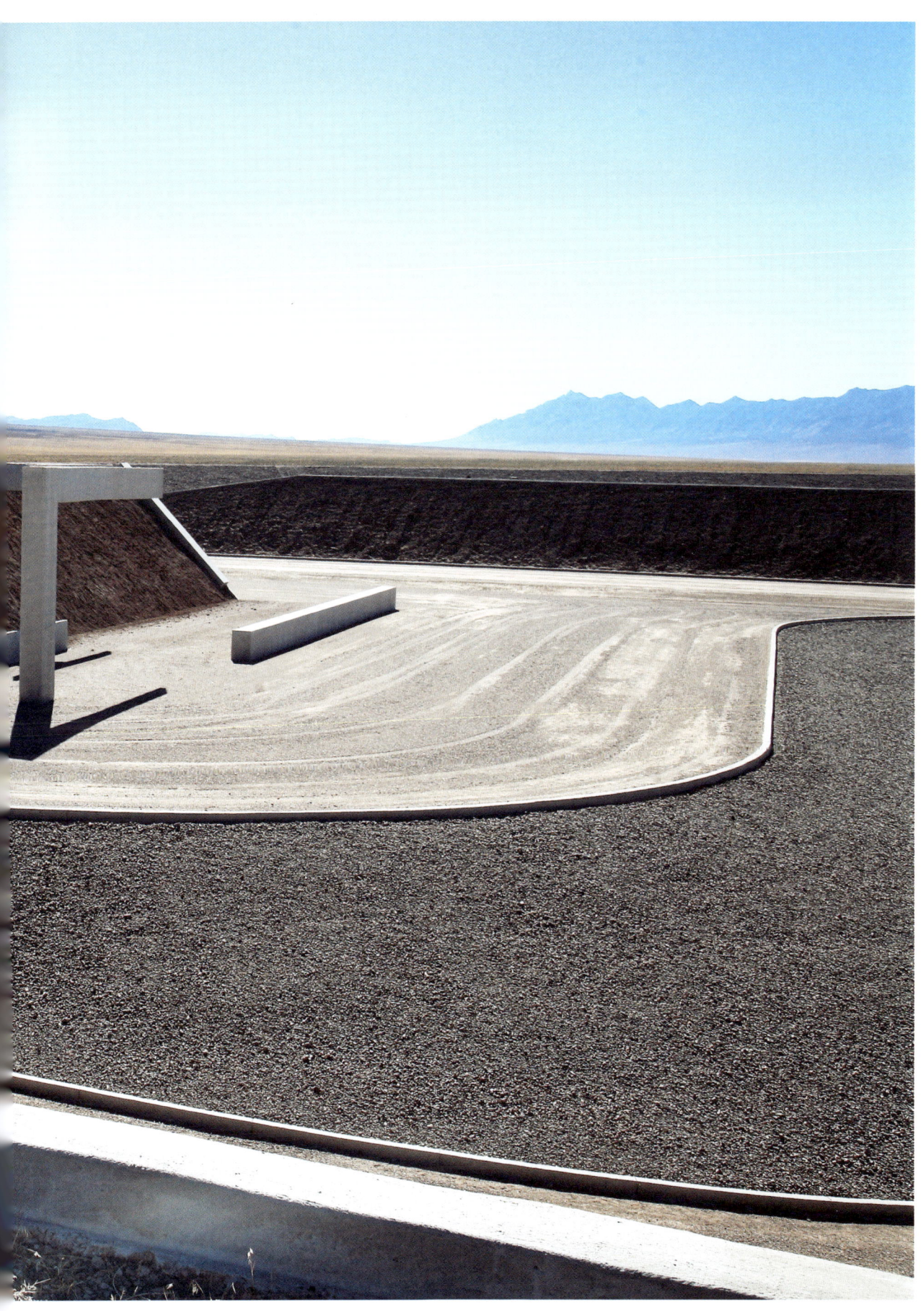

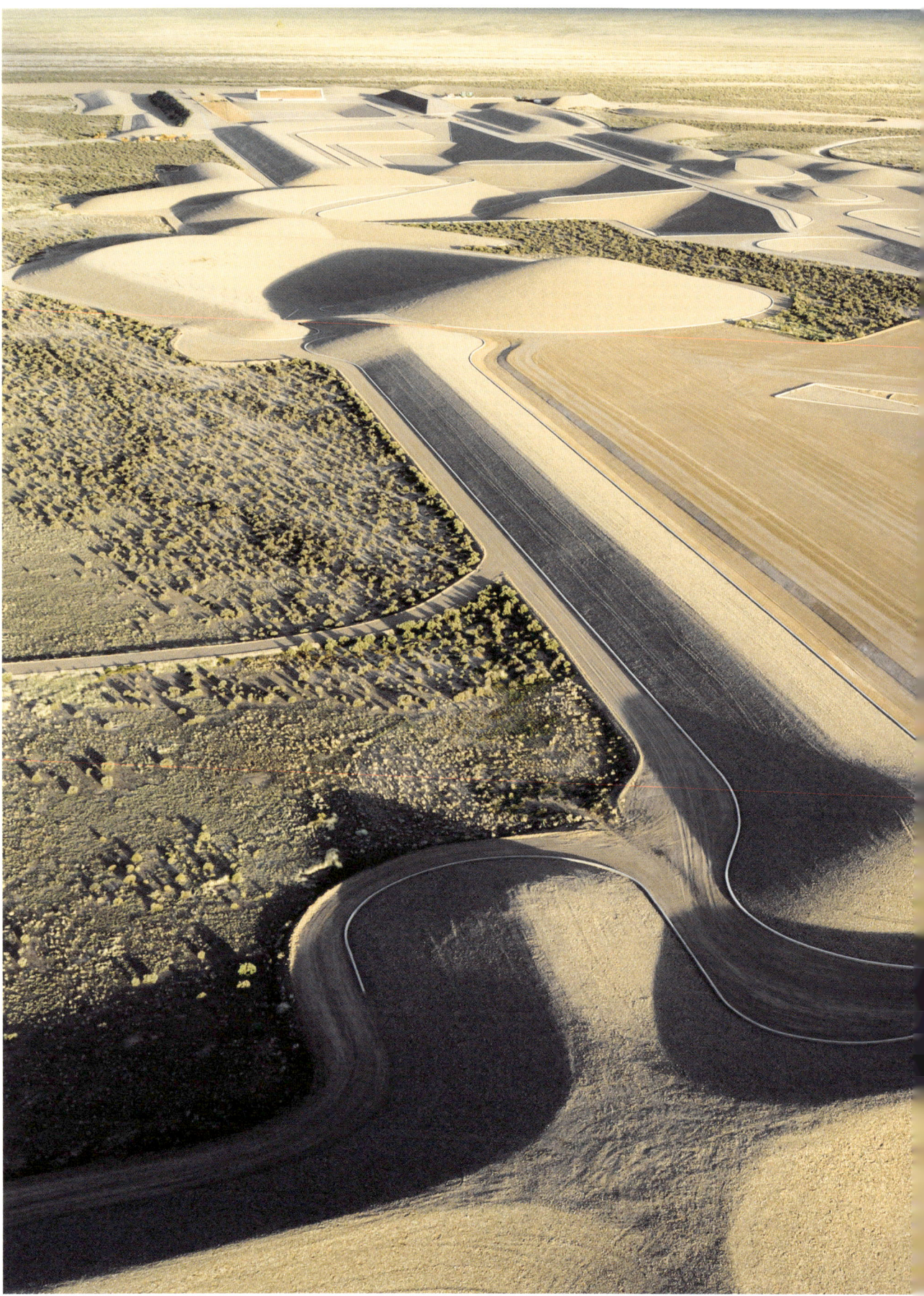

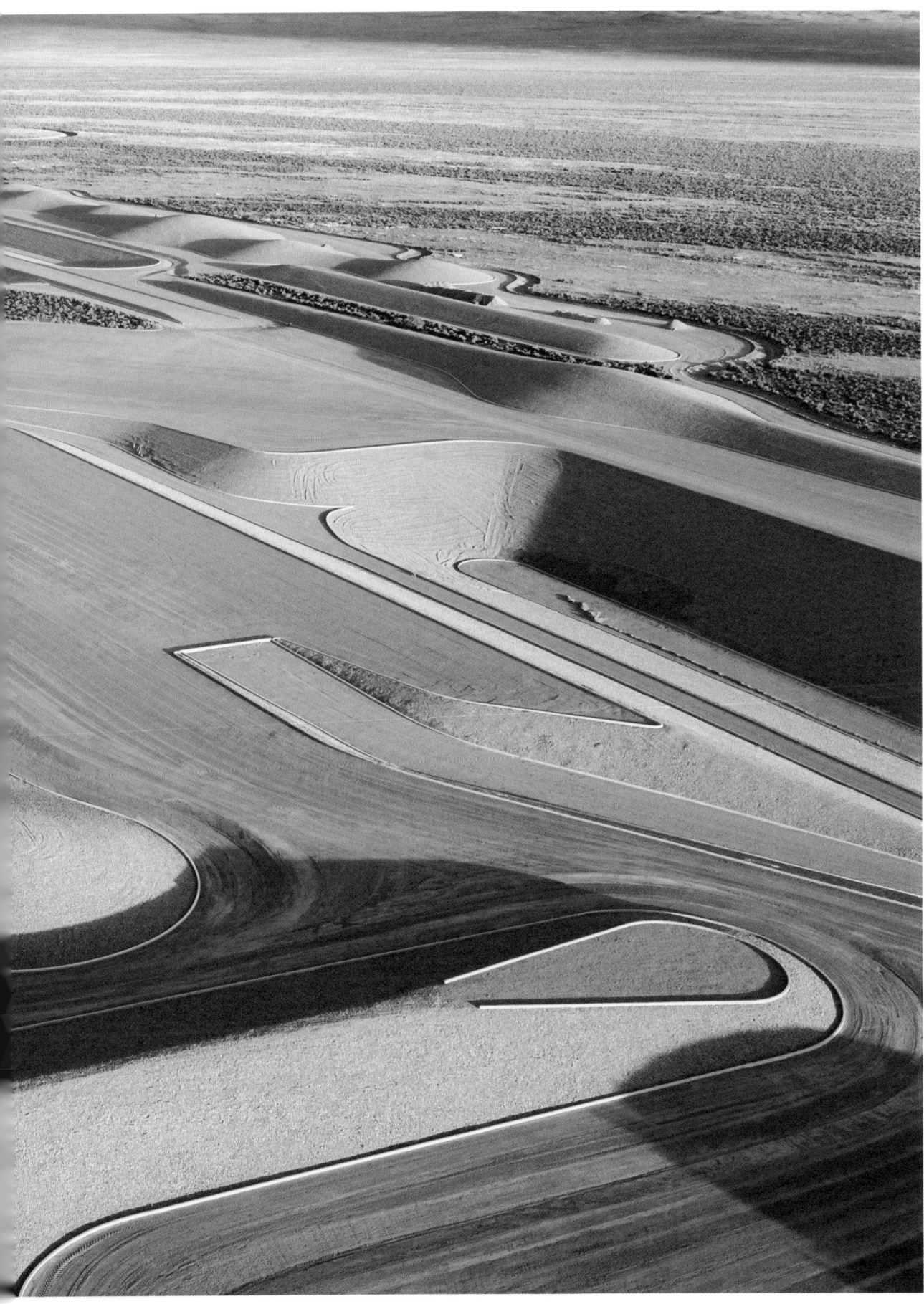

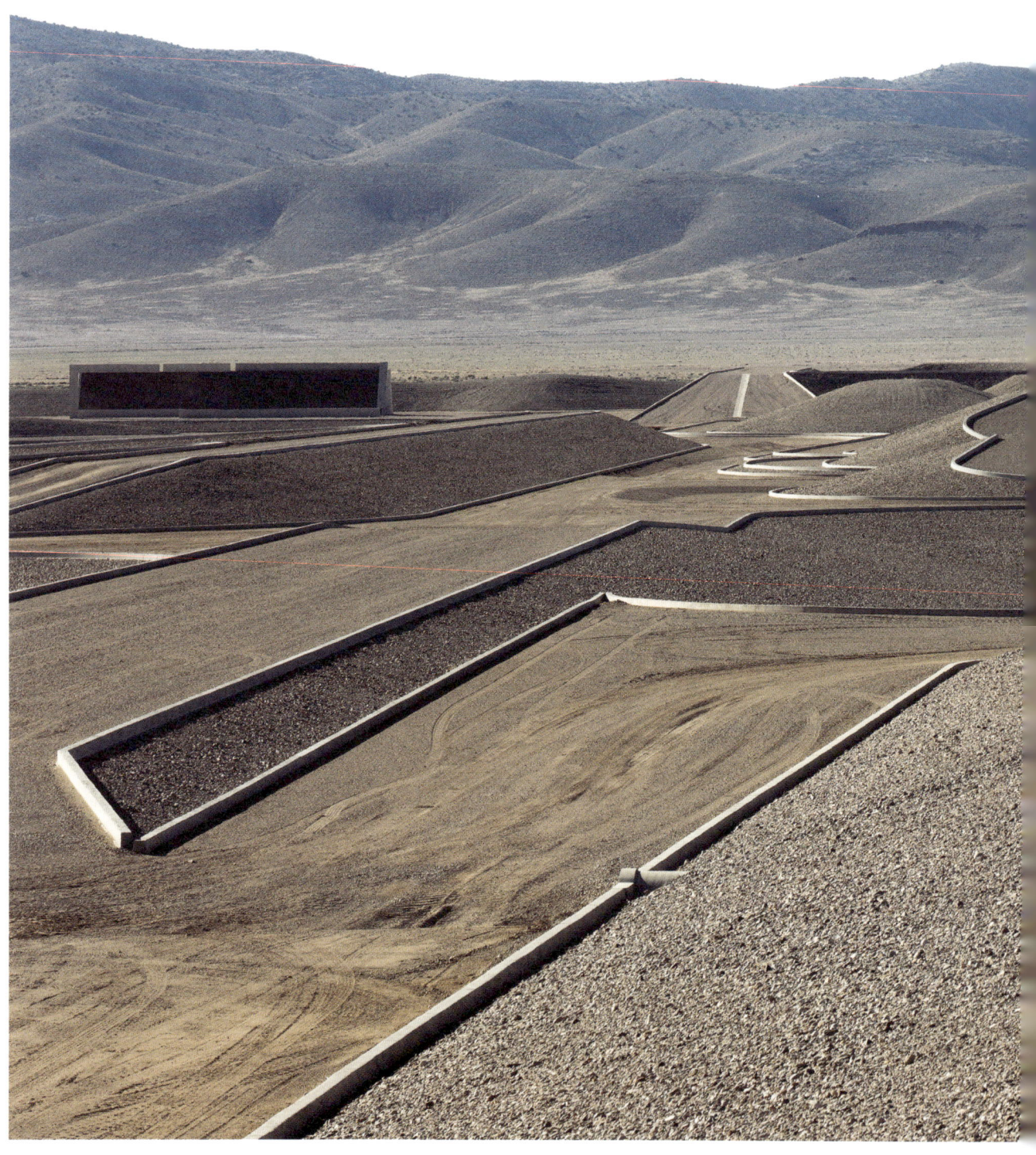

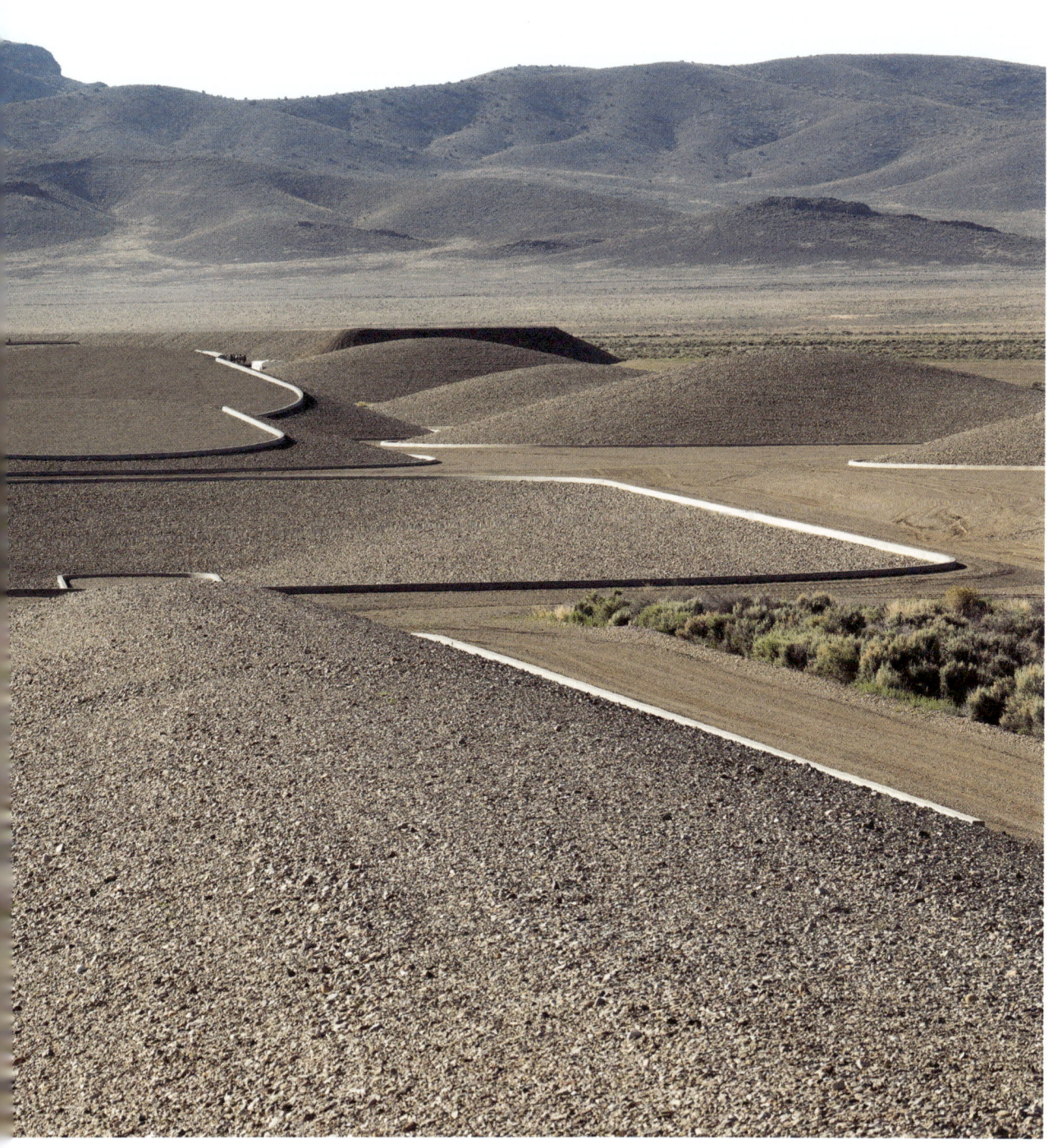

Afterword by Shohei Shigematsu
Architect, Partner at the Office for Metropolitan Architecture

Designing for a museum can be a way of investigating its potential. On the surface, a new building or an addition simply increases an institution's footprint or moves it somewhere else. But as this book makes clear, by responding to urban, natural, social, and historical conditions, architecture intensifies a museum's relevance as a generator of culture in diverse forms. For example, the Louvre's position at the heart of the Parisian cultural system relies entirely on its building: a palace that is the central node in an urban network, a quality that I. M. Pei's ingenious overhaul of internal circulation expresses. Pei's project created an intensely public concourse that establishes close connections between museum, city, and transportation infrastructure. The famous discussions between the architect, the client, and the media transformed the design process into a platform for examining the Louvre in the late twentieth century, contributing to its changing but enduring relevance. This is a good result for any contemporary museum project.

Our work as architects makes us participant-observers, to borrow a term from anthropology, allowing us to examine and contribute to the evolution of museums. OMA New York's projects for the expansion of the Buffalo AKG Museum and the Musée National des Beaux-Arts du Québec respond to opportunities at both sites to question the natural and the urban as separate categories, reacting to what we observed as a need to host more than the conventional exhibition program and accommodate concerts, parties, classes, and spontaneous gatherings. Both projects attempt to connect the park and the city through the intermediary of the museum and to extend all three with open, unprogrammed space.

The choice of site represents a museum's public ambition and influences any architectural intervention. The leap from Left Bank to Right Bank for the Fondation Cartier, the close cohabitation of the New Museum's two buildings on the Bowery, and the hyperactive decade (2014–2024) of Marcel Breuer's 945 Madison Avenue as a space for the Whitney Museum of American Art, the Metropolitan Museum of Art, and the Frick Collection are, in different ways, reflections of the changing cultures of Paris and New York and proposals for what could come next for the city. Museums evolve as cities evolve, as we see in this book, and they are increasingly becoming connectors across domains. The work of an architect should always reflect the changes in behavior taking place around us, which means contributing to the potential of museums as flexible zones for our anticipation and experience of culture.

Acknowledgments

I had the idea for this book when I visited Wang Shu and Lu Wenyu in Hangzhou in the summer of 2023. Their most recent project, which I discuss in the first chapter, was a material manifestation of a hypothesis I had been toying with since first moving to Paris in 2020 to work as a curator on the design phase of the new spaces of the Fondation Cartier, opposite the Louvre in Paris. This is where I truly began to understand and experience the agency of architecture in formulating our relationship to art and its power in shaping cultural policy in an urban context.

The book would not have been possible without the many critical encounters that followed in the years it took to write it: in Zanzibar with Aziza Chaouni, in Rotterdam with Rem Koolhaas, in Tashkent with Gayane Umerova, in Alula with Bernard Khoury, in Beirut with Hala Wardé, in Shanghai with Gong Yan, in São Paulo with Thyago Nogueira, in Paris with Jean Nouvel, in New York with Shohei Shigematsu, in Madrid with Cristina Iglesias, in Beijing with Xu Bing, in Memphis with Jeanne Gang, and in Milan with Junya Ishigami, as well as in Montreal with Giovanna Borasi.

The long-standing dialogues I have had with Chris Dercon, John Rajchman, and Cai Guo-Qiang, over the years have profoundly shaped my thinking.

A conversation with Emanuele Coccia on the Left Bank of Paris was decisive and sparked a turning point toward a new direction in my thinking. I'll never forget it and all that followed; our dialogue has been essential since.

My obsessive optimism regarding the museum as a catalyst for change pushed me to follow my interrogations about its contemporary form and manifestation, leading me to the Great Basin of the United States to the small town of Hiko, Nevada, where I had the most shattering aesthetic and profound philosophical encounter with art while visiting Michael Heizer's *City*. Warm thanks to Kara Vander Weg for making this possible.

Andrew Goodhouse was a generous conversation partner throughout a summer of writing in Berlin and read all the versions of the manuscript, providing invaluable feedback at different stages of the book. His insights helped me sharpen my thinking.

I learn every day from the friendship and unwavering support of Dorothée Charles and the intellectual camaraderie, warmth, and attention of Gui Trotti, whom I both thank for their presence in my life. Thank you to Louise Heywood and Chris Mills, who opened the door to their home countless times and provided the quiet and still air necessary for concentration and isolation from all else that could impede the fragile process of writing.

Catherine Bonifassi, my editor, materialized this project with the intelligence, sharpness, strength, and conviction that none other is capable of.

This book is dedicated to my parents, Louise Plante and Raymond Grenier, who, perhaps unbeknownst to them, were the first to suggest to me what architecture could do—in the household that they built for our family, the world was transformed into a museum of all possibilities.

Picture Credits

Cover: Interior of the Richard Gilder Center for Science, Education, and Innovation, ©Studio Gang, Photo ©Iwan Baan.
Pages 12–13: Photo Wang Dachou; pp 14–15: Photo Chen Lichao; p. 16: Library of Congress, Asian Division; p. 17: All rights reserved, Courtesy Amateur Architecture Studio; pp. 18–19: Photo Wang Dachou; p. 20: ©Amateur Architecture Studio; p. 21: Photo Laksana Studio; pp 22–23: Photo Ji Yun; p 24: Photo Zeng Han; p. 25: Attributed to: Li Cheng, Chinese (919–967 CE) *A Solitary Temple Amid Clearing Peaks*, Chinese, Northern Song dynasty (960–1127), hanging scroll; ink and slight color on silk, 44 × 22 in. (111.8 × 55.9 cm), The Nelson-Atkins Museum of Art, Kansas City, Missouri. Purchase: William Rockhill Nelson Trust, 47-71, Courtesy of Nelson-Atkins Digital Production & Preservation; pp. 26–27: Photo Laksana Studio; pp 28–29: All rights reserved, Courtesy Amateur Architecture Studio; pp. 30–31 top: All rights reserved; p. 31, bottom: Pexels/Taha Abbas; pp. 32–40: Photo Ji Yun; p. 41: Maurice Jarnoux/Paris Match/Scoop; p. 42: Photo Zeng Han; p. 43: Photo Ji Yun; pp. 44–45: Pexels/Luke Webb; p. 46: iStock/Repianatoly; p. 47: Courtesy of I. M. Pei, Photo Pexels/Josh Withers; p. 48: ©2025 Jean Nouvel/Musée du Quai Branly/Artists Rights Society (ARS), New York/ADAGP, Paris; p. 49: ©2025 Jean Nouvel/Musée du Quai Branly/Artists Rights Society (ARS), New York/ADAGP, Paris, Photo Philippe Ruault; p. 50: *Les statues meurent aussi* by Chris Marker and Alain Resnais ©Revue Présence Africaine, 1953; p. 51: ©2025 Jean Nouvel/Musée du Quai Branly/Artists Rights Society (ARS), New York/ADAGP, Paris, Photo Philippe Ruault; p. 52: Unsplash/Inha Bea; p. 53: iStock/legna69; pp. 54–55: ©2025 Jean Nouvel/Artists Rights Society (ARS), New York/ADAGP, Paris, Photo iStock/Liz Coughlan; pp. 56–57: ©2025 Jean Nouvel/Artists Rights Society (ARS), New York/ADAGP, Paris, Photo Courtesy TDIC; pp. 58–59: All rights reserved; pp. 60–61: ©2025 Jean Nouvel/Artists Rights Society (ARS), New York/ADAGP, Paris, Photo Pexels/Kent Zhong; p. 62: ©2025 Jean Nouvel/Artists Rights Society (ARS), New York/ADAGP, Paris, Photo Pexels/Sandhu Jassi; p. 63, left: ©2025 Jean Nouvel/Artists Rights Society (ARS), New York/ADAGP, Paris,Photo Unsplash/Dan Calderwood, right: ©2025 Jean Nouvel/Artists Rights Society (ARS), New York/ADAGP, Paris, Photo ©HW Architecture; pp. 64–65: ©2025 Jean Nouvel/Artists Rights Society (ARS), New York/ADAGP, Paris, Photo Unsplash/Agnieszka Stankiewicz; pp. 66–67: Unsplash/Etienne Boulanger; pp. 68–69: ©2025 Renzo Piano/Artists Rights Society (ARS), New York/SIAE, Rome, Photo iStock/no limit pictures; p. 70: ©2025 Renzo Piano/Artists Rights Society (ARS), New York/SIAE, Rome, Photo ©Cyril Masson, Courtesy Nike Inc.; p. 71: ©2025 Renzo Piano/Artists Rights Society (ARS), New York/SIAE, Rome, Photo iStock/StockByM; p. 72: CC0 Paris Musées/Musée Carnavalet – Histoire de Paris, Photo Roger Henrard; p. 73: Atelier parisien d'urbanisme, Archives de Paris, 1514W 99; pp. 74–75: ©2025 Renzo Piano/Artists Rights Society (ARS), New York/SIAE, Rome, Photo ©Cyril Masson, Courtesy Nike Inc. and Eliud Kipchoge; p. 76: ©2025 Jean Nouvel/Artists Rights Society (ARS), New York/ADAGP, Paris; p. 77: ©2025 Jean Nouvel/Artists Rights Society (ARS), New York/ADAGP, Paris, Photo iStock/Sergio Delle Vedove; pp. 78–79: ©2025 Jean Nouvel/Artists Rights Society (ARS), New York/ADAGP, Paris, Photo ©Zhang Yong; pp. 80–81: ©Harvard Art Museums/Fogg Museum, Anonymous Loan in honor of Branden W. Joseph ©Ed Ruscha ©President and Fellows of Harvard College, Courtesy Gagosian; p. 82: ©2025 Frank Lloyd Wright Foundation, All Rights Reserved, Licensed by Artists Rights Society, Photo Pixabay/Kai Pilger; p. 83: ©2025 Frank Lloyd Wright Foundation, All Rights Reserved, Licensed by Artists Rights Society, Photo Unsplash/David Emrich; pp. 84–85: ©2025 Jean Nouvel/Artists Rights Society (ARS), New York/ADAGP, Paris; p. 86: CC0 Paris Musées/Musée Carnavalet - Histoire de Paris, Photo Hippolyte Blancard; p. 87: Courtesy Parramatta ©Moreau Kusunoki and Genton; p. 88: Public domain, Ferdinand Dutert; pp. 89–93: ©2025 Jean Nouvel/Artists Rights Society (ARS), New York/ADAGP, Paris, Photo ©Martin Argyroglo; p. 94: ©REX , Rendering ©Luxigon; p. 95: ©Diller Scofidio + Renfro; p. 96: ©2025 OMA/Artists Rights Society (ARS), New York/Pictoright Amsterdam, Photo ©Delfino Sisto Legnani and Marco Cappelletti; p. 97: ©2025 OMA/Artists Rights Society (ARS), New York/Pictoright Amsterdam; p. 98: ©2025 Jean Nouvel/Artists Rights Society (ARS), New York/ADAGP, Paris, Photo ©Luc Boegly; p. 99: ©2025 Jean Nouvel/Artists Rights Society (ARS), New York/ADAGP, Paris; pp. 100–105: ©2025 Jean Nouvel/Artists Rights Society (ARS), New York/ADAGP, Paris Photo ©Martin Argyroglo; pp. 106–107: ©The New York Public Library; pp. 108–109: Public domain; p. 110, left: Unsplash/Aditya Chinchure, top right: Pixabay/dariasophia, bottom right: ©Studio Gang; p. 111, top: ©Studio Gang, Photo Tim Gersten, bottom: iStock/Andrea Astes; p. 112: ©Studio Gang; p. 113: ©Studio Gang, Photo Tim Gersten; pp. 114: Asher B. Durand, *Kindred Spirits*, 1849, oil on canvas,

44 x 36 in. (111.8 x 91.4 cm), Crystal Bridges Museum of American Art, Bentonville, Arkansas, 2010.106, Photo Edward C. Robison III; p. 115: ©Stephen Ironside, Courtesy Crystal Bridges Museum of American Art; p. 116: Courtesy Safdie Architects; p. 117: Unsplash/Arvid Høidahl; pp. 118–119: ©2025 Jean Nouvel/Artists Rights Society (ARS), New York/ADAGP, Paris, Photo ©Luc Boegly; p. 120: ©2025 Jean Nouvel/Artists Rights Society (ARS), New York/ADAGP, Paris; pp. 121–123: ©2025 Jean Nouvel/Artists Rights Society (ARS), New York/ADAGP, Paris, Photo ©Luc Boegly; pp. 124–127: ©Arch-Exist Photography; pp. 128–129: 123RF/storyteller2k20; p 130: iStock/Sohadiszno; p. 131, top: iStock/powerofforever, bottom left: Public domain, bottom right: All rights reserved; pp. 132–133: Pexels/Salim Kombo; p. 134, top left: Map data ©2025 Google Earth, bottom left and right: All rights reserved; p. 135: Pexels/I am Alex; pp. 136–137: ©Aga Khan Trust for Culture; p. 137, right: Pexels/Julia Volk; pp. 138–139: iStock/chriss73; pp. 140–141: Pexels/I am Alex; p. 142: iStock/Moiz Husein Storyteller; p. 143: ©Aziza Chaouni; p. 144: iStock/chriss73; p. 145, top: Stock/Dkart, bottom left: iStock/Clement Olivier Meylan, bottom right: iStock/Moiz Husein Storeyteller; pp. 146–147: Pexels/Ahmed Bates; p. 148: ©2025 OMA/Artists Rights Society (ARS), New York/Pictoright Amsterdam; pp. 149–150: ©Madelon Vriesendorp/www.point101.com/madelon-vriesendorp; p. 151: ©2025 Ludwig Mies van der Rohe/Artists Rights Society (ARS), New York/VG Bild-Kunst, Bonn, Photo ©Ezra Stoller/Esto, Yossi Milo Gallery; p. 152: ©UNESCO; p. 153, top: iStock/chriss73, bottom: ©Aziza Chaouni; pp. 154–155: ©Iwan Baan; p. 156: iStock/nycshooter; p. 157: ©The Metropolitan Museum of Art, Image source, Art Resource, NY; p. 158: Public Domain, the Metropolitan Museum of Art; p. 159: ©The Metropolitan Museum of Art, Image source, Art Resource, NY; pp. 160–161: All rights reserved; pp. 162–164: Courtesy of Herzog & de Meuron, Photo ©Kevin Mak; p. 165: iStock/Chunyip Wong; p. 166: Courtesy M+, Hong Kong, Photo ©Dan Leung, Background photo ©Tomio Ohashi; p. 167: Courtesy Herzog & de Meuron, Photo©Kevin Mak; p. 168: iStock/josephmok; pp. 169–171: iStock/winhorse; pp. 172–173: ©Iwan Baan; p. 174: ©Fondation Le Corbusier/ADAGP, Paris/Artists Rights Society, New York 2025; p. 175: ©The Metropolitan Museum of Art. Image source: Art Resource, NY; p. 176: CC0 Paris Musées/Musée Carnavalet - Histoire de Paris, Photo Lucien Cresson; p. 177: Public domain; p. 178: iStock/rmcguirk; p. 179: Artvee/E.J. Stanley; pp. 180–181: All rights reserved; p. 182: Public domain; p. 183: ©Steve Hall, Hall + Merrick + McCaugherty; p. 184: ©Studio Gang; p. 185: ©Jeanne Gang; pp. 186–187: ©Iwan Baan; p. 188: ©2025 Cristina Iglesias/Artists Rights Society (ARS), New York/VEGAP, Madrid, Photo ©Attilio Maranzano; p. 189: ©2025 Cristina Iglesias/Artists Rights Society (ARS), New York/VEGAP, Madrid, Drawing ©Cuauhtli Gutiérrez; pp. 190–191: ©2025 Cristina Iglesias/Artists Rights Society (ARS), New York/VEGAP, Madrid, Photo ©Roland Halbe; pp. 192–193: ©2025 OMA/Artists Rights Society (ARS), New York/Pictoright Amsterdam; pp. 194–195: *45°, 90°, 180°, City* ©Michael Heizer, Courtesy Triple Aught Foundation, Photo Ben Blackwell; p. 196: Pexels/Oscar Ruiz; p. 197: Pixabay/u_7tm48tvmle; p. 198: Pixabay/nhluoj; p. 199: ©Robert Polidori; pp. 200–201: ©Gilles Bensimon; p. 202: Pexels/Omar Zetina; p. 203: Pexels/Roberto Shumski; pp. 204–205: ©Michael Heizer, Courtesy Triple Aught Foundation, Photo Joe Rome; p. 206: *Complex Two, City* ©Michael Heizer, Courtesy Triple Aught Foundation, Photo Michael Heizer; p. 207, top: *Displaced/Replaced Mass* (1/3), 1969, 30-ton granite block in concrete depression, 22 ft. 7 ⅝ in. x 5 ft. 11 ⅝ in. x 4 ft. 11 ¾ in. (6.9 x 1.8 x 1.5 m), bottom left: Michael Heizer, *Displaced/Replaced Mass* (3/3), 1969, 68-ton granite block in concrete depression, 41 ft. 4 in. x 10 ft. 11 ½ in. x 9 ft. 2 ¼ in. (12.6 x 3.3 x 2.8 m), bottom right: Michael Heizer, *Displaced/Replaced Mass* (2/3), 1969, 52-ton granite block in concrete depression, 50 ft. 2 ⅜ in. x 15 ft. 9 in. x 9 ft. 2 ⅜ in. (15.3 x 4.8 x 2.8 m), Silver Springs, NV, no longer extant ©Michael Heizer, Courtesy the artist and Gagosian, Photo Michael Heizer; pp. 208–209: *45°, 90°, 180°, City* ©Michael Heizer, Courtesy Triple Aught Foundation, Photo Joe Rome; p. 210: Pouring volcanic cinder concrete for the stele at *Complex Two, City* ©Michael Heizer, Courtesy Triple Aught Foundation, Photo Mary Shanahan; p. 211: *Complex Two, City* ©Michael Heizer, Courtesy Triple Aught Foundation, Photo Joe Rome; pp. 212–213: *Complex One, City* ©Michael Heizer, Courtesy Triple Aught Foundation, Photo T. Converse; pp. 214–217: *City*, 1970–2022 ©Michael Heizer, Courtesy Triple Aught Foundation, Photo Eric Piasecki.

Every effort has been made to contact copyright owners to obtain permission to reproduce copyrighted material. However, if any permissions have been inadvertently overlooked, we will be pleased to make the necessary and reasonable arrangements at the first opportunity.

Architecture for Culture: Rethinking Museums

First published in the United States of America in 2025 by
Rizzoli International Publications, Inc.
49 West 27th Street
New York, NY 10001
www.rizzoliusa.com

Copyright ©2025 Béatrice Grenier

Texts: Béatrice Grenier
Foreword: Chris Dercon
Afterword: Shohei Shigematsu

All rights reserved. No part of this publication may be reproduced, stored in a retrieval system, or transmitted in any form or by any means, electronic, mechanical, photocopying, recording, or otherwise, without prior consent of the publisher.

Publisher: Charles Miers
Editorial Director: Catherine Bonifassi
Production Director: Maria Pia Gramaglia
Managing Editor: Lynn Scrabis
Proofreader: Kim Scott, Tricia Levi

Editorial Coordination, Design, and Production:
CASSI EDITION
Vanessa Blondel, Candice Guillaume,
Andrew Ayers, Martha Torbey, Ilinca Neculcea, Marie Donzelli

ISBN: 978-0-8478-4571-2
Library of Congress Control Number: 2025932615

Printed in Latvia
2025 2026 2027 2028 / 10 9 8 7 6 5 4 3 2 1

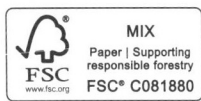

The authorized representative in the EU for product safety and compliance is Mondadori Libri S.p.A., via Gian Battista Vico 42, Milan, Italy, 20123
www.mondadori.it

Visit us online:
Instagram.com/RizzoliBooks
Facebook.com/RizzoliNewYork
Youtube.com/user/RizzoliNY